Nietzsche in Hollywood

THE SUNY SERIES

MURRAY POMERANCE | EDITOR

RECENT TITLES

David Venditto, *Whiteness at the End of the World*

Fareed Ben-Youssef, *No Jurisdiction*

Tony Tracy, *White Cottage, White House*

Tom Conley, *Action, Action, Action*

Lindsay Coleman and Roberto Schaefer, editors, *The Cinematographer's Voice*

Nolwenn Mingant, *Hollywood Films in North Africa and the Middle East*

†Charles Warren, edited by William Rothman and Joshua Schulze, *Writ on Water*

Jason Sperb, *The Hard Sell of Paradise*

William Rothman, *The Holiday in His Eye*

Brendan Hennessey, *Luchino Visconti and the Alchemy of Adaptation*

Alexander Sergeant, *Encountering the Impossible*

Erica Stein, *Seeing Symphonically*

George Toles, *Curtains of Light*

Neil Badmington, *Perpetual Movement*

Merrill Schleier, editor, *Race and the Suburbs in American Film*

Matthew Leggatt, editor, *Was It Yesterday?*

Homer B. Pettey, editor, *Mind Reeling*

Alexia Kannas, *Giallo!*

Bill Krohn, *Letters from Hollywood*

Alex Clayton, *Funny How?*

A complete listing of books in this series can be found online at www.sunypress.edu

Nietzsche in Hollywood

Images of the *Übermensch* in
Early American Cinema

Matthew Rukgaber

Cover: Marlene Dietrich in *The Scarlet Empress* (Josef von Sternberg, Paramount Pictures, 1934). Courtesy Photofest New York.

Published by State University of New York Press, Albany

© 2022 State University of New York

All rights reserved

Printed in the United States of America

No part of this book may be used or reproduced in any manner whatsoever without written permission. No part of this book may be stored in a retrieval system or transmitted in any form or by any means including electronic, electrostatic, magnetic tape, mechanical, photocopying, recording, or otherwise without the prior permission in writing of the publisher.

For information, contact State University of New York Press, Albany, NY
www.sunypress.edu

Library of Congress Cataloging-in-Publication Data

Name: Rukgaber, Matthew, author.
Title: Nietzsche in Hollywood : images of the *Übermensch* in early American cinema / Matthew Rukgaber.
Description: Albany : State University of New York Press, [2022] | Series: SUNY series, Horizons of Cinema | Includes bibliographical references and index.
Identifiers: ISBN 9781438490274 (hardcover : alk. paper) | ISBN 9781438490298 (ebook) | ISBN 9781438490281 (pbk. : alk. paper)
Further information is available at the Library of Congress.

10 9 8 7 6 5 4 3 2 1

For Niti

Contents

Acknowledgments		ix
Abbreviations of Nietzsche's Works		xi
Introduction: Approaching Film with Nietzsche		1
1	The Inhuman in the Human: Social Darwinism and the *Übermensch* in the Silent Era	15
2	The Weakness in Strength: The *Übermensch* as Degenerate in the Films of Erich von Stroheim	37
3	The Criminal Law: The *Übermensch* as Gangster and the Will to Power	61
4	The Salvation of Sin: The *Übermensch* as Superwoman and the Role of Gender	85
5	The Truth of Lies: The *Übermensch* as Genius in the Comedies of Ben Hecht	113
6	The Freedom in Fate: The *Übermensch* as Dionysius in the Films of Josef von Sternberg	141
7	The Revealing Mask: The *Übermensch* as Free Spirit in the Comedies of Ernst Lubitsch	169

Conclusion: A Nietzschean Philosophy of Film	197
Notes	221
Bibliography	263
Index	277

Acknowledgments

This work would never have come to be if Edward Minar had not introduced me to the thought of Stanley Cavell as an undergraduate. While he also presented me with my first formal introduction to the thought of Nietzsche, it was through the teaching and mentorship of Richard Schacht that I was presented with a unified model through which to read Nietzsche. I owe them both a huge thanks for the philosophical evolution that led to this book.

Abbreviations of Nietzsche's Works

A	*The Antichrist*
BGE	*Beyond Good and Evil*
BT	*The Birth of Tragedy*
D	*Daybreak*
EH	*Ecce Homo*
GM	*On the Genealogy of Morality*
GS	*The Gay Science*
HC	*Homer's Contest*
HTH	*Human, All Too Human*
NCW	*Nietzsche Contra Wagner*
PT	*Philosophy and Truth*
TI	*Twilight of the Idols*
UM	*Untimely Meditations*
WP	*The Will to Power*
Z	*Thus Spoke Zarathustra*

Citations of *A*, *BGE*, *BT*, *D*, *GS*, and *WP* are by section number.

Citations of *GM* and *UM* are by essay number and section number.

Citation of *HTH* is by part (P, Volume 1, *AOM*, *WS*) and section number.

Citations of *EH* and *NCW* are by chapter ("Wise," "Clever," "Books," etc.) and section number.

Citation of *Z* is by part (Prologue, I-IV), chapter title (e.g., "On Apostates"), and, if applicable, section number.

Citation of *TI* is by chapter (P, 1-11) and section number.

Citations of *HC* and *PT* are by page number. The page numbers of *HC* refer to *The Portable Nietzsche*.

Modern translations have been used rather than the early translations in the Oscar Levy edition of *The Complete Works of Friedrich Nietzsche*. All translations used are by Walter Kaufmann, except *D* and *HTH*, which are by R. J. Hollingdale, and *PT*, which is by Daniel Breazeale.

Introduction

Approaching Film with Nietzsche

ALTHOUGH NIETZSCHE'S PRESENCE in American culture at the start of the twentieth century has been documented, his influence on early Hollywood cinema prior to the Second World War has gone entirely unnoticed.[1] One of the few mentions of Nietzsche in conjunction with classical Hollywood is the analysis of the films of Orson Welles offered by Deleuze. He calls Welles's work, which begins in 1941, a *precursor* to "a critique of veracity," which implies that the Nietzschean insight that "the ideal of the true was the most profound fiction, at the heart of the real, had not yet been discovered by cinema."[2] Similarly, when linking Nietzsche with director Leo McCarey's *The Awful Truth* (1937), Cavell thinks the connection so unlikely that he wonders whether the connection might be mere chance and settles on the idea that they happened upon a shared idea because they are "each originals."[3] Many scholars have noted Nietzsche's explicit mention in *Baby Face* (1933), but it is often seen as an exceptional case that was heavily censored, because "1930s Hollywood just couldn't handle the philosophical overman, let alone the unashamedly promiscuous overwoman."[4] And so the conclusion that "Nietzsche's time had not yet come" is again reached.[5] The present work challenges this consensus.

Nietzsche's influence on film is suggested by Lea Jacobs's remarkable work *The Decline of Sentiment*, which details the turning of cinematic taste against the norms of "middle-class correctness and tact" and toward the naturalism of "explicit descriptions of sexual urges and encounters; an interest in the body and emphasis on the primacy of instincts; exploration of the modern city or ugly industrial milieu that bore down and sometimes controlled the naturalistic protagonist."[6] It is telling that the people that Jacobs associates with this movement in culture—H. L. Mencken, Emma Goldman, Theodore Dreiser, Floyd Dell, Randolph Bourne, Carl Sandburg, Margaret Anderson, Ben Hecht, Van Wyck Brooks, Sherwood Anderson, Eugene O'Neill, and Upton Sinclair—were all influenced by Nietzsche's challenge to traditional values. "The Nietzschean creed," Mencken claims, is essentially "a counterblast to sentimentality" that lies at the heart of this shift in taste.[7] Yet this move toward naturalism in film and culture that Jacobs details was consistent with the humanistic morals and progressive politics of the time, while Nietzsche's ideal of the *Übermensch* indicates a more radical opposition to the "moribund gods" of the Victorian Age.[8] His thought suggests a darker, anti-humanistic, and amoral tradition, which was often used as proof of the error of naturalism.[9] The cinematic expressions of this challenging idea are especially valuable, because they show that it is not actually a valorization of a hateful, racist, misogynistic, and fascistic life. I will interpret the *Übermensch* as being an open-ended idea about human possibility that does not point us to a specific end but indicates the superhuman task of embracing both the relentless process of transformation and the inescapable hands of fate. This figure points to a conception of time itself that Nietzsche names the eternal recurrence of the same, which is cinematically expressed via images of remarkable individuals that are committed to both the tragedy and comedy of fate. Through such images, this cinematic tradition can be thought of as engaged in philosophizing via its ability to visualize a form of life that philosophy itself has been unable to adequately picture.

This cinematic tradition precedes and stands in juxtaposition to the genres outlined by Cavell, the comedies of remarriage and the melodramas of the unknown woman. Both sets of films identified by Cavell are "working out the problematic of self-reliance and conformity."[10] They depict a pursuit of happiness and integrity via "a step into selfhood or into nationhood," as well as the task of becoming human through "the virtues that allow you to become at home in the world, to establish the world as a home," either through (re)marriage or through the achievement of self-esteem and selfhood.[11] In both sets of films, Cavell argues that the principal characters (who are women) demand a life that, "if it is to be shared," must be one of "equality, mutual education, transfiguration, [and] playfulness," a vision he describes as "Emersonian perfectionism."[12] The Nietzschean tradition of film that I will explore offers a more radical conception of "a singular life," by which I mean that the *Übermensch* is an exception to morality, law, reason, and norms like equality and mutuality that define and make possible human society.[13] We can see the more egalitarian cinema that Cavell explores as a response to the cinema and philosophies of the earlier part of the century that led many poets, playwrights, and philosophers down a dark path toward futurism, nihilism, pessimism, eugenics, and fascism. While I do not believe that Nietzschean philosophy necessarily leads to those outcomes, the potential for them was dangerous enough that the *Übermensch* had to be either condemned, humanized, or entirely ignored in the films that followed the Nietzschean cinematic tradition that flourished in the early and mid-1930s. In other words, the genres that Cavell explores offer us accounts of how to marry again and be human again in the wake of the earlier cinematic tradition of the *Übermensch*.

According to Rancière, Schopenhauer and Wagner influenced a tradition in late nineteenth-century literature, "the era of Ibsen, Strindberg, and Maupassant," where "beneath life's schemes" there "lies the nihilistic logic of illusion as the real truth of existence."[14] These Nietzschean films place this subterranean logic on the visual surface of the world. Even the self is shown to be an illusion, a consequence of what Jules de Gaultier called "Bovarysm" or the fact that "any living reality" exists only insofar as it conceives itself otherwise than it is and continually differentiates itself.[15] Rather than the search for selfhood and equality that Cavell details in films of the late 1930s and 1940s, the Nietzschean film tradition of the early 1930s points to a life of immoral passions and self-overcoming, where deception and illusion are how meaning, reality, and selfhood are created only to then be destroyed by the *Übermenschen* themselves and by fate. Scholars have been skeptical that such a tradition could find a footing in classical Hollywood cinema. According to Rancière, there is "a gap between literary nihilism and the straightforward faith of cinematic artifice," which kept the former from making its way onto film.[16] This is a strange remark given the tradition of German Expressionist filmmaking. My sense is that faith in cinematic realism is also disrupted by the American films that are my focus, because they offer a metaphysical challenge to the very distinction between reality and artifice.

Yet before delving deeply into the dialogue between Nietzschean philosophy and film philosophy, it should be noted that there is not a single thing called "Nietzschean philosophy." There are many different and conflicting accounts of what his texts mean. I will be using an interpretation of Nietzsche that makes the most sense of the Hollywood films that are my focus. This interpretation can be found among many public intellectuals and artists during this era, and it is admittedly more cynical, inegalitarian, and more "metaphysical" than the academic interpretations of his thought that would follow the Second World War. Much of mid- to late-twentieth century Nietzsche interpretation is a response to the perceived dangers of this and other interpretations that dominated the early part of the century. While I will be discussing this iconoclastic interpretation of Nietzsche *as if* it were the truth of Nietzsche, this is not because I aim to defend it as the one and only true interpretation. Rather it is simply the one that is most historically relevant to the films that I will be discussing.

In presenting this vision of Nietzsche's thought, I am also not advocating for the philosophy of the *Übermensch* or for a rejection of morality and truth. My aim is descriptive and historical. These Nietzschean ideas aid us in better appreciating the depth of these works of art. By elaborating the "superhuman" visions in the films of this era, we are able to see how they challenge traditional moral and humanistic norms, and they will act as illustrations of a Nietzschean film aesthetics. I see Nietzschean film aesthetics as resisting, by showing it to be subjectively and "politically compromised," what Devereaux calls the "narrative illusionism" that places the viewer in a passive position to receive the truth revealed by the director and the camera.[17] While it is often held that classical Hollywood film is dominated by this narrative illusionism and, thus, fails to announce itself "as a fiction, a construct," I maintain that the Nietzschean films that are my focus adopt the aestheticist position that reality is the construction of fictions.[18] Furthermore, they avoid the passivity that results from "playing to our existing desires, fantasies and fears" by exposing the "human, all too human" elements of our impulses and ideals and by presenting us with inhuman and superhuman alternatives.[19] Cinema's artificial world allows it to explore socially destructive, contradictory, and illiberal value systems, to detach from the ordinary and the everyday in order to become farce and tragicomedy. It reveals and revels in its artificiality. Furthermore, during this time of monumental advances in cinematic technique and technology, I think it plausible that the widespread endorsement of Nietzsche as *the* philosopher of the age informed how these writers and directors thought of the artistic medium of film itself. Film, as illusionism par excellence that announces itself as such, could match Nietzsche's challenge to truth, morality, and the metaphysics of Being by creating a truly Dionysian art. Such art captures the human being's capacity to embrace the destructiveness of fate, the reliance of life on forgetting and deception, and the ceaselessness of change. Thus, to expose this Nietzschean tradition in film is to offer a challenge to what, following Bordwell, is called the model of "classical Hollywood film."[20]

Many readers will still be surprised by the idea that Nietzsche had a pervasive influence on Hollywood film prior to 1938. Part of that surprise can be traced to the opinion that Cavell continually resists. "Philosophy and Hollywood movies occupy separate cultural intentions, with nothing to say across their border, indeed with not so much as a border between them."[21] The preconception that Hollywood films are little more than escapes from serious philosophical reflection on our existential predicament has been weakened by Cavell's texts and other more recent studies, but it still persists. We would not see the same incredulity if my thesis were that Nietzsche's philosophy infused German films from the same era. After all, what Eisner calls the core of Expressionist filmmaking obviously has deep affinities with Nietzschean thought: "Human life, transcending the individual, participates in the life of the universe; our hearts bear with the rhythm of the world itself and are linked with everything that happens: the cosmos is our lung. Man has ceased to be an individual tied to concepts of duty, morality, family and society: the Expressionist's life breaks the bounds of petty logic and causality. Free from all bourgeois petty remorse, admitting nothing but the prodigious barometer of his sensibility, he commits himself to his impulses."[22] It is actually surprising that no book-length study of Nietzsche's influence on German film has yet to emerge.[23] If I were to argue that the popularity of Nietzsche's philosophy in France had a profound influence on its traditions of *Lebensphilosophie* and avant-garde aesthetics, which inspired both cinema and cinematic criticism in that country, then there would be little resistance.[24] Again, it is more remarkable that no one has actually argued for this in significant detail.

Skeptics of the merits of forging this connection between Nietzsche and major Hollywood films of the era are perhaps unaware of how widespread Nietzsche's ideas were and how central they were to a series of debates in international politics, psychology, sociology, education, biology, and the arts. German-language magazines and newspapers in America began transmitting Nietzsche's thought to the over two million German immigrants in America in the 1890s, a group that remained the largest population of non-English immigrants through the 1910s, nearly equal to the number of immigrants from the whole of the British Isles. Nietzsche's works began being translated into English as early as 1896, and several volumes appeared before this initial translation project was abandoned.

It was then taken up again by Oscar Levy, who oversaw a complete eighteen-volume edition that was published by 1913. As Levy notes in the opening essay of the eighteenth volume of this edition, this was "the most complete and voluminous translation of any foreign philosopher into the English language."[25] The first monograph on Nietzsche published in America was by Grace Neal Dolson in 1901. She justified her study by the rather hesitant remark that "in some way Nietzsche appeals to the thought of the time."[26] What she did not say was that Nietzsche was already the most widely read philosopher in Germany, a full-blown "public event."[27] Several years earlier English authors were already speaking of a "Nietzsche vogue," and not long after Dolson's book there was a full-scale "Nietzsche revival" taking place in the English-speaking world.[28] In 1913, Paul Elmer More remarked that "if the number of books written about a subject is any proof of interest in it, Nietzsche must have become one of the most popular of authors among Englishmen and Americans."[29] Nietzsche's influence was not halted by World War I, leading Dolson to remark in 1918 that some of his ideas had "permeated every civilized country and greet one at every turn."[30] Yet Nietzsche's influence did wane in England and France after the First World War, while it continued to flourish in America and in Hollywood until around 1938, when the dangers of German aggression, anti-Semitism, and talk of supermen were recognized as existential threats to the world. Not even the Leopold and Loeb murder case of 1924, with its well-publicized arguments equating Nietzsche's philosophy with murder, was able to staunch the appeal of his thought.[31] Ultimately, this "cult of Nietzsche" was associated with a diverse and influential collection of writers that would inspire, directly and indirectly, many significant Hollywood films.[32]

While the appearance of several key concepts from Nietzsche's philosophy will be explored in this work, the one that dominated his early reception was the *Übermensch*. Early in the first wave of his reception in America, many argued that he offered no philosophical system. "The superman is the crowning stone in the whole fabric of Nietzsche's beliefs and teachings," which reduced simply to a "a kind of titanism, which has had a very broad sway in art."[33] One might immediately worry whether it is a specifically Nietzschean concept of the *Übermensch* in these films, rather than an idea inspired simply by mythic heroes, the cult of genius and Romantic hero worship, or Emerson's praise of "representative men." Walter Kaufmann argues that Nietzsche gets the concept from Goethe,[34] while others have found the idea to be an anodyne restatement of the Aristotelian notion of the *meglopsychia*.[35] Leo Berg's 1897 book *Der Über-*

mensch in der modernen Litteratur spends more time discussing the sources of the idea in Kierkegaard, Carlyle, Emerson, Goethe, and Renan than in Nietzsche.[36] Yet it was Nietzsche's thought that refined the idea from mere vagaries about geniuses and heroes into something that challenged the very notion of what it means to be human. One of the reasons it is the specifically *Nietzschean* superhumanity found in these films is that what one finds is not a hero or genius who, for example, redeems civilization, culture, selfhood, the truth, beauty, morality, or the community. Instead, we find a character capable of a previously unimaginable undermining of traditional values associated with human society and culture. This seems to be Nietzsche's unique contribution, which, in Derrida's words, is a "stepping outside the human" and which is expressed in a form of art "that would be *unheimlich* [uncanny] because in this art one would find at home (*zuhause*) these apparently inhuman things" that challenge our notion of the self and the oppositional limits that sustain it.[37] The ways in which these Nietzschean films present us, both formally and narratively, with *unheimlich* and *unmenschlich* images will be central to understanding this cinematic tradition and the aesthetic that governs it.

What is the *Übermensch*? For many scholars, this idea is less about overcoming *the human* and more about overcoming the beast or the herd. Kaufmann argues for a conception of the *Übermensch* as simply "the man who has overcome himself" and achieved "unique individuality."[38] It is reassuring and non-threatening to think that this ideal refers to just "our true self" acquired through "self-integration, self-creation and self-mastery."[39] To be "beyond-humanity" apparently means simply to be a person who has organized their passions and given their character style. This view is not much different from the view of Danto, who argues that about all that can be said about the *Übermensch* is that it is "a joyous, guiltless, free human being, in possession of instinctual drives which do not overpower him."[40] Do such ideas really do justice to the idea that "Man is a rope, tied between beast and overman—a rope over an abyss. A dangerous across, a dangerous on-the-way, a dangerous looking-back, a dangerous shuddering and stopping. . . . he is a bridge and not an end: what can be loved in man is that he is an *overture* and a *going under*" (Z Prologue §4, emphasis in original)? The idea of the joyous human is given a more exhaustive treatment by Richard Schacht, who sees the *Übermensch* as a person who is highly cultivated and who brings about a higher level of culture through their creativity: "Overflowing vitality and great health; powerful affects and the ability to control and direct them; high spirituality and refinement of sensibility and manners; independence of mind and action; the capacity to befriend and to respect and disdain and deal justly with others as they warrant; intellectual honesty and astuteness; the strength to be undaunted by suffering and disillusionment; persistence in self-overcoming; the resources to undertake and follow through on the most demanding of tasks; and the ability to love and esteem, and above all to create—this configuration of qualities well warrants identification as the consummation of human existence."[41] Undoubtedly these notions can be found being praised at different times in Nietzsche's works, but such a description is strangely compatible with a variety of humanistic ethical programs. It certainly does not suggest a radical rejection of the entire Western moral tradition. For Schacht, this figure transcends the "merely animal" and the "all-too-human."[42] But one might wonder: Why did Nietzsche call it the *Übermensch* rather than the *Übertier*, the beyond-animal? The picture of Nietzsche's ideal that I will be utilizing is one that refuses to offer a prescriptive, general ethics, to support traditional pro-social values, or to simply endorse a list of human virtues. What is beyond the human is also beyond comprehension through such mundane concepts. It remains the idea of a limit and a gesture to something beyond it. Perhaps our reflections on this idea will lead us toward the humanistic virtues that Schacht describes, but that outcome is not equivalent to the *Übermensch*.

The conception of the "beyond human" that I will be utilizing is seen when, for example, A. R. Orage states that the *Übermensch* is the "earthly end" to replace all "other-worldly ends," which has "never existed on earth."[43] He argues that if the *Übermensch* is to the human what the human is to the tiger, then using human traits to speculate on that future state is as absurd as understanding the human to be "a tiger writ large."[44] The *Übermensch* is an ideal that contains multiple visions of how life may "become ever and ever more moving, more splendid, more Dionysian" and may strive toward a self- and species-overcoming, thus making "life more tragic" by enlarging "the will of man" to the point that it engages in "conflict with gods."[45] The beyond-human is a symbol of an unknown future to which we have to remain continually open. It is a promissory note of a new culture and a new set of values.[46] The *Übermensch* is a goal, an ever-becoming but never-being future to which we are directed but that is always deferred (*WP* §1001). This is not a goal that we as individuals can hope to achieve. All humanity will ever be is a "bridge" or a "herald of the lightning" (Z Prologue §4). The *Übermensch* is a "metaphor" intended to replace the concept of god or any other organizing principle of human life and society that has had the enervating result of "an overall diminution, a value diminution of the type man" (*WP* §866). The superhuman is one who unifies with creative, cosmic becoming and not with a reductive notion of nature thought as a return to animal impulses. This non-prescriptive idea of a form of life is committed to the pursuit of great things, to remarkable transformations of morals, society, and selfhood, often with tragic outcomes.[47] Nietzsche thinks that we as a species require such an aim, which he identifies through a trifecta of ideas: eternal recurrence of the same, the love of fate (*amor fati*), and the *Übermensch*.[48] This approach to the *Übermensch* is expressed on film, I maintain, via inhuman worlds where the individual is subsumed (even rushes headlong) into and embraces the impersonal forces of fate. *Fate* is just another word for time, understood as the fact that "everything becomes and recurs eternally" (*WP* §1058). Such a view necessarily challenges classical conceptions of Hollywood filmmaking, which supposedly gained "full formulation in 1917" and stabilized in the 1920s.[49] That classical model relies on a common-sense causal structure, understandable characters with rational psychologies, and a humanistic and realistic worldview that results in passive spectatorship. Yet the ordinary assumptions that underlie these components are notoriously challenged by Nietzsche's philosophy.

Placing Nietzsche alongside Hollywood film requires us to confront the fact that Nietzsche himself thought poorly of the theater and surely would have thought the same about cinema.

> What is the theater to me? What, the convulsions of [Wagner's] "moral" ecstasies which give the people—and who is not "people"?—satisfaction? What, the whole gesture hocus-pocus of the actor? It is plain that I am essentially anti-theatrical: confronted with the theater, this mass art par excellence, I feel that profound scorn at the bottom of my soul which every artist today feels. . . .
>
> No one brings along the finest senses of his art to the theater, least of all the artist who works for the theater—solitude is lacking; whatever is perfect suffers no witnesses. In the theater one becomes people, herd, female, Pharisee, voting cattle, patron, idiot—Wagnerian: even the most personal conscience is vanquished by the leveling magic of the great number; the neighbor reigns, one becomes a mere neighbor. (*NCW* "Where I Offer Objections"; *GS* §368)

While this foreshadows well-known criticisms of Hollywood films as mere entertainment, Nietzsche does not give us a reason to think that theater or film *must* give rise to this "leveling magic." By being comforting rather than challenging, the theater gives rise to passivity and ease. Such art is in the service of "declining life," but there certainly is art, even theater and cinema, that is in the service of "growing" life or the Dionysian "*overfullness* of life" (*NCW* "We Antipodes," emphasis in original). Cinema, to the extent that it is able, must, as Nietzsche once said of history, "stand in the service of life," which means to stand "in the service of an unhistorical power" and, we might add, of an uncinematic, impersonal, and unethical power that is called fate (*UM* 2 §1).[50] Life for Nietzsche is "existence as it is, without meaning or aim, yet recurring inevitably without any finale of nothingness: '*the eternal recurrence*'" (*WP* §55, emphasis in original). He would agree with Devereaux's call for cinematic art that creates a "critical spectator," who is "less likely to be victimized by the text."[51] Yet cinema in the service of life is more than merely critical. It imagines the possibility of embracing the cosmic course of our lives and, thereby, becoming absorbed in grand, dangerous, and revolutionary tasks. If cinema is capable of this, then we must say that the films themselves, through their "use of images, sounds, montage, narration, the conversion of bodies and words into forms, the regulation of duration," are able "to fashion our reception, to mould our perception" and, thereby, arm us with tools to actively and critically turn life itself into artifice, masquerade, dangerous experimentation, and joyous playing with fate.[52]

Nietzsche was aligned with the modernist idea that the very foundation of life is the creative urge. In the scholarship of the day, it was recognized that Nietzsche adopts a philosophy of masks that holds that the "only thing certain . . . is Life itself," which implies that one ought to be "continuously experimenting with life, with ideas, with himself."[53] When Nietzsche describes an aesthetic model of life, it is through the recognition that "the superficiality of existence is its essence" and that everything profound is just a "veil" (*GS* §64). "Life—that means for us constantly transforming all that we are into light and flame—also everything that wounds us; we simply can do no other" (*GS* P §3). The application of this idea to film is striking. Film quite literally transforms life into light. Cinematic realism is here reversed. Rather than being the mere appearance of real life, "real" life is nothing but the cinematization of existence, the conversion of our Being into light and appearance. If we call our construction of meanings, images, and self-interpretations "appearances" or "veils," then we should also say that they are both a phantasmagoric revelation of "truth" and the continual denial of truth for the sake of deceptions that we can call self-invention. The self mirrors what Comolli calls the "*fictional fatality*" of cinema, its deep ambiguity, and its placing us into "an endless tourniquet where 'true' and 'false,' nature and artifice, spontaneity and preparation, freedom and work are brought together without ceasing to be opposed to each other" (emphasis in original):[54] "The screen is not a window, and if the cinema shows, it also hides. It opens and shuts. It inscribes a dissemblance within resemblance, and this is why it constitutes a lure. The screen is ambiguous. Outside-inside. Front-back. Bright-dark. Surface-depth."[55] When we think of the metaphor of converting life to light and flame, we must recognize that this conversion is not the creation of a representation that captures some pre-existing reality. Rather, as Nietzsche says, it is a transformation of *all that we* are, without remainder, because all that we are is the creative process of becoming.

Given this aesthetic conception of life and Nietzsche's famous criticisms of the illusoriness of traditional metaphysical and epistemological categories, one might well think that if classical Hollywood contains such a Nietzschean vision, then it would align rather well with Cavell's notion that film is "a moving image of skepticism."[56] According to Cavell, the "photographic basis of movies" results in "an artistically unheard of relation between the presence and absence of its objects"; that is, film and photography "transcribe" the existence of things, but those things do not actually exist before us, and yet our senses are satisfied with what is given.[57] The modern mind is plagued by skepticism, in which we are (or at least take ourselves to be) distanced from what is real, and modern philosophy and art can be thought of as our efforts to recover ourselves and the world from this situation.[58]

> At some point the unhinging of our consciousness from the world interposed our subjectivity between us and our presentness to the world. Then our subjectivity became what is present to us, individuality became isolation. The route to conviction in reality was through the acknowledgment of that endless presence of self. What is called expressionism is one possibility of representing this acknowledgement. But it would, I think, be truer to think of expressionism as a representation of our *response* to this new fact of our condition—our terror of ourselves in isolation—rather than as a representation of the world from within the condition of isolation itself. It

would, to that extent, not be a new mastery of fate by creating selfhood against no matter what the odds; it would be the sealing of the self's fate by theatricalizing it. Apart from the wish for selfhood (hence the always simultaneously granting of otherness as well), I do not understand the value of art. Apart from this wish and its achievement, art is exhibition.[59]

Cavell explicitly says that "what we wish to see . . . is the world itself—that is to say, everything" and that modern philosophy, Nietzsche included, says that this is "beyond our reach metaphysically."[60] Modern skepticism is a "new realization of . . . human distance from the world, or some withdrawal of the world, which philosophy interprets as a limitation in our capacity for knowing the world."[61]

I do not actually think that Nietzsche is overly concerned with this skeptical problem nor subject to it. Nietzsche's perspectivism holds that truths are relative to forms of life and that what we call *ultimate truths* are simply "*irrefutable* errors" (*GS* §265, emphasis in original).[62] Beneath all truth claims are value systems. "Truths" began as metaphors and illusions in the service of life, but this has been forgotten (*PT* p. 84). Thus, any number of conflicting "truths" are "*applicable* to life," resulting in a sort of "skepticism," which he calls a "noble and frivolous tolerance" of different truths (*GS* §100; *BGE* §46; see also *GS* §358, emphasis in original). Nietzsche would agree with Merleau-Ponty that "ambiguity is of the essence of human existence."[63] This is not a concession to skepticism as it does not deny that such irrefutable errors do not get at some aspect of reality that is relevant to that value system. But this is but one view on the world among many. The screen reflects this ambiguity, the multiplicity of perspectives, which is a feature of all expression, perception, and the human body itself. Contrary to Nietzsche's noble perspectivism, an ignoble and intolerant skepticism comes about as a pessimistic reaction to this multiplicity and partiality of truth. Rather than acknowledging perspectivism as the very foundation of meaning, ignoble skepticism maintains that there can be no meaning among this plurality, ambiguity, and partiality. Perspectivism exists not because of some separation from reality but because of the multiplicity within reality of which we are a part (and not apart). What Cavell calls skepticism is a dissatisfaction with finitude, contingency, and perspectivism. It dwells still in the shadow of god according to Nietzsche. It is a result of the failure to recognize the creative course of life that adheres to no rational system and admits of a multitude of truths and perspectives. Cavell believes that the foundation of the problem is a "natural or inevitable presentment of the human mind" that manifests as "the human denial of the conditions of humanity," the motive and result of which he calls "the horror of being human itself."[64] This horror is a response to "human vulnerability, or, say, finitude," and Cavell would hold that the doctrine of the *Übermensch*, or beyond-human, perpetuates it.[65] But the beyond-human does not strive to overcome vulnerability or finitude. Instead, it is a superhuman embrace of these features of all life.

Cavell calls film a "moving image of skepticism" because it recreates that skeptical distance from the real world. It is not without reason that the metaphor for this distance is called the Cartesian Theater (or, we might say, Cartesian Cinema). By contrast, a more Nietzschean approach sees film as a *moving image of perspectivism*. Rather than entreating us with a philosophical error, Nietzschean aesthetics looks to how film disrupts the metaphysical, epistemological, and moral distinctions that enforce static notions of reality, selfhood, and humanity. Nietzsche's perspectivism has been described as the idea that "*all* doctrines and opinions are only partial and limited by a particular point of view" (emphasis in original), which also recognizes itself as opinion or assertation of a particular perspective that cannot be made absolute or definitive.[66] Famously, Nietzsche argues that the notion of a "true" or "real" world can be done away with and recognized as a sort of fable (*TI* IV). What that means, in the domain of art, is that we cannot devalue the things on film as unreal, nonexistent, or appearance. Nor is there any value in contrasting them to the more real and existent things outside of film, at least from an affective and value perspective. Art and its objects as embodiments of meaning can be as real and true as the world outside of art. Merleau-Ponty's conception of art and meaning has striking similarities with Nietzsche, and he argues that "a movie has meaning in the same way that a thing does," because both the film-world and the non-film-world present us with "that special way of being in the world, of dealing with things and other people, which we can see in the sign language of gesture and gaze and which clearly defines each person we know."[67] This aestheticization of "the real" is not due to the fact we are trapped in our own perceptual prison and isolated from others or from meaning. Quite the opposite is the case for Nietzsche.

In the following chapters, this brief description of Nietzschean film aesthetics will act as a foundation for my analysis of what these films do. And what they do, in addition to their explicit thematic intersection with the concepts of the *Übermensch*, the love of fate, and eternal recurrence of the same, is allow us to see them as constituting a sequence of multidimensional Nietzschean art objects.

1

The Inhuman in the Human

Social Darwinism and the *Übermensch* in the Silent Era

Introduction

THE FIRST APPEARANCES OF the *Übermensch* in American cinema are within films that morally condemn the figure. According to these works, the superman is an inhuman monster, a mere beast who is *below*, not *above*, the human. Although all these films can be regarded as part of the naturalistic movement insofar as they dare to present the bestial *Übermensch*, they remain within the moralistic tradition of naturalism. They misinterpret the *Übermensch* as a return to brutal forces that threaten to destroy society. The films discussed in this chapter constitute a prehistory to the Nietzschean films that present the *Übermensch* as, at least, an ambiguous figure, if not a noble one, who legitimately challenges the moral, epistemological, and metaphysical foundations of human society. It is no real surprise that the *Übermensch* first appeared on the screen as "blond beast of prey . . . avidly prowling round for spoil and victory" (*GM* I §11). Nor is it surprising that this is how the concept would appear on screen, in films such as *Rope* (1948) and *The Sea Wolf* (1941), after the rise of Nazism returned Nietzsche's philosophy to the caricature that had marred its initial reception.[1] Nietzsche's naturalism led him to be initially introduced to the American public through the raging discussion about evolutionary biology and its significance for social, political, and economic thought.² Whether textually justified or not, Nietzsche was interjected into the stormy debates about heredity, eugenics, and human evolution that swirled around the works of Darwin, Malthus, Lamarck, Spencer, Huxley, and Haeckel.³

I tend to agree with Heidegger that such "biologism presents *the main obstacle* to our penetrating to [Nietzsche's] fundamental thought" and that it is an "illusion" that covers up the metaphysical notion of life as "Becoming" (emphasis in original).⁴ As Fink argues, Nietzsche "conceals his deep and abysmal concept of life beneath a biological concept" only for polemical reasons: the seemingly natural concept of "life" actually represents the flux of becoming, or the "infinity of the Dionysian world-ground."⁵ This means that an essential aspect of the films that *actually* depict a recognizably Nietzschean conception of the Übermensch is that they visualize a Dionysian transformation of "the human subject" by detailing its deconstruction via its combination with that world-ground, whether that is called fate, the eternal recurrence of the same, a passion for great and terrible deeds, the beyond-human, or even love.⁶ Such films offer criticisms of existing moral and metaphysical distinctions and point us toward an ever-evolving form of life. As Derrida notes, the notion of "life" in Nietzsche must be read as a "perhaps" and "in a much more suspensive manner to avoid these reductive gestures *and* affirm something else" (emphasis in original).⁷ Such an idea is not hard to find in both Nietzsche's early and late texts. For example, it is visible when he endorses the "true but deadly" belief in "the doctrines of sovereign becoming, of the fluidity of all concepts, types and species, of the lack of any cardinal distinction between man and animal" (*UM* II §9). Such an idea challenges even the difference between life and death by claiming that the aim of life is "perishing (*animae magnae prodigus*), in pursuit of the great and impossible" (*UM* II §9).⁸ But before we can see such a figure represented on film, we must see its misrepresentation.

Nietzsche's contribution to the debate about sociobiology was taken to be little more than praise of "the strongest." This philosophy of the strongest seemed to result not in human progress but in egomaniacs that failed to evolve the species. It offered nothing but an atavistic return to the primitive. The conversion of "a belief in natural selection as the main factor of human progress" into "the moral field" is proclaimed by H. G. Wells in 1897 to be "the glorification of a sort of rampant egotism—of blackguardism in fact,—as the New Gospel," which gives us "the Gospel of Nietzsche."⁹ The great irony is that Wells would go on to argue for the need of a new society, dominated by a racist doctrine of eugenic selection, which would produce "the kinetic men of the coming time," so while he supports Darwinism in terms of species development and social planning, it must be guided by a socialist morality and faith in God.[10] This conception of Nietzsche's *Übermensch* is a common one. In 1899 in *The Monist*, it was argued that the *Übermensch* is that individual who can "dominate the masses" and who is "strong, healthy, powerful, arbitrary, selfish, cruel" and "a master."[11] That article states that Nietzsche held that "the weak must perish because they hinder the development and delay the coming of the *Übermensch*," although such a claim is an open contradiction with the idea that the *Übermensch* will emerge from the "quagmire of plebeianism."[12] Such a being could hardly emerge from a population that has been annihilated. Nevertheless, people believed that Nietzsche advocated for "the extermination of whatever stands in the way" of the *Übermensch*'s will, which was concerned only with "appropriating, robbing, overcoming, destroying" and was "supremely happy" only when he could "rise on the dead and wounded bodies of the weak."[13] Today this reading is widely and correctly dismissed as a profound misunderstanding of Nietzsche's philosophy.

Such visions of enslavement and extermination were present even in the writings of members of what Upton Sinclair called the "Nietzsche cult."[14] For example, Mencken's popular account claimed that Nietzsche held that "the proletariat" are to be considered "draft animals made to be driven, enslaved, and exploited."[15] Of course, Nietzsche no more advocates for a simple return to the exploitative aristocracy of the Greeks than he does a return to the "beasts of prey" that preceded modern humanity. Furthermore, Mencken assumes that Nietzsche promotes the "law of natural selection" and survival of the fittest, which means that humans are no different than "lions in the jungle and the protozoa in the sea ooze."[16] Nietzsche explicitly rejected this philosophy in favor of the ideal of the human that is incredibly careless with their life while in the service of something great (*animae magnae prodigus*). It is of course true that some passages from Nietzsche appear amenable to social Darwinian thought, particularly his criticism of pity and Christianity: "Pity crosses the law of development, which is the law of *selection*. It preserves what is ripe for destruction; it defends those who have been disinherited and condemned by life; and by the abundance of the failures of all kinds which it keeps alive, it gives life itself a gloomy and questionable aspect" (*A* §7, emphasis in original). But rather than an endorsement of "the survival of the fittest," Nietzsche's law of development is a principle that directs one to the difficult task of selecting those values that will enable one to meet fate courageously or perish in the process. Rather than being concerned that the fittest or strongest survive for the health of the species, Nietzsche's concern is the individual's fulfillment of their own destiny.[17]

Culturally speaking, there was an obvious reason for the moral condemnation of the Nietzschean ideal, however it was interpreted. America was undergoing a radical shift in its fortunes and values, as expressed famously by Santayana in a lecture from 1911 where he noted that the "American Will inhabits the sky-scraper; the American Intellect inhabits the colonial mansion"—its outer world was that of masculine "aggressive enterprise," and its inner life was dominated by the feminine "genteel tradition."[18] The ethical cinema of the Progressive Era could depict the will that inhabits the skyscraper only in order to criticize the greed of the few and highlight the terrible circumstances of the many. The glamourization of the brutal egoism of a leading man like Warren William in *Skyscraper Souls* (1932)—a film that seems to take its name from Santayana's distinction—could not have appeared only a few years earlier. William's character makes money by shady loans and cutthroat capitalism, lives in an open marriage, sleeps with his secretary for twelve years, and then abandons her for a younger woman. While such deeds and worse were depicted in earlier films, they were not the defining and sole deeds of the suave and sophisticated lead character. Notably, this film has positively Nietzschean odes to achievement, to the monolithic skyscraper formed out of pain and suffering, and to the joy of possession and freedom. Yet even in 1932, *Skyscraper Souls* concludes on a profoundly moral note, albeit one that is not sufficient to counteract the attraction that we have for the amoral lead character. Ending in a tragic murder-suicide, the film's lesson is that to fully embrace the nature of the "American Will" is to court death. This lesson persists in many films of the early sound era. And yet the skyscraper soul (and the *Übermensch*) was so attractive to American culture that it needed to be rescued, for example by being clothed in Christianity. In Bruce Barton's book *The Man Nobody Knows* from 1925, Jesus is interpreted as the "Founder of Modern Business," whose doctrine of "service" was a great public relations campaign to create the greatest organization in the world. Without a touch of irony, Barton argues that God's "business" on earth, which his Son came down to institute as CEO, was "to develop perfect human beings, superior to circumstance, victorious over Fate."[19] Jesus and Nietzsche seem to share the same aim, to create the *Übermensch*.

It is unsurprising that filmmakers had such a negative impression of Nietzsche. After all, a professional philosopher like Santayana summarized Nietzsche's thought in brutal terms.

> This egotism is romantic; it does not ask to be persuaded that evil, in the end, is good. It feels that evil is good in the present; it is so intense a thing to feel and so exciting a thing to do. Here we have what Nietzsche wished to bring about, a reversal of all values. To do evil is the true virtue, and to be good is the most hopeless vice. Milk is for babies; your strong man should be soaked in blood and in alcohol. We should live perilously; and as material life is the power to digest poisons, so true excellence is the power to commit all manner of crimes, and to survive.[20]

While this is a ridiculous description, Nietzsche does proclaim the aim of a "reversal of all values." And this is what essentially happened with the economic crash of 1929. It has been said that "when the stock market crash precipitated the Depression, Americans were not only traumatized by financial hardship but also betrayed by the religion they had believed in so fervently."[21] The idea of American progress with its skyscraper soul had tied itself to socioeconomic reformist philosophy and forms of Darwinian, eugenic social planning. Both sat alongside traditional sentimental values despite the cognitive dissonance. When both perspectives fell to ruin, radical philosophies, cynicism, and pessimism could flourish. Thus, it was in this space that a new type of film with a new type of *Übermensch* could emerge, one that could learn to live with and even embrace the destructive course of fate. A remarkable convergence of events gave Nietzsche's philosophy new legs in Hollywood after its initial flourishing in literary circles. Alongside the monumental economic disruption of the American identity and values and the advent of sound in film, a massive influx of writers to Hollywood took place, many of whom were inspired by the first generation of members of the "cult of Nietzsche."

Nietzsche, Darwin, and the Progressive Age on Film

Nietzsche's *Übermensch* still appears within our present culture as a figure who proclaims, "Let us have the struggle and the combat. Then the weak will die, and those who yearn for other worlds."[22] This idea has a long history of association with eugenics or "science of race culture" and the hope for a creation of the "Super Race" made up of "Super Men" or the "acme of human perfection."[23] His philosophy was (and sometimes still is) described as a "harsh, hard-hearted, purely biological program for destroying the weak and arbitrarily giving all the prizes of life to the strong" and as "a worship of a super-race, a race of strong men who 'live dangerously,' dangerously especially to those weaker and less fortunate than themselves."[24] This vision of Nietzsche obviously conflicts with the humanistic values of the Progressive Age, with its more beneficent approach to the new scientific reality. This conflict between Nietzsche and a more humane social science was the theme of the first explicit mention of Nietzsche in an American film, *A Disciple of Nietzsche* (1915) from Thanhouser Film Company. This lost film offers what many people believed to be the distilled essence of Nietzsche's philosophy through the following intertitle:[25] "That the lifting up of the weak, in the long run, is an unprofitable and useless business, is evident upon very brief reflection. Philanthropy, considered largely, is inevitably a failure. Nothing is more patent, indeed, than the fact that charity merely converts the unfit—who, in the course of nature, would soon die out and cease to encumber the earth—into parasites, who live on indefinitely, a nuisance and a burden to their betters."[26] As it turns out, this is not a quote from Nietzsche. Instead, it is from Mencken's book on Nietzsche. This would not be the last time that Mencken's words would be substituted for Nietzsche's on film. This quote appears in a book that a professor of philosophy is reading, who agrees that "only the strong were of any consequence." The film contrasts the professor's cruel Nietzschean philosophy to the progressive values of his daughter, who brings home a "poor emaciated, hungry-looking bit of humanity," namely, an unemployed factory girl, as a charity case. The girl soon flees the home, in part because of the unwelcoming professor, who calls her one of the "unfit." The professor senses his own hypocrisy when he attempts to intervene in his daughter's engagement to a "reformed gangster," because Nietzsche's idea that "the strong must grow stronger, and that they may do so, they must waste no strength in the vain task of trying to lift up the weak" would suggest that he allow nature to take its course here. This quote is once again attributed to Nietzsche, but it is from Mencken.[27] The "unfit" factory girl ultimately is successful at the factory, gets a boyfriend, and exposes that the professor's daughter has fallen in love with a thug who is just using her for money. Ultimately, once the professor recognizes that the unfit may become fit, largely through their moral virtues, he remarks that "Nietzsche has lost one disciple. Never more will I despise the weak." This three-reel serial is a remarkable exposition of how Nietzsche's philosophy was understood as standing in stark opposition to the progressive politics and moral reformism of the era. While the film's depiction of the unsavory and criminal elements that were a part of modern industrial life speaks to the literary naturalism that we have seen associated with Nietzsche, the film essentially agrees with H. G. Wells that Nietzsche's philosophy threatens the species.

Nietzsche's supposed brutalism conflicts with humanistic sociobiology, a view seen in Ritchie's *Darwinism and Politics*, which argues that evolutionary principles did not support the ideas of an aristocracy, laissez-faire politics and economics, war, or inequality in general.[28] Yet it was sometimes recognized by scholars that "Nietzsche expressly opposes the Darwinian theory," at least in the sense that he denies that the "environment" is the "supremely important factor in evolution."[29] Adaptation to the environment is less significant than "the inner, spontaneous, assimilating power" that strives to individuate and become more complex and richer.[30] Although a minority view, a Nietzschean conception of progress could be found at the time, which claimed that species and types are rather fixed and that their limits are exceeded only by a "genius" who "gathers up and assimilates the preceding stages" and creates a new type or species.[31] This idea of the *Übermensch* as cultural reformer, genius, and prophet, rather than a heartless predator, was available even within Mencken's influential book on Nietzsche, from which the quotes in *A Disciple of Nietzsche* were drawn to endorse indifference, if not active cruelty, toward those who were deemed unfit. This points to the confusion surrounding the *Übermensch* at the time, even within Mencken's book, which allowed it to become a symbol reflecting both nightmares and dreams.

The discourse on eugenics and its alignment with a morally progressive viewpoint famously appears in numerous early "social problem" films, such as D. W. Griffith's *The Escape* (1914) and several Lois Weber films, including *Where Are My Children?* (1916), *The Hand That Rocks the Cradle* (1917), and *The Blot* (1921).[32] The eugenics discourse that informed Weber's films was likely drawn from the work of Margaret Sanger, who was aware of Nietzsche's thought and advocated for contraception as a way of refusing to "populate the earth with slaves," that is, with those who would find unfavorable conditions in an overpopulated society and who would end up exploited.[33] The eugenics debate continues even as late as Katharine Hepburn's first film, *A Bill of Divorcement* (1932), where hereditary madness requires Hepburn's character to abandon her marriage and dreams of children in order to care for her lucid but excitable father.[34] The genetics of madness and the need to give birth to a "fit" rather than "unfit" child remained at the core of several other films in the 1930s, such as *A Strange Interlude* (1932), based on the play by noted Nietzschean Eugene O'Neill. Much of the eugenicist tradition in film is rooted in putatively egalitarian values, the welfare of society, the happiness of individuals, and the progress of the human species. Ultimately, Nietzsche does not belong either to this brutalist interpretation or to the contrasting sociobiological humanism.

Indeed, Nietzsche wrote on such a Darwinian ethics when criticizing Strauss, who wanted to create a naturalistic ethics and religion of the future.[35] Nietzsche describes Strauss as wrapping himself "in the hairy cloak of our ape-genealogists" and praising "Darwin as one of the greatest benefactors of mankind" (*UM* 1 §7). Strauss offers us traditional platitudes wrapped in pseudo-scientific musings, which is to say, according to Nietzsche, he offers nothing "whatever offensive, that is to say productive" (*UM* 1 §11). Strauss is engaged in demythologizing religion and philosophy via Darwin to arrive at the traditional moral precepts of society that are an homage to the Ten Commandments, natural law, Kantian ethics, contractarianism, the golden rule, Rousseauian equality, and Schopenhauer's ethics of sympathy.[36] The lawfulness of nature, the teleology of progress, the natural elevation of man, and nearly every article of Enlightenment reason and faith can be found on display in Strauss's "new" faith. Nietzsche challenges whether there could even be "Darwinian ethic," not because Strauss's version is insufficiently naturalistic and brutal, but because "the concept of man yokes together the most diverse and manifold things" (*UM* 1 §7). Nietzsche thinks that Strauss sugarcoats his scientific worldview, which could just as well lead to nihilism, brutalism, mechanism, materialism, and amoralism. Strauss fails to see that what he advances "as culture [is] precisely that which negates culture" (*UM* 1 §2). It is clear, even in this early work, that Nietzsche is concerned with the hegemonic consequences of any ethics, whether naturalistic or not, because they constitute a system of rules that limits human possibility. Ethical systems fail to recognize that human beings are manifold and inconsistent. They ascribe to the person a unified notion of the self. As such, they fail to offend. Being offensive means being productive in the challenges to the moral and metaphysical concepts that restrict the diversity of forms of life.

Another way in which the inhumanity of the *Übermensch* emerged in literature and film was through the notion of atavism. In the debate about social Darwinism, atavism was spoken of in frightening terms as the fact that "the past will not let go" and that "dead hands from older graves" are holding recessive and unimagined traits within us.[37] Yet the atavism was regarded as a specific hereditary result that could be healthy *or* morbid.[38] The two most important cinematic atavisms are Tarzan and Dr. Fu Manchu.[39] Tarzan is a beneficial sort of atavism, a return to traits of vitality, strength, and nobility, whom Edgar Rice Burroughs explicitly calls a "super-man" in the first novel, *Tarzan of the Apes*.[40] The popularity of this modern myth in American film was remarkable: there were five silent films based on the Tarzan novels, followed by over twenty sound films. Fu Manchu is found in three early sound films with Warner Oland and then the Boris Karloff film *The Mask of Fu Manchu* (1932). He represents the brutish form of atavism, a return to a murderous life of cruelty and hate. Such bestial atavism was commonly tied up with racist ideas, as in Cecil B. DeMille's Asian stereotype in *The Cheat* (1915). But the most obvious form of this atavistic *Übermensch* was the barbaric Hun, which flooded theaters in anti-German propaganda films such as *The Little American* (1917), *The Kaiser, the Beast of Berlin* (1918), Raoul Walsh's *The Prussian Cur* (1918), *Kultur* (1918), *Wolves of Kultur* (1918), *The Hun Within* (1918), *Kaiser's Finish* (1918), *The Claws of the Hun* (1918), *The Heart of Humanity* (1918), D. W. Griffith's *Hearts of the World* (1918), *Behind the Door* (1919), and *Beware!* (1919).

Perhaps the most influential anti-German propaganda film is *The Battle Cry for Peace* (1915), by J. Stuart Blackton. Here social Darwinism is used to advocate for military preparedness and for a positive atavistic return to strength against modern decadence. But the film also shows the Germans as nihilistic atavisms that seem to have no aim but to burn the world to the ground.[41] The alignment of this story with social Darwinist philosophy is found clearly in the inspiration for the film, Hudson Maxim's book *Defenseless America*, which argued, among other things, that "self-preservation is the first law of Nature," that war was always inevitable, and that luxury had led to weakness and effeminacy.[42] Maxim's inspirations came from Teddy Roosevelt, Thomas Carlyle, and a theory of life pulled from Ernst Haeckel and Herbert Spencer. The result was a conception of human evolution based on strife and war, and a theory of life based on the need for strong stimuli and the balance of opposing forces. This led him to the social Darwinian conclusion that the "the reward for strength and the penalty for weakness" were as great today as they ever had been in human existence, and that the Christian teaching of pity could not change human nature.[43] Whether Maxim was a reader of Nietzsche or not, it seems unlikely that a person as involved as he was in discussing the threat of "German militarism" would not have heard of Nietzsche.[44] Thus, it is surprising when we find him essentially adopting ideas commonly associated with Nietzsche: "The best of us are at heart barbarians under a thin veneer of civilization, and it is as natural for us to revert to barbarous war as for the hog to return to his wallow."[45] A nearly Nietzschean analysis of the hypocrisy of the peace-lovers also appears in Maxim's book when he points out that their doctrine of "mildness, meekness, self-sacrifice, and lowly-spiritedness" is paradoxically enforced with violence and cruelty.[46] He adopts the idea that "war" is the foundation of "all the high virtues and faculties of men" from John Ruskin, which sounds not unlike Nietzsche's praise of the virtues of his own warlike nature in *Ecce Homo* (*EH* 1 §7). Maxim also arrives at such an idea from Emerson as well, whose influence on Nietzsche has been often noted: "War educates the senses, calls into action the will, perfects the physical constitution, brings men into such swift and close collision in critical moments that man measures man. On its own scale, in the virtues it loves, it endures no counterfeit, but shake the whole society until every atom falls into the place its specific gravity assigns it."[47] In the end, *Defenseless America* ultimately endorses the "survival of the fittest" and a philosophy of war, arguing that it is primarily the weakest and "stay-at-home incompetents" who are killed in times of war rather than the strong.[48] Such a naïve viewpoint surely would have been impossible by the time that the First World War came to an end.

While *The Battle Cry for Peace* is lost, its details are available to us in the story and images that Blackton published. Advertising from the film identifies war and the destruction of morality and civilization with a hairy caveman-like figure, but it paradoxically also associates such a return to barbarism with "the hatred and passion of nations" and "the crime of weakness." The enemy is found in both the brutal, atavistic barbarian and the weaklings who are unprepared for war. The film depicts the enervating effects and decadent behaviors of the "Peace-at-any-Price" groups, which are infiltrated by spies from the fictional Ruritania.[49] The Ruritania spies are monsters, while the pacifists are hedonistic elites. After bringing about a severe weakening of national defense, Ruritania immediately invades in an extremely cruel attack on the civilian population by a sexually rapacious army. This brings about a change of heart in the remaining pacifists in favor of a philosophy of "Peace thru Power."[50] The film simply contrasts the forces of barbarism against the forces of civilization and sees the former as embodied in the Nietzschean *Übermensch* and the latter only in those warriors fighting for home and country. To explain the connection between the weak pacifists and the invading barbarians, the film must show that the activists do not care about "human brotherhood" as they proclaim and are instead corrupt egoists. It is this egoism that unifies the threats within the film.

In addition to the previously mentioned Tarzan films, the clearest presentation of the positive atavism on film was through the work of Jack London, who had encountered Nietzsche's thought early in his career around 1903. London made the obscure notion of the atavism, as both a noble and brutish return to nature, into a prominent idea in popular American literature and cinema.[51] His work was made into numerous short and feature-length films in the 1910s, primarily by Hobart Bosworth and his production company. Films such *The Sea Wolf* (1913), *John Barleycorn* (1914), *Martin Eden* (1914), and *The Chechako* (1914) would present London's vision of men who were hardened by extremes both in the external world and in their own hearts. Addiction, madness, and suicide seemed to be the fates of many who experienced atavistic recapitulation. Yet rather than a mere brute who simply wants to trample on the weak, London often managed a truer Nietzschean vision of *animae magnae prodigus*. Traits of the positive atavism, such as strength, courage, and single-mindedness, were recognized as incompatible with the modern world and needed to be aired in isolated climates. The result of the de-civilization of the human being was an inhumanism that was at once awe-inspiring and ephemeral due to its self-destructiveness. This vision appeared again and again in London's hereditary *Übermenschen* in films such as *Burning Daylight* (1920), *The Sea Wolf* (1920), *The Mutiny of the Elsinore* (1920), *The Little Fool* (1921), *The Son of the Wolf* (1922), *Abysmal Brute* (1923), *Call of the Wild* (1923), and *Adventure* (1925).[52] Zweig's famous account of the literary trope of "adventure" makes Nietzsche into the primary philosopher of the "'inhumanity' in human nature," which is what makes the "adventurer" into a "source of values, expressing the essentially human adventure of man engaged in the economy of struggle which is the world."[53]

The debate about the animality within us and the threat of atavistic return is outlined in Jack London's novel *Before Adam*, an unnerving tale of our ape ancestors. Central to the tale is the evil character "Red-Eye," who is explicitly called an atavism and is aggressive to the point of killing his own wives. He is the most primitive and cruel of the proto-human "Folk" (essentially, Neanderthals), a return to something more monstrous than even what is found in "lower animals" (the more primitive apes, or Tree-People). Such atavism borders on insanity and is a foreshadowing of "the coming of man," namely, the more advanced Fire-People (humans).[54] London's tale is the dramatization of the Nietzschean idea of a being who is an evolutionary rope between something higher and something lesser. But the lesson in London's novel appears to be that both ends of the rope are problematic: the higher Fire-People engage in genocide, and the lower Red-Eye is an unthinking psychopath. Evolution toward something higher seems an inescapable fact of the novel, but the in-between "Folk" have characteristics of playfulness, curiosity, joy, lack of seriousness, and a lack of attachment and forgetfulness, which are lost on either the ascending or descending path.[55] Develop the "Folk" must, but how and at what cost? London presents an intriguingly Nietzschean world of figures who fluidly transform between these types.

While London's *Before Adam* may be a paean to a future of open possibilities as well as a cautionary tale of the dangers of such growth, the silent films that envision our Darwinian roots often lack this sophistication. D. W. Griffith's *Man's Genesis* (1912) was directly inspired by London's work and is described as "psychological comedy founded upon the Darwinian theory of the evolution of man." Ultimately, Griffith's story of cavemen has little to do with London's novel and, instead, simply concerns the creation of tools by a human called "Weakhands" after he is defeated by "Bruteforce," a saga that he would continue in *The Primitive Man* (1914) (originally titled *Brute Force*). Here we find a simple story of our hominization, of the value of the reasoning mind over mere physical strength and a criticism of the *Übermensch* as commonly understood. A year before Griffith's cinematic anthropology, Thanhauser released *As It Was in the Beginning*, which had the working title *Her Master*. In this misogynistic tale, a modern woman reflects on prehistoric times and on a "masterful" man who could be brutish and resistant to feminine charms, a pure, no-nonsense Tarzan of a man. While Griffith clearly sees the atavism as beneath us, a morally condemnable hindrance to progress, *As It Was in the Beginning* sees the atavism as morally praiseworthy due to his ability to dominate and add vitality to the species. The two atavisms can be found together in the 1916 film version of *20,000 Leagues under the Sea*, in which Captain Nemo is a black-faced maniac hell-bent on some unspecified form of revenge, whereas on the "mysterious island" a black-faced female "child of nature" is found frolicking. We can see the two types of atavisms in the documentary films of the time as well. It has been argued that a Nietzschean philosophy of a joyous, natural form of life underlies *Nanook of the North* (1922),[56] whereas the atavistic return to "humanity at its lowest ebb" on the "island that God forgot" is found in exploitation films such as *Shipwrecked among Cannibals* (1920) and the "headhunting" films (1923, 1928, 1931) by Edward Salisbury.[57] But it is surely the case that both types of depiction of the atavism miss Nietzsche's point. The *Übermensch* presents neither the noble savage nor an atavistic horror. Perhaps the sort of careless, laughing, and forgetful lives that we see in the prehistoric farces, such as Charlie Chaplin's *His Prehistoric Past* (1914), *Clubs Are Trumps* (1917) with Harold Lloyd, Cecile B. DeMille's *Adam's Rib* (1923), Buster Keaton's *Three Ages* (1923), Sydney Chaplin's *The Missing Link* (1927), and Laurel and Hardy's *Flying Elephants* (1928), are closer to the childlike, amoral innocence of the *Übermensch*.

The moral response to the threat of an atavistic return to nature is at the heart of Cecil B. DeMille's *Male and Female* (1919). Even if our primitive natures hold some sort of basic truth, it must be resisted for the sake of preserving tradition and civilization. The film is based on *The Admirable Crichton* (1902), by J. M. Barrie, the creator of *Peter Pan*. This Robinsonade is structurally identical to Ludwig Fulda's *Robinsons Eiland* (1896). But unlike Fulda's more egalitarian tale, Barrie's tale articulates the "radical view" that servants and lords should drink tea together only to reject it and, thus, maintain traditional class divisions. This tale of blue-blooded aristocrats, who learn the virtues of the red-blooded butler Crichton, dances ambiguously between scandalous ideas and images. It tantalizes us with perversions of the natural and social order only to then preserve that order. The film is fascinated with the erotic powers of the primitive, the exotic, and the mixing of classes. But these temptations are ultimately regarded as too destructive. The film asserts that between different types and things, "comparisons are odious—and sometimes dangerous." Neither this socially conservative core of the film nor its ode to the vital powers and ingenuity within the more primitive lower class constitutes anything like an acceptance of Nietzschean ideas. In fact, the radical philosophy that advocates for a naturalism and that destroys both class distinctions and Christian morality is the ultimate threat in the film. The key to the film is William Ernest Henley's poem "Or Ever the Knightly Years." In that poem, a Babylonian king reflects on his brutal use of force to break the "pride" of a "Virgin Slave" and force her to "love" him. She curses "the gods" and kills herself, and now this haunts him. He is filled with regret. The specter of such a return to barbarism, seen as pagan violence against Christian morals, shows us how *Male and Female* is engaged with the Nietzschean-Darwinian onslaught that was permeating American culture.

Before being stranded, Gloria Swanson's Lady Mary rejects the idea of love between the classes and argues that it is "kind to kind." She asks, "Would you put a jackdaw and a bird-of-paradise in the same cage?" She is completely against these "democratic" notions. Like the pacifists who praise peace over all other values in Blackton's film, DeMille has Lady Mary's friend Lady Duncraigie, who will marry her chauffeur, praise the value of love over all things. Whereas Fulda's original work seems to have accepted such idealistic visions, neither Barrie's text nor DeMille's film goes down this route. In fact, it is love—in the lovelorn tears of Tweeny, the maid who loves Crichton—that leads to the boating party being stranded on the island. Love is a cataclysmic disruption and is named "Destiny" in the film. Presumably, this destiny gives them the opportunity to test the Darwinian philosophy that Crichton articulates: "One cannot tell what may be in a man, my Lady: if all were to return to Nature tomorrow, the same man might not be master—nor the same man servant—Nature would decide the matter for us!" I do not think that this point is actually proven by the fact that Crichton becomes the leader once they get stranded on an island. In fact, Crichton refrains from becoming a "master" in any true sense. He becomes the group's savior and says that on the island what must happen is that *everyone must be of service*. He takes charge so that they all survive. While he takes on the appearance of being their leader, it is not clear that his position is much different from still being a servant. Is there really a return to nature that disrupts civilization, or do the moral values that define society remain?

As the feelings grow between Crichton and Lady Mary on the island, he allows himself to fantasize a true return to nature and to brutal mastery. The tale of the poem comes to life. Crichton is the Babylonian King, and Lady Mary is the Christian slave. But rather than be his, she marches herself into the lion's den and is devoured. Lady Mary's status is reaffirmed as she annihilates herself rather than allow pagan passion to flourish. Crichton's fantasy of the Henley poem shows him that moral and religious values must hold, even if the social order is disrupted by "Destiny." Radical philosophies like Nietzsche's cannot be allowed to define us. Their egoism threatens civilization. But this misunderstanding of Nietzsche's philosophy, as a nihilistic, anarchical primitivism, continually keeps these works from recognizing their affinities with Nietzsche's thought. Just as H. G. Wells attacked Nietzsche and then advocated for the social engineering of a new kinetic man of the future, and just as Maxim attacked German militarism but advocated vitalism and animalistic power beneath the veneer of civilization, so also does DeMille's film criticize the atavistic myth for the sake of an aristocratism that aligns with at least a superficial reading of the Nietzschean praise of the "pathos of distance."

Upon being saved from the island, Crichton says that he must return to normal life and "play the game" of a servant, which he does. Has the island shown that these class divisions are a mere game? If that is so, then why must he return to this game? It seems to me that this game is endorsed as essential. Not only that, but Crichton, the pagan and potential rapist in that fantasy, shows himself to be unworthy of Mary, the good Christian. His brutish impulses erupt several times, in intimidating motions he makes toward Tweeny so that she goes to tend the fire, in dunking the head of a loafer in a water bucket, and in his first scene in the film, where he smiles about a young peeping tom before scolding him. So, despite his red-bloodedness, ingenuity, and leadership, it is not clear that Crichton overcomes his "lowness." His ingenuity does not show him worthy of Mary's love or of ascension into the aristocracy. Such hybridization of the classes is rejected when Mary's friend marries her chauffeur and is ruined. When Mary expresses that she would give up everything for "someone," Lady Duncraigie tells her, "Love *isn't* everything! There is Heredity—and Tradition—and London!" The idea that the elite are soft and degenerated by luxury and that the working class are more self-sufficient is undoubtedly stated in the film for comedic effect. But that does not deny the principle of "kind to kind." Lady Mary's self-sacrifice in the fantasy effectively overpowers the passion within Crichton, leading him to also make a "great sacrifice." He and Tweeny leave their jobs of service and form a new life together in America. The types remain separated. Even if Crichton represents a type a strength, it is one that flares up in violence, both in reality and in fantasy. But Lady Mary's grace, beauty, and morals remain unmatched even as Crichton makes his great sacrifice for the preservation of tradition. If *Male and Female* is correct, human progress does not take place through survival of the fittest or through an appeal to atavistic traits that may upend the social order. It takes place through Christian morality and respecting the division between classes even when it appears that the slave has become the master.

Unnatural Knowledge and the Monsters It Creates

The films discussed so far all belong to the genre of the "social problem" film. Whether the themes are eugenics, peace, war, charity, or class division, they all are concerned with what we might call the threats to civilization that typically looked like German soldiers, Neanderthals, ne'er-do-well decadents, thugs, or philosophers. The enemy is, in every instance, the egoist, who represents the threat of an atavistic slide into the primitive side of nature, the destruction of civilization, and, in many cases, the philosophy of Nietzsche. These same concerns appear in early horror films, which often make explicit their appeal to the *Übermensch*, Darwinian concepts, and esoteric Teutonic philosophy. The most obvious example of this is in the various Frankenstein films.[58] Take, for example, the 1910 Edison short film *Frankenstein*. It is explained that Dr. Frankenstein will attempt to "create into life the most perfect human being that the world has yet known." This idea of creating a *perfect* human being is absent from Mary Shelley's novel, in which all that is really said of Frankenstein's ambitions is that he wants to bring light to the world by conquering life and death, which will be of service to all mankind and will, in the process, bring about "a new species."[59] The idea of creating a *perfect* being, or a superman, seems to a direct result of the discourse surrounding Nietzsche. There is said to be an evil in Dr. Frankenstein's mind in the 1910 film, which is the reason why his creation is a monster rather than a perfect human being. That evil is his focus on his research, his isolation from other persons, and his failure to love, which causes him to favor science and knowledge over his sweetheart. Once again, the main threat is egoism. When this evil is eliminated and he sets aside his research for the sake of love, then the monster magically fades away from existence.[60]

Dr. Frankenstein's failure to love and his temptation away from the shared, human world by dark philosophies is quite similar to the masterful 1919 film *Victory*, based on the Joseph Conrad's 1915 Schopenhauerian novel of the same name. There is some evidence that Conrad knew Nietzsche's work, although the character Axel Heyst more clearly follows Schopenhauerian pessimism.[61] He has retreated to an isolated island with his father's philosophy books, living ascetically and denying his will. Conrad calls him the "man of universal detachment," and the film describes him as mysteriously, for inscrutable reasons, choosing "a life of invulnerable solitude and loneliness." Such stoicism sometimes appeals to Nietzsche, who describes his free spirits as those who are "born, sworn, jealous friends of *solitude*, of our own most profound, most midnightly, most middaily solitude" (*BGE* §44, emphasis in original). The film version expresses Heyst's regret at disrupting his own isolation to save a mistreated woman, Lena, with the Nietzschean remark that "pity makes meddlers of us all." Heyst and Lena are plagued on their volcanic island by several thugs sent to rob and kill them by the foul Schomberg, who represents the "the psychology of a Teuton" according to Conrad.[62] But it is Lon Chaney's Ricardo, a bloodthirsty, double-crossing, sex-crazed atavism, who clearly is the greatest threat. Ultimately, against such barbarism, the film tells us to love, act, and even kill. Written on the eve of the First World War, both the novel and the film reject the life of peace and of separation from the herd. Such isolationism is said in the film to be slavery to an idea. Yet rejecting that idea leads to war and death. While this is an ambiguous outcome in the novel, in the Hollywood ending, Heyst finds love to be life's greatest adventure and praises the freedom "to slay and die for his woman." He seems to have turned from the life of contemplation to the law of the jungle. What the film offers us is a criticism of a type of egoistic, idealistic, and isolationist philosophy that goes against human emotion and ignores human society. Such egoism is rejected for a life of courage, defending civilization from the threat of Nietzschean and Darwinian philosophies that would return us to primitive islands of madness.

The aim to create a perfect *Übermensch* unifies many early horror films. In the 1915 film *Life without Soul*, life is imbued in a statue, like the famous Golem tale, but the result is a reanimated being without a soul.[63] This film explicitly states that the aim of "Victor Frawley" is to "create a superman," but the result is a being of "tremendous of physique but possessing no conscience."[64] We find the idea of creating superhuman geniuses in *The Crimson Stain Mystery* (1916), which results only in producing lunatic criminals. And in the lost Lon Chaney film from 1922, *A Blind Bargain*, based loosely on Barry Pain's novel *The Octave of Claudius*, from 1897, mad scientist Dr. Arthur Lamb is attempting to prolong life, but the side effect of his experiments is to revert humans to prehuman form. In 1925, Lon Chaney plays another mad scientist and hypnotist, Dr. Ziska, in the comedy-horror film *The Monster*, where he rants about power and superiority while engaging in some sort of soul transference experiments. The aim of creating new life is found in *The Magician* (1926), from W. Somerset Maugham's novel. Oliver Haddo is an *Übermensch* figure who stands "apart from humankind," beyond love and at the nexus of infinite knowledge and the "kingdoms of darkness."[65]

Maugham clearly knew of Nietzsche's thought but, like H. G. Wells, saw it as destructive egoism. Haddo is attempting to create a new race of human beings through the "manufacture of *homunculi*."[66] The notion of creating a new race of persons is here equated with black magic, alchemy, and human sacrifice. In the novel, Haddo kills Margaret and uses her blood to create a series of monstrous, deformed creatures, while the film has her rescued before this can happen. We can assume such hideous mutants are what Maugham thought of the outcome of any attempt to engineer the *Übermensch*.

The theory of human atavism is obviously at the core of *The Strange Case of Dr. Jekyll and Mr. Hyde*, by Robert Louis Stevenson.[67] The regular treatment of this story in Hollywood film shows an interesting variation of concerns across time. The first two versions, the 1908 version with Hobart Bosworth and the 1912 version with James Cruze, both seem to tell a story about the collapse of the human being into bloodlust because of drugs. They come across as morality tales telling us little more than that drugs can separate us into evil and good. To be evil is to be something entirely unredeemable, and to degenerate fully into it is to warrant death. But the 1920 film is quite different. It begins by saying that there is a battle between good and evil and that we have "the power to choose—what we want most to be, we *are*." That strange, morally ambiguous statement, echoing the Nietzschean sentiment to become who we are, is followed by a description of Henry Jekyll as a selfless idealist and a "professionally progressive" doctor of medicine who treats the poor at his own expense. His saintlike nature irritates his acquaintances, including the father of his fiancée, Sir George Carewe, who argues that he is "neglecting the development" of his own life. The life of service to others *is* self-development, Jekyll argues. But Carewe argues that a man has two selves. One is the "really strong man" who "fears nothing," and the other is the "weak one who is afraid of experience." This remarkable reframing of the problem in terms of strength and weakness, rather than moral terms of good and evil, suggests that a rather Nietzschean (or at least social Darwinian) logic is being used by screenwriter Clara Beranger. The 1920 film gives two distinct justifications for the separation of Jekyll into Hyde. The good, moral, and selfless person is a construct of weakness. We are afraid of our true nature and passions, and to separate is to become strong. But Jekyll himself justifies the transformation by arguing that the essentially good, immortal soul could live without stain or conflict if the evil side could be spent by being cast out into a different body and persona. But it is not the dream of being more Christlike that ultimately motivates Dr. Jekyll to drink his chemical concoction. It is the superimposed face of Carewe tempting him to be strong and to indulge his baser self. The fact that this evil nature comes to dominate both sides of his existence suggests that it is in fact the good self that is weaker. Carewe's cynicism makes Jekyll ashamed of his kindness and leads him to turn to evil. Thus, in 1920, the scourge that threatens modern humanity is not drugs or even his base desires, which can be controlled; it is precisely the sort of moral skepticism that Nietzsche represented.

This idea of the division of the self into two beings had its female expression in the lost film *The Two-Soul Woman* (1918) and in the remake *The Untameable* (1923), based on the novel *The White Cat*, by Frank Norris's associate Gelett Burgess. This is a gothic horror story of a woman with a split personality (Joy/Edna) who is created and controlled by the malevolent hypnotism of Dr. Copin. The figures of the scientist and mentalist are often thought of as one of the many types of degenerative "dwellers on the borderland between reason and pronounced madness," of which Max Nordau warns his readers as being the consequence of Nietzscheanism.[68] Forbidden knowledge, as seen in Mary Shelley's mention of the esoteric philosophies of Cornelius Agrippa, Paracelsus, and Albert Magnus, is regularly linked with a sort of Germanic or Semitic occultism. The figure of Svengali has become synonymous with this idea. Svengali, with his "German accent," possesses the mind of Trilby in the film of that name from 1915 and then again, with John Barrymore, in *Svengali* from 1931.[69] The idea that such unnatural knowledge could lead to a degeneration of humanity into something lower is seen in an early story by Frank Norris, whose ideas will be important in the next chapter. In his story "Lauth," a young scholar experiences "a mighty flame of blood-lust" and reverts to his "savage Celtic ancestors."[70] This atavistic regression leads to his death, after which several scientists attempt to prove that there is a "vivifying spark" but no "soul" by reanimating the dead scholar through mechanical and chemical means. The result is a horrifying regression through the entire evolutionary history of humanity. The scholar ascends from an incoherent, quivering mass of flesh to humankind, and then back down to "apish savagery." This even has a physical effect and causes him to grow animal hair, claws, and fangs and to revert to walking on all fours. Eventually, his senses wither away and all human shape disappears until he is a "horrible shapeless mass," a sort of "jelly-fish."[71] Norris's *Vandover and the Brute* also contains an atavistic return to wolf form seemingly caused by inhuman circumstances.[72] Similar ideas can be found cinematically, for example, in *Lola* (1914), in which a woman is brought back to life via a machine, but without a soul, which leads her to become a vamp and hedonist.

While I have focused on silent films from the 1910s in this chapter, it is worth mentioning that these critical encounters with Nietzsche's thought continue into the sound era. Parasitic egoism is at the heart of *Dracula* (1931), and criminal degeneration, which will be discussed in future chapters, is manifest as a "scarcity of convolutions on the frontal lobe" of the monster's brain and results in his violent behavior in the 1931 film *Frankenstein*. Unsurprisingly, films based on H. G. Wells's work tend to illustrate the evils of Nietzschean blackguardism. The clearest instance of this is in *The Invisible Man* (1933), which links obsessive egoism and worship of knowledge with invisibility. In the novel, it is said that "an invisible man is a man of power," and that he plans to establish a "Reign of Terror" by judicious slayings in some small town that will terrify its citizenry and convince them to do his bidding.[73] The character Kemp describes him as follows: "He is mad, inhuman. He is pure selfishness. He thinks of nothing but his own advantage, his own safety."[74] In the film, Claude Rains's madness and cruelty are profoundly exaggerated as he constantly proclaims his "power, power to rule" and "to make the world grovel at [his] feet." He wants to cause wanton destruction, to rob, rape, kill, and derail trains. His explanation for this is little more than the demand for power, which devolves into mad ramblings about how the moon and the whole world fear the power of his little invisible finger. Similarly, the horror of atavism is on full display in *Island of Lost Souls* (1932), the first English-film version of H. G. Wells's *The Island of Dr. Moreau*.[75] In the novel, Moreau aims to make "a rational creature" of his own, a man, but bestial traits continually return.[76] The 1932 film says very little about Moreau's motivations except that he is pursing scientific knowledge, although his real motivation is perhaps revealed when he talks about feeling like god. His main project, the Leopard Woman, is referred to as his attempt to make "the perfect woman." Of course, all Dr. Moreau ends up making are mixtures of beast and human, who, being neither and coming to realize this, begin screaming in rage that he has made them mere "things."[77] Overall, the horrors of these atavisms, soulless resurrections, divided natures, human-animal fusions, formation of homunculi, creations of new life, and experiments of black magic represent the existential threat that many people saw in the philosophy of Darwin and Nietzsche.

Conclusion

Admittedly, the link to the thought of Nietzsche is rather indirect in several of the films discussed in this chapter, as his influence on film was initially through the larger sociobiological debates, which included many other writers as well. Nevertheless, there is some evidence that several of the authors on which these films are based were aware of Nietzsche. This moralistic reckoning with a biologistic account of the *Übermensch* constitutes little more than the crude first steps of an increasingly sophisticated intersection between Nietzschean philosophy and cinema. Eventually this intersection would lead to films capable of expressing a uniquely modern challenge to traditional values and ethics, as well as to American culture and identity. The films and cultural discourse examined in this chapter present us with a conception of the inhuman within the human. The inhuman is largely considered evil in these films, but the fact that there is within us what Kant once called a "radical evil," a deep-seated resistance to law, is something that we will see being recognized as the source of value and of life itself in future chapters.

2

The Weakness in Strength

The *Übermensch* as Degenerate in the Films of Erich von Stroheim

Introduction

WHILE NATURALISM INFILTRATED Hollywood cinema in its early decades, Nietzsche's thought appeared on film more like as a social ill than an alternative value system. The *Übermensch* was akin to other social problems like drugs, the loss of one's soul, atavistic de-evolution, bestial passions, warmongering, occult knowledge, immoral science, isolationism, animal blood-mixing, and congenital madness. Nietzsche's influence was usually indirect within the "narrative formula of the social problem film" but was rather direct in early horror films.[1] While both genres condemn the egoistic *Übermensch*, the films of Erich von Stroheim present us with the first positive cinematic evaluations of the *Übermensch*. They also present us with an opportunity to see a Nietzschean aesthetics of film in practice. In particular, Stroheim relies heavily on sequences of conflicting symbols to illustrate the degeneration of different value systems. Each worldview has its weaknesses exposed when faced with the irrational forces of fate and history. The metaphysics of becoming, the waxing and waning of life through degeneration and regeneration—that is the heart of Stroheim's world. He offers us, we might say, a cinema of *différance*, an illumination of the traces that make possible a subversion of every sign into its opposite.[2] The noble and the traditional are inextricably linked to the perverse and the modern. Within Stroheim's work, there is also the sense of entering into a singular, obsessive set of interests of the director. Not only are these films disruptive of any sort of cinematic realism by being clearly symbolic, psycho-sexual, and socio-historical myths, but they also suggest that the myth of director as "master manipulator" is being undermined by Stroheim's own obsessive passions.[3] It seems as if he cannot film anything but this decline of civilization. While there is a gesture at "mimesis," in which Stroheim presents us with the Italian Alps or Monte Carlo, this in fact acts as "parodic strategy" in which *reality* is another word for "the inevitable perpetuation of myth" and the singularity of Stroheim's memory and fantasy.[4] Realism, naturalism, and materialism, aspects of Stroheim's work that are often praised, are used only to show their limitations in contrast to the powers of the irreal, unnatural, and symbolic.[5] Were Stroheim's elaborate sets striving for verisimilitude or for an embodiment of his own imagination? Material objects are symbols of spiritual aspirations and degeneration. Nature itself becomes a site of cultural and spiritual conflict. There is no escape from fate's conversion of one thing to its opposite. Nor is there any escape from the process of attempting to make sense of this process through representation and self-invention, and this is the power of the *Übermensch*.

In these films, appearances are always deceiving. One value is always exposed as its opposite, illustrating what Deleuze describes as "the power of the false of life, the will to power," or the fact that "there is only becoming."[6] The aristocracy is buffoonish, crude, and low. The most civilized and polite figures are also the most passionate and cruel. Hubris is always crushed. The lowly are elevated. The moral choice is as dangerous and disastrous as the immoral one. The symbols and settings of the sacred are the playground of a pagan heart. Reality is revealed as impersonal fate, as time itself, which leaves the "human" as the unstable attempt to retain stability. Stroheim develops a vision of the *Übermensch* as a tragic figure, a piece of fate, whose tremendous will and strength leads to a dangerous challenge to existing circumstances and, whether intentional or not, an exposure of reality's fractures.[7] Often selfish and parasitic, the *Übermensch* is a form of degeneration in Stroheim's works, but that does not preclude a positive evaluation of the figure or its effects in a world where *everything* is undergoing degeneration. This figure, even when morally abhorrent, can point to a radical relation to life and time itself. It suggests a form of life that manifests as a dangerous and heedless existence, which can degenerate into purely destructive desires or can point to the possibility of regeneration, if not for the *Übermensch* himself, then for those who surround him.

Nordau, Norris, and Degeneration

Any examination of Stroheim's biography will show how his colorful life of self-invention and passion appears modeled on the notion the *Übermensch*. He was committed to self-invention, to life as an aesthetic phenomenon, and to the strength of passions. Furthermore, we know that he must have been intimately familiar with the defining early moment in the Anglophone Nietzsche reception, Max Nordau's criticism of Nietzsche from 1892 in his book *Degeneration*. That Nordau's thought was influential for Stroheim is seen in his first written work, "In the Morning" (1912), where he praises Nordau's *Paradoxes* as "a philosophy of every day, for everyone."[8] *Paradoxes* is essentially Nordau's positive philosophy, a strange mixture of Lamarckianism, materialism, *Lebensphilosophie*, and social conservativism, whereas *Degeneration* is his criticism of Schopenhauer, Tolstoy, Wagner, Romanticism, modernist forms of poetry and painting, Ibsen, Zola, Nietzsche, and numerous others. Nordau could have led Stroheim to have a rather negative conception of Nietzsche as a thinker and person, yet "In the Morning" does not obviously condemn the idea of a Nietzschean *Übermensch* who overturns society's standards. The character of "the Stranger" articulates a philosophy opposed to traditional notions of honor and bravery and praises a heroic rebellion against the world: "But to fight alone—to match your wits and your nerve against a whole world—a hostile world. To fight to every tomorrow, in a world which does not understand—which does not want to understand. To fight alone—always alone. That takes courage."[9] We can find similar ideas in the novels of Frank Norris, who was a tremendous influence on Stroheim. Norris often gives voice to the *Übermensch*, as in *Vandover and the Brute*, published in 1914, where Geary expresses the concept of *animae magnae prodigus* through the idea of achieving "something on a tremendous scale" and doing so by abandoning "friendships, fortunes, scruples, principles, life itself, no matter what . . . to attain the desired object in spite of the whole world, to ride on at it, trampling down or smashing through everything that stood in the way, blind, deaf, fists and teeth shut tight."[10] But no member of "the infinite herd of humanity" can escape the fact that "all life was but a struggle to keep from under those myriad spinning wheels that dashed so close behind" and inevitably overtake us.[11] Although Norris's vision may be more representative of Stroheim's worldview than the conservativism of Nordau, Nordau's key concept of "degeneration," a concept also found in Nietzsche, is still crucial for Stroheim.

This idea was part of the confusing pseudoscientific discourses of the time and amounted to the idea that there could be a reduction in the "complexity" of a thing's structure rather than the normal evolutionary "elaboration" or increase in complexity.[12] One idea of degeneration was that once food and safety were easily attained, then complexity and ability to innovate and do different sorts of work collapsed. The idea was directly connected to human cultures that had an excess of wealth and luxury and, thus, gave rise to individuals and groups who were degenerate, unadaptable parasites.[13] Nordau's very influential notion of degeneration is Lamarckian, arguing that a "*morbid deviation from an original type*" caused by "noxious influences" will then be transmitted to the offspring, eventually creating a subspecies that dies out after a few generations (emphasis in original).[14] Human degenerates are "dwellers on the borderland between reason and pronounced madness."[15] They have a "moral insanity" designated by "unbounded egoism," "impulsiveness," "emotionalism," mysticism, and pessimism.[16] The type of degeneration that plagues Nietzsche, according to Nordau, is egomania, in which a person is essentially an "invalid who does not see things as they are, does not understand the world, and cannot take up a right attitude towards it."[17] Unable to adapt to the conditions found in the world, the egomaniac descends into "immorality" and "moral madness," although they may be a mere "theoretic malefactor" who constructs a philosophy to "justify depravity."[18] Despite this criticism, there are clear, albeit unacknowledged, Nietzschean affinities with Nordau's own Lamarckian philosophy, which rejects the notion of static natural laws and endorses a *Lebensphilosophie* in which truth, art, and the self are unique constructions of genius. This may well have been another way in which Nietzschean ideas reached Stroheim.[19] Nordau's own conception of genius suggests a positive *Übermensch* that avoids reductive, biologistic accounts of it. The question is whether the traditions of the community should be continued and preserved as a source of truth, as Nordau believes, or whether the genius must turn that history on its end. Stroheim presumably saw that history itself had undergone such upheaval in the twenty years since Nordau's works were published that the question was now how to live among the ruins of the past rather than how to preserve it.

Stroheim's films embody the modernist trope of the tragicomedy. Orr describes tragicomedy as making "the reversal of fortune a matter of laughter as well as sorrow, of comic error as well as lament" and having the "role of play, role, and masquerade" become "increasingly reflexive, knowing, volatile, a property of the stage as much as the soul":[20] "Tragicomic heroes are helpless prisoners of performance, diminished by circumstance, prisoners of action, not its authorizers. Their world is circular and change of fortune merely moves them round a fixed circumference. . . . Life at all social levels, in all affairs of the heart, crosses over and is tragic and farcical at the same time. . . . The tragicomic generates images of fear, distrust, extravagance, desire and vanity. It points to the fragility of class power and the dubious morality of its cultural advantages, to gross mismatches of technology and culture, power and desire."[21] In terms of the symbolic worlds that Stroheim creates, his mise-en-scène is famously crammed full of objects, furtive expressions, and ceremonial behaviors all in service to detailing and undermining both human pretension and the myths and values that are the bedrock of society. It was this overdetermination and symbolic density of his worlds that made his films so expensive and cost him his career. But it was also what allowed them then to show the power of history and of circumstances over the prisoners of these worlds. Persons are suffocating and literally made small by their surroundings. Eventually he shows how each value system tragically and comically degenerates into its opposite. These deconstructive films cannot picture any positive future: it always lies beyond the frame. These *Übermenschen* are mixtures of both the *Unmensch* and *Übermensch*, which can act only as a rope leading to a future form of sustainable life.

Stroheim Directs the Collapse of Civilization

Stroheim's first film is *Blind Husbands* (1919), which he originally entitled *The Pinnacle*, after the mountain that is "as old as the world itself" that figures so prominently in it.[22] The opening description of the mountain already points to the temporal and cosmic aspects of this cinematic universe. The mountain's eternal perspective is immediately contrasted to the traditional, religious values of the "little" village Cortina, which is said to be "choked" by the Alpine magnitude surrounding it. We are presented with its chaotic town square on "the Seventh Day," followed by church bells and simple, faithful people praying at an outdoor chapel. Half of the film takes place at the "White Cross" (*Croce Bianca*) Hotel, while the rest takes place on the Pinnacle. The contrast between this religious village and the cosmic power of the mountain suggests that these are two contrasting perspectives on the world. The first statement of any human, given to us by the intertitles, is the question "What time is it?" Thus, we are presented with an explicit statement of the human's temporal finitude in contrast to the perspective of the eternal. The insignificance of human aims and intentions is also made evident in the hubris of the three Americans who attempt to climb the north side of the mountain and meet their demise. This early example of the *Bergfilme* presents us, as does Nietzsche, with the "eternities" during which human meaning and value do not exist (*PT* p. 79).

The film's main degenerate, Lt. Erich von Steuben, played by Stroheim himself, appears as a third value system. He represents not only "the Other man" but modern decadence in general. As previously mentioned, the notion of degeneracy is a notion of specialization: a being has focused on one set of skills to the exclusion of a more complex and sustainable existence. Steuben's area of specialization is, as announced by the intertitles, "wine, WOMEN and song." He attempts to seduce three women in his first night, a "village blossom," a "vamp" waitress, and the American doctor's wife. The three women also present to us contrasting value systems: the sentimental tradition, the primitive atavism, and the modern, bourgeois woman who is separated from passion and life itself. The village is not as simple and pastoral as it first appears. There is a homegrown degenerate, a sexually promiscuous and jealous waitress, who pursues Steuben from the moment he appears on screen. Degeneration is not just a modern sickness. So it is not surprising that the film ends with the assertion of Steuben's degenerate philosophy that we are "created for nothing but love—love with its longings and ecstasies," rather than offering some traditional moral conclusion. Dr. Armstrong and his wife are clearly suffering from another sort of degeneration—a passionless exhaustion caused by the modern world. The husband's degeneration has manifested as his "blindness," "self-complacency," and the "alienation of affection," in which he "forgets the wooing wiles of his prenuptial days." With remarkable economy, the opening scenes provide us with a complicated set of modern and traditional values, each showing signs of degeneration and finitude, as opposed to the perspective of the eternal mountain.

This cosmic symbolism was even more explicit in Stroheim's original vision for the film. During one of Steuben's attempted seductions of Mrs. Armstrong, the scene was supposed to cut to a shepherd boy playing a flute, before Steuben himself appears "in a faun costume playing the flute into the ear of Margaret, who is depicted as a cowherd nymph."[23] It is worth noting what Nietzsche says of such "Dionysian companions" as the satyr or faun.

> The satyr, like the idyllic shepherd of more recent times, is the offspring of a longing for the primitive and the natural; but how firmly and fearlessly the Greek embraced the man of the woods and how timorously and mawkishly modern man dallied with the flattering image of a sentimental, flute-playing, tender shepherd. Nature, as yet unchanged by knowledge, with the bolts of culture still unbroken—that is what the Greek saw in his satyr who nevertheless was not a mere ape. On the contrary, the satyr was the archetype of man, the embodiment of his highest and most intense emotions, the ecstatic reveler enraptured by the proximity of his god, the sympathetic companion in whom the suffering of the god is repeated, one who proclaims wisdom from the very heart of nature, a symbol of the sexual omnipotence of nature which the Greeks used to contemplate with reverent wonder. (*BT* §8)

This passage from Nietzsche could have easily been an influence on *Blind Husbands*. The village and locals like Sepp, the mountaineer, are sentimental images like the flute-playing shepherd. It is important to see that Stroheim is, like Nietzsche, not embracing the mawkish symbol of the tender shepherd and simply condemning Steuben, the Dionysian satyr. We can clearly see what condemnation of this symbol of our most intense emotions looks like in D. W. Griffith's extremely moralistic and profoundly un-Nietzschean film *The Avenging Conscience* (1914), where the satyr is a "ghoul" and the product of madness. For Stroheim, the satyr proclaims the Dionysian wisdom of the sexual omnipotence of nature, which the blind husband has forgotten.[24] One might believe that his placing of an adulterous seduction during the festival of Christ's transfiguration or in front of three crosses recreating the scene of the Crucifixion to be a moral condemnation of these passions. Instead, a Nietzschean approach to these layers of symbols would be to see their juxtaposition as pointing to their similarities, to the omnipotence of sexuality underlying both symbolic orders. All are expressions of the will to power. Steuben's degenerate philosophy of passion more honestly captures the temporal, human perspective than either the sentimental, the religious, or the polite bourgeois value perspectives. Each value tradition can be thought of in mythological terms, a nexus of possibilities unified around a classical, cultural symbol. Each scene is an intersection of these value systems constructed in the shadow of the eternal abyss of the mountain. Deleuze argues that such a cinematic embrace of "irreducible multiplicity . . . shatters the system of judgment because of the power of the false" and results in false rather than "truthful narration."[25] We see this false narration in how Stroheim's work veils itself in religious symbols, seemingly in support of traditional marriage and the sentimentality of the flute-playing shepherd, but it is actually subverting those value perspectives through the mountain's cosmic indifference and the constant degenerating and regenerating inversions of life. We might call that process of constant inversion the will to power, but the film calls it love.

Who should we consider to be an image of the *Übermensch* and why? Is it Sepp, the local mountain man, the American doctor, or Steuben? What is the function of the *Übermensch*? Is it to act as the sentimental symbol of the idyllic shepherd, the seductive Dionysian satyr, or the dispassionate American who recovers his passion for his wife? The *Übermensch* in Stroheim's world is a precarious figure. He embraces life's passion and the universal process of endless becoming, but to do so is dangerous. The soul that expends itself on great things is always near complete degeneration. The *Übermensch* acts as a symbol of a power of ardent love that invigorates the society of *Menschen* to strive for greatness. This is not the role of Sepp, the mountaineer, who acts as the Superego, guarding moral traditions and values. Identified as the son of the mountain, he is a Christlike figure, a symbol of a lost, sentimental past that was one of humanity's early attempts to stave off the crushing weight of eternity. While some have thought that Dr. Armstrong represents American strength and cleanliness in contrast to the European degenerate, this fails to recognize Dr. Armstrong's own weakness and his need for Steuben. The American doctor specializes in altruistic and dispassionate behavior. Like Dr. Frankenstein, who ignores his fiancée, he needs to return to the world of love, to no longer see the body through his medical eye. While we might say that Stroheim's work here is an example of cinematic naturalism, it is not one that is particularly "caught up in realism" and, thus, unable to arrive at the subjective world of the affects.[26] In fact, what Stroheim's work seems to recognize, as Deleuze notes, is the process of "natural degradation," the entropy of violent passions and impulses, which cannot make it onscreen through (psychological) realism and action.[27] Instead, they require the lyricism of myth. Such passions are put to film by exposing the conflict of symbols that sits at the heart of the real.

To interpret Steuben as the *Übermensch* requires us to reckon with the comedic aspects of his character and his weaknesses, which lead to his death. The wild children of Cortina mock his regimented walk, and everyone sees through his politeness and ceremonial behavior to recognize him as an egoist. But Stroheim, the director, lavishes attention on his immaculate style. His clothes, his perfumes, his monocle, his cigarette, and the affected behavior by which he manipulates these objects is both comic and, yet, effective as part of his specialism in seduction. His words and feelings are fake—he repeats them to each of his conquests—but they provoke real emotion and real crises. Stroheim was clear that Steuben was meant as a depiction of the "kulturist," which means that he is a proud egoist, an aesthete, and a hedonist.[28] This is the *Übermensch* thought of as a modern, urban, intelligent, cultured, and refined degenerate. His greatest strength and greatest weakness are his egoism. This is the problem of degeneration: specialization is both a strength and weakness. His degeneration is such that he has hindered the multiplicity within himself and lost access to the "incompossible presents, or the coexistence of not-necessarily true pasts" that make up human possibility, including the possibility of regeneration.[29] That is, he cannot shift from his own perspective to any of the others. The result of this is that once placed in a new environment outside of human society and confronted by raw nature in the guise of a predatory bird, he panics and falls to his death.

While the human world is littered with religious iconography, the mountain itself is an eternal inhuman force. It passes judgment on the characters of the film, nearly killing Sepp in a flashback and then wounding Dr. Armstrong, after he makes the *moral* decision to return to help Steuben rather than leave him alone to die. The mountain is described as merely "lifting itself to immortal Heaven" rather than actually being a holy place. Instead, it is "forbidding and still, still as everlasting death." The Pinnacle is an altar of sacrifice, a purifying and terrifying judge. When Stroheim was asked to rewrite the story for a sound film, the mountain was no longer called the Pinnacle. Its true nature was revealed. It was called "The Teufelsberg. Monte Diablo. The Devil's Mountain." The mountain kills not because of a concern for justice or morality. It kills anyone who, as the mountaineer Sepp says, "does not leave behind all worldly troubles." Of course, to leave all worldly troubles behind *is to die*. Thus, Sepp says that they will die on the mountain only if they fail to die to the world. Paradoxically, it is this death to the world and, specifically, the death of sexual desire in Dr. Armstrong that has led to the alienation of affection from his wife and to the seductions of Steuben. Humans are in a terrible situation: to survive the deadly altar of sacrifice, they must forget their "baser self." Doing so allows "the soul beneath the mind" to "grow clean." But the actual lesson of the film is that the death of the "baser self" is also to degenerate. So we are trapped between the holy path of purification of our soul and the pagan path of the passions. Each seems to be a path to death and degeneration. This is the tragicomic logic of Stroheim's world: the only way to avoid death is to deny passion, but in denying passion, one is denying nature, and that is surely a fate equal to death.

Foolish Wives (1922) is an even bleaker film. While a seductive "kulturist" does again invigorate an American marriage, the film presents a criminal hedonism that is hardly attractive. The Dionysian metaphysics hinted at in *Blind Husbands* now loses its romantic sheen and becomes a "wisdom" that destroys "the rigid law of individuation," plunges "nature into the abyss of destruction," and leads the Dionysian sage to "suffer the dissolution of nature in his own person" (*BT* §9). Life and time, identified with love and all its ecstasies in *Blind Husbands*, has been replaced with a darker destructive force, which is now symbolized by the image of a roulette wheel. This image was probably a reoccurring theme throughout the film, although the New York Censor Board had the filmmakers cut out five separate shots of it so as not to promote immorality. The roulette wheel of fate suggests that there is no rational story to be told about the incalculable, random events and choices that lead one either to degeneration or regeneration. The world in this film is profoundly contradictory. Monte Carlo is introduced as "irresponsible and gay," defined by its games of chance, suicides, endless ocean waves, kings, and crooks. The main casino itself is paradoxically called Hell's Paradise. There are continual juxtapositions of symbols of the sacred and the profane, the low and the high, and strength and weakness. Stroheim's world is filled to the brim with such contrasts, such as Captain Count Cladislaw Sergius Karamzin, played by Stroheim, seducing a dim-witted child who makes the sign of the cross. Similarly, we are confronted with the image of a cross swallowed up in the inferno started by the suicidal maid who the Count has also seduced. We are shown a counterfeiter and murderer whose room is overwrought with religious icons. We are brought into a demonic hag's hut, who seems to conspire with Steuben in his attempted rape of Mrs. Armstrong, a plan thwarted by two contrasting symbols, a goat and a monk. This irrational world is positively inhuman, filled with floods, lightning strikes, uncontrollable desires, raging infernos, wild animals, luck in the casino, and the psychological break that leads one to suicide.

Stroheim's work seems to embody Deleuze's power of the false, which we might call a way of image-making that fractures the unity and primacy of our notions of "reality" and "truth" by making "the forger" into "*the* character of the cinema" (emphasis in original).[30] This film's uncanny power is found in how its counterfeit world "provokes undecidable alternatives and inexplicable differences between the true and the false, and thereby imposes a power of the false as adequate to time, in contrast to any form of the true which would control time."[31] The "false" and counterfeit nature of the whole of Monte Carlo is what makes it an adequate image of time. The characters are all fakes, but the Count and his "sisters" are master counterfeiters. Their past and present are illusions, and the future is nonexistent, a degenerative flight toward death. The present is out of everyone's control. Whatever appears real and true in this counterfeit world is undone by the randomness of events, which both requires and undermines the posturing that is required to survive in this world. We must all engage in forgery and form a performative belief in what we forge to find some sort of stability on the roulette wheel of life.

The basic plot of *Foolish Wives* is that the Count and his two "cousins" are parading around Monte Carlo as Russian aristocrats attempting to ensnare and compromise the wife of an American diplomat. That minimal plot is just an excuse for an unrelenting sequence of cruel and grotesque behaviors. But to what end? Did Stroheim simply want to shock people by presenting the uncanny?[32] The film concerns the degeneration of Europe in the aftermath of the First World War and the question of whether America and its values will go down the same path. The Old World is represented through the wanton cruelty of these criminals. Count Karamzin abuses, deceives, extorts, and seduces his servant, shoots helpless doves, drinks oxblood, passes counterfeit money, spies on and plans the rape of the diplomat's wife, and ultimately rapes a mentally immature girl. The result of his actions on those around him is to drive them to arson, suicide, and murder. This world is elegant, cultured, perfumed, opulent, fashionable, and polite on the outside. The question is whether the Americans will be able to penetrate these outer appearances and see the brutal forces that motivate all things. How foolish with they be? Initially the Americans are deeply impressed by Monte Carlo and the ceremonial aspects of the aristocracy. Mrs. Andrew Hughes, the American diplomat's wife, is encountered by the Count reading a book called *Foolish*

Wives said to be written by Erich von Stroheim, thus exposing the artifice of this world within the frame. We see the following passage on a page opposite a chapter on "Titles and Society." It is a commentary on the conflict, already discussed, between the values of aggressive enterprise and the genteel, sentimental tradition: "To the average American, written or unwritten codes of honor and etiquette are unessential, as, in his tiresome chase after the dollar, he has no time to cultivate that, for which the European mainly lives. In his battle of wits fought for commercial superiority the fatigued body forgets sometimes to react even to the most primitive and fundamental laws of politeness." There are multiple ironies here. Firstly, the idea that there is a primitive law of politeness is laughable. Secondly, the Europeans in the film who operate by these fundamental laws of politeness, honor, and etiquette are in fact complete charlatans who are simply chasing after money themselves. Thirdly, the Americans in the film are more representative of the genteel tradition, as Santayana called it. They do not appear to be chasing tiresomely after the dollar. Fourthly, and most importantly, the fixation on norms of politeness is shown to be a sort of cruelty and as self-serving as the chase after the dollar. In other words, this supposed division between value systems is exposed as illusory as each is little more than a desperate attempt to deal with fortune's favor and disfavor.

Both value systems—the life of manipulative passions and the life of polite society—are exposed as idols in their twilight. Each is just another manifestation of human vanity, a desperate attempt to retain meaning when faced with the degeneration of all human structures in the course of time. The identification made between Mrs. Hughes and the Count is a crucial, cynical point. It is found in the subtle moment where he gives a military salute to the soldiers who walk past him, but he refuses to salute the wounded soldiers in wheelchairs. They disgust him. We soon see the Count and Mrs. Hughes both lift their noses up at a wounded veteran who does not help pick up a fan that she drops, although they do not know him to be maimed. The false politeness of the Count, which Mrs. Hughes's book chides Americans for not having, is shown to be both snobbery and cruelty. She glares at the same veteran when once again he fails to be gentlemanly when she drops her purse in an elevator. But these "high" norms of politeness are shown to be inhuman and "low," as we could clearly see when they were embodied in the Count. On Mrs. Hughes's third encounter with the veteran, it is his cape that drops, exposing that he has no arms with which to pick anything up. Mrs. Hughes's cruelty is a function of her foolishness, vanity, and being conned by the "primitive and fundamental" but also counterfeit "law of politeness."

The veil of European manners is finally revealed as fakery to the Americans when the sheer cowardice and inhumanity of the Count are exposed. But why has there been any reprieve from the cruel hands of fate for anyone in this world? What has this encounter with these European degenerates accomplished? What possibilities has "the power of the false" and the revelation of the world itself as counterfeit revealed? We are awakened to the razor's edge between life and death, between civilization and barbarism. The two are essentially equated by the Count when he pressures Mrs. Armstrong into gambling her money at the roulette table, saying, "To me this means life—but sometimes it means death." In essence, this is the lesson of all *Übermenschen* in Stroheim's world. The dangerous life beyond morality, immersed in desire and passion, can just as well lead to a flourishing life as it can a terrible death. But the life of mere tradition—of foolishness trapped in norms of politeness—also leads to degeneration and death, just at a slower pace. All life in the film seems careening toward this abyss. Is there no hope? How have the Americans won their reprieve at the end? Can it be understood, or is it simply luck? Undoubtedly, Mrs. Hughes's difference from the Count is seen in her tearful regret upon finding out that the soldier that she has been condemning is without his arms. American naivete and ignorance are their saving graces, for these traits shield them from the destructive force of Dionysian wisdom. But once they encounter that wisdom and see its abysmal truth, can simple faith in politeness remain? Or will they learn to stand on their own and develop their own values and culture? Perhaps the latter is the future, as shown when Mr. Hughes throws off the politeness of being an "officer and a gentleman" and punches the Count in the face, declaring that he is "not even a man." Might this mean that he (as well as Dr. Armstrong in *Blind Husbands*) is a new type of *Übermensch*? I do not think so. But even if that were so, they can never be shown on film to be anything but the elusive promise of a new future in the final fadeout.

Lennig claims that these early films show that the Americans are "basically good people" but also show that they are quite stupid.[33] The "proofs of man's irrationality, destructiveness, and lust for financial, social, and sexual goals" do not just apply to the Count: "none of the characters comes off unscathed."[34] As Lennig states, Stroheim's vision is one that does not offer any "grace," no "City of God" without "ironic overtones."[35] The film ends with the following remark: "And thus it happened that disillusionment came finally to a foolish wife, who found in her own husband the nobility she had sought for in—a counterfeit." Does this mean that Mr. Hughes is our *Übermensch* and that the Count is a counterfeit version of him? We must remember that Stroheim is most likely influenced by Nordau and Norris and sees the *Übermensch* as a singular figure, part genius, part madman. This figure cannot be duplicated or incorporated into human society. Its degeneracy cannot be willed or adopted. Its specialization in desire, will, power, and the style of aristocratic culture means that it stands as a spur, an extreme endpoint of human possibility. It reminds the American couples in these films of their own power and desires. But it also awakens them to the counterfeit nature of all human systems. Yet it does not make them into that which is beyond the human.

Stroheim's most well-known film, *Greed* (1924), is based on Norris's novel *McTeague*. It offers us a clearer and uniquely American picture of the *Übermensch* in contrast to his European-based films. Furthermore, it offers a more complete picture of the development and demise of this figure rather than merely showing it at its final stages of degeneration. McTeague (Mac) is literally a "blond beast," in the book and the film, "carrying his shock of blond hair six feet three inches from the ground."[36] In the film, we initially find him mining for gold. He gently picks up a baby bird and kisses it. When an old man knocks the bird from his hand, Mac picks the old man up over his head and throws him off a cliff. This sensitivity combined with brutal rage captures a complexity in the *Übermensch* that we have not seen in the previous films. This superhuman seems to point in multiple directions toward a wealth of possibilities. *Greed* shows us what happens to such a being who is caged, whose possibilities are slowly taken from him by a world that is crueler than even he is. Nature has given rise to a person of great vitality in McTeague, one of its many pointless, excessive expenditures. Mac has power, but he is trapped within a soulless existence. He is worn down by a deep despair that comes from the fact that the whole world seems like a cage.[37] Stroheim's work depicts the human as driven relentlessly by the nonrational to act. Even when such action seems pleasurable, it is tinged with desperation and with uncontrollable passion that is equal parts pleasure and pain. It calls to mind a pessimistic moment in Norris' novel *The Octopus*: "Men were naught, death was naught, life was naught; FORCE only existed—FORCE that brought men into the world, FORCE that crowded them out of it to make way for the succeeding generation, FORCE that made the wheat grow, FORCE that garnered it from the soil to give place to the succeeding crop."[38] While Mac, thanks to Norris's novel, is the most unambiguous "strong man" in Stroheim's films, this perhaps made it necessary to subject him to the most rigid and inhuman laws of fate. What little agency and humanity Mac has is continually crushed by circumstances, by the greed of Trina, by the jealousy of Marcus, by economics, by class, and by social regulation. While Mac begins the film as a sort of brute, there are clear signs that he could ascend in life to something better than how he began. Instead, due to forces outside of his control, he descends into madness, murder, and a futile death. Like Stroheim's other films, *Greed* captures a deterministic world governed by uncontrollable natural and unnatural forces.[39]

Stroheim is called by Deleuze as one of the "great masters of naturalism in the cinema," which is to say that he turns to the "impulse-image" as a more direct expression of time, psychological duration, and (de)evolution.[40] This is a naturalism that is "saturated" with "the death impulse" according to Deleuze but, in his opinion, is still tied to a type of realism.[41] But by connecting Stroheim with the Nietzschean vogue of the era, we have a way to read his works as moving past the cinematic limitations of depicting "Nature" and "the Real." According to Deleuze, post-realism and post-naturalism take place though the notion of time as repetition. The result is a cinema that moves beyond "action images" and the empirical surface of things in order to construct "the actual image of the present which passes" and "the virtual image of the past which is preserved" within a single ambiguous image that is divided and "perpetually *self-distinguishing*" (emphasis in original).[42] While degradation, entropy, and parasitism in all forms of life are recognized by Deleuze as part of Stroheim's work, he argues that he stops there and does not move toward a cinema of time as "repetition" that can open up the possibilities and hope of a life "beyond good and evil."[43] But this seems to me to read Stroheim, like many have read Nietzsche, as attempting a realistic depiction of the "true" nature of the inhuman animal impulses beneath the human. But Stroheim explores these "impulses" only as the recollected past that is woven into every present moment, filling it with unstable possibilities. The actual image on the screen is not only depicting a relentless recapitulation of the past in the present, but it is always fracturing toward either a deeper degeneration and death or the increasingly unlikely regenerative act. Furthermore, natural impulses are recognized as being unable to be made visible and, instead, must constantly be symbolized through conflicting value systems.[44] It is not clear that Stroheim presents the natural as "true" as opposed to showing it to be a multiplicity that can be made manifest only through self-invention and counterfeiting. Mac immediately begins to move past the simple natural, impulsive strongman. He attempts to escape from degeneration and destruction through the deceptive invention of himself as a dentist rather than simply following his natural tendencies. Neither nature nor society is real, true, or a salvation from the hands of fate. We must cage ourselves to survive, and to do so is also to destroy ourselves. But that death impulse is not a natural, animal force in the living being: it is time manifest as repetition through all of history, society, and the cosmos.

Stroheim's symbolic alternative to mere naturalism is seen when he cuts from Mac kissing Trina while she is under anesthetic to extreme, almost abstract close-ups of Mac's twisted expression and Trina's corpse-like face, seemingly wrapped in a nun's habit, then showing us a bird leaping about in its cage. We cannot help but see in this an atavistic past in the uncontrollable impulses as well as a premonition of their future life and death together. Life and death, freedom and determinism, the sacred and profane are all encapsulated in this fraught moment. The bird in its cage, eventually attacked by a cat as Mac's world begins to crumble, presents us with both animality and sociality, impulse and restraint, nature and technology, destructive forces and social structure. Stroheim shows us the hereditary past, the desirous present, and the fated future all at once. In each moment of will, there is an aspect of fate. It is a fulfillment of the past and a leap to the future, a resounding and futile "yes" filled with life and death. As a cinematic depiction of Nietzsche's comment that "the concept of man yokes together the most diverse and manifold things," *Greed* is unparalleled in early American cinema (*UM* 1 §7). Yet our appreciation of the film is currently hampered by the fact that its two subplots have been edited out and lost, one of which shows a regenerative life in the two elderly boarders who are Mac and Trina's neighbors and the degenerative madness of the junk dealers. That there are these two possibilities does not mean that human choice will decide the outcome rather than fate. When Mac tells Marcus that being close to Trina, smelling her hair and her breath, made him unable to control himself, Stroheim cuts to the pianola moving on its predetermined course. The randomness of fate symbolized by the roulette wheel in *Foolish Wives* has been replaced with the constrained future of the self-playing piano. Mac and Trina kiss, and Stroheim cuts to a train barreling past them and then to intertitles discussing "mysterious instincts, as ungovernable as the winds of the heavens." These passions are as inscrutable as Trina's winning of five thousand dollars in the lottery. This promise of life is also a promise of death, a fact openly stated by Marcus and Mac when they promise eternal friendship. That human promise is quickly broken, but the inhuman fate of their bargain remains.

The previous discussion of Stroheim's three most successful films makes a plausible case for their attempt to capture the superhuman possibilities of the human being who wrestles with fate and the collapse of all traditional crutches that prop up civilization. The *Übermenschen* of these films must specialize to survive, causing them to be both geniuses and degenerates, whose death seems the inevitable outcome of the struggle to live a life based on their own passions and inventiveness. Such hubris inevitably fails. While his later films continue to support these ideas, they also begin to show us the regenerative possibilities of the *Übermensch*. In *Merry-Go-Round* (1923), *The Merry Widow* (1925), *The Wedding March* (1928) (and its lost sequel, *The Honeymoon* (1930)), and *Queen Kelly* (1932), there is an interesting bifurcation of the *Übermensch* into the descending, degenerative path and the ascending, regenerative path. The ascending path is found in Count Hohenegg in *Merry-Go-Round*, Prince Danilo in *The Merry Widow*, Prince Nicki Wildeliebe-Rauggenburg in *The Wedding March*, and Prince Wolfram in *Queen Kelly*. Their degenerative counterparts are, respectively, Schani Huber, Prince Mirko (and the even more degenerate Baron Sadoja), Scani Eberle, and Queen Regina. Just as in Stroheim's previous films, symbols that represent fate are made central, and it is in their shadow that regeneration, insofar as it is possible, must take place. The most Nietzschean of these symbols is found in *Merry-Go-Round*, where there is an image of Pan (or perhaps Dionysius himself) laughing while standing in front of a miniature rotating merry-go-round populated by people and animals. When this symbol appears in the film, it is accompanied by the words "the merry-go-round goes round and round."[45] This symbol suggests Nietzsche's theory of the eternal recurrence of the same. As stated in *The Gay Science*, this is a challenge posed by a "demon" who proclaims that "this life as you now live it and have lived it, you will have to live once more and innumerable times more" (*GS* §341). Reconciling with that idea is essential for nearly all understandings of the *Übermensch*—a reconciliation that is eventually symbolized by some form of Dionysian existence. This endless cycle is characterized in the film as "our little world of good and evil, innocence and guilt, love and hate." In case one wondered what Stroheim thought of this little world, named "Vienna" in *Merry-Go-Round*, it is made clear in the first action of the film: a mother abandons her child on bridge as she leaps off to her death.[46]

The scenario of the film was novelized by Gladys Adelina Lewis (Georges Lewys), who makes clear that it is meant to be a "frank weighing of values in the scale of depravity and regeneration."[47] Stroheim continues to tie degeneration to hereditary, but also to the historical past and its atavistic presence. In *The Merry Widow*, *The Wedding March*, *The Honeymoon*, and *Queen Kelly*, it seems that the source of degeneration is traced to a distinctly premodern or medieval heritage. This is symbolized by the statue of the "Iron Man" in *The Wedding March*, who is said to be an artifact of medieval times that signifies war, unimaginable cruelty, and death. An explicit connection is made between Queen Regina's sadism and the vestiges of her medieval past. Each of the figures who are capable of regeneration are nevertheless princes and counts, suggesting a natural aristocracy. Thus, there is power and life within that tradition as well. It is difficult to watch Stroheim's final silent films and see anything like an endorsement of traditional values despite the romances that exist between Sally and Danilo, Mitzi and Nicki, and Kitty and Wolfram. Indeed, calling these temporary reprieves from degeneration rather than regenerations might be more apt. Nevertheless, these love affairs are between strong, sensual types, which point to a future happiness that is neither the pedestrian, traditional love in Stroheim's earliest films nor the appetitive love of *Greed* nor the rule-bound medieval relations of the royals. These lovers gesture toward an ideal that cannot be shown or named in Stroheim's fatalistic universe. But that their futures are offscreen does not mean that they are nonexistent. Regeneration is found in *Merry-Go-Round* in the hedonistic Hohenegg's irrational and spontaneous transformation within the course of his violent and deceptive seduction of Agnes. This moment of fate is symbolized by a violin string snapping, a moment seemingly borrowed from Chekhov's *The Cherry Orchard*.[48] According to Stroheim's original script, we were to see other strings on the violin violently cut by a hand as the First World War begins, suggesting that the original breaking string is a random moment of passion and fate, while the cuttings of strings is deliberate human irrationality.[49] Similar spontaneous eruptions of love, which challenge the weight of tradition and hereditary degeneration, are found in his final films. Yet these are far from happy endings. While *Übermenschen* may survive the effects of internal (physiological) and external (cultural) degeneration, they do not escape unscathed. While these films certainly deserve more detailed analysis, it would merely confirm the interpretation seen already in his first three films.

Madness and the Herd in *The Great Gabbo* (1929)

I want to conclude by discussing *The Great Gabbo*. This is Stroheim's first sound film, but it is directed by James Cruze. *The Great Gabbo* is based on a short story by Ben Hecht, who says that it was told to him by Groucho Marx.[50] Unsurprisingly, given the intersection of talent behind and on the screen of *The Great Gabbo*, it offers a remarkable revaluation of egoism and, thus, approaches the *Übermensch* in a significantly different way than the Stroheim-directed films. The film poses an interpretative puzzle: Is Gabbo's strength and inhumanity to be valued, or should it be overcome for a more humane life? Is human sentiment—love and kindness—shown to be a weakness that the genius must avoid, or is it central to life? From the perspective of the *Übermensch*, those moral values are seen as weakening, but from the human perspective, the selfish worldview of the egoist is inhuman. While it is possible to read *The Great Gabbo* through either value perspective, I believe that the one that positively values the *Übermensch* as an artistic genius divorced from human sentiment is the dominant one.

The film concerns Gabbo, a ventriloquist played by Stroheim. Egotistic and cruel, he dresses like an Austrian prince in military regalia and spouts German when he is angry. Hecht's original story describes Gabbo as the "loneliest, stuck-up professor," who "never looked at a dame" and used to "walk around like Kaiser Wilhelm."[51] The point of Hecht's story is that Gabbo makes a fool of himself by falling for a gold-digging, talentless vaudevillian tramp, named Rubina, who tortures him out of "morbid viciousness" by flirting with the ventriloquist dummy (called Jimmy in the story, but called Otto in the film). It is clear in the story that Gabbo has descended to base desires and feelings rather than ascended out of his egoism to join humanity. In other words, the tale is a typical bit of Hechtian cynicism in which human sentiment and love are viewed as a *human, all too human* weakness. Does the film retain this Nietzschean contempt for traditional moral sentiment, or does it condemn Gabbo for his lack of humanity? After proclaiming, "I'm the greatest living artist in my line in the whole world," Gabbo is chided by Mary, who exclaims, "You are so wrapped up in yourself that you are blind to anyone else. It is always, 'You, you, you!'" Mary offers us the human assessment of Gabbo and his relation to his dummy: "Little Otto, there is the only human thing about you. . . . The only sweet things that you have ever said to me have come from Otto. . . . Goodbye, Otto, I'm sorry to leave you, because you are the only thing about him that seems to have a soul." Mary articulates her moral philosophy as she leaves Gabbo: "To get along, to succeed, forget yourself once in a while. Think of someone else. Give in sometime. And listen, we only take out of this life what we put into it." This philosophy will be articulated by Gabbo later in the film, but it is a poor fit on him. Immediately after stating it to his manservant, Louie, he explodes, scolding and firing Louie for making him late, even though it was Gabbo's own moral philosophizing that caused this. But is it the rejection of this philosophy that drives Gabbo insane, or is it the attempted adoption of it that does so? I believe that the film shows us that Gabbo's genius, his artistry, and his sanity depend on his pursing his inhuman destiny, excluding human sentiment, and placing his "human, all too human" self in the ventriloquist dummy.

There are several reasons why I believe this to be so. While Mary is right that Otto is Gabbo's humanity, his heart, and his conscience, I think that he also represents a decadent desire for useless pleasures and sentimental nonsense. This is seen from the fact that Otto is continually "fresh" with the audience. He appears as an imbecilic optimist in his song "I'm Laughing" and as a perverse child in "The Lollipop Song." Otto may stand for what is human in us, but he also shows that the human is a self-deceived idiot who cannot face reality without tranquilizing sentimentality and nonsense. If this is Gabbo's "heart" and "soul," then it is better to objectify it and externalize it in something artificial and artistic rather than embrace it and unify with it. Secondly, when Mary and Gabbo meet after their two-year separation, her behavior is inexplicably cruel, although she appears to be attempting to be thoughtful. But it is that thoughtfulness that is cruel, as she is married and has no real interest in rekindling her relationship with Gabbo. There is no rational reason that she begins to behave like his assistant again, creeping into his dressing room and preparing things as he likes them, even returning a second time to paint a part of Otto's face. She oddly repeats lines that Gabbo had said on the day that he ran her out of his life ("Okay, Mr. Bones, what are the flowers for?"), thus echoing that earlier cruelty. Thirdly, although Mary is presented in a rather angelic way, this is undermined by the story told by the musical numbers in the film. The musical revue presented in the film is essentially an expressionist depiction of Gabbo's mental state, from loneliness and longing ("Every Now and Then") to infatuation and desire ("I'm in Love with You") to disorientation ("The New Step") to humiliation (the song missing from the existing print "The Ga-Ga Bird") and death ("The Web of Love"). In that final song,

Mary is dressed as a fly, and her husband, Frank, is dressed as a spider. Eventually Frank hauls Mary like a corpse up into his web. Rather than a tale of redemptive power of love over egoism, we get a story about love's destructive power.

Unlike the horror movies discussed in the previous chapter, in which isolation from human sentiment and the pursuit of genius were regarded as giving rise to monsters, Gabbo's pursuit of his genius, while clearly inhuman, is nevertheless how he should live his life. The philosophy of kindness and love should be rejected so that he can remain the best at what he does. Gabbo is driven insane when he attempts to become human. Of course, one might regard this madness to be a result his *failure* to become human and his inability to accept Mary's rejection of him. On that reading, the film is exhorting us to become human. No one ought to be such a cruel, idiosyncratic genius who ignores social norms for the sake of success. But if Gabbo's madness is punishment for his inhumanity, notice that it is excessive, worse than anything that Gabbo perpetrates. I suggest that he is driven mad not because he has failed to become human, but because he has failed to remain inhuman and has been weak. He has not remained true to his genius. Gabbo's madness is directed toward a world that requires him to step out of his artistic creation, to give up his genius to get along in the world. Gabbo's final march away from the theater is his abandonment of the world, which he only really connected with through his art.

Nietzsche's idea of the "pathos of distance" is that this external difference between human types is transformed into a *distance within the self* and that this allows us to experience "comprehensive states" that place us above the crowd, capable of laughing at it and at ourselves (*BGE* §257). It is the collapse of that inner difference that leads to madness: it is this internal distance that allowed Gabbo to become a great artist.[52] In particular, we find that the destruction of Gabbo comes from his uniting with Otto. That human part of him, which is the only thing that has a soul, must remain a separate self. Gabbo's shift from egoist to mere human is explained by his servant, Louie: Gabbo is human only when he *thinks that he is Otto*. But he succeeds in his art only because, like the dream of Dr. Jekyll, he has divided his self into two distinct persons. Otto has literally been the tool of self-sublimation, of the inner pathos of distance. It is in that gap that subjectivity and Gabbo's creative power emerge. It is also from the closure of that gap that his madness emerges. It is not his egoism but attempting to overcome it and unify himself with Otto that causes him to lose his mind and his art.[53] We ought not criticize

Gabbo's egoism. Instead, we ought to criticize his vain and ridiculous hope to unify with Otto, to make himself into something he is not, to strive for a vision of happiness that is not his own. Gabbo has confronted the emptiness of the *principium individuationis*, the fact that the identity that we call "human" is a fiction, a wooden dummy that we make talk, and that we can retain dignity only insofar as we are a will that strives inhumanely for our own highest art. When he abandons that hardness with himself for the comfort of Mary and the web of love, he is taking up the common feelings that he has excluded from himself and placed within the dummy. Thus, Gabbo the artist collapses, disappearing into a world not of his own making.

Conclusion

Stroheim's films do not advocate for the *Übermensch* as a general, ethical ideal for humanity. We should not allow such an attempt to arrive at a positive, human ethics to distract us from the other ways in which *Übermenschen* might be revalued as a positive phenomenon, even if unstable, destructive, and egotistical. The *Übermensch* can act as an illustration of the complicated and fluid relation between the ascending and descending, the strong and the weak, the human and the animal. Derrida describes another way in which Nietzschean concepts and figures may be valuable, as revelations of the inescapable "law of inversion."

> Nietzsche is fascinated (intrigued and alarmed) by the way in which reactivity causes the weakest to become the strongest, by the fact that the greatest weakness becomes stronger than the greatest strength. This is the case with Platonism, Judaism, and Christianity. This law of inversion is, of course, what makes the promise just as easily strong as very weak, very strong *in* its weakness. As soon as there is reversibility, this principle of inversion, Nietzsche himself cannot prevent the most puny weakness from being at the same time most vigorous strength. The logic of force reveals within its logic a law that is stronger than this very logic.[54] (emphasis in original)

In Stroheim's films, we can see that the laws of the supposedly civilized and humane society are a thin veneer over the impersonal forces of fate.

Force relations, social relations, and interpersonal relations in general are all essentially subject to the cosmic pull of fate. Yet what this means is that the divisions between strong and weak, rich and poor, moral and immoral, and virtuous and vicious are all subject to the law of inversion. The divisions that define us and our society can suddenly shift, leading to tragic consequences. Although degenerates die and regenerated egoists survive, albeit maimed but at least in the arms of someone they love, it is hard to feel that there is a satisfactory *moral* resolution within Stroheim's fantasies. Their *deus ex machina* resolutions suggest only a temporary reprieve from the crushing force of circumstances. Whereas the films of the previous chapter show how society and film seemed to recognize within Nietzsche's moral genealogy only a praise for the blond beasts of prey, I believe that we can see in Stroheim's films a rather more complex and cyclical struggle in which both the strong and the weak are subject to fortune's whim.

Rather than offering a prescriptive ethics that suggests that we become the *Übermensch*, Stroheim's films cast positive light cast on the *Übermensch* in at least three distinct ways. Firstly, it is a depiction of a certain type of refined, stylized, and specialized existence that is creative, powerful, and connected to the Dionysian power of the passions. Secondly, the *Übermensch* has positive social and interpersonal benefits to many that encounter this unique specimen, who combines both positive and negative atavisms and degenerative and regenerative possibilities. Thirdly, his films critically outline the conditions that caused the *Übermensch*'s degenerative specialization and that hinder its regeneration. Insofar as these films offer us a first glimpse at a Nietzschean cinematic aesthetics and philosophy of film, we can say that among Stroheim's many contributions to cinema, the layering of multiple and often conflicting symbols atop one another is a significant expression of the philosophy of perspectivism. While he is regarded as offering a naturalistic cinematic vision of brutal impulses, I think it sells his work short if we do not see how his characters are trapped in tragicomic myths, bound to history, fate, and the irrational events that break down the barriers that keep us divided between the Apollonian realm of self-serving stabilizing symbols and the Dionysian passions that obliterate the social self. Stroheim's characters are not isolated animals working out their desires according to their own individual rationales: they are subject to cosmic forces, ancient history, international catastrophes, social codes and barriers, and inescapable weaknesses. Central to Stroheim's films are their locations, their placement in mythical, symbolic spheres. These forgotten and foreign worlds for most moviegoers and the obsessiveness of the stories placed within them challenge the idea that they offer us psychological or social realism as opposed to fictional autobiography, self-mythologization, and the reality-creating fantasies of one of early Hollywood's most powerful and philosophical directors.

3

The Criminal Law

The *Übermensch* as Gangster and the Will to Power

Introduction

RATHER THAN TRACING how the discourse of degeneration continues within films about criminals and gangsters in the 1910s and 1920s, this chapter will concentrate on several key films of the later, more developed, and more Nietzschean gangster film genre. While the long cinematic life of the discourse of degeneration and sociobiology is historically interesting (and disturbing), it remains tied to moralistic criticism of perceived social ills. I will focus on the fundamental revaluation and even glorification of the criminal at the end of the silent era and the first few years of the sound era. At the heart of these films is an unlawful rebellion, which might be thought of as being a step toward a higher and more just law or to a form of life beyond law altogether. Following Derrida, we might see the figures in these films as attempting to "*change things . . .* in what one calls the city, the *pólis . . .* not to change things in the no doubt rather naïve sense of calculated, deliberate and strategically controlled intervention, but in the sense of maximum intensification of a transformation in progress" (emphasis in original).[1] In essence, the examples of the *Übermensch* in this chapter exemplify a challenge to the laws of economy and opportunity, or to what Hegel calls "state power" and "wealth," the two initial manifestations of "the ethical order" (*Sittlichkeit*). What is important in Derrida's quote is that that challenge is not done in a deliberate and calculating way. Rather, their way of challenging existing hegemony is through a sort of affective intensification, through letting passions loose in a way that is violent, illegal, and amoral. Although they may be egoists concerned only for themselves, gangsters' destruction of themselves for the sake of greatness may enact a new law of enterprise, a new form of life for others. Whether they know it or not, they may be leading to a more just world, defined as one that admits a more diverse set of future possibilities.

We can see these figures as "ripping apart" the "homogenous fabric of a story or history" through a radical and egoistic "decision," which consists of a "performative and therefore interpretive violence that in itself is neither just nor unjust and that no justice and no earlier and previously founding law, no preexisting foundation, could, by definition, guarantee or contradict or invalidate."[2] There is something excessive and irrational in these characters, which makes it difficult to see their behavior as ending in something like a traditional notion of justice, which is tied to notions of equality and peace. The gangster's explosive performances disrupt the whole of society and gesture toward new forms of life and new laws. The *Übermenschen* in these films are something like the flux of life itself, or the ceaseless force that Nietzsche names the will to power.[3] T. E. Hulme speaks of the "universals of thought" as attempting to present "the flux in some kind of order, *as the police might arrange a crowd for the passage of a procession,*" but this sort of "fixity," for example in a conception of justice, amounts to little more than a belief that reality is whatever fits into law, a belief in "the ultimate reality of the police" (emphasis in original).[4] Just as the police are unable to contain the power of the gangster, so also are the universals of thought and metaphysics incapable of capturing in some formula the *Übermensch*, which is why their singular projections on film are so valuable. The hope that either the revolutionary violence of the gangster, the counterrevolutionary violence of the police, or the conceptual violence of categorizing the flux of the *Übermensch* into an ethical doctrine will lead toward a stable, utopian end that we can call justice or progress is to be rejected on Nietzsche's view. We must instead accept "the joy of the circle," or the eternal recurrence of the same (*WP* §1067). Part of reconciling with this idea is recognizing that whatever occurs must be faced, endured, and taken up into our singular acts of valuation and revaluation. In the words of Rico in *Little Caesar*, whatever happens, one must be able to "dish it out and take it." Eternal recurrence is total commitment to the decision, to fate.

The gangster expresses "the *essence* of what lives," which is "the will to power," or the desire "to grow, spread, seize, become predominant" and to appropriate, injure, suppress, incorporate, and exploit, actions which Nietzsche recognizes as having "a slanderous intent" (*BGE* §259, emphasis in original).[5] Yet we must not misunderstand the will to power as the primitive atavistic violence discussed in the first chapter. The life committed to the will to power is a life of *"value-creating,"* which then allows the will to honor what is a "part of itself," including other people with their own created set of values (*BGE* §260, emphasis in original).[6] Nietzsche was no simple nihilist and believed that one could "destroy only as creators" of new values (*GS* §58). These creations of new values, these "highest insights must—and should—sound like follies and sometimes like crimes" (*BGE* §30). But is the gangster simply an expression of the American skyscraper soul? De Casseres argues that "the cult of the Superman in America began long before Nietzsche first gave poetic and philosophic vitality to a biological and psychological law as old as the race: the superior man is a law unto himself."[7] Is the gangster just a version of John D. Rockefeller, who spoke of the "zest of work" and to be "active-minded" in pursuit of more than "the mere accumulation of money?"[8] To intellectual readers of Nietzsche, figures like "Ford, Rockefeller, Edison, [and] Coolidge" only appear to "mass-consciousness" like "Supermen," because the American public is "innately philistine, conservative, without vision, without imagination, without daring" and receives its values from "politics, business, [and] machinery."[9] They lack the *Übermensch*'s power of value-creation. In other words, the gangster film is only Nietzschean when we recognize that the criminals within them are heralds of a set of values and a future that is not just a repetition of existing capitalistic values.

Whereas Stroheim's films are focused on how the past is woven into the present, the gangster films are focused on how the future fills every image of the present. That future seems to be the only real thing for the gangster, a vision in which power is complete and total, but this aim is also impossible. Striving in the present and directed toward an impossible future, the gangster is no rejection of finitude. Rather, it is a positive valuation of the power to embrace the most rewarding and revolutionary possibilities no matter their danger or impossibility. Whereas Stroheim's degenerates are nearly all fated to be undone by the grip of the past, the gangster's destruction is at the hands of their own impossible future. However, this destruction takes place, much as it did for the ventriloquist Gabbo, because of a remnant of humanity, an unfortunate adoption of sentiment. The isolation of the gangster from the "Other," from any human sentiment, places them in a world of themselves. These egoists are driven by a gnawing void, a nonexistent future, that remains more real to them than the world around them. The essential doctrine of the gangster genre can be seen in Emerson's claims that "the only sin is limitation" and that "as soon as you once come up with a man's limitations, it is all over with him."[10] The criminal power of transformation is also seen in Emerson's prophecy that when a true "thinker," unencumbered by tradition, lives "with no Past at [their] back," then "all things are at risk" through experimental actions and concepts that strike many as "crimes."[11] For Nietzsche, the idea of the will to power is a sort of growth that is "cruel and inexorable against everything *about us* that is growing old and weak," which can be recognized as more Emersonian than Darwinian (*GS* §26, my emphasis).

The development of a Nietzschean aesthetics of film requires us to think of how film is used to express the philosophical ideal of the *Übermensch*, not as anything recognizably human but as an unimaginable future. That idea is explicated by the notions of *amour fati*, *animae magnae prodigus*, and the eternal recurrence of the same. These ideas do not lend themselves to either a realistic or naturalistic interpretation, for what they present is the image of a being who no longer recognizes *Being itself* as anything but comic, as "less than nothing," as Rico says in *Little Caesar*. The gangster sees only the forever opening future as what is "real," although it is also entirely virtual, impossible, and untrue. I have also said that a Nietzschean approach to film is itself a moving image of perspectivism, presenting to the viewer a juxtaposition of different values and an exploration of their ambiguity and relativity to lives that are beyond good and evil. While I do not mean to endorse any particular film theory, it is useful to draw from Deleuze's for the simple fact that it appeals to Nietzsche's thought with some regularity. He envisions filmic moments that may act as "the test of the eternal," moments that point in different directions ("Saved" or "Doomed"), which he describes as "the bursting forth of life, of time, in its dividing in two or differentiation."[12] Deleuze also describes these types of images as being "inseparable from a process of decomposition which eats away at them from within."[13] While I do not think it necessary to tie my account of Nietzschean film to this particular theory, I find it suggestive that the penetration of Nietzschean philosophy in early Hollywood enables us to find this cinematic approach to time and to humanity in the films of the era, including the gangster film. Deleuze does not see within classical Hollywood cinema the deconstruction of truth, the creation of amoral characters that are beyond *ressentiment* and beyond judgment, and the development of a cinema of conflicting wills and powers. Only Orson Welles points in this direction, leading him to postulate an "authentic or spontaneous Nietzscheanism in Welles."[14] This introduction of film theory helps us to challenge the idea that these very familiar Hollywood films are simply governed by the rationalistic and realistic presuppositions of the "classical Hollywood" model. Such a challenge is needed for us to consider not only that such Nietzschean ideas are depicted in the content of films but that they may also be present—as they are in German Expressionist filmmaking—in how the films themselves are constructed, thus potentially generating the sort of *unheimlichkeit*, or uncanniness, in the spectator that can bring about the revaluation of values.

Early Crime Films and the Reform of the Gangster

After documentary-style crime films such as *The Burglar on the Roof* (1898), *How They Rob Men in Chicago* (1900), *The Great Train Robbery* (1903), *The Black Hand* (1906), and *The Silver Wedding* (1906), the crime film developed significantly in terms of its narrative complexity with such films as D. W. Griffith's *The Musketeers of Pig Alley* (1912), *The Wages of Sin* (1913), *Traffic in Souls* (1913), and *The Gangsters of New York* (1914).[15] In these early films, the gangsters, thieves, and thugs are menacing threats to innocent folk, but there is little else in terms of development or understanding of the criminal mind and world. Instead, the narratives are focused on the social consequences attributable to these thugs. At the same time, the nature versus nurture debate regarding criminality began to be explored in films such as *A Victim of Heredity* (1913), *Heredity* (1915), and *Are They Born or Are They Made?* (1915).[16]

Raoul Walsh's *Regeneration* (1915) offers an alternative to the bleaker vision of the "instinctive criminal."[17] Walsh himself called this film the "first feature-length gangster picture."[18] Loosely based on the book *My Mamie Rose: The Story of My Regeneration*, by Owen Kildare, it is the story of a small-time ruffian finding "education, inspiration, and love."[19] *Regeneration* shows us the steps by which Owen is brought out of the darkness and into the light by being taught to read and write by the charity work of an upper-class woman, Marie. This story of reform is not isolated to the 1910s; in Walsh's last silent picture, *Me, Gangster* (1928), we find, according to the film's marketing, another tale of the "regeneration of a gangster" through love. The transformation of the heart and mind of the criminal is an essential aspect of most of the crime films of the 1920s. For example, many of Lon Chaney's films during this time, most of them directed by Tod Browning, all show criminals who come to regret their actions and be reformed, often through love and sometimes through religion. These include films such as *The Wicked Darling* (1919), *The Miracle Man* (1919), *Outside the Law* (1920), *The Shock* (1923), *The Unholy Three* (1925), and *The Big City* (1928). The sheer number of thieves, safe crackers, bootleggers, and murderers that find redemption in films of the 1920s certainly justifies generalizing that this was the dominant way in which crime and gangsters were represented on films of the progressive era. It could be seen in other Tod Browning films such as *Drifting* (1923), *The White Tiger* (1923), and *The Mystic* (1925), the three different versions of *Alias, Jimmy Valentine* (1915, 1920, 1928), *Big Brother* (1923), the remake of *Regeneration*, entitled *Fool's Highway* (1924), *Going Crooked* (1926), *The Wise Guy* (1926), *Ladies of the Mob* (1928), and *The Lights of New York* (1928).[20]

The film from this early regenerative sequence of crime melodrama that most explicitly draws upon Nietzschean ideas is *The Penalty* (1920) with Lon Chaney, who plays a criminal mastermind and double amputee. I say the film is explicitly Nietzschean because it adds concepts and dialogue not found in the original novel by Gouverneur Morris IV.[21] Lon Chaney's Blizzard is said, in the film, to dream of becoming the "master of a city" and acquiring the "pleasures of a Nero and the powers of a Caesar." His goal is also to have legs again and be "a tower of strength" and "a Caesar." Most telling is when hearing of Blizzard's plans to have a leg transplant and to take over the city, Dr. Ferris says, "You're right—you'd be a superman." These are not statements found in the book. Ultimately *The Penalty* is more like the horror films discussed in chapter one. Blizzard is more like the Invisible Man or Dr. Frankenstein's monster than the *Übermensch* gangster of the 1930s. Chaney's character has degenerated into a criminal because of his physical maladies: he suffers from a "contusion at the base of the skull," which causes "pressure on the brain" and which means that "he has never been wholly responsible for his acts." This is revealed when surgery is performed and the evil within Blizzard is removed. Thus, it is clearly part of the morally progressive film tradition, in which criminality and immorality might be cured, either by breeding or surgical intervention.

It is interesting and ironic that Nietzsche's own philosophy would be identified with the ills of modern decadence and degeneration rather than a response to it. As Moore notes, the same sort of physiological analysis of the degenerative nature of Nietzsche's mind and art is closely related to the analysis that he himself gives of Wagner and his art.[22] Nietzsche is one of the central critics of the decadence of the modern age, even though he becomes the number one symptom of that illness. He argues that the problem with "crime" results from the weakening of humanity by destroying its "basic instincts" (*WP* §39). The social straitjacket makes people less willful and, thus, less in control of their own desires. The result is a "low" sort of crime that comes about from those who heedlessly pursue the values of society. What those decadents lack is self-control and the ability to "wait" and "postpone action," which is required to pursue the sort of great and terrible tasks that Nietzsche values (*WP* §45). From the perspective of the herd, "those who tower above" are a sort of criminal (*WP* §285). But it is a mistake to label them "sinner" or "villain" when in fact they are merely foolhardy and an enemy to the existing order (Z I "On the Pale Criminal"). This sort of criminality might be praiseworthy, "awakening us from our slumber" about some aspect of society "against which war ought to be waged" (*WP* §740). Nietzsche revalues the criminal's act, at least if it emerges from strength and for the sake of rebellion against the social order, possibly enacting a new understanding of values such as "truth or loyalty or justice" (Z I "On the Pale Criminal"). The superhuman expression of the will to power is a sort of "luxury cultivation of the exception, the experiment, of danger, of the nuance" that appears as a criminal figure of great passion and great tragedy, who is careless with the values of society and with their own life (*WP* §933, 936, 939). Thus, the criminal has virtues that "lack public approval" and is treated as an outcast. This creates in the criminal "a feeling of hatred, revenge, and rebellion against everything which already *is*, which no longer *becomes*" (*TI* 9 §45, emphasis in original).[23]

As much as headlines about Al Capone, the Nietzschean idea of the will to power is at the core of these gangster films. This notion is meant to describe "the really fundamental instinct of life, which aims at *the expansion of power* and, wishing for that, frequently risks and even sacrifices self-preservation" (*GS* §349, emphasis in original). While the gangster may sacrifice himself, it is not done from a spirit of moral kindness. It is done from the natural impulse of life to squander itself and to be excessive in its power and expansion. The notion of the will to power is inseparable from Nietzsche's rejection that there is a given *telos* to life in general, whether thought of in natural, moral, or social terms.[24] In other words, we misunderstand the will to power if we understand it as a story about individual agency, the struggle for sensuous feelings, or even some sort of individualistic perfectionism. We cannot overlook the cosmic aspects of Nietzsche's doctrine, in which to live according to this fundamental instinct is to recognize that "one is necessary, one is a piece of fatefulness, one belongs to the whole, one is the whole" (*TI* 6 §8). We should not read the gangster and the will to power as a story of survival of the fittest and the individual struggle for the goods of society. Instead, we should see within it a Dionysian unification with the cosmic flow of life itself, represented by *amor fati* (*GS* §276) or the "joyous and trusting fatalism" that Nietzsche attributes to Goethe (*TI* 9 §49).

Underworld (1927) and the Justice of the Gangster

Insofar as the gangster genre is defined by the presentation of an unrestrained, unrepentant, and unreformable man driven by the will to power, *Underworld* is its clearest first example.[25] The story was written by Ben Hecht, who will be the subject of a subsequent chapter, and then rewritten by Robert Lee, who would go on to polish the script for *Little Caesar*. *Underworld* was directed by Josef von Sternberg, whose films with Marlene Dietrich show another aspect of the *Übermensch* ideal and will be discussed in detail later in this work. Yet it is Hecht's inspired cynicism that is the heart of the film and that makes it truly the first gangster film, even though, according to Hecht, Sternberg softened his original story by adding "sentimental touches," such as having the main character, Bull Weed, not die onscreen.[26] Although Hecht had a cynical attitude toward philosophy and the pretensions of intellectualism, he respected Nietzsche's thought. He remarks that a philosophy should be judged according to "how unwelcome" it is "to the churchmen, politicians, and other majorities of his time."[27] The experience of Nietzsche's philosophy was "as exciting as melodrama," which offered a "heals-up-head-down-in-a-storm ideology" and a "mad call that aped the wind and rain of freedom."[28] By 1924, he describes Nietzsche's work with the metaphor of being "an obsolete Spanish cannon," something that "roared in its youth" and that was now admired for "its ornamental iron work."[29] But his assessment fluctuated;

in 1958, Hecht, who had converted to Judaism, still praised Nietzsche as "the most explosive and wildly exciting anti-social, anti-conventional, anti-Christian, anti-Jewish, anti-everything philosopher that Europe has hatched."[30] In *Underworld*, Hecht's first film script, we see a rather flat-footed depiction of the *Übermensch* as pillar of strength, a fearless individual overflowing with vitality, laughing at everything sacred, and expressing a radical sort of hospitality. Hecht often valorized those who found "the grin of life, however ironic, more important and persuasive than all its defeats," a trait that he attributed to "Supermen with soiled collars" who were "cynical of all things on earth."[31] Hecht's future screenplays would capture this ideal far better than *Underworld*.

The story of *Underworld* is a love triangle, where love is interlinked to friendship and loyalty, between Bull Weed, the strong gangster, Rolls Royce, an ex-lawyer that Bull Weed pulls from the gutter, and Feathers, a stereotypical gangster's moll. The film begins with the description of "the city" as empty as "cliff-dwellings of a forgotten age," and its opening shot is of a clock face superimposed on a skyscraper. Time stands monumental on the face of a building, but on its lower lever Bull Weed is blowing a safe, shattering windows, and robbing the establishment. With great economy, the ancient past is woven into the monoliths of the present, as the *Übermensch* dynamites the foundations of modern society. George Brent's Bull Weed is introduced as a laughing, joyous tower of strength, slinging the spoils of war under one arm and Rolls Royce, the drunk who witnesses the crime, under the other. These two items symbolize the life of crime and the life of friendship, and it is the latter that causes a "human, all too human" sentiment and weakness in Bull Weed that spells his doom. That sentiment is jealousy, which forms as an attachment to the world and disrupts his normal lighthearted and generous displays of power. Sternberg's film does not take place in the real world; rather it takes place in a gloomy "underworld" and in places like the Dreamland Café. The encapsulation of past and future in the present moment is also seen in the first shot of Rolls Royce after Bull Weed has gotten him a job at that café. Kneeling over and sweeping the ground, he remains close to his past, to the gutter out of which he came. But at that moment a feather floats off Feathers's dress and lands in front of Rolls Royce's face. Their future together is foretold, but it is also a chance event like the breeze on which the feather drifts.

The character of Rolls Royce is particularly intriguing. He does not have the same joyous, laughing nature of Bull Weed. But he is transformed by the power and generosity of the *Übermensch*. Rolls Royce may be a refinement of the *Übermensch*. Perhaps Bull Weed is just the lion in Nietzsche's story of development in *Thus Spoke Zarathustra*, a "beast of prey" whose ambition is to fight and to destroy "values, thousands of years old" (Z I "On the Three Metamorphoses"). Perhaps it is Rolls Royce who will embody the final stage of development, the child. As an ex-lawyer, who is sometimes called "professor" in the film, he shows that he is in control of his desire, unlike the wild and overflowing Bull Weed. This is seen in his denial of Feather's advances despite his own feelings for her. Such control for the sake of great and tremendous goals is central to the *Übermensch*. His nickname is earned because he is the "Rolls Royce" of silence, a trait that suggests the "innocence and forgetting" that is necessary for a "new beginning" (Z I: "On the Three Metamorphoses"). And yet that control is not absolute as he begins the film as an unwashed drunk. He contains multiple contradictions, behaving like an aristocratic gentleman while also being the lowest of the low. He contains the values of the upperworld and the underworld.

Bull Weed's generosity may seem an unusual trait for an egoistic gangster. He offers no explanation for his action when he places a large sum of money in Rolls Royce's hand. He simply says, "I'm either a missionary or a sucker, but I'm going to put you on your feet." Effectively, he is acting on an instinct. Rolls Royce asks, "But what could I do to help you?" Bull Weed, the murderous bank robber, responds "Help me? Nobody helps me. I help other people." If we look at Nietzsche's passage "On the Gift-Giving Virtue," we can see that Bull Weed is acting according to this "highest virtue" (Z I "On the Gift-Giving Virtue" §1).[32] He approaches "all values as a robber," wanting to take all that is good and life-enhancing, so that everything of value will then "flow back out of your well as the gifts of your love" (Z I "On the Gift-Giving Virtue" §1). When reflecting on the soul that lacks this virtue, like Buck Mulligan, Nietzsche says, "we shudder at the degenerate sense which says, 'Everything for me'" (Z I "On the Gift-Giving Virtue" §1). That degeneracy has a "sick selfishness," which manifests as a criminal who acts based on the desires of others and not from the inner source of power, not from the heart that "flows broad and full like a river" (Z I "On the Gift-Giving Virtue" §1). This sick selfishness is found in Buck Mulligan, who is jealous of Feathers, cruel to Rolls Royce, and filled with *ressentiment*. These two different types of crime, one emerging from a lowly need and one from overflowing power, are made evident when Bull Weed sees a young boy stealing an apple. He grabs his hand and tells him, "Don't you know it is wrong to steal?" before giving him some cash, violently kicking him down the street, and then stealing the apple himself. Here we see the moving image of perspectivism—how the same exact act can be seen as both crime and law, moral and immoral, an act of weakness or of strength.[33]

Looking at a sign that says "The City is Yours," Rolls Royce tells Bull Weed that he is "Attila the Hun at the gates of Rome" and was "born two thousand years too late." The echoes of the past are manifesting in the present and in the rare exception that is the *Übermensch*. Another remarkable image that depicts the gangster's relationship to time is given when Bull Weed robs a jewelry store to please Feathers. What we see is a clerk reaching for a clock in a cabinet, right before Bull Weed shoots out the middle of the clock with his pistol. The gangster's violence both marks and stops time. It defines the moments of time in the city for both the lawful and lawless alike, yet it also interrupts the social mechanisms of keeping time. After that shot, cinematic time is fragmented: a hand grabs a bracelet; a flower—Buck Mulligan's calling card planted by Bull Weed—falls on the floor; the legs of a crowd frantically run from the gunshot; a legless beggar sits on the street; Bull Weed's hands are shown bending a coin—his calling card—and from inside the store looking out a window, we see a huddled crowd as police fire at the perpetrator. It is a remarkable sequence of frantic, fractured time unfolding, spiraling out of the *Übermensch*'s excessive expression of power.

Unsurprisingly for a Hecht script, Bull Weed's downfall comes about because of a woman, a theme that we have already seen in *The Great Gabbo*. The moment Bull Weed stops laughing and screams at Rolls Royce for dancing with Feathers, he is doomed. Feathers tempts Rolls Royce toward the so-called "decent" or "straight" life, out of the underworld and away from Bull Weed's grasp. While life in the upperworld and away from the "devil's carnival" of the criminal life is "decent" in the eyes of some, it is also indecent, because it is an abandonment of the life of constant becoming for a life of stasis. There are two laws in this film world. At Bull Weed's sentencing for killing Buck Mulligan after he attempted to rape Feathers, the judge says that "no man can defeat the Law." But there is a higher law in which Rolls Royce and Feathers must remain true to the power that made them who they are, namely Bull Weed's disruptive strength and generosity. This law of the underworld requires Feathers and Rolls Royce to break Bull Weed out of prison and to subvert the judge's law. When they do remain true to him, this also is called *decency* in the film but in a revalued sense. While the judge says that "the Law" ends Bull Weed's career, he actually escapes from jail with ease when he believes that Feathers and Rolls Royce have broken the law of loyalty. The end of Bull Weed's career comes about when he realizes that he was "wrong all the way" to stop laughing, to attempt to possess Feathers, and to doubt the loyalty of his friends. So it is this self-enforced law of the gangster that rules the underworld, a law of honor, and a demand to stay true to the spirit of power, laughter, and the gift-giving virtue. Bull Weed recognizes that he had shown weakness, like his enemy Buck, by attempting to hold on to the present rather than rush headlong into the unknown future. This leads him to give himself up to the police. The only way to overcome his jealously and lowliness is to move on from Feathers, even if that means to die. *Underworld* is sometimes compared to Frank Capra's *The Way of the Strong* (1928), in which there seems to be a similar sacrifice. The heavily scarred gangster Handsome Williams gives himself up so that his romantic rival (Dan) can escape the law with the girl (a blind pianist).[34] But it is clear that Capra's gangsters are all moved by love and human sentiment. *Underworld* clearly ranks the law of love below the law of development, which Nietzsche tells us requires us to not preserve that which is ripe for destruction even if that is oneself. It is that law which we might call the gangster's concept of justice.[35]

Little Caesar (1931) and the Becoming of the Gangster

Unlike the other two Ben Hecht–scripted films that I focus on in this chapter, *Little Caesar* does not have an obvious Nietzschean influence. It is based on a novel by W. R. Burnett, whose works are not particularly Nietzschean in spirit. In fact, Burnett's *Little Caesar* started from a work that he called *The Furies*, which suggests that he saw the story to be about justice and Rico's inevitable fall.[36] Although I have no reason to suspect that Burnett was attempting to write a Nietzschean novel, he does confess that he intended to write in such a way that "all conventional feelings, desires, and hopes" were "rigidly excluded."[37] He recounts that he began his time in Chicago thinking that murder was "morally wrong and that the murderer was bound to suffer pangs of conscience and remorse."[38] What he found was that this was not the case and that the gangsters he met had an "entirely new and fresh way of looking at the world"—everything boiled down to what was "practical."[39] There is evidence that Burnett's novel was an attempt to translate Stendhal's *The Red and the Black*, a story of a young upstart on a Napoleon-like quest for power, into Prohibition-era Chicago. The clearest proof that this was on Burnett's mind is that his novel starts with a quote from Machiavelli: "The first law of every being, is to preserve itself and live. You sow hemlock, and expect to see ears of corn ripen."[40] This quote is attributed to Machiavelli in chapter 53 of *The Red and the Black*, but the epigraphs of Stendhal's chapters are notoriously fake.[41]

I also do not have any direct evidence that director Mervyn LeRoy aimed to present an especially Nietzschean film. And yet a case could be made that several of LeRoy's films have Nietzschean themes. For example, Paul Muni's character is a sort of *Übermensch* in *I Am a Fugitive from a Chain Gang* (1932). Unable to be a member of the crowd who works in the shipping department of a shoe factory, Muni's character wants to be an engineer. He wants to build, create, and do great things, which he manages to do by the power of his own will after he escapes the chain gang. Yet a series of parasites, liars, and imbeciles, including representatives of the law, brings him down. They embody the corrosive effect of *ressentiment*. Leroy's other film with Muni, *The World Changes* (1933), is another depiction of pure ambition, which seems to morally condemn the degenerative effects of wealth and success. *Little Caesar* was produced by Darryl F. Zanuck, who also has a story credit for *Baby Face* (1933), which is the most explicitly Nietzschean of all Hollywood films from the 1930s. While these components make a potential Nietzschean reading of *Little Caesar* plausible, they do not establish that the film was constructed with that in mind.

Because these films often end with the violent destruction of the gangster, there is a tendency to read them in moralistic terms. For example, Shadoian argues that Rico in *Little Caesar* is continually plagued by "internal malfunctioning" and that his drive for power is a sort of corruption:[42] "The nakedness of his power drive and his stubborn purity are forceful, to be sure, but not pleasurable, and offer little impetus for emulation. He leads a compulsive, joyless existence. Purity is a difficult quality to warm to; very few people have it. The pure man is unnatural, a freak, a pervert."[43] While it is clearly not the case that Rico leads a joyless life, it is important to note that it is not obvious, from a Nietzschean perspective, that being pure, compulsive, unnatural, a freak, or a pervert is a necessarily bad thing. Even if such factors are what ultimately lead to his death (and I do not think that they are), that does not show that Rico is to be condemned. We might recall Nietzsche's statement from *On the Genealogy of Morality*, "All great things bring about their own destruction through an act of self-overcoming" (*GM* III §27). According to Nietzsche, "the law of life" is not mere survival of the fittest but is the "law of the necessity of 'self-overcoming'" (*GM* III §27).[44] This self-overcoming may be violent and even lead to death, but it is also constructive. It is important to see that Rico has such alternative values and is not simply attempting to achieve "the American Dream" by illegitimate means: "Dancing? Women? Where do they get you? . . . I figure on making other people dance. . . . Money's all right, but it ain't everything. Be somebody. Look hard at a bunch of guys and know that they'll do anything you tell them. Have your own way or nothing. Be somebody." To have your own way or nothing, to have power over others, and to be somebody—these are Rico's articulations of positive valuations of the pure, stubborn, and perverse power drive. In the words of Nietzsche's *Ecce Homo*, he wants to "become what he is," and to do so requires "courage," "hardness against oneself," and "cleanliness in relation to oneself" (*EH* P §3). His aim is not the decadent values of the "soft" world around him.

The gangster film, if it is to articulate the idea of *Übermensch* and to point toward a radical relation to time and fate, must do more than just present a realistic tale of the rise and fall of a power-hungry criminal. It must create ambiguous cinematic moments such as the first clear shot of Rico, turning the hands of a clock in a roadside dinner back twenty minutes to create an alibi. This is not only an attempt to erase their past (a murderous hold-up), but it shows "the old bean" working and how Rico is always thinking ahead. The present is asserted to be nonexistent by being erased. Rico says that he and Joe are nobodies, nothing, and yet they also show their power over time, to literally be able to reach out and grab it. Another major appearance of a clock in the film is a watch given to Rico by his gang, acquired by their throwing a brick through a window and grabbing it. This watch is significant for several reasons. Because it is stolen, it shows Rico that others have power over time as well. But it also begins to pollute him with human sentiment. Ultimately, he is wounded in a drive-by shooting because, rather than paying attention to his surroundings, he is handling his watch and admiring it. The aims of having power and being his own man slip from his mind as he reflects on this gift and on the present moment. The metaphysics of time at work here is stated in the novel: "What distinguished him from his associates was his inability to live in the present. He was like a man on a long train journey to a promised land. To him the present was but a dingy way-station; he had his eyes on the end of the journey."[45]

The concept of time is everywhere in the film: Joe's lateness to a meeting, the clocks on New Year's Eve during a robbery, the slowness of

Tony's funeral procession, the fact that they have "plenty of time" before the banquet, and Rico running "out of time" at the end. It is through the grasping of time and by leaping ahead of it that one endures and even succeeds. This is the philosophy of becoming, which for Nietzsche means that "Being" is the relentless process of "living" (*WP* §582). "Becoming" is not simply being swept along by the relentless push of time as in Stroheim's films. The gangster as *Übermensch* handles time itself, turns its hands, marks it out, and even dances to its rhythm. The *Übermensch* views time as repetition, as eternal recurrence, which should not be understood as passive or reactive. Instead, this relation to time should be thought of as the power to cause an eruptive event, to make each moment of life an eternal moment by disordering the lawfulness of "human, all too human" time. Dancing into the future endlessly away from both the past and the present is another way of making each moment eternal. Rico's statement of this philosophy of repetitive mythologizing of each moment is that one must be able to dish it out and take it, to take risks, to grab hold of the future, and to deal with whatever emerges in the present. In Deleuzian terms, one *might* think that the relentless action of the gangster places these films in the domain of realism and the "action-image." But we should not overlook how the film challenges a linear, temporal, and human world. It is through superhuman control of time, risking its fracturing and ultimately stopping in death, that one can become somebody.

Much like Rolls Royce in *Underworld*, the figure of Joe in *Little Caesar* is suggestive of an alternative set of values. Joe seems to match the will to power of Rico by a value inversion that converts the gangster's violence into a life of artistry and dance. The screenwriter made the explicit choice to make Joe into a major figure of the film and into Rico's only friend. This contrasts to the opening pages of the novel, in which not only do Joe and Rico not have a past together, but Rico also says that he hates Joe.[46] Most importantly, in the film, Rico's fall from power is entirely a result of the fact that he "likes" Joe too much. Rico is worried that Joe will talk, but he is also threatened by the fact that his "pal" left him to become a dancer. Like Bull Weed's possessiveness of Feathers, Rico's possessiveness of Joe is his downfall. Rather than continue to change and grow or protect himself by "shooting first and asking questions later," Rico remains attached to the past and, thereby, abandons his status as *Übermensch*, for such a being must embrace *différance*, or "the displaced and equivocal passage of one different thing to another, from one term of opposition to the other."[47] It ends up being Joe who can best transform and "be somebody" in this "Tipsy Topsy Turvy" world, as the sign advertising his dance routine and under which Rico dies proclaims. Joe is someone who can move across multiple worlds. Rico speaks of Joe's power as being able to walk into a fancy hotel and rent a suite without raising any eyebrows. That ability to inhabit both worlds shows that Joe has the power to make his own time. But rather than just grasp the future as one's own, Joe has the ability to move between times, to capture moments of his own past as a dancer, to escape from the gang, and to reinvent himself in the big city. He has shown us a greater power of self-overcoming, to shift from an accomplice to murder and robbery to being a dancer.

Joe's presence suggests there is a third law in addition to Rico's law of "dishing it out" in the underworld and the law of the police in the upperworld. According to Nietzsche, the law of development sometimes requires one to recognize that one's "*fighting instinct* wears out" when "everything hurts" and "memory becomes a festering wound" (*EC* 1 §6, emphasis in original). If one cannot accept this, then the result is "anger, pathological vulnerability, impotent lust for revenge," or *ressentiment* (*EC* 1 §6). This is what we see with Rico, who cannot let Joe go. The fighting spirit of having it your own way or not at all will eventually come up against limits. While Rico moves from "nothing" at the start of the film to "somebody," he cannot continue that transformation any further. Thus he no longer adheres to his own law—"*patere legem, quam ipse tulisti*," or "submit to the law you yourself proposed"—and forfeits his life (*GM* III §27).

Mason has argued that rather than a law of self-overcoming, the gangster acts as a force of chaos.[48] She argues that modernity expresses an inversion of values that turns into a chaos of excess, and that *Little Caesar* (and the gangster film in general) shows us the struggle of the individual to organize themselves. If this approach is correct, then the lesson of the film is that Rico is too chaotic and that he cannot handle the modern world or form into a coherent self. This reading fails because it does not incorporate the actual reasons for Rico's fall into the overall meaning of the film. Rico does not fail because of his own chaotic violence. Instead, the problem is that he cannot let Joe follow his own law, nor can Rico be violent enough when it comes to Joe. Rico says, "You're my pal. . . . Who else do I have to give a hang about? I need you, Joe. . . . I need somebody, somebody to work in with me, a guy like you, someone I can trust." But he also cannot square that with his desire to "look hard at a bunch of guys and know they'll do anything you tell them." When

Joe will not do as Rico says, all that is left for Rico to do is to accept fate and to forget about the past friendship, which means that he must kill Joe. To do so would not be out of anger or *ressentiment*—it would be survival. To not do so would be to continue to seethe with *ressentiment*.

Ultimately, the film presents us with a feverish dream of conflicting moralities: the lazy, decadent code of the "made" gangsters who enforce the status quo, the law of the police, the Catholic guilt of Tony, who is gunned down on the church steps, the worshipfulness of Otero for Rico, Rico's ethics of violently dishing it out, and Joe's graceful balancing act between worlds and loyalties. Perhaps it is that ambiguity, Joe's liminality, that makes him so troublesome for Rico. Joe wants Rico to "forget" him. Forgetting even one's enemies is required to live in power, to overcome oneself, and be without *ressentiment*. Everything has changed for Rico, so why is he unable to focus on the future in front of him, such as replacing "the Big Boy" and ruling the whole city? Rico cannot forget, because he cannot understand Joe's dual loyalty. He cannot grasp that Joe could "quit" the "man's game" of gangsterism but not abandon his loyalties. Rico's problem is not his power, his violence, his chaos, his passions, or his intellect. His weakness is ultimately a sentimentality about the past. On the one hand, the *lived Übermensch* is one who forcefully asserts their own value system and, like Rico, may look at other value systems as "nothing," even "less than nothing." On the other hand, the *philosophy of* the *Übermensch* must recognize the plurality of values and the multiplicity of forms of life. The conflict of values and the violent assertion of one value set in response to the other is captured in the two most memorable cinematic moments in the film. The film is dominated by static medium, single, and two shots, but when Rico realizes that Joe has abandoned their meeting, even after Rico has threatened to kill Joe and Olga if he does not agree to work for him, we receive a shot like no other in the film until that point, a low angle zoom on Rico's determined face in full recognition of what he must do. This movement enforces Rico's strength, his antipathy to anything "soft." But it is soon followed by Rico's fateful walk toward the camera, eye level, as he pulls a gun on Joe, followed by a close-up of Rico with almost tearful eyes, slowly backing away from the camera, moving out of focus. These are the key moments of Rico's decline. The camera announces itself in them. In the first movement, it models the narrowing of future options as the will to power decides on a course of action. In the second movement, it shows the disorienting breakdown of that future when confronting a past that it cannot overcome. Rico's ultimate sin is, according even to the police, that he contradicted his own boast that he could dish it out and take it. He failed to live up to his own law. Joe, even after being shot, does not give up Rico. He stands unflappable before his almost certain death as Rico takes aim at him. He shows us that the revolutionary intensification of the gangster requires one to be able to pivot in this "Grand Theatre" of life, to laugh, sing, and dance over the past and toward the future in this "Tipsy Topsy Turvy" world, as the final shot of the film tells us.

Scarface (1932) and the End of the Gangster

Scarface is another intersection of creative forces that suggests the influence of Nietzschean ideas. The first is Ben Hecht, who produced the script in around eleven days. The second is director Howard Hawks, whose work often skirts around Nietzschean themes, especially in his other films based on screenplays by Hecht, such as *Viva Villa!* (1934), *Twentieth Century* (1934), *Barbary Coast* (1935), and *His Girl Friday* (1940). In fact, the classic Hawksian themes of the camaraderie within a "man's world," heroics in the face of death, and the disruptions caused by women draw upon a conception of manhood and the strenuous life that, although widespread in the culture, did align with a rather pedestrian notion of the *Übermensch*. Given how far Hecht's script for *Scarface* deviates from the original novel, a clearer source of the script is one of Hecht's first publications, which is on criminality. It is an article in *The Little Review* from 1915, entitled "The Sermon in the Depths (Phosphorescent Glows of Spiritual Putrefactions)." This review of Dostoevsky's *The House of the Dead* begins with the following reflection: "American criminals, are as rule a petty lot given to sentimental regrets and griefs and reforms and periodicals. There is nothing which reflects the smugness of a people so much as the manner and temperament of its vice. And the temperament of American vice is more distinctly and monotonously bourgeois than any of its virtues."[49] Hecht is drawing on his experience of criminality in Chicago, but his criticism applies to the criminals of early Hollywood, prior to the emergence of figures such as Lon Chaney's Blizzard and Hecht's own Bull Weed. He says that the American criminal "is an artificial and uninteresting disappointment" who recites poems and sermonizes. Against such banality, Hecht relishes the "swaggering monstrosities," "bestial grotesques," "Herculean villains," and "the irritable gargoyles innocently steeped in insatiable perversion and dripping with infamy" within Dostoevsky's novel.[50] He is fascinated by these "terrifying lusts and passions and distorted rages," which "make the mind quiver."[51] Dostoevsky offers a "Sermon of the Depths" comparable to the "Sermon on the Mount," which if understood will enact in the reader an "exclusiveness which will merit them the flattering curses and derisions of their fellow men."[52] Hecht would ultimately write a story of just such an amoral, perverse, misogynistic, and insane criminal mind in *Fantazius Mallare*. Tony Camonte, the Al Capone clone of *Scarface*, offers his own sermon of the depths, and it is written with the gun.

Tony is a Dionysian, ecstatic figure: he is a charmer who continually winks, jokes, mimics, laughs, and, of course, shoots his way to the top.[53] He is also intelligent, inventing his own bulletproof shutters for his apartment and going to see the play *Rain*, based on the W. Somerset Maugham story. Tony is a creator: his gun is his typewriter, he says, and he will write his name all over the town. While the reoccurring sign proclaiming "The World is Yours" may seem to point to Tony's rise, it also points to the impossibility of such an aim, and its inevitable collapse. To possess the world suggests an end to the path of the will to power. The collapse comes because Tony's world includes no one else as a true agent, and this includes his sister. Mason reads the downfall of Tony as a result of his excessive "desire for absolute obedience and control which is also an act of enforcing discipline on others."[54] I find Tony's downfall to be the result of an inner contradiction in values that is signified and explored through his perverse relationship with his sister, Cesca, who even remarks in her first scene that he acts more like a jealous lover than her brother. Rather than make a more traditional love triangle be Tony's undoing, Hecht chooses the fixation on the sister to be what breaks Tony, much as the relationship with Joe is what breaks Rico in *Little Caesar*. This incestual spiritual putrefaction, the repetitive warlike nature of things, and the transformation even of the *Übermensch* into sniveling swine in the final scenes are a result of the fact, as Poppy notes of Tony, that people are a "funny mixture." They are contradictory: smart and stupid, courageous and fearful, hedonistic and ascetic, generous and greedy, and filled with irrational spurts of love and hate. No single force or value can remain on top within them for very long. The other shoe always drops. While internal contradictions mark Tony throughout the movie, his downfall is a result of the contradiction between the value he places on the virginal purity of his sister versus his own way of life. Undoubtedly, Tony is a sort of *Übermensch*, but Hecht is distrustful and sees the terrifying outcomes, like Nietzsche looking at the Greeks and telling us that we cannot understand them and, if we could, we would "shudder" (*HC* p. 33). Tony illustrates an inhuman *Übermensch*, with his childlike glee, Herculean mental and physical energy, insatiable appetites, and utter fearlessness, but he also shows the crippled soul behind such unrestrained flights of love and hate when he collapses. The *Übermensch* is a glorious monster and an unsustainable contradiction that, like Nietzsche himself, succumbs to madness. Rather than offering moral condemnation of this figure or some ethical model that we ought to follow, Hecht is simply an observer of inhuman humanity.

Although the film is the most action-filled of any early gangster movie, it is also the most episodic. We can see each scene not so much as a linear progression from the previous but a spontaneous eruption of some contradictory force from Tony. In Hecht's universe, time truly is repetition: there is constant motion, and nothing changes. Journalism is war; politics is war; crime is war; policing is war; love is war. It was the "war" that gave Tony his scarred face. The law of war and of life, according to Tony, is the law of repetition. Pointing to his gun, he explains that "there is only one law that you gotta follow to keep out of trouble. Do it first, do it yourself, and keep on doing it." War is hell, and at its start and its conclusion we see that it changes nothing. It will simply repeat. There is no new law or justice in *Scarface*. As an irrepressible cynic, Hecht sees the law only in Hobbesian terms as authority, punishment, and control of the feckless and the depraved. On several occasions the film addresses the role of government directly: it must control both the weak and the strong, and if it will not, then we must hold it accountable. "What are *YOU* going to do about it?" asks the opening titles, as does the speech by the publisher of *The Evening Record*, Mr. Garston. Outlaw guns, enforce martial law, and kick out the immigrants seems to be Garston's answer, which is to say that there is no regeneration and reform of the criminal because the problem is not something like degeneration. It is humanity itself. Aristocratic control of the decadent herd seems to be the only possible response: force will always be met with force and, eventually, with a greater force. This aristocratic approach to the "herd" was common among the members of the cult of Nietzsche. Mencken regularly articulated this idea, and Huneker's and Thompson's magazine *M'lle New York* bemoaned the fact that the ancient aristocracy of force was dead, which meant that we were faced with the "monstrous fallacy that all men are born free and equal."[55] In the end what was needed was an "intellectual aristocracy" to rule the masses. The *Übermensch* is a rebellious and tragic supplement that appears without reason or cause within any existing order, so one might as well have the herd under control. After all, the problem the *Übermenschen* in these films face is not restrictive laws: it is the weakness and decadence of the world around them, which eventually penetrates their own wills.

The openly didactic moments of the film, addressed directly to the audience, explicitly shatter the illusionism of the film and make its narration explicit. It is as if the film had to contrast a socially responsible perspective with its ceaseless depiction of violence. But rather than simply providing a lesson to appease the censors, the clatter of social do-gooders, journalists' typewriters, police sirens, and machine-guns all become similarly deafening and ultimately ineffective. Ironically, Mr. Garston's proposals about how to eliminate wholesale defiance of the law and gang warfare are not what stops Tony. Instead, it is Tony's own internal contradictions that lead to his self-annihilation. That final collapse happens when he kills his second in command, Guino Rinaldo, after he finds him with his sister. Even though Tony threatens to kill his sister simply for being in the Paradise nightclub, actually acting on that threat after finding out about Cesca and Guino shatters his world. At first glance, this shift in Tony's demeanor does not make much sense and might be dismissed as a result of the time pressure on Hecht's rewrite. But the best explanation of this breakdown in Tony is one we have already seen in *The Great Gabbo*. Just as Gabbo and Otto are a divided person that, when unified, results in madness, so also does the film make it explicit that Tony and Cesca are "the same." Cesca, her mother, and Guino all note how she is just like Tony. Tony's frantic and stupefying final moments are a result of his unification with Cesca. The breakdown results when he sees that it is true that they are the same, because she is now caught up in gangster life rather than being his innocent sister. He begins to stumble around like a drunk as soon as he sees Cesca with Guino, even before killing him and before she tells him that they are married. What breaks him is merely that she has turned into a gangster's moll.

The contradiction in Tony is his attempt to preserve some sense of the human amid all his inhumanity. He was able to operate by keeping Cesca, his other half, separated from the underworld. This Jekyll and Hyde division between selves was essential for him to continue to see himself as some sort of human being. When that illusion is destroyed, he resigns himself to death in a suicidal haze, wishing that Cesca would kill him. A maelstrom of passions and despair overtakes Tony. He eventually pivots to a wildly laughing madman with a godlike delusion that he and Cesca will gun down the entire police force outside their window. This occurs when he reconciles with their unity: "You're me and I'm you. It has always been that way." Until that moment, I suspect that Cesca and his family had been a remnant of the past and of a more traditional value system. Tony perhaps believed that he needed Cesca to remain virginal and separate from him both so that he might remain human and so that his own family's recognition that he hurts everything would not in fact turn out to be true. As Cesca dies, Tony pivots again, now acting like a child, afraid of being left alone and claiming that he is "no good by himself." So now we see, that until that moment, Tony has thought of himself and needs to think of himself as, in some sense, "good." With his final attachment to humanity gone, chaos overtakes him. This is Hecht's cynicism at work, taking us from suicidal depression to godlike fantasies to complete panic in a matter of minutes. Hecht is illustrating an idea he learned early in life: "That's the easiest thing people can do, change into swine."[56]

Conclusion

Underworld, *Little Caesar*, and *Scarface* remain three of the most influential gangster movies in the initial run of this genre. Films such as *Me, Gangster* (1928), *The Big City* (1928), *The Way of the Strong* (1928), *Alias, Jimmy Valentine* (1928), *The Lights of New York* (1928), *Chinatown Nights* (1929), *Thunderbolt* (1930), *The Doorway to Hell* (1930), and *City Streets* (1931) all depict some sort of moral reform on the part of the gangster. The films that people often take as defining, foundational moments for the genre are the most obviously Nietzschean ones, each of which gives us a different glimpse at the *Übermensch*. Of the films that I have discussed, *Underworld* provides us with the most positive conception of the *Übermensch*, the one most clearly advancing its own conception of law and justice. Bull Weed has overflowing strength that challenges the existing legal and economic order by blowing up banks and literally bending coins with his hands. His will to power manifests as generosity and criminality, both of which flow impulsively like his good-natured laughter. Cinematically, Sternberg presents us with a sparse world seemingly without sun. This underworld is utterly divorced from the upperworld, and the proclamations of the latter have little relationship to justice. Bull Weed's robberies and murder of Buck, who tried to rape Feathers, are hardly wrong within the context of the film. His ultimate demise is obviously a result of his failure to adhere to his own will to power when he gives in to *ressentiment*.

Little Caesar offers a conception of the ever-expanding circle of power that reaches its limits when it cannot relinquish the past and its own present self for an unknown future. That inability to forget is central to *ressentiment*. Rico's need for Joe disrupts his power over time and over himself. This suggests that Joe, who participated in two murders that we know of and is clearly at home in the world of the gangster, may be the superior conception of the *Übermensch*, as may be Rolls Royce in *Underworld*. For it is Joe who can leave the past behind for a life committed to creation through dance. Rather than the relentless pursuit of power or its generous yet explosive expenditure, the will to power has to diversify into different worlds and value systems, or else it will find itself haunted by *ressentiment*. Whereas *Little Caesar* shows us that the past and the present are "nothing" or even "less than nothing," *Underworld* presents us with an atmospheric, sunless world where an ancient warlike past and the upperworld's laws of decency haunt the shadows. The inverted world of shadow that Sternberg creates reflects the *Übermensch*'s value inversion and, thus, offers another visual way of capturing a moving image of perspectivism. Finally, *Scarface* presents us with the most challenging of the gangster *Übermenschen*, an incestuous, relentless killer, whose internal contradictions and perversions drag him down into madness. But lest we think Tony is simply condemned, we must recognize that this "strange mixture" of a person is, at least from Hecht's perspective, supposed to be the sort of gloriously amoral criminal that inspires us toward unimaginable human possibilities. The film addresses us directly: What are we going to do? We must enact our will—whether that means enact martial law or our own law. There is nothing to do but create out of our contradictions. But no one is an inexhaustible well. Our contradictions have their price.

4

The Salvation of Sin

The *Übermensch* as Superwoman and the Role of Gender

Introduction

THE FILMS OF STROHEIM and the gangster genre have presented images of the *Übermensch* as a degenerative specialist in desire and a power-hungry criminal. Yet they have also presented us with commentaries on the *Übermensch*'s inhuman relationship to time itself. That relation is expressed in how fate is bound to degenerative histories, random events, and eruptive exceptions at the heart of civilization. Or else it appears as existence without a past, in which forgetting everything is essential to the relentless striving toward an impossible future. We have seen how the mythological time of these films results in a cinematic time that challenges two central aspects of classical Hollywood cinema. It challenges a narrative analysis that is centered on rational subjects. It also disrupts any cinematic realism that approaches these films as presentations of the visible world. Instead, we are confronted by an ontology of forces that are not, strictly speaking, visible—fate, history, social tradition, degeneration, irrationality, atavistic heritage, will to power, and time itself as eternal recurrence. True, these forces are inseparable from the visible world, but they also challenge the metaphysical division between the visible and invisible, the real and the illusory, that we commonly take to define the world. Furthermore, we have seen that while these films belong to a broad movement opposed to Victorian sentimentality identified as literary and cinematic naturalism, there is something particularly excessive and inhuman within these *Übermenschen*. This is captured in Nietzsche's notion of the spirit that ruins itself in the pursuit of something great (*animae magnae prodigus*), a notion that can hardly be called "natural" and, instead, aligns with the idea of loving fate and the embodiment of the eternal recurrence of the same. I take these notions to be central to coming to terms with the *Übermensch* not as some ethical prescription that we should adopt or some moral monster that we ought to condemn. Instead, the tragicomic presentation of these figures in film does what philosophy has often failed to do. It presents this figure as something utterly singular, a piece of fate, a stroke of luck, a freak expression of power that is awesome and terrible, something beyond any sort of law, even beyond the law that it imposes on itself. Philosophy seems unable to avoid being prescriptive.

Presenting such an image is one way in which Nietzschean cinema can be said to be doing philosophy rather than simply representing something already fully articulated by philosophy. These figures are not simply "illustrations" of philosophy.[1] Rather, language cannot capture the singularities that are the quanta of power and pieces of fate that we call the *Übermensch*. The challenge that Nietzschean philosophy faces is to make sense of that which is beyond the available human concepts. "His goal . . . is to synthesize things that stand in a peculiar relationship by their very opposition. But again and again what Nietzsche tries to articulate into a unity ultimately breaks apart."[2] Philosophy aims to give accounts of things and is "subject to the claims of reason"; thus, insofar as it is contradictory, even if the phenomena themselves are contradictory, it will seem to have failed.[3] Philosophy needs to reconcile opposites, make sense, and give epistemic and ethical norms. But it seems like a category mistake to criticize these visions of *Übermenschen* because they are contradictory or irrational. I find this cinematic possibility—namely, the ability to present to us that which is not subject to the claims of reason—to be more suggestive of film's philosophical potential than the idea that it is engaged in the reflection or "critical evaluation" of the "condition of its own possibility."[4] Thus, the Nietzschean films give a visual account of something that is outside the limits of philosophy itself, but that still is the object of philosophizing. It can present within its visuals something that is beyond justification or reasonable explanation, which is to say beyond the human, a task that is particularly difficult within the language of philosophy, even a philosophy as untraditional in its form as Nietzsche's.

In this chapter, I will turn to a series of films often referred to as "gold-digging" films, but it is more accurate to call them films of liberated women who use sex to succeed in a patriarchal society. For that reason, they are also sometimes referred to as films of "sin and success." I will refer to them as films of the *Überfrau* and will concentrate on several that have a direct connection to Nietzsche's thought. Rather than reading these liberated women as female versions of the gangster, which is possible, I want to draw upon Derrida's understanding of Nietzsche's comments on the notion of truth and its relation to the metaphor of "woman." We can also continue to draw upon Deleuze's Nietzschean notion of the "power of the false," which understands the *Überfrau* as paradoxically containing "incompossible presents" and embodying an "artistic, creative power" that does not rely on the distinction between illusion and reality or between the virtual and the actual.[5] A film that adopts "the power of the false" accepts the "indiscernibility of the real and the imaginary," abandons truthful narration for farce, and embraces playfulness with the division between the true and the false.[6] Such untruthful narration means that even if the films give the appearance of subverting the "liberated woman" for the sake of the patriarchal norms that govern the culture, there are clear reasons why we cannot trust those moments.

One *might* look at these films as pursuing a form of justice, namely equality or a life in which there is a "single standard" rather than one set of rules for men and one for women. While justice and a single standard for the sexes regarding their freedom to sin and to succeed might be possible, the superwoman points to a more radical form of life that does not deceive or sin simply as the means toward a level of "success" equal to that of men. Instead, as Deleuze says of "the power of the false," the person who embodies this power realizes that they never stop lying because, as a creator or "forger," there is simply a series of "metamorphoses" and not "something" real or true behind these forgeries.[7] We can follow Derrida's suggestion and identify two different symbols of the liberated woman. But before any liberating movement takes place, there is what he calls the "castrated woman" or "the woman, taken as a figure or potentate of falsehood," who "finds herself censured, debased and despised . . . in the name of truth and metaphysics" and in contrast to the "virtuous man."[8] We might think of her as the woman under patriarchal law. Then Derrida describes the first form of liberation: the "castrating woman" who is "the figure or potentate of truth."⁹ This image of the woman is of one who challenges the patriarchal order yet still operates within "the economy of truth's system."¹⁰ Derrida says that she may identify with truth or she may play with truth and manipulate it to her own advantage without believing in it.¹¹ Either naivete or guile is at work here, but Derrida's point is that a simple inversion has taken place, either an inversion of the predominant gender of truth (from male to female) or an inversion from valuing truth to not valuing it. Derrida's description of these women is intended as a translation of Nietzsche's account of how the "true world" became a fable in *Twilight of the Idols*, an account in which the idea of the true world is said to become "more subtle, insidious, incomprehensible—*it becomes female*" (*TI* 5 §2, emphasis in original).¹² The first stage of liberation is meant to indicate the moment of Nietzsche's fable, in which the true world is seen as entirely unattainable and indemonstrable. Thus, the woman appears as mystery to be uncovered and, thus, as a "figure or potentate of truth."¹³ Woman was labeled as everything false, but she is now revealed as absent truth. While I think that there are certainly reasons to think that the liberated women in many of the films that I will discuss intersects with this category of "woman as mystery," Derrida is clear that this negation of patriarchal law remains bound to it, just as the middle stages of the true world's becoming a fable remain bound to its truth even if it is unattainable.¹⁴

A more radical conception of the liberated woman is aligned with Nietzsche's abolishing both the notions of the true world and the merely apparent one. He calls this the "high point of humanity" and the birth of the superhuman (*TI* 5 §6). Derrida describes this final stage as the "affirming woman" and in the following terms: "Beyond the double negation of the first two [the castrated and castrating woman], woman is recognized and affirmed as an affirmative power, a dissimulatress, an artist, a dionysiac. And no longer is it man who affirms her. She affirms herself, in and of herself, in man."¹⁵ What would be the more radical depiction of a woman outside of this so-called economy of truth, beyond what Derrida calls phallogocentricism? Rather than using "parody or the simulacrum as a weapon in the service of truth," this figure's use of the power of the false is a radical force that cannot be assimilated or fully brought to intentional consciousness or to language.¹⁶ This is because the *Überfrau* is utterly singular in her creative acts, while the "sign-world" of language and consciousness is "shallow, thin, relatively stupid, general, sign, herd signal" due to its being bound by "the snares of grammar (the metaphysics of the people)" (*GS* §354). This "dissimulatress" and

Dionysian artist does not simply play at truth for her own advantage.[17] She embodies *animae magnae prodigus* and acts, creates, and dissimulates even when it is not to her advantage.[18] To use others and truth as mere appearance to gain power, status, position, wealth, and even a husband is to remain oscillating within what Derrida calls the two reactive positions—the pre-liberated state and liberation still under the sign of "truth." The truly affirmative woman appears cinematically through her excess, which converts everything into dissimulation, including her own stated ends. Such excessive self-overcoming looks like her destruction, but it takes place though her own power.[19] The concept of the Dionysian woman that Derrida has given us is an example of his notion of the logic of "the supplement," that is, the excessive or frivolous expenditure that lies outside the phallogocentric system but also reveals what is lacking within that system. I use this notion to combat a hasty reading of the sometimes tragic fate of woman in these films as the reassertion of the power of patriarchy. Even if there are such explicit disruptions of the fate of these liberated women, which likely are inserted for the sake of satisfying the censors, they come across as narratively dishonest, leading us to continue to read them through the expression of the power of the *Überfrau*.[20]

Derrida's reading of Nietzsche in *Spurs* uses a philosophical metaphor, which is found in Nietzsche's texts and which is obviously a long-standing misogynist notion, that links women and deception. The sexist history of the idea is clearly present in the demonization of the sexually liberated woman as the vamp. But presumably Derrida's reading of Nietzsche is attempting to revalue that association. Nietzsche's famous claim that "truth is a woman" must sit alongside the claims that he makes about the deep skepticism of women, who are able to see that there is no truth, only a masquerade (*BGE* P). Derrida captures this apparent contradiction in the following terms.

> There is no such thing as the truth of woman, but it is because of that abyssal divergence of the truth, because that untruth is "truth." Woman is but one name for that untruth of truth. . . . Because, indeed, if woman *is* truth, *she* at least knows that there is no truth, that truth has no place here and that no one has a place for truth. And she is woman precisely because she herself does not believe in truth itself, because she does not believe in what she is, in what she is believed to be, in what she thus is not.[21] (emphasis in original)

The point here is that the shift that Nietzsche makes by calling "truth a woman" is to show that the power to establish "truth" necessitates that the creator has "no place" for and does not believe in "truth" in a traditional sense. The creation of truth is a sort of "veiling dissimulation," a construction of meaning that both reveals and covers up.[22] If we take as our starting point that language and all truths expressed in it are static and partial, incapable of capturing the creative flux of life itself and its multiform possibilities or the singularity that is each piece of fate, then the association of woman with deception is to associate her with the one fundamental truth, the "untruth" (the interpretability, perspectivity, and deconstructability) of every "truth." This amounts to the association of woman with *différance*, with the "play of differences" that is "the possibility of conceptuality" as the "non-full, non-simple, structured and differentiating origin of difference."[23] While it may seem (and Derrida has been criticized for this) as misogynistic to link woman to non-presence and untruth, his point is that such misogynistic associations are a result of the privileging of presence and truth. His aim is to revalue these seemingly negative notions and identify them with the positive, creative striving behind all meaning. Woman paradoxically exists as "non-being" in a world where the myth of "being as presence" is dominant. The *Überfrau* exposes this myth of presence, which opposes illusion, as violence.

I will explore these ideas within three films: *Female* (1933), *Baby Face* (1933), and *Red-Headed Woman* (1932). The first two were written by Kathryn Scola and the writer and illustrator Gene Markey, who knew Ben Hecht from the heyday of organized crime in Chicago and from the literary scene in New York City before both moved to Hollywood.[24] There is no doubt Markey and Scola were familiar with Nietzsche's philosophy and explicitly infuse it into each of the films under discussion here. *Red-Headed Woman* was written by Anita Loos, one of Hollywood's most prolific screenwriters, who was also friends with Ben Hecht and was certainly aware of Nietzschean ideas.[25] For example, in her one-act play *All Men Are Equal*, she has an intellectual named Brill spout the sort of Mencken-inspired elitist philosophy commonly associated with Nietzsche and Hecht. He rails against the "common herd," praises "aristocratic" taste, and argues that, rather than reforming the herd, we should strive for passion.[26] The main Anita Loos screenplay to articulate such an amoral expression of the will to power is *Red-Headed Woman*.[27] The character in this film was intended to be an utter egoist "deeply in love with herself" and no one else.[28]

The *Überfrau* in American Silent Film

The depiction of liberated superwomen in films of the 1930s stands in sharp contrast to their earlier representation. Initially they were contained within the "social problem film" as the degenerative vamp. Among such films are Alice Hollister's *The Vampire* (1913), Helen Garnder's *Vampire of the Desert* (1913), Olga Petrova's *The Vampire* (1915), and *A Fool There Was* (1915), with Theda Bara.[29] These morality tales condemn vamps: Theda Bara's vamp in *The Devil's Daughter* (1915) goes insane, as she does in *The Eternal Sappho* (1916), while she is blinded and redeemed in *Gold and the Woman* (1916) and killed in *The Tiger Woman* (1917). The vamp is sometimes formed through split personality in *The Two-Soul Woman* (1918) and *The Untameable* (1923), through soulless resurrection in *Lola* (1914), through satanic hypnotism as in *Saint, Devil and Woman* (1916), or through a dream-state sent by an evil demon in *Miss Jekyll and Madame Hyde* (1915). While the glut of vamp movies faded in the late 1910s, they certainly did not disappear. The most famous literary and cinematic depiction of the *Überfrau* as a degenerative vampire is W. Somerset Maugham's *Of Human Bondage* (1934). Bette Davis's Mildred is the definition of a parasite, returning to Leslie Howard's Philip Carey several times and devouring his future. She is a cruel egoist who crawls deeper and deeper into the gutter. Yet her pathetic existence ultimately teaches Carey how to live and to freely accept himself and his own weaknesses.

Yet silent cinema did not condemn all liberated women to be parasitic vamps. Although I have no direct evidence of her being influenced by Nietzsche, Mary MacLane was one of early twentieth-century America's most radical feminists, whose tale of her different love affairs was made into a film *Men Who Have Made Love to Me* (1918), in which she plays herself. Her writings, while terribly self-centered and often juvenile, were revolutionary, widely read, and widely critiqued by leading intellectuals of the day. MacLane's confessional writing "sings only the Ego and the individual" and reveals her pagan heart, her "savage" incongruity, the absence of God, her love of her body and of sex, and her desire to "do a murder."[30] In her newspaper article "Mary MacLane Meets the Vampire on the Isle of Treacherous Delights" from 1910, the vampire is New York City, which teaches Mary the doctrine "'More Life, More Life!'—to turn everything outward, to let slip all one's emotions, all one's glimmering passion, all one's dormant lights-o'-love."[31] MacLane quickly disappeared from the public eye, but in her 1918 film, she made a remarkable appearance. She says that she became "a 'film star.' . . . Nay, more, a vampire."[32] MacLane felt that film in general had "more of sheer beauty—world beauty, life beauty, human beauty" than any popular expression of everyday life.[33] This unfortunately lost film advertised MacLane as a genius, albeit an erratic one, who would bear her soul to the world, as she had done in her writings.

As we begin to see the depiction of superwoman on the screen in the 1920s, it is worth noting how Nietzsche's thought and feminism combined in Britain and America.[34] The idea of whether Nietzsche would accept the notion of the "superwoman" was a question raised as early as 1907.[35] It was a pressing issue as several early commentators on Nietzsche were also women, such as Grace Neal Dolson and the British Catholic nun Maude D. Petre, who wrote several articles on Nietzsche, including the article "Nietzsche the Anti-Feminist," prior to Mencken's influential book.[36] Petre argued that the Nietzschean critique of equality and egalitarianism suggested women ought not to strive for the same sort of freedom available to men, which was an unrealistic ambition, but should strive for a type of womanly freedom that had a "natural fitness" for them.[37] Other feminist approaches to Nietzsche translated his individualism into a rebellion against patriarchy.[38] For example, Margaret Sanger's "The Woman Rebel" famously proclaimed "No Gods No Masters" after Nietzsche.[39] Sanger was less explicitly Nietzschean than Dora Marsden in England, who promoted her egoism in *The Freewoman* (1911–1912), *The New Freewoman* (1913), and *The Egoist* (1914–1919). Marsden distinguished freewomen from bondwomen. The latter were not "separate spiritual entities" from men, and most women were forced into this category because "all those activities which presuppose the master qualities, the standard-making, the law-giving, the moral-framing, belong to men."[40] She defined feminism as the effort of woman "to find her place among the masters."[41] Her conception of the freewoman is that of the genius, because any "individual revelation of life-manifestation made realizable to others in some outward form" is an act of genius and personal vision.[42] Marsden, unlike Sanger, who was focused on the downtrodden and the poor in spirit, wanted to create a vanguard of women who would point "towards a higher race, for which their achievements will help to make ready, and their strivings and aspirations help to mould."[43]

Marsden's vision of the freewoman is perhaps expressed in Raoul Walsh's film *The Strongest* (1920), based on Georges Clemenceau's novel. This novel is essentially a meditation on Nietzsche's idea of the "*surhomme*" and the egoistic life devoted to power and success. Take, for example, the following remarks from Clemenceau's novel, where Claudia aims to be an *Überfrau* and rejects, for the sake of her own pursuit of power, the generous man who loves her.

> I have already experienced the desire to command, and I feel, in spite of myself, that the power of the world is the strongest.[44]
>
> I am in the camp of the strongest, as my father calls them, and you are deliberately taking place among the conquered.[45]
>
> I am going in for the pleasure of ruling the world.[46]

The book is filled with profoundly illiberal, Nietzschean, and elitist political philosophy, punctuated by ridicule of the "crowd" and praise of the "noble joy of power."[47] Although the film seems rather cliché, there is no way that Walsh could have penned the screenplay of this novel around 1919 or 1920 and directed it without having a full understanding of this prominent interpretation of the Nietzschean worldview. The film is unfortunately lost, so we do not know how much of this philosophy made it onto the screen.

While Marsden looked to the higher "freewomen," depictions of bondwomen struggling against the world provide some of the most memorable early depictions of the *Überfrau*. In Thomas Ince's film *Anna Christie* (1923), from Eugene O'Neill's play, we find a series of tragic figures cast about like driftwood on "that old devil sea." In effect, the characters are in flight, escaping from forces they cannot control, but they must come to understand their fate and to love it rather than flee from it, even if that means to love someone who has had to live an "immoral" life. Anna Christie has been a prostitute and is brought to the edge of suicide, not so much because of her moral conscience or guilt, but because of a hatred of men, the lack of freedom of her conditions, and the endless monotony of the future. To will her way through this nightmare world shows us a sort of *Überfrau*. In *Anna Christie* we see characters struggling under the yoke of moral conceptions of good and evil. They come to recognize a force that is more powerful than human civilization. That force is fate and time, understood as the eternal recurrence of the same.

Hermann Sudermann's works are another source of the *Überfrau* on film in the silent era. His work *Heimat* was the basis for *Magda* (1917), with the remarkable Clara Kimball Young, who portrays a strong, successful Wagnerian opera singer. She is a version of the "freewoman" who is beyond traditional notions of good and evil. Sudermann's work is also the foundation of *The Song of Songs* (1918), which was remade with

Pola Negri as *Lily of the Dust* (1924) and then in the sound era with Marlene Dietrich, again entitled *The Song of Songs* (1933). In Dietrich's version of *The Song of Songs*, we find her entering Dionysian states, first of love, which is so powerful that it frightens the sculptor with whom she is having an affair. When she is abandoned to Baron von Merzbach, who attempts to be her Svengali and to mold her into a "great woman," she falls into a state of despair and self-destruction, which culminates in her nihilistic life as a prostitute. Sudermann's *The Undying Past* was made into *Flesh and the Devil* (1926), which is an ode to male friendship between John Gilbert's character, Leo von Harden, and Lars Hanson's character, Ulrich von Eltz, whom Greta Garbo's Felicitas marries. In effect, this love triangle takes place from an amoral perspective in which the fundamental principle that should be followed is, like in *Underworld*, that people be upfront and honest with one another rather than sneaking around and being filled with *ressentiment*. Finally, Sudermann's story "The Excursion to Tilsit" inspired F. W. Murnau's masterpiece *Sunrise* (1927), in which modern decadence and weakness give rise to despair and murderous passions that are dissipated only by recovering the joy of life through a series of fateful events. These presentations of Sudermann's work provide important artistic visions of *Überfrauen*, whose lives are able to transcend the limitations of their past, to endure the indignities of the world of men, and whose happiness, even in death, is an enactment of their expansive soul.

Vivente Blasco Ibáñez was also influenced by Nietzsche, as is seen in his novel *The Four Horsemen of the Apocalypse*, which contains an insightful discussion of Nietzsche's thought. This work was made into a lengthy anti-war film in 1921 by the same name. The film begins with the idea of the world being weighed down by its history of violence and possessing "fires of resentment smoldering beneath the crust of civilization." This resentment is represented in the difference between the two husbands, one French and one German, of two Argentine daughters. The father of the family is a sort of *Übermensch*, capricious, despotic, and feared, who had created his own success as a cattleman. As the family and civilization are torn apart by war, the film concludes that love must ultimately replace hate. Greta Garbo's first American film, *Torrent* (1926), was also based on the Ibáñez novel *Entre Naranjos*, which is a strikingly similar story to Sudermann's *Heimat*. Garbo's second American film, *The Temptress* (1926), based on Ibáñez's *La Tierra de Todos*, shows a surprising revaluation of the vamp. The opening intertitle explains that "vamps" or "temptresses" are the creation of men and not the product of the inherent evil and sexuality of women: "Oh Woman! Thou art not alone the creation of God—but of Man." As seductive and destructive as Garbo is, she legitimately argues that it is she that has been exploited. When it is pointed out that "men have died for you, forsaken honor and work for you," she points out that it has been "not for me but for my body! Not for my happiness, but for theirs!" Ultimately, her collapse into a life of prostitution, abandonment, and near insanity is no indictment of her actions. Although it seems a cruel irony when the intertitles announce, "Woman! Born to rule the world!"—the recognition of the power of women to endure and to command shows a shift away from the previous duality, in which women were either angels who had to retain their purity at any cost (castrated women) or were devils who had lost that purity (castrating women).[48]

A final notable depiction of the liberated woman in 1920s silent film that I want to discuss is *Sadie Thompson* (1928), which was then made into *Rain* (1932). Maugham, as mentioned earlier when discussing *The Magician* and *Of Human Bondage*, was not an advocate of Nietzschean thought, but his criticism of traditional morality and religion was not entirely dissimilar to Nietzsche's.[49] Maugham's story is not originally representative of the *Überfrau* ideal. The prostitute he describes in the story is rather ordinary. By focusing on Sadie's intellect, her toughness, and her energy, both films produce an image of the *Überfrau* as a woman who has acquired the power of "the masters." The 1932 film draws upon Nietzsche explicitly through the character of Joe Horn, the owner of the general store where the travelers sleep after being stranded on the island of Pago-Pago. In his reflections, he begins to quote Nietzsche. He draws from "The Convalescent" in the third part of *Zarathustra*. Horn recites a passage where Zarathustra's animals claim that all things "are dancing." According to the modern translation, Horn quotes the song of the animals: "Everything goes, everything comes back; eternally rolls the wheel of being. Everything dies, everything blossoms again; eternally runs the year of being" (Z III "The Convalescent" §2). Undoubtedly, the endless rain on the island is used to capture this expression of the eternal recurrence of the same. After stating this, Horn concludes, "Thus spoke Zarathustra . . . Ah, good ol' Nietzsche." There is no such reference in the short story by Maugham or in the play. Part of the lesson of this passage in *Zarathustra* is that "man is the cruelest animal" and that his attempt to redeem the world is the invention of hell (Z III "The Convalescent" §2). Both films and the original story make it clear that the Christian reformers are turning paradise into hell. This reforming cruelty is called "pity," and yet the reformers approach it with their tongues "hanging from lasciviousness" (Z III "The Convalescent" §2). There is "voluptuous delight" in the persecution of "sinners" and "cross-bearers" (Z III "The Convalescent" §2). The film in general seems to draw upon this passage from Nietzsche's *Zarathustra* because it captures the nausea and disgust at these "smallest men" and reformers like Mr. Davidson, who hate life and who attempt to kill the "evil" in us that is our "best power" (Z III "The Convalescent" §2). It also shows the connection between religious reform, cruelty, pity for the sinful souls, and the true psycho-sexual motives underlying such behavior that result in the surprise ending of the film.

From this brief overview of some very influential cinematic depictions of *Überfrauen* in the 1920s, which were inspired by literary sources familiar with Nietzschean philosophy, we can certainly see that the representations of women were changing in a multitude of ways often characterized as part of "the New Woman" concept, which stressed women's independence and the rejection of patriarchal norms.[50] The depictions of "flappers" in, for example, the films of Clara Bow present a far more comic and less tragic conception of women's liberation and sexuality. If we were to try and read Bow's films such as *Mantrap* (1926), from a Sinclair Lewis story,[51] and *It* (1927), from Elinor Glyn's story of animal magnetism, through a Nietzschean perspective, we would have to do so (and certainly could do so) through the ideal of the "free spirit" and the attempt to establish those alternative values of "caprice and gaiety."[52] But I do not think that these films from the 1920s always constitute a complete shift in values entirely beyond good and evil. They often remain within the humanistic strand of socially progressive films, which see the establishment of "justice" as merely raising women to the single standard set by phallogocentric discourse. In other words, women remain the mysterious symbol of a higher truth in a lot of these films, as seen in the continual appeal to the "prostitute with a heart of gold," and, thus, it is hard to say that they go so far as reveal the fully Dionysian figure who is beyond good and evil, truth and falsity, or the real world and the apparent one.

Baby Face (1933) and *Red-Headed Woman* (1932): The *Überfrau* and the Circle of Exploitation

Baby Face is the early Hollywood film in which Nietzsche's philosophy—more specifically, Mencken's interpretation of it—is most prominently on display, at least in the uncensored version. We have seen that it is not accurate to call the main character, Lily Powers, "Hollywood's first self-conscious representation of the Nietzschean superhuman."[53] What distinguishes the *Überfrau* from the gangster is her capacity for deception and self-transformation. *Baby Face* takes part in the "abolition of the true" by transforming the classical, unified subject into an "irreducible multiplicity" rooted in "passion" or will to power.[54] I find it instructive to compare Scola's and Markey's *Überfrau* to their depiction of the male counterpart in their exceedingly lifeless movie *A Modern Hero* (1934), a flat-footed and joyless depiction of the *Übermensch* directed by G. W. Pabst, his only Hollywood film. This "modern hero," Pierre Radier, is a horse rider in the circus and the son of a female lion-tamer who is an *Überfrau*. Through affairs with affluent and powerful women, he becomes a rich industrialist. But not only does he not deceive any of these women, each seems to volunteer both her body and her pocketbook to him before setting him free to continue to climb higher in the world. His mother characterizes him as a restless egoist for whom "no woman means as much to him as he does to himself." Yet he is not a cruel person. He is honorable, kind, and loving. Everyone seems to recognize that Pierre is always thinking about the future, which only his mother interprets as rooted in the passions for money, power, and ambition. In making this film, Markey and Scola seemingly took the plot of *Baby Face* (as well as the circus plot from their earlier film *Lilly Turner*) and applied it to a male protagonist. This translation somehow meant that they had to *eliminate all deception*. From a Nietzschean perspective, such a change meant that they lost the very magic of life, that "veil of beautiful possibility, sparkling with promise, resistance, bashfulness, mockery, pity, and seduction" that seems both philosophically (if we follow Nietzsche and Derrida) and cinematically associated with women (*GS* §339).

It is worth describing the explicit references to Nietzsche in the uncensored version of *Baby Face* before looking at Barbara Stanwyck's Lily Powers in closer detail.[55] Obviously, her name, like Tom Powers in *The Public Enemy* (1931), expresses her status as the embodiment of the will to power. The articulations of Nietzschean philosophy in the film are contained in scenes surrounding the cobbler named Cragg. He enters Nick Powers's speakeasy in Erie, Pennsylvania, and tells Lily that he has not been to there recently because he does "not care for the crowd here"—an articulation of Nietzschean disgust for the herd. Cragg acts as Lily's mentor, her educator, and tells her to "go out into the world" and "to make something of herself," because "she has power" even though she does not recognize her "potentialities." She shrugs and responds with sarcasm, "I'm a ball of fire, I am." Soon she will become a ball of fire, when her wish for her father's death becomes reality, igniting his distillery and consuming him in an explosion. Before that, Lily is literally the bondwoman that Marsden describes, the castrated woman of Derrida, enslaved to her father, who prostitutes her. Cragg has lent Lily a book to read "by Nietzsche, the greatest philosopher of all time." Although she says she "never got much" out of books, she eventually educates herself, for example, by reading a book on manners. Cragg gets irritated by Lily's dismissive attitude but refuses to offer her pity: "If you are content to stay here like a dumb animal, in this miserable life, then I wash my hands of you." His lack of pity is also seen in his refusal to accept his beer for free: "I accept no favors," he exclaims. The shock of the refusal of pity has a profound result on Lily's behavior, and she begins to rebel.[56]

After the death of her father, there is a cut to the spine of Nietzsche's *Will to Power*, held by Cragg. The page opens to sections 172 and 173, a set of scathing aphorisms against religion that argue that Christianity enables "the sickest and unhealthiest elements and desires to come to the top." I doubt that the specific aphorisms were intended as significant for the film, although the supposedly respectable and moral people, such as the politician Ed Sipple, that Lily meets along her path are all wretched creatures motivated entirely by the basest of desires. Cragg warns Lily that, while what she does "is up to her," if she stays in this town, then she is lost. She makes the excuse that she cannot leave because of money, after which he admonishers her, saying, "You let life defeat you. You do not fight back." Lily still does not get it, and asks, "What chance has a woman got?" Cragg gives her a lecture on Nietzsche.

> More chance than men. A young beautiful woman like you can get anything she wants in the world because she has power over men. But you must use men and not let them use you. You must be a master, not a slave.[57] Look here, Nietzsche says: "*All life, no matter how we idealize it, is nothing more or less than exploitation.*" That is what I am telling you. Exploit yourself. . . . Use men. Be strong. Defiant! Use men to get the things you want!

I do not think that anyone has noticed it, but that is not actually a quote from Nietzsche. Like the quotes from the 1915 film *A Disciple of Nietzsche*, it is from H. L. Mencken's *The Philosophy of Friedrich Nietzsche*: "We are taught to believe that the only true happiness lies in self-effacement;

that it is wrong to profit by the misfortune or weakness of another. But against this Nietzsche brings the undeniable answer: *All life, no matter how much we idealize it, is, at bottom, nothing more or less than exploitation. The gain of one man is inevitably the loss of some other man*" (my emphasis).[58] Nietzsche actually says that non-exploitation can be the norm of behavior among those who are similar in strength, possessing the same value standards, and "belonging together in *one* body" (*BGE* §259, emphasis in original). There are exceptions to purely exploitative relations such as friendship. We find this in the film in the relationship between Lily and Chico, who form a "healthy aristocracy" (*BGE* §259).

The final explicit mention of Nietzsche in the film is when some of Cragg's books and the news of his death arrive at Lily's upscale apartment. She has slept her way up to J. P. Carter, the first vice president of the bank. Lily opens a copy of *Thoughts out of Season*—the early translation of *Untimely Meditations*—and we see a page of text. Most of the page is in shadow, but an illuminated quote says, "Face life as you find it—defiantly and unafraid. Waste no energy yearning for the moon. Crush out all sentiment." The page shown us is not actually a printed text from that book or any other book. Unlike the earlier presentation of pages from the *Will to Power* at Mr. Cragg's, where we could clearly see both pages and edges of the backing of the book, here we cut from the shot of the spine of the book, telling us what it is, to Lily looking through it, to a close-up on a single page of text. We cannot see the edges of the book, page numbers, or any adjoining page. The page clearly has been constructed for the sake of showing this highlighted quote. We know that this is not an actual page in a book because on the visible page, the preceding and following paragraphs that surround the highlighted quote *are identical*. That repeating paragraph says: "Remember that sentiment is opposed to reason and rational thought. Individual success and achievement, being the goal toward which humanity strives, can be reached only through the strictest application of mental faculties. The dead weight of sentimental superficial observations and impractical theories have no value for the man who intends to surmount all difficulties." Although I am unable to find this repeated paragraph in any source, the highlighted passage in the film is nearly a match to a quote from Mencken: "a being who *faces life as he finds it, defiantly and unafraid* who knows how to fight and how to forbear, who sees things as they actually are, and not as they might or should be, and so *wastes no energy yearning for the moon* or in butting his head against stone walls. 'This new tablet, O my brethren, I put over you: Be hard!'" (my emphasis).[59] Undoubtedly, the filmmakers have used an alternative articulation by Mencken of these lines from something else he wrote, or else the filmmakers have made a pithier statement of Mencken's sentiment and surrounded it by some text, perhaps an exegesis of Nietzsche. There are no such exaltations of this sort in the *Untimely Meditations*. Nietzsche certainly would never say that the "goal toward which humanity strives" is something as practical-sounding as "individual success and achievement." Lastly, it is utterly unlike Nietzsche to say that the way one achieves this goal is the strictest application of *mental* faculties, that is, "reason and rational thought," which sentiment pollutes. This is pure Mencken, not Nietzsche.

Rather than simply detailing the actions by which Lily Powers exploits, controls, and ultimately destroys men, I want to focus on Lily's internal contradictions, her potentialities, as Cragg calls them. How is it that she is being prostituted by her father in the first place, when she so clearly has the power to defend herself? She pushes the men away, breaks bottles over their heads, and causes her father to fearfully crawl away from her. The opening scenes barely contain the contradictoriness of her character: raging power and masterful passion sitting alongside dead-eyed slavery and suicidal impulses. But the fact that there is no clear picture of who or what Lily is speaks to her multiplicity, to her status as having no truth. Lily is seen through the male gazes that surround her, and so she is never seen. She appears as mystery, truth, pleasure, beauty, happiness, and innocence. They treat her as the false or castrated woman, a "kept woman," but they also value her and praise her as "intelligent" and "head and shoulders above the other girls." Her paradoxical position as castrated and castrating shows how a patriarchal viewpoint layers these values on Lily. But the Dionysian position eventually manifests. Only the Nietzschean cobbler sees her as the power to be both anything she wants or nothing at all.

Lily is the most real force in the world for these men, but she is also never present to them except as a simulacrum. This is visible in one of the more remarkable cinematic moments in the film, where Lily's power is shown but her presence is also seen as illusory, a reflection of light in eyes of men. When Mr. Stevens finds Lily and Mr. Brody in a compromising situation in the women's restroom, we see Mr. Stevens framed in the doorway, standing tall and exemplifying male authority. The camera's position, looking out at Mr. Stevens, seemingly places us amid the sexual rendezvous. After he fires Mr. Brody, we see a remarkably composed shot: Mr. Stevens looks in through doorway, but now a mirror on the wall next to him shows both a reflection of Lily's back and the reflection of another mirror in which we see Lily's face as she applies makeup. Lily appears as a reflection to Mr. Stevens. She appears as the (photographed) reflection of a reflection to us, the audience. She is also creating a mask with her cosmetics.[60] Her power, like Medusa, seemingly cannot be directly gazed upon. The camera cannot look at her when this power manifests—for example, cutting to a pair of gloves and a lantern when Lily seduces a guard at the trainyard as she escapes Erie for New York City. The presence of censorship in the film requires it to be deceptive, to show discarded gloves or the application of lipstick to signify sex. If the *Überfrau* exposes that all life is power and exploitation, then there is really no difference between reality and appearance and so no difference between *really* showing desire as opposed to deceptively substituting for it. For example, consider the scenario where Lily dishonestly plays the part of the innocent victim to Mr. Stevens, and he, presumably being honest and forgiving, has pity on her. But Mr. Stevens is lying as well: his pity is an expression of his power over Lily. His forgiveness of her transgression is an exploitation that will lead him down the same path as everyone else, even though he is an "extraordinarily fine person," has "high ideals," and is "not like other men." Thus, the "truth" of his pity is just as deceptive as Lily's innocence: both lead to the same place. Mr. Stevens has an affair with Lily, which his fiancée discovers. Mr. Carter says that this is not "the end of the world," but, ironically, it is. The men in the film continue to see Lily as something other than what she is. She is *in fact* the end of their worlds. Mr. Stevens kills Mr. Carter and himself over Lily.

The question remains whether the concluding moments of the film "reframe Lily as an affectionately submissive woman" through an "unmerited sentimentalism."[61] The closing of the film is odd in both the edited and unedited versions. I do think it helps to recognize Lily as "a dissimulatress, an artist, a dionysiac," who has the power to become anything for anyone; we must not think that any of her forms is "authentic."[62] Why is this apparently "submissive" form adopted? Even if it is simply an adoption for the sake of the censors, this dishonest shift in the film's narrative perspective exposes the lie that undergirds the moral perspective itself. The return of Lily to the moral herd could take place only by a violence against her own will that is imposed on her from without, from literally outside the filmic universe that she inhabits. But more can be said than that. The scandal of the love-nest murder-suicide sends Lily to the bank's Paris branch. Not only does Lily play the victim to the bank's board of directors and new president, Trenholm, but when she moves to

Paris, she takes on a new name and becomes a hard worker making an "honest living." This too is entirely unlike Lily in the rest of the film, but, strangely, *that* transformation does not strike scholars as odd and submissive. Only her final outburst is regularly considered a collapse of her power. But isn't she putting on a mask of traditionalism throughout the film? Her traditional life at the Paris branch is rationalized as part of a long (and completely improbable) con job. But if that is seen as just another of Lily's forgeries, why is the final scene not also read in this way? In that scene, financial hardship hits Trenholm and the bank. Lily first refuses to help him, proclaiming that she is not like other people because "all the gentleness and kindness in me has been killed." But she then returns to him and gives him the money she has saved. There are reasons to see this as just another forgery.

Lily's choice to not abandon Trenholm begins with a flashback of the faces of *all* the men she has seduced to get where she is. It is not a vision *only* of her husband's face. She is not recounting her love for her husband but the struggle to get where she is, which the censors recognized and cut the sequence down so that we see only Trenholm's face. Her original vision tells her that the logical conclusion of the "long con" is to give away her wealth, act the dutiful wife, and articulate ordinary human sentiments even if they are dead within her; otherwise the sequence will go on indefinitely. She envisions Trenholm saying that he loves Lily *even though* she has been with other men. But this shows his love retains its patriarchal double standard, as he has been with other women. His confession of love should not have the qualification "*even though*." This does not distinguish Trenholm from all the men in the film, who also love her "*even though*." The failure to love Lily for her power to do just as Cragg advocates suggests that the love at the end of the film is corrupted, conventional, and a type of weakness. Trenholm's qualified and patriarchal love, even though she has been false, shows that he does not understand that her falseness is what makes her most loveable. So is Lily's emotional return to Trenholm "true"? She screams at his semi-conscious body, "Darling, don't leave me. I'll do anything. I love you so much," after she finds him with a self-inflicted gunshot wound. It is a moment of sentimentality that does not fit with a film that has argued that the *Übermensch* must crush all sentiment. But that emotion instantaneously dries up, and she is back to her stoic self. In the ambulance with Trenholm, her case of money and jewels spills on the floor, and she seems to have returned to her emotionless stare that she dons earlier in the movie when tragedies occur. She mutters that "it doesn't matter now," which suggests that she has recognized that all life is exploitation. For this reason, her path to the top of the bank does not look so much different than her life back in Erie. She has returned to the state of despair that we see her in when we first find her in her father's speakeasy. Her moment of hysteria in the ambulance seems to be a desperate attempt to awaken what she has admitted is dead inside her.[63] The *Überfrau* can play the *Frau*, but it is only momentary. Jacobs believes that the original ending of the film was that Lily returns and finds Trenholm dead, which would confirm that her choice to return was a mistake, one from which fate saved her.[64]

Ironically, the ambiguous ending of the original film is less cynical than the censored version. Although Jacobs reads this censored ending as forcing the film to punish Lily for her immorality and to establish "the formation of the couple," I see the possibility of a quite different reading.[65] The edited ending is a scene in which the bank managers discuss "Mr. and Mrs. Trenholm" and the fact that they have sacrificed everything for the bank. They are now penniless and "working out their happiness together," back in Erie, Pennsylvania. However, I would argue that the censored ending makes it clear that the decision to return to Trenholm was the wrong decision. It was a sacrifice in vain. It has returned us full circle: the final shot is of the steel mill seen at the start of the film. But if we are back where we started, do we really believe that they are living in wedded bliss in Erie as a coal miner and a coal miner's wife? It is much more likely Lily is back to the life of prostitution, the life of "men, nothing but filthy men," which she tried to leave but which she recreated at the bank. Thus, both endings of the film suggest the eternal recurrence of the same rather than redemption and a return to the unliberated woman. The film, even in its censored form, does not offer a criticism of the life of the *Überfrau* or a rejection of the idea that all life is exploitation. We are left with both tragedy and farce, which is the result of repetition.

In *Baby Face*, Lily Powers seems to successfully deceive and hypnotize the men around her. None of them have pangs of remorse, and none of them seem to see through the counterfeit personas that Lily adopts. None of them scold her for her deceptions or suggest that she is not a hardworking secretary or a sweet and loving companion. Even when she harshly rejects them: their response seems to be to either agree with her rejection or simply try harder to get her to love them. Jean Harlow's character in *Red-Headed Woman*, Lillian Andrews or Red, is a rather different *Überfrau*. Red creates forgeries that everyone sees as a forgery, but they work all the same. It has been said that lies require ignorance: to shine the light of truth on the deception eliminates it. But in *Red-Headed Woman* everyone sees that Red is a "dirty little home-wrecker" whose aim is to ensnare wealthy and powerful men for her own benefit. Yet her illusions work. Deceptions can work even when they are recognized as deceptions, if everyone chooses to support the deception or has the mechanism to cause themselves to forget that it is a lie. To call the *Überfrau*'s actions deceptions, although everyone accepts and adopts these deceptions regardless of their truth or falsity, seems like a misunderstanding because they are just as much the construction of a truth.

Lily Powers and Lillian Andrews can be thought of as embodying one of Orr's modernist categories, the cool apocalypse, which "highlights the unspoken fears which lie behind the banalities of everyday life, the constrained anguish at the rapid fluctuation of unpredictable emotion."[66] The polite life of the elite members of society is not only undermined by these *Überfrauen*, but they show that elite society itself is built on the sexual and economic exploitation of women. The *Überfrau* coolly faces the apocalyptic consequences that come from challenging the fear of women's power that props up the sham values of society: "[Cool apocalypse] charts the material excess of a bourgeois existence. . . . Here the presence of time is unyielding. It hangs heavy because the *durée* of human existence is always open. Any closure would seem utopian. Nothing complete, nothing too tangible ever unfolds."[67] Lily Powers exudes coolness in the face of unyielding time, material excess, and the ephemerality of the sentiments that (Mencken's) Nietzsche instructs us to crush. I can see why Orr might think that Hollywood films fail to sustain this; yet, the films of the *Überfrau* expose not only the mass delusion of bourgeois existence, but also the bad faith of those that inhabit it. Bourgeois existence attempts to mask time and unpredictable passions for the sake of patriarchal control, while it leaves those passions and the illusion of respectability an open secret for men. Bill Legendre Jr., who is Red's initial conquest, expresses the hidden fears beneath bourgeois existence when he makes explicit that there is only "one filthy idea" in Red's "whole rotten makeup," namely, sin and success. But this is of course true of the men in the film as well, which Red expresses by saying that regardless of the moral uptightness of the man, at the end of the day, "he's a man, ain't he." Jean Harlow's character never fools anyone and is not fooled by anyone. Nevertheless, the power of her sexuality still manages to subjugate men.[68] Whereas there is very little moral criticism of Lily Powers, Red must constantly hear the peals of traditional morality. While Lily's men all seemed held fully in her sway, the "despisers of the body" in *Red-Headed Woman* speak the morality of "castratism" against the passions and, in so doing, reveal themselves to be hypocrites (*Z* 1 "On the Despisers of the Body"; *TI* 5 §1). When the open secret of the sexual and "material excess of bourgeois existence" is no longer an *unspoken* truth, Bill can no longer stand himself or Red. He claims that he is degrading himself by even talking to her and that every time he touched her that he hated himself for doing it. But Bill is transparent in his attempt to convince himself that the veils that have fallen remain intact and that the truth that is out somehow can be put back in the closet. It is at those moments, as Nietzsche argues, the suppression of the passions backfires, resulting in a savage and sadistic counterreaction, as seen in the violence that Bill lets loose on Red (*GS* §47).[69]

If Bill's moralizing were correct, then it would presumably be true that Red would end up in the gutter as people commenting on the newspaper reports of her attempted shooting of Bill proclaimed would happen. However, at the end of the film, we find out that she has moved to France, continued her romance with Albert the chauffeur, and has married a rich old idiot. This final scene tells us something about life itself. Life is a race, and we find both Red and the reconstituted Legendre family at a horse racetrack in France. The Legendres are excited because the horse they bet on has won the race. As it happens, they have won only fifty-six dollars. But Red and her decrepit French husband own the horse that has won the race. By not despising the body or following the morality of castratism, she retains the power to deceive without destroying herself or the bourgeois order. That is possible because that order is created upon exploitation and deception. The Legendres are now mere spectators to true life and to its creative Dionysian energy. Unlike the dual endings of *Baby Face*, in which Lily's exploitation takes on a repetitive, eternally recurring aspect by either returning her to a nihilistic state of mind in which she starts the film or literally returning her to Erie, *Red-Headed Woman* allows Red to continue her successful upward trajectory. Here we see the cool apocalypse of the *Überfrau* who flourishes rather than despairs in the absence of closure and completeness.

Anita Loos's farce pushes us toward the more radical affirmation that life itself is this unrelenting energy of desire, self-creation, and deception. *Red-Headed Woman*, with its images of cupid in the closing credits, dares us to think of Red's life of endless and obvious deception as what love, romance, and marriage actually are. It is worth noting that this film is entirely the opposite of Cavell's remarriage comedies.

It offers the farcical and cynical conclusion that there is just as much deception in the reconciled marriage of Bill and Irene as there is in the union of the grizzled old French millionaire and Red. The Dionysian joy and inhumanity of Jean Harlow's Red is easily seen as farce, but *Baby Face* seems more serious and tragic. Does Lily Powers learn how to be human at the end? As I have argued, this is so out of character for her that we should see it as a moment of false narration, either imposed on the film by the demands of censorship or imposed within the film by Lily herself, who is attempting and failing to feel human sentiment for a brief moment. This does point to a difference in the two film worlds. In *Red-Headed Woman*, everyone, even the "narrow-minded, strait-laced old dodos," sees passion, the creative power of lust, as that one filthy thing on everyone's minds. Everyone sees the Dionysian abyss, but only the *Überfrau* can flourish within it. Everyone else must retreat to their bourgeois existence. The world of *Baby Face* is filled with men ready to commit murder and suicide as they are absorbed into the Dionysian power of the *Überfrau*. While it is true that they must continually coat their passions with romantic notions of love and marriage, the tragic rather than the farcical dominates because of how hopeless and self-deceived they all are. The result is destruction for everyone but the *Überfrau*. The repetition of exploitation seems to be the fate of both characters, but Lily has a moment of despair because of the benighted and destructive world in which she lives. The cinematic world that Red inhabits is less benighted and, thus, less suicidal when confronting the abyss. Lily has reason to lament the endlessness of her struggle and to attempt to anesthetize herself with human sentiment as the men do.

Red-Headed Woman announces its challenge to realistic cinema and trustworthy narration in the opening shot, where Jean Harlow has her face unwrapped from a towel and she asks the audience, "So gentlemen prefer blondes, do they?" a reference to Loos's own 1925 novel. Next, there is a swipe transition to Harlow asking us if we can see through her dress, which we learn is what she wants, followed by a swipe cut to her legs. She pins Bill Legendre's picture to her garter, and tells us that she hopes to use it to seduce him. The montage of her preparations for her gold-digging is directed toward the audience, showing us her construction of an illusion and how cinema itself constructs illusion by splicing space and time and making the private public. This fantasy she is building, like the film itself, is one that ensnares everyone from an innocent soda jerk to multimillionaires. And yet the fantasy she spins is not one that fools, just as we are not fooled as we watch its cinematic construction. The

Nietzschean moving image of perspectivism is also present, for example, in the fade from Bill's wife's face in tears to Red's smiling face, laughing and retelling her adventure that she likens to an "uncensored movie." Morality and immorality are placed face to face; one is filled with tears and the other with laughter. The explicit mention of cinematic censorship in the movie itself and the way the camera plays with this notion, for example as Red and her friend Sally switch pajamas as the camera gazes at their bodies from the knees down or the shoulders up, makes evident the edited, perspectival view that we are receiving. Whether intended or not, the film and Red are co-conspirators, eschewing the value of the true, and recognizing the desire to luxuriate in the false. To buy into those illusions is called a sickness, a form of insanity, by Bill's wife and aunt. It is a madness, a Dionysian ecstasy that accepts, as Red puts it, that "nothing's ever impossible," as long as everything is a fiction. Is this not the lesson of film that has broken from the demands of realism and morality?

Female (1933) and the Single Standard

If, as Dora Marsden argues, the *Überfrau* must take her place among the "masters," then we should be able to look to films that depict gender role reversals to see this in action. In such films, the woman does not simply strive for social status and wealth while remaining entirely in the role of "the woman," the wife or the lover of a rich and powerful man. Gender role reversal, in which the wife becomes the breadwinner and the husband raises the children, can be found in *The Home Maker* (1925), but this was considered good wholesome entertainment that did not liberate female desire. On the other hand, Norma Shearer's films famously explore the hypocrisy and double standards of patriarchal society, as in *The Divorcee* (1930), *Let Us Be Gay* (1930), *Strangers May Kiss* (1931), and *Strange Interlude* (1932). Undoubtedly Rouben Mamoulian's *Queen Christina* (1933), the famous Greta Garbo vehicle, is a radical depiction of an *Überfrau* taking her place among the masters. But rather than simply occupying the male position, the more revolutionary possibility, according to Derrida, is one that is beyond the true and the false. This is to show a woman as a creative Dionysian who simply invents. I mention this because I want to turn to *Female* (1933) by Scola and Markey, which is often interpreted as starting with a radically liberated woman, an explicitly Nietzschean notion of the *Überfrau* who rejects the traditional roles of women, but is thought to end with her collapse back into something very traditional.[70] I want to challenge that by arguing that this apparent return to the traditional role is expressive of her power of invention. Rather than simply inverting the male-female order, she has the power to create and control both value systems.

In *Female*, Ruth Chatterton plays Alison Drake, who is the CEO of her deceased father's automobile company. She is introduced sitting in a boardroom in front of maps of the earth, suggesting her power over the globe. Drake says that she never has time for anything that does not interest her, including love. At her ultramodern house (the Ennis Brown House by Frank Lloyd Wright), Drake uses her male employees for sex. She asserts that "to be a woman in love is such a pathetic spectacle" and that she has "decided to travel the same open road that men travel." Her life is devoted to "the battling and the excitement" of business, but it is also the case that she has "never found a real" man. Her first seduction in the film is the young Mr. Cooper, which includes a ceremonial serving of vodka, explained by her butler as "a custom of Catherine the Great" to fortify the courage of her soldiers. While Drake is battling with and easily wining over Mr. Cooper, her visiting friend is reminding her husband to de-ice the icebox and take his mineral oil. Such is the sad life of marriage. Her assistant at work, an elderly man named Mr. Pettigrew, articulates explicitly the *Überfrau* doctrine. Pettigrew goes down to the comptroller to give Cooper a bonus for his "work" in the "business conference" last night with Miss Drake. The comptroller says, "I'm afraid that young lady is riding for a fall." Pettigrew responds: "Oh no, not Miss D. She's a superwoman. . . . She's the only honest woman I've ever met. There's nothing of the hypocrite about Miss D. That's more than you can say about the men she comes in contact with. Look at them. A pack of spineless yes men all after her for her money. She sees through them. That's why she tosses them aside. Just as Napoleon would have dismissed a ballet girl. Why, she's never met a man yet that's worthy of her. And she never will." Drake's honesty and exploitation of men require her to take on a very masculine persona, like Catherine the Great. She is literally crushing out all human sentiment, and the men around her are continually mistaking her expression of desire as her being human.

Chatterton's Miss Drake is a coiled spring of energy, doing calisthenics, swimming, having massages and cold showers. She may strike suggestive poses for the men around her, but we can see that they are fake and, thus, we see her as the master forger. All of the men she meets are mentally and physically inferior to her. They are easily exhausted, while she is an indefatigable. The men around her never understand her, mistaking her as a goddess, cold and pure, an issue that famously arises for Katharine Hepburn's character Tracy Lord in *The Philadelphia Story* (1940). She *wants* men to see themselves as "Kings in Babylon"—the opposite lesson of DeMillle's *Male and Female*—but they continually fail, and she has to meet them at their lower "human, all too human" level, which does not mean the level of based desire but is the level of moralistic self-deception. This is true even of Thorne, the engineer that she poaches from another company, whom she eventually pursues romantically. Pettigrew explains that Thorne cannot be seduced by Drake's normal means because he wants "someone gentle, feminine, someone he can protect. That's because Jim Thorne is strong. And rather primitive, perhaps. The dominant male, my dear." While Thorne has the appearance of the dominant male initially, he nevertheless turns out to be as traditional as the rest of the men in the film.

I maintain the apparent conversion of Drake to the "pathetic spectacle" that she initially condemns is just part of her power over her own persona. After lying to Thorne to get him to a staged romantic picnic, he says that she has been four women. First, she was amusing when they initially met and did not know who each other was. Second, she was a thinking machine at the office. Thirdly, she was a seductress at her home, which he did not like because "I'm a man and I prefer to do my own hunting." Fourthly, she was the woman at the phony picnic, which is in fact the fakest one of the bunch. She asks him, "Which one is real?" He believes that the obviously false, helpless woman at the picnic is the most real. Her adoption of a traditional "female" role is not an actual conversion to the castrated woman. Nor should we think that any of these roles is the "most real." As Drake fluidly occupies these roles, we see her as significantly more powerful than simply engaging in a gender reversal or taking on the role of the castrating woman. By showing us her fluidity and deceptiveness, she is more like the affirmative and Dionysiac woman that Derrida discusses. Thorne's upright, American honesty is obviously built upon self-deception and a misogynistic projection that do not allow him to see Drake as "real" in any other form except when she is the fakest damsel in distress. As proof of the illusoriness of this traditional female form, she laughs off the possibility of marrying him after he comes in the next day with a marriage certificate, proving again that he is traditional and inferior to her. His response to her laughter is patriarchal nonsense: "Is it old-fashioned to want to be decent? I suppose you think you're too superior for marriage and love and children. The things that women were born for. Who do you think you are? Are you so drunk with your own importance you think you can make your own rules? Well, you're a fake. You've been playing this part so long you've begun to believe it. The great superwoman. Cracking your whip and making these poor fools jump around. You and your new freedom. Why, if you weren't so pathetic, you'd be funny." For anyone who admires Chatterton's character in the first half of the movie, this is stupid sexist claptrap. As disgustingly misogynistic as this speech is, it *seems* to strike home with her. But which part? Is it the part about women being born for marriage, love, and children, or is it the fact that she has been merely conquering "poor fools" and that her superwoman status is fake if it does not conquer true challenges? While it is quite possible to read the film as turning against the *Überfrau* doctrine for the sake of a being a traditional *Frau*, I do believe an alternative reading is possible. Our interpretative options seem to be either that the film is endorsing Thorne's sexism or else her *übermenschlich* power remains and that she is engaged in a different sort of seduction more fitting to a more challenging male.

I favor the second interpretation due to the final sequence of events in the film. It ends with Alison tracking Thorne down after he has left town. She bullies her male chauffeur out from behind the wheel and drives with the speed and recklessness of a race car driver. Nevertheless, when she finds Thorne, she becomes traditional: "I can't go on without you. I am not playing a part. I'm not a superwoman. . . . I had to find you. Oh, Jim, take me wherever you're going. I'll marry you, if you still want me to." Here we see a juxtaposition of her superwomanly self at work followed by her own verbal disavowal of her power to occupy multiple and dissimilar roles. Why is she doing this? Firstly, it ensnares Thorne and gets him to return to her. It gives him the illusion of power. But has she *actually* forfeited her power? She states in Thorne's car that he will run the business and that she will stay home and have nine children. This hyperbole is obviously not true. But if she should leave the business world, there are ways of seeing her as preserving her superwomanly power. Why is Alison Drake chasing after Thorne and making this promise of a sacrifice of her freedom for being a traditional housewife and mother? She is having problems keeping the business afloat. She needs a loan. And she is distracted by Thorne, the man she could not conquer. We know her "feminine and gentle" act is a ploy to get Thorne, which she has been putting on since her phony picnic. Because she cannot run the business while thinking of him, she is playing the role of a damsel in distress in order for him to feel like a hero. He needs a woman to look up to him, as Pettigrew noted earlier. She explodes at work and says that she wants to give up and that the boardroom is no place for a woman, something we know to be false based on the first half of the film. She composes herself, asks the boardroom (and us) to forget that that ever happened, and solves all her own problems. She sets up a meeting to get a loan, and she decides to go play the "female" role to capture Thorne. Once she has Thorne, she will not be distracted at work and will not have these emotional outbursts.[71] Maybe she will let him run things and maybe not. But she will still retain power and her automobile business through him, rather than to lose it to a bank or to competitors. Given that Chatterton's character is the most self-assured and self-conscious depiction of the *Überfrau* among the early instances of this theme on film, the turn toward the traditional values of motherhood appears to be the fakest moment of the film and invites alternative explanations. The title *Female* suggests that the traditionalism of the latter part of the film is a part of her superhuman power to play that role, and every other role as well, to get what she wants. In a way, Thorne was right: she is a fake through and through, which is just to say that she has the power of complete self-invention, of Dionysian becoming. Yes, the superwoman role was fake, insofar as it was just an adoption of the role of Napoleon and Catherine the Great. But, as Nietzsche points out, what made Napoleon great was not his belief in the reality of the persona he created. It was his power of strategy and the capacity to invent and play these roles. While some see the second half of the film to be a reversion back to that phallogocentric world of the double standard, I wonder if it is not instead a more radical embrace of the fakery and deception essential to human life itself. Drake can be all four roles ascribed to her by Thorne without making one more real than any other.

Conclusion

While censorship certainly is a part of the story of how these films were constructed, I think it a mistake to believe that it somehow kept Nietzschean *Überfrauen* from populating the screen in the mid-1920s and early 1930s. The filmmakers and writers that I have discussed were surely able to make their point even within the confines of cinematic standards of the time. In fact, because the *Überfrau* is identified with a creative power to adopt any role and, thus, to elude any notion of a true or real self, her power of illusion is made more potent by the forced shifts between roles that she must occupy. As an onlooker says of Red, she is "strictly on the level, like a flight of stairs." But the story of such a person is not hindered by constraints (whether inside or outside the frame). The superwoman's power is visible only through her plasticity in the face of those constraints. The more wildly implausible and whiplash-inducing these shifts are, the more powerful and the more unnatural the *Überfrau* appears. By showing the *Überfrau* as such a multiplicity, capable of remarkable self-fracturing, we come to see in a cinematic way what the "innocence of becoming," or form of life that is "not to be judged or justified" looks like in a way that philosophy can accomplish only by becoming fiction, as in Nietzsche's own *Thus Spoke Zarathustra*.[72]

5

The Truth of Lies

The *Übermensch* as Genius in the Comedies of Ben Hecht

Introduction

IN THE COMEDIES OF Ben Hecht, the *Übermensch* appears both as a deceiver and as an artistic genius. My specific focus within four essential Hecht comedies—*The Front Page* (1931), *Design for Living* (1933), *Twentieth Century* (1934), and *Nothing Sacred* (1937)—will be how life and the natural use of the intellect are aimed at "dissimulation," and how "truth" indicates the life of the bored, the average, and the compromised (*PT* p. 81).[1] The Hechtian *Übermensch* is a master of life, power, and art. Importantly, unlike the *Überfrauen* of the previous chapter, Hecht's geniuses are masters of the *word* and, except in one instance, masters of the *written* word. Their ability to play with, distort, and bamboozle with language is their very lifeblood. Hecht's characters almost always mean other than what they say and cannot say what they mean, exposing how language is much less a mirror of the mind than a shifting field of graphemes and phonemes with elusive meanings, unstable interpretative circumstances, and risky performative acts. Like Nietzsche, Hecht describes language and words as the "inevitable canonizations of life," like "property loaned me and not my own" in his novel *Fantazius Mallare*.[2] Simply using language is not enough: it must be made one's own. The problem is not that borrowed language does not get at the truth and that we need a new use of language that does. The problem is that borrowed language is boring, uninspiring, and lacking vitality. The alternative is witty and willful manipulation of language, a rhetorically intoxicating and bewildering barrage, that is inspiring and vitally expressive. Hecht's *Übermenschen* do not simply deceive to live. Rather, they recognize that to live is to deceive. They are truly alive only when enveloped in artistically fashioned illusions, words, and roles, deceiving themselves as much as everyone else. They are innovators unencumbered by morality and, therefore, are what Nietzsche calls geniuses. While Hecht was an enthusiastic reader of Nietzsche, this idea would have been clear to him from other sources as well. For example, Nietzscheans like Benjamin de Casseres argued that "make-believe is the eternal Fact. Appearance, semblance, illusion, seduction, lying, constitute the elements of life."[3] This idea was widely disseminated in the intellectual culture of the time, for example, by Jules de Gaultier's *Le Bovarysme* (1902) and by Mencken, who remarked that "there is something in the human mind that turns instinctively to fiction."[4] These fictions are neither true nor "truths in decay"; in fact, one might think "they are simply better than truths," because they make life agreeable.[5] Hecht's geniuses show us something even more radical than that lies are pleasing: communication and life itself thrive on deception and that to be honest and truthful is to collapse into stupidity, mediocrity, and death.

I call the *Übermenschen* in these films geniuses, in part, because of their connection to the arts and the printed word. Nietzsche often sees the genius as tied to artistic creation and deception: "*Genius of culture.*—If anyone wanted to imagine a genius of culture, what would the latter be like? He would manipulate falsehood, force, the most ruthless self-interest as his instruments so skillfully he could on be called an evil, demonic being; but his objective, which here and there shines through, would be great and good. He would be a centaur, half beast, half man, and with angel's wings attached to his head in addition" (*HTH* vol. 1 §241, emphasis in original). The geniuses of these films tear down everything sacred, but they always elevate those few around them who are inspired by their creativity, bringing these acolytes to their highest passions and possibilities. Another passage on the genius from Nietzsche also fits the *Übermensch* of Hecht's universe rather precisely: "A human being who strives for something great considers everyone he meets on his way either as a means or as a delay and obstacle—or as a temporary resting place. His characteristic high-grade *graciousness* toward his fellow men becomes possible only once he had attained his height and rules. Impatience and his consciousness that until then he is always condemned to comedy—for even war is a comedy and conceals, just as every means conceals the end—spoil all of his relations to others: this type of man knows solitude and what is most poisonous in it" (*BGE* §273, emphasis in original). Here we see the "gift-giving virtue" in the genius's graciousness—a virtue that was discussed when considering Hecht's *Underworld*. The egoistic genius does not strive for something low, like security or recognition by others, but for one's own highest possibilities. Once one achieves one's highest self, through cultural warfare and the creative transfiguration of thought, value, and human possibility, then one can be "gracious." But the struggle toward that end, that war, is a "comedy," which is to say that whatever fills the present is laughable and not half as serious as the great end toward which one is striving. The genius is impatient with the world as it is presently configured and, thus, all human relations are "spoiled." His laughter and impatience alienate others. And yet solitude can also be poisonous. The genius needs others to thrive, to achieve the great end that is concealed in the comedic war. They must effectively cloak their exploitation of others in dissimulation to avoid ruining all human relations and ending up in isolation. In Hecht's film, this exploitation is a sort of love, whether between two men or between a man and a woman, but it is an amoral love, one that must deceive, even about love itself.

In another passage on genius, Nietzsche gives us a division that will also appear in Hecht's films: "There are two types of genius: one which above all begets and wants to beget, and another which prefers being fertilized and giving birth. Just so, there are among peoples of genius those to whom the woman's problem of pregnancy and the secret task of forming, maturing, and perfecting has been allotted. . . . These two types of genius seek each other, like man and woman; but they also misunderstand each other—like man and woman" (*BGE* §248). The geniuses of pregnancy in Hecht's comedies are reporter Hildy Johnson, who is fertilized by his editor, Walter Burns, in *The Front Page*, Wallace Cook, who is fertilized by Hazel Flagg in *Nothing Sacred*, and Lily Garland, who is fertilized by Oscar Jaffe in *Twentieth Century*. And in the Hecht-penned and Lubitsch-directed *Design for Living*, Tom Chambers and George Curtis are fertilized by Gilda Farrell. Nietzsche's doctrine of the genius is articulated in *The Will to Power* in a section called "Anti-Darwin." The genius is "*sui generis*: such things are not inherited"—only general types are inherited and not individuals. Geniuses are "lucky strokes of evolution" who "perish most easily," because they are "exposed to every kind of decadence" and "are extreme" (*WP* §684): "The higher type represents an incomparably greater complexity—a greater sum of coordinated elements: so its disintegration is also incomparably more likely. The 'genius' is the sublimest machine there is—consequently the most fragile" (*WP* §684).[6] This complexity, this mixture of robust will to power, decadence, and fragility, is found within the sublime and often manic geniuses of Hecht's films. If they are not on the verge of suicide, as with Oscar Jaffe and Hazel Flagg, then they are on the verge of prison for debts, deceptions, and outright crimes. But most importantly, they all "*have need of lies* in order to conquer this reality, . . . in order to live" (*WP* §853). The "problem" of life is solved by the artist with a "will to art, to lie, to flight from 'truth,' to *negation* of 'truth'" (*WP* §853, emphasis in original): "This ability itself, thanks to which he violates reality by means of lies, this artistic ability of man *par excellence*—he has it in common with everything that is. He himself is after all a piece of reality, truth, nature: how should he not also be a piece of *genius in lying!*" (*WP* §853, emphasis in original). Here we see how Nietzsche connects being a genius with both deception and his metaphysical picture of everything that exists as creative becoming.

The Genius of Manipulation: *The Front Page* (1931) and *Design for Living* (1933)

Before *The Front Page* cynically opens with the gallows for Earl Williams, being tested with a bag of Sunshine Flour that has the motto "Insures Domestic Happiness" printed on the front, we see the cast of the film as images in a newspaper. Their presence as artifacts of the paper suggests that all the characters exist only insofar as they are printed and read in the daily rags. Rather than a realistic tale of newspaper life, we are told that the film transpires in a "mythical kingdom." The director, Lewis Milestone, offers a disorienting series of constantly moving shots, clever angles, and startling cuts, from the initial rapid pan out to expose the gallows, to close-ups of faces eating and spitting, to shots looking up and down through the gallows' trap door, then on to the constant camera movement inside the criminal court's press room and around the never-ending poker game in the center of the room, to a series of lengthy tracking shots of Walter Burns as he strides through his newspaper offices in the search for Hildy Johnson, to Burns's thugs moving with a line of dance-hall girls, to the ride up an elevator into a bordello, and so on. It is a tour de force of early camera movement and editing. While one certainly could see Deleuze's point that movement is here being used as an indirect image of time, I do not think that we can ignore how the rhythm of the movement, both on screen and by the camera, is effectively powered by sound, by phone calls, typing, shouting, questioning, bickering, joking, and pleading. The action of the camera and of the figures on screen are, to quote one of the reporters, like the proverbial "milk wagon" tied to a "fire horse," which is the torrent of verbal wit that pours from the mouths of the characters and visual wit that flows from the camera. The shift from movement to pure "sound situations" is representative of a cinema that explores "the power of the false," and no set of early Hollywood films love the sound and fury of the human voice as much as Hecht's.[7] The moving image of perspectivism that I have said represents a Nietzschean aesthetic on film is a constant presence as well, as in the equivalence drawn between the two dollars that Burns owes the prostitute with the two-dollar cost of a marriage certificate. In this world of cynical equivalence, the power of the written word reigns supreme, as the prominent image of the marriage license reminds us. The written word constitutes the couple itself, whether that is a legal document or legal tender.

The film concerns Burns's attempt to retain Hildy as his best reporter, who is in the process of getting married and going to work in advertising. Hecht once remarked that marriage requires people who are violent, fearless, invincible, and steadfast.[8] It requires "genius of character, of self-hypnosis, or wit, or merely that of endurance."[9] While this was his comedic "Yes to Marriage," he also gave "A No to Marriage" and described them as "wearied disasters, epilogues of ennui" that are based primarily on revenge and on proving to one another that each is "a source of pain and misery."[10] Marriage contrasts to male friendship for Hecht. *The Front Page* so easily enables the translation of the two male leads into a romantically entwined male and female in the remake, *His Girl Friday*, because Hecht's story is of the love of two men for each other. Such a love between men, Hecht says, is many ways superior to the love of a woman. "In loving a man, one does not have to contort oneself into a hundred pretenses of devotion and fidelity in order to wrest a cry of ardor from his lips. . . . The beauties men find in kinship lie in the pleasure of being known and not judged, of being admired and not bagged and clapped into a marital zoo, of being intimate without the inconvenience of turning into a Siamese twin."[11] Although the relationship between Walter and Hildy is filled with deception, manipulation, and blackmail, none of it is a matter of revenge or resentment. These are the sorts of deceptions that are done in innocence and without malice. In fact, Walter's deceptions, although selfishly motivated, are also attempting to save Hildy from marriage and to keep him living the life of a great journalist. In other words, the deceptions are done in such a way that they sustain life rather than vitiate it.

Hildy is the sort of genius who gives birth, whereas Walter Burns is the genius who impregnates. Peggy, Hildy's fiancée, is an interloper, and she sees it herself. When she and Hildy receive the marriage license, all he can talk about is what the reaction will be from Walter Burns. Peggy sees this fixation and asks, "So that's why you are going to marry me . . . Walter Burns?" It is clear that his heart is less interested in marriage than it is in irritating Burns in their game of one-upmanship. Consider the moment when Hildy pulls Peggy into a phone booth to confess how she is breath of cool, fresh air and that he has emerged out of a sewer. To make this confession, they must engage in deception, to act as if they are making a phone call. But we also know he is not entirely on the level here, because if he were so steadfast in his rejection of the foul air of his past, then he would take Peggy's advice and go resign to Burns's face. Rather than doing so, Hildy's odd response is "What, and have him get his hands on me?" Does the sewer have such a draw for him, and is Peggy's "clean air" so weak? Why do Burns and Hildy have such a hold on each other?

When Burns claims that he has Hildy's best interests at heart, we have an essential Hechtian moment. In what appears like a moment of high deception, in which Burns is selfishly trying to manipulate him so that he does not get married, this "lie" turns out to be largely true. This is an instance where what is "real" is the illusion. The "reality" is that Burns is lying to him about having his best interests at heart so that he will remain a journalist. While we all read that as *really* a lie, because Burns's motivations are selfish, his deceptions *will* make Hildy into his highest self. This ironic inversion of appearance and reality is central to Hecht's work. Whatever appears to be a confession or statement of truth is inevitably the biggest lie. Whatever appears like the biggest lie holds the most truth. Similarly, when Hildy says that he wants to be his own man, it is clear to everyone that he is doing the opposite in getting married. The life of a journalist is the best life he can lead because he both is and is not his own man. He can be his freest and highest self only when he is basically a slave to Burns's passionate leadership. Burns is able to provoke Pavlovian responses in Hildy. At the sound of fire engine sirens, created by Burns's fakery, Hildy starts writing headlines in his head and flees his fiancée and mother-in-law. Being one's own in some absolute sense is to dwell in solitude. The genius needs impregnation and to give birth through their combative, comic art and, especially, through the written word. They need people they can trust rather than living in isolation. They trust those fellow geniuses to respond to their words with their own creations and to match their energy and wit. Part of that trust is that the exploitation that takes place does so in the comic mode rather than a serious one. Burns needs Hildy to be able to literally get the story and to metaphorically *get* it as well, to understand the power and vitality of getting the story above all else. He trusts Hildy to locate "the sage" in himself that is a "willingness to change" and is "what remains after all our social positionings."[12] But unlike Cavell's moral conception of this recovery of sagacity, which he describes as the alternative to "the endless debasements" of the self, to sophistry, and to the skepticism in everyday "meanness of thought" and "hardness of glance," Hecht's world embraces these.[13] Cavell's perfectionist description certainly does not capture the world that Hecht has given us in *The Front Page*, even if the main action can be called the pursuit of Hildy's highest self. This is because that pursuit takes place only through adventure, sophistry, journalistic skepticism, and endless debasements. We cannot become who we are through the "undramatic, repetitive, daily confrontations" of everyday existence.[14]

Such a cynical "black world," as Cavell calls it, is the core of all of Hecht's films, a world of "rumor, distortion, falsehood, corruption, [and] brutality."[15] Distortion and falsehood are present at every turn, as when Burns and Hildy talk about the respectability and grandeur of marriage and children, where the words *respect* and *grand* clearly are slanderous and calling their present life "idiocy" and "craziness" is high praise. Binswager, one of the reporters in the press office, is a germophobe and says that the germs of the mouth are the most contagious, suggesting the viral contagiousness of language itself. Thinking of language as a virus helps us to see how it is inescapably bound to persuasion and deception, infecting us with the values of others.[16] It is a great irony that Hildy is leaving the news business in Chicago to go into the business of advertising in New York City, which is a business entirely predicated on deception and is surely just a different sort of sewer. Both advertising and journalism create germs that infect us. In the advertising business, Hildy will be "writing poetry about my lady's panties," whereas the function of journalism is "that a million hired girls and motormen's wives and housewives will know what's going on." While Hildy is clearly attempting to ridicule journalism with that comment, a Hechtian reversal is taking place. He is waging a much more serious criticism at his own flight into advertising and inadvertently exposing the value of the newspaper business. Hildy adopts a standard, everyday criticism of journalism that one might hear from "the man on the street," and that another reporter notes is actually Peggy's opinion rather than his own. So much for "being his own man."

The secondary story in the film and the one that Burns wants Hildy to report on is the execution of Earl Williams, who is possibly an innocent patsy, possibly suffering from a split personality, and who may have killed an African-American police officer, which leads the mayor to want to hang him to earn that demographic's vote. Earl Williams is a self-professed anarchist, a philosophy to which Nietzsche was often aligned in his early reception. Williams spouts a philosophy that "guarantees every man's freedom." But what is the "truth" of Williams's situation? It is entirely unknown what the "truth" of Williams's crime is. What matters is the "copy" that it generates. Sheriff Hartman, who is in the pocket of the mayor, gives the journalists a piece of written copy that is pure propaganda. It is mere fearmongering over the "Red Scare" to re-elect the mayor. Moreover, it is also an especially unbelievable lie, promising death to every "bum, truant, un-American Red" in Chicago. They are going to "reform the Reds with a rope." These hyperboles are not only lies, but they are the "big lies" that Hitler once said had the "force of credibility." But the journalists are not beacons of the truth either. They joke, twist the facts, and eventually hound Molly, the prostitute who visits Earl Williams in jail, until she leaps out of a window and almost kills herself. When they report on Williams's eventual capture, they simply make up one fantastic story after the other. Of course their lies are significantly different in aim than the sheriff's.

Ironically, although Molly is a prostitute and Williams is a murderer, they are the most innocent figures in the film, for which reason they are trampled underfoot. Life in modern Chicago is a struggle that Burns likens to a war when he takes charge of the newsroom at the courthouse after Williams escapes prison and hides in a rolltop desk. The resulting criminal chaos and Burns's numerous "traps" to capture Hildy are minimized by Cavell when talking about the remake *His Girl Friday*: "They [Burns's manipulations] are the expression of his nose for news, which is to say, for a pair of convictions: First that the world at all times presents a false face to its inhabitants, second that under the opportune eruptions of a big story there is a truth behind that face that the right nose can track down."[17] While I cannot here analyze whether Cavell's point is true of the remake, it certainly does not hold in the original film. There is no real way to make Burns's "deviousness" into something moral by, for example, saying that in fact what he is doing is telling some deeper truth.[18] There is no evidence that Burns has any motivation other than to enact his will and to bamboozle the world.

Peggy sees the ephemerality of the newspaper life, pointing out that every day is just a story, each story is "the biggest story in the world," and then forgotten the next day. This is a perfect description of life as adventure and creation. Its value is entirely lost to Peggy, who expresses shame about having to face her mother and worries that the money that Hildy has lost to Burns is "all they've got in the world," the perfect expression of bourgeois values. Hildy is harder to pin down. When he confesses his love for Peggy and proclaims, "If I am not telling the absolute truth, may I fall dead. I'm going to cut out drinking and swearing and everything connected with the crazy newspaper business," he certainly seems earnest. But the problem is that when each subsequent moment is the biggest story in the world—one moment a jailbreak and the next his marriage—then the ephemeral nature of his commitments and the falsity of his promises are made clear. On the phone to Peggy, he says Earl Williams's escape is the greatest thing to happen to him in his life. That must also mean that it is greater than Peggy accepting his marriage proposal. Of course, he does eventually manage to leave Chicago, although Burns plans to have him arrested for theft and returned to face charges. We can see this as Hecht's way of capturing the idea of the eternal recurrence of the same, a concept he explicitly made into the forgettable film *Turn Back the Clock* (1933) with Lee Tracy. I have suggested that film might be able to do philosophy, in the sense of explore concepts in a way that philosophy itself cannot. Eternal recurrence has never had as plausible or intriguing exploration in philosophy as it has in the radical form of life that Hecht pens and that directors of his work project on screen.[19] We might say that the implication of the eternal recurrence of the same is that each moment is a story, the biggest story in the world, and our fate, should we accept it, is to live heedlessly in pursuit of those stories.

Another appearance of the written word, a reprieve for Williams from the governor, shows us how life and death are the product of fictions, for the reprieve is just a piece of paper that is fictionally imbued with the power of the state. Rather than lawfully follow the reprieve, the mayor substitutes his own piece of paper, a business card with the address of a brothel on it. Not only can we can use these moments to recognize the juxtaposition of values representative of the moving image of perspectivism, but we can also see the role of the written word as part of a critique of logocentrism and its prioritization of the spoken word. What comes out of the mouths of these characters are lies, exaggerations, outbursts, platitudes, and jokes. Rather than a direct expression of the mind, the spoken word is a series of distractions—either rationalizations and jokes that keep us from fully embracing the life of restless change and endless "big stories," or else deceptions that keep us manipulating the world in this comic war. The newspapers, paper money, train tickets, legal and political documents, IOUs, business cards, and Williams's written statement are, on the other hand, the lynchpins of this biggest story in the world. Not only is the written word a crucial tool of the film's plot and these characters' lives, but these documents are always shown to be dictating the nature of what is real rather than depicting some "true" preexisting reality. They act like engines of *différance*, spinning the characters in different directions, toward law and criminality, order and chaos, marriage and prostitution, success and failure, freedom and death.

In Cavell's analysis of the conclusion of the remake of *The Front Page*, he argues that there is a way to escape the black world of Hecht's cynicism. Cavell sees something like an appeal to justice when Burns places his faith in an "unseen power" that protects him and his newspaper after he is arrested. That justice comes via the intervention of the governor. But what is the "power that always looks over *The Post*" that Burns appeals to except the fate that the strong will conquer, that the weak will be vanquished, and that Burns's own power will come out on top? Call it fate, nature, an unseen power, or the will to power, but it is certainly not an appeal to the authority of the state, to justice, or to love and marriage. The corruption and stupidity of the mayor and the sheriff are the actual saviors of Burns and Hildy. The mayor and sheriff kick the governor's messenger out of the office and send him to a brothel rather than simply take the reprieve from him, send him on his way, and then destroy it. Their action causes the messenger to return—a good moral man married for nineteen years who is now returning drunk from a brothel and with remorse for his deeds. The "unseen power" is life as the will to power, namely, the inevitable failures of the weak, the power of guilt and bad conscience, and the triumph of genius. There is no reprieve from this dark world of struggle and constant inversion: all we can be sure of is that the tables will always be turned. Rather than justice, what remains is a trail of human carnage—shootings, car crashes, tear gas grenades, attempted suicides, theft, kidnapping, broken marriages, moral corruption, debauchery, blackmail, and a host of other crimes and catastrophes big and small.[20] The film does not offer an escape from the black world to a green one, as Cavell believes is central to remarriage comedies and even to *His Girl Friday*, which, like *The Front Page*, has no world outside of the newsroom. Instead, there is only the eternal repetition of the same.

In *Design for Living*, the love between men seen in *The Front Page* must find a way to navigate the fact that both men are the type of genius that requires impregnation and that a third figure, a woman, is who must impregnate them. While much can be said about this film and its direction by Ernst Lubitsch, I want to discuss only some of the Hechtian themes concerning genius and language that are similar to the ideas at work in *The Front Page*. The film concerns the love triangle of Tom Chambers (Fredric March), a playwright, George Curtis (Gary Cooper), a painter, and Gilda Farrell (Miriam Hopkins), a commercial artist in the advertising business. The central conceit of the play is stated by Tom as he works on his play *Good Night Bassington*. He tries two lines and settles on the second: "I'm afraid, Bassington, that you are wrong," and "I'm afraid, Bassington, that you are right but nonetheless boring." This encapsulates Hecht's philosophy that right or wrong are far less important than whether one is boring or not. The moving image of perspectivism is seen clearly in the conflict between the advertising executive Plunkett, who wants to speak delicately and politely while Tom praises speech that is crude and objectionable. "Delicacy is the banana peel under the feet of truth," says Tom, but of course he is not indelicate. He is witty and articulate, elusive, and forthright. He paradoxically criticizes speaking with "ribbons" on one's tongue even though he is the most ribbon-tongued of all the characters. Such contradictoriness is how one is not boring. His genius is seen in how his writing precedes and determines reality. His fictional character Bassington says, "There is only one thing that I have to say to you," right before Plunkett says the same thing. Plunkett's "one thing" is that "immorality may be fun, but it isn't fun enough to take the place of 100 percent virtue and three-square meals a day." This is both right because poverty is crushing and wrong because the moral distinction is useless. Right or wrong: it is boring. This scripted platitude by Plunkett becomes comedic gold in the mouth of Bassington, but then it is recognized in the real world by George as evidence that Tom and he are both seeing Gilda romantically. After all, they have both been given the same speech from Plunkett for, presumably, the same reason. Plunkett's simple moral fiction makes the world go round, but not because it is true. Rather it is a platitude, a self-deception, made into a laughable literary deception, that comes to be as truthful as anything else, not because of its content but because of its performance. That is to say, the conversion of Plunkett's words into literature and the conversion of literature into reality show how the division between the two is unsustainable. Plunkett is a believing fake. We see how artificial his purity is, even if he does not, when it becomes caricature in the play. But we also see how the artificiality at work in the play transfigures what we ordinarily call "the real world" and turns it into myth and comedy.

The love between Tom, George, and Gilda can never take on a traditional form or be expressed in traditional words without sounding like the fictional embodiment of all that is average. How to love without being boring is the question. Sincere love really "gets their goat." They must ultimately commit to the shifting seas of a nontraditional threesome, because their peculiar and dreadful feelings cannot be captured in words, pictures, or social forms. Such feelings are said to be "abnormal" by Plunkett, but that abnormality is life *qua* the power of overturning the normal. The moving image of perspectivism in this film is not simply a presentation of different value sets. It offers an image of a life dancing between all value sets, much like the migration across worlds seen by Rolls Royce in *Underworld*, Joe in *Little Caesar*, and Miss Drake in *Female*. Tom and George themselves represent two different values, like two different types of hats, explains Gilda, one civilized and one barbaric. When faced with their failed attempts to form Platonic relationships, their response is not to return to something traditional. The end of the film tells us that they must simply start again in their untraditional form of life, even if it careens into something traditional and comes off the rails from time to time. Although they may be "unreal" by "trying to play jokes on nature" by avoiding sex, it at least does not translate into a life that is boring. Yet they must not avoid their passions, which are something more "honest than all the art in the world," says George. Nevertheless, whenever a Hechtian character makes such an honest, romantic remark, it must be looked at suspiciously. We get the exact opposite view from Gilda: staying a true artist is the most important thing. But then how should we deal with these feelings? The first two options we are given are either crude "burlesque"—just giving in to our desires—or "high-class comedy" with "grown-up dialogue"—sublimating passion into art. A third option is pure violence to "beat some decency" into a person, which is identified with cheap and very dull melodrama. In this option, Tom and George should just fight for Gilda. The three options are sensuality, sublimation, or primitivism. But the film itself offers a fourth option, which is the conclusion of the film. The solution is to move between all these options, recognizing the cyclical, repetitive nature of life that we must make not boring by continually inverting it. That life translates into their bohemian existence of continual illusion-making. Such a life allows one to strive for impossible values both in life and in art, as if there is any difference between the two.

The Genius of Acting: *Twentieth Century* (1934)

Twentieth Century was directed by Howard Hawks and written by Hecht and Charles MacArthur. The opening shot announces that Oscar Jaffe (John Barrymore) is a genius as well as an egoist—a Napoleon of Broadway—by showing us an advertisement for his new play *The Heart of Kentucky*, in which he is the only thing mentioned besides the title.[21] Oscar's ego is such that he openly calls himself a genius, although the play he is putting on is obviously melodramatic garbage. But perhaps that is part of his genius: his gives the public what it wants. Yet Carole Lombard's character is something of a genius too, although one who gives birth rather than one who impregnates. Her initial problem is that she cannot act. She is too honest. The film's lesson is that the greatest, most vital form of life is one that can endure and even thrive within a self-generated or jointly generated illusion. Art is both nothing (illusion) and everything since the will to live is the will to illusion. As opposed to the bleakness of the constant war found in *The Front Page*, *Twentieth Century* is more expressive of a creative, artistic approach to life. What we see is what Jules de Gaultier called "Bovarysm"—the combination of Schopenhauerian will to live and Nietzschean will to power—into a conception of life as will to illusion or "the ability of humans to conceive of themselves as other than what they are."[22] Nietzsche's remarks on the actor are worth noting here. He attempts to understand the "dangerous conception of the 'artist'" through the work of the actor: "Falseness with good conscience; the delight in simulation exploding as a power that pushes aside one's so-called 'character,' flooding it and at times extinguishing it; the inner craving for a role and mask, for *appearance*; an excess of the capacity for all kinds of adaptations that can no longer be satisfied in the service of the most immediate and narrowest utility—all of this is perhaps not *only* peculiar to the actor?" (*GS* §361, emphasis in original). Nietzsche's two types of genius, the one that is fertilized and gives birth as opposed to the one that fertilizes, are represented, respectively, in Lombard's Lily

Garland and Barrymore's Oscar Jaffe. Both are the epitome of falseness with good conscience, not because they are misleading for *morally* good reasons, but because their falseness comes from an inner need to transform themselves and the world around them into something witty, fascinating, and passionate.

Often when Hechtian geniuses lie, they do so when they appear most earnest. Oscar softly and sensitively tells his actors that he loves them all, no matter what his behavior says. But they are simply tools to be used to make his art. After saying that he loves everyone in the theater, he calls the actress Francine Anderson a piece of human tripe. Yet it is never enough to simply lie. Part of the nature of deception in Hecht's films is that everything is true in one sense and false in another because of the double meanings at work. When he says he loves his acting troupe, that is a way of saying, "Disregard my outbursts; I do not really mean them." And this is certainly the case, because Oscar is an actor at all times. Oscar's first outburst is due to Lily's inability to enact the will to illusion. While Oscar sees in Lily the possibility of a profound power of deception, having found her already engaged in illusion as a lingerie model, her power of illusion is a merely external one. What is required is that she begin to have lies come from within, to be expressions of life. Oscar is a wizard, because he can enact the inner lie to oneself that breeds self-confidence.[23] His job is to transform the inner world of people—first the actors and then the audience. He needs Lily to be "vital," to have "vibrations," and to be able to provide reactions that come from deep "inside." He will find the "soul" within her and "release it." But this is a painful process. Indeed, to get Lily to scream requires him to jab her with a needle, which we later learn that she keeps as a sacred object.[24]

Ultimately, Lily stands up to Oscar and says that she will not take his bullying: "No man living can kick me around for eight hours until I can't see straight. I'm a human being, do you hear, a human being. . . . I wanted to be an actress, but I won't crawl on my stomach for any man." This viewpoint is exactly the opposite one that Lily takes later in the film. Here she articulates her humanity. She is being moral. Later, she receives a lecture from a lover she is trying to dump, who says that Lily needs but is not earning his respect. Lily responds, "Who cares about your respect? I'm too big to be respected. Men I've known have understood that." Oscar is the type of man who knows that her call to be respected early in the film is limiting her growth and power. Her outburst against his bullying is for him a lie. Beneath it he sees something else: "She's marvelous. Just as I thought, fire, passion, everything. The gold is all there. But we must mine it." Lily's appeal to moral dignity is just noise. Her language is just the parroting of those inevitable canonizations of life. So, in typical Hechtian fashion, an exaggerated expression is made, in which the literal truth (an assertion of her dignity) is a lie and the rhetorical form of it (an angry outburst at Jaffe) is also a lie. But what is true is the passion, the unintended, unspoken, unspeakable demand to be treated unjustly, to have the genius mine the gold within her. But that cannot be stated, or else the illusion will fail. One cannot truthfully state the request to be made a *complete* fake. To do so would be too honest.

After Lily and Oscar have success with their first play, she says that everything that was applauded for onstage was really just Oscar. Thus, her fakery (the performance) was also fake. Even her acting is a lie, because she says that she felt that it was Oscar and not herself out there going through the performance. But this apparently humble confession is, like all moments of honesty and confession in Hecht's films, itself a lie, because it is surely Lily's ability that is moving the audience. In spite of this false humility, the performance of her speech itself is expressive of her passion and succeeds at flattering Oscar and hitching him to her star. At this point in the film, we know that two geniuses, two *Übermenschen*, have met and that the war between them will be a comedy, a farcical "no" to everything real, honest, and average. This helps to explain Derrida's remark that the genius "never yields anything to the generality of the nameable" and as an "absolute singularity subtracts itself from the community of the common, from the generality or the genericness of the genre and thus from the shareable."[25] Derrida ties this specifically to the notion of the *Übermensch* when he remarks that when "one allows oneself to say 'genius,' one suspects that some superhuman, inhuman, even monstrous force comes to exceed or overturn the order of species or the laws that govern genre."[26] He describes the genus as creating an "undecidable" and deeply ambiguous "line" between reality and fiction, a sort of performance that gets its power, its limitless generation of *différance*, through play with the notion of a secret, a truth that is always hidden and, thus, a fiction.[27] He goes on to describe this in Nietzschean terms as "the instant of the eternal return."[28]

Whenever Oscar says something seemingly deep or profound, like "the sorrows of life are the joy of art," he is occupying a role, putting on a mask, and portraying a melodramatic artist for the sake of some goal.[29] His melodrama is used to provoke Lily into enacting her own melodrama. She is not fooled. His lies are recognized as invitations to provide her own lies. He puts a star on Lily's dressing room door and says that it "henceforth sets you apart from the world, beyond the reach of any one man to have and to hold." Of course, this is a lie: his goal is precisely for one man to have and to hold her, namely himself. But this statement is, like many in Hecht's comedies, a half-truth. The star is a statement of the Nietzschean pathos of distance. Lily *is* set apart from the rest of the world, both because of the fame she ultimately achieves and because of her remarkable power to inhabit fictions. And although Oscar means to be the one man that has and holds her, he must also suspect (or at least it turns out to be the case) that no one man will be able to have and hold her. Similarly, when Lily says that she is nothing without Jaffe and will never be, it is a half-truth. It can be said that this is an exaggeration. It is false because she will go on to be a movie star without Oscar. But it is true that she becomes nothing without him because she must survive in a world surrounded by average idiots and performing in Hollywood trash. Without Oscar's genius, the pathos of distance is lost.

Things begin to go wrong in the Jaffe–Garland "producer-star combination," when their collaboration becomes, according to a newspaper, an "institution," like a marriage. This means, in the Hechtian universe, that it has become a sort of hell. Oscar and Lily are fighting because he has become very possessive of her. He is driven by "senseless, neurotic, egomaniac jealousies," according to Lily. She complains that he does not want her to go out and, instead, they just sit at home and "discuss his genius." This is supposedly an indictment of Oscar, but in fact what he is doing, although certainly selfishly motivated, is preserving Lily's genius. The rest of the world is "riff raff" from Oscar's perspective, but Lily wants to go out and see some "plain human beings" and to act like one. That is supposed to sound like a reasonable aim, but from the perspective of the genius, there is no reason to want to be with plain human beings. To keep Lily from abandoning her distance above the herd and becoming a plain human being, Oscar threatens suicide, a slang term for it being "the Dutch act." The use of that phrase for suicide tells us explicitly, which everyone knows, that Oscar's gyrations and threats to throw himself from the window are just *an act*. As he threatens suicide, Lily stops acting and becomes a theater critic, saying, "You horrible fake. Be a man. . . . You cheap ham." It is this remark from Lily that really shocks Oscar. She has broken the illusion that they were weaving together, their comedy. Such play-acting is how they live, allowing them to shift moods and personas at the drop of a hat.

When Lily and Jaffe end up on the *20th Century Limited* train together, the artificiality of the interactions becomes even more manic and explicitly artificial. What I mean by that is that it becomes clear both to the audience and to Oscar and Lily that what they are doing is playing a part. All their behavior is mere acting to stimulate the other do so the same.[30] There are several breakdowns in their acting that show how measured their hysterics are. Lily starts to play the part of someone in love, seemingly taking lines from her plays once she realizes she is stuck on the train with her date, George. She says to him he does not know the "real Lily Garland." This is another half-truth because, of course, there is no real Lily Garland. But it is also true in that George does not understand that to live for her is to live in an illusion. Lily, continuing her fake confessions, says that she has died and made love so much on the stage that she has "lost track of what is real."[31] This shows that her first remark about the real Lily was false. George tries stupidly to match Lily and stutters, "Well, uh, w-w-what is real?" recreating, as de Casseres once described, "the astonishment of a cow looking at the changing colors of the dawn."[32] Her answer is a lie, perhaps taken from the play *The Heart of Kentucky*: "a house, a home with a little attic and a cookie jar, and a doorstep and little feet patterin' up and down." That is not real. That is the biggest lie of all. When Lily's controlled hysterics start and stop abruptly, he calls her fake, as she once did to Oscar. She is of course a fake, but the sentiment of this criticism is mistaken. What George does not understand is that fakery is all there is.

Neither Lily nor Oscar wants to be a *real* human, where that means an ordinary, moral, and boring human. They do not even want to be human beings. They want to be pure fictions. When George, for example, says that Lily is the most horrible excuse for a human being, we are supposed to see this as an insult. It is not. It is praise. She is a terrible excuse for a *Mensch*. She is an excellent example of an *Übermensch*. In their scenes on the train, everything that is said between Lily and Oscar is a lie. Oscar says that he was jealous because "love blinded him," but he was not blind. He was trying to protect the illusion they had created together and to keep idiots like George from ruining it. But there is a partial truth to these lies, as Oscar surely has come to love her in his own exploitative way. Lily lies and tries to convince everyone, including herself, that the problem was that he was deluded to think that he was "a Shakespeare and a Napoleon and a Grand Lama of Tibet all rolled into one." Again, this is true and false. It is false in a moral sense, and true in a nonmoral sense. That is, insofar as Lily is scolding him for being an egoist and saying that *that* was the problem, she is wrong. They are suitable for each other *because* they are egoists. It is true in a nonmoral sense in that the problem in their relationship was due to the pressure of keeping up the genius-level deceptions. At the peak of their mutual deceptions, Oscar takes all the blame and praises Lily: "You're absolutely right. I'm big enough to admit. I never appreciated your real greatness until I lost you. How small, how cheap, what egotism not to know that it was Lily Garland instead of Oscar Jaffe that really mattered." Lily sees that he is lying and challenges him to lie even more. She suggests that he lied when he told people that he put chalk marks down to show her how to walk, where to stand, and even how to talk, which he in fact did do. Oscar takes up this challenge and agrees, "It was despicable." What Lily says is factually false. He was not lying when he told people about how he made her. In a nonmoral sense, Oscar is right: it was despicable to tell the truth. They should have lived a lie together.

The core cynical truth of the film is stated clearly: "We're not people. We're lithographs. We don't know anything about love unless its written and rehearsed. We're only real in between curtains." To live is to live creatively, artistically, and wrapped in fakery. De Casseres called this "the stage-instinct"—"the stage is life because life is a stage."[33] As the lies and deceptions reach a fever pitch, one might expect a moment of truth or of romance, a marriage proposal, perhaps. But instead, we find Oscar conning Lily into signing a contract with him. It is a selfish and egotistical thing to do, but it is also a good thing for Lily too. The film concludes with a repetition of the first scene of the film, signaling the eternal recurrence of the same. The central point of the film is to show us the superhuman as lithograph, as that being who has the deceptive energy to face the cynical truth that we are reproductions. The written plays and screenplays that Lily and Oscar live are what is most real, even though they are obviously entirely fictions. The selves that they create are artistically fashioned from these written sources. What makes them geniuses is the inhumanity of the task of such self-creation. Ordinary people also allow screenplays of films, newspapers, and sentimental garbage, like Oscar's play *The Heart of Kentucky*, to create the selves they inhabit. They simply do not recognize this fact and, instead, believe this fictional self is sacred, stable, real, and worthy of respect.

The Genius of Deception: *Nothing Sacred* (1937)

What makes *Nothing Sacred* remarkable is the degree of deceptiveness in it. The truth in lies and the lies in truth are manifest in nearly every line and scene.³⁴ Everything normal, average, human, and truthful lacks value in Hecht's world, and everything that promotes deception, illusion, genius, and life is of value. However, this is not openly stated. Instead, everyone talks as if the same value order is still in place. People and institutions will be criticized as being phony and fake, when in fact that trait is what makes them valuable and gives them life. The opening titles announce that "this is New York, Skyscraper Champion of the World . . . where the Slickers and Know-it-Alls peddle gold bricks to each other . . . and where Truth, crushed to earth, rises again more phony than a glass eye."³⁵ The meaning of this is initially obscure. Truth being "crushed to earth" presumably means that we are entering a society in which there is no regard for truth. But what does it meant to say that "Truth" *rises again* and that when it does that it is *even phonier than a glass eye*? The idea of truth being crushed to earth suggests the idea of idol smashing, the reduction of something to its earthy, material foundations. Having Truth (with a capital *T*) smashed to its earthly components surely leaves people confused and without illusion. Faced with what Derrida calls the untruth of truth, or what Deleuze calls the fact that "truth is not to be achieved, formed, or reproduced; it has to be created," we must have truth rise again. But how can we call it truth anymore except though a deception, through a fictional claim to truth?³⁶ And to say that what emerges is "truth" that is *phonier* than a glass eye means that it is *a lie that everyone can in fact see*.³⁷ The glass eye does not fool anyone. So we might say that the lies that carry truth are circulated and accepted, because it pleases people to peddle fake gold bricks to each other. After all, the value of gold is an illusion, albeit a practically meaningful one. But at least those who are sophisticated enough to flourish in New York City are in on the con. Rather than being entirely fooled, there is a certain primitive, unstated grasp of the material ground of our actions, the artificiality but necessity of our invention of value and exchange. And so we come, in every practical way that is important, to accept the glass eye as an eye. To point it out as false is to misunderstand the situation.

The first scene of the movie is a pageant of fakery, a banquet to raise money for the "Morning Star Temple"—a complex of museums and culture centers to enrich humanity. The name of the newspaper that the main character, Wallace Cook (Fredric March), works for as its star reporter is the *Morning Star*.³⁸ The main deception at the banquet is Ernest Walker, a local shoe-shiner, who is being presented as an "Oriental Potentate," "Sultan," and major donor to the Morning Star Temple.³⁹ Who is Ernest, a shoe-shiner or a sultan? Which is true? Which is phony? And which is truth crushed and risen again phonier than a glass eye? His American family comes into the banquet and exposes him as a fraud. But is that the true Ernest? When the "Sultan" speaks he is eloquent, exclaiming without any accent, "Peace be unto you, my friends. Peace and the blessings of culture." But after his exposure he becomes a stuttering fool, who says, "Yas, suh" and "Ain't Mr. Cook a reporter no mo'?"—enacting the worst sort of stereotypical behavior. But should we take this transformation of Ernest to be the truth of Ernest? After all, it is clearly the enactment of the stereotypical (and racist) representation of African Americans that is often found in early Hollywood cinema. If truth is crushed to earth and arises as phony, then maybe the representation of Ernest Walker as a shoe-shiner is what is phony. After all, such representations are lies, both in the sense that they were dehumanizing racist depictions *and*, insofar as such servile behavior was actual, it was a result of the necessity that African Americans play a *role* to pass in white society. Such behavior is inherently a mask. Maybe Ernest is a sultan.[40] His family was brought to America from Africa in slavery, and so perhaps the truth of Ernest Walker the shoe-shiner is that he is indeed a prince. He may be the prince of a society to come, as the actual person who inspired Hecht to make this character proclaimed. The servile shoe-shiner that we see may be a disguise of his true nature in more ways than one. It is the case in this film (and in all of Hecht's early comedies) that the lie, the scam, and the con job are truer than the so-called truth. The ordinary world of just being a shoe-shiner (for Ernest) or being a bumpkin from Vermont (for Hazel), even if they are facts, is a lie. Reality is becoming who you are through lies and illusion. It is the untruth of truth.

Cook's moral criticism of the fakes in New York society is entirely mistaken. These condemnations ring hollow and do not recognize the nature of a world where truth has been crushed and risen again as phony. In Hecht's world, the lies are always closer to the truth than the honest, boring, moral interpretation of the situation. For example, Hazel deceives and pretends that she is dying (from radium poisoning), but she *really is* dying (of boredom) in Vermont. The moral reading that she and her admirers are phonies is a serious misunderstanding. If that were how we should read the film, then the lesson of the film would be the moralizing remark that "the Big City" is simply a land of opportunists, liars, cheats, and scoundrels. I see the lesson of the film to be that such deceptiveness is essential to communication and to life. If Cook was correct about the fakery of New York City, then when he arrives in Warsaw, Vermont, one would expect to find truth. However, what is found are a bunch of monosyllabic Neanderthals. We can understand this contrast in Derridean terms. According to Derrida, the "very emergence of speech and of appearing" (language and the phenomenal world it names) is identified with a "transcendental violence."[41] That is, discourse itself, the stock and trade of the journalists and elite in New York City, is a sort of violence, concretizations and categorizations that are necessarily also a constant deferment of truth. It is an act of will to power. To criticize the inventiveness, partiality, perspectivity, willfulness, and fictionality of discourse from an objectively moral or epistemic perspective is, however, to undermine the foundations of language itself. Thus, the honest people in Vermont, who do not buy into the false discourse of the Slickers and Know-it-Alls, have descended into a sort of a non-verbal "peace," an elimination of the creative and conflictual nature of language. But in so doing, they have sunk into "the worst violence, the violence of primitive and prelogical silence, of an unimaginable night."[42] Therefore, Cook does not find truth and honesty in Vermont. The land of phoniness is in fact the only choice there is. It is the land of rich human discourse. What he finds in Vermont are the blank faces of the "last men" and women. New York is the place of chaos, which is required "to give birth to a dancing star" (Z "Prologue" §5). These last men and women in Vermont lead a life focused on their health and digestion: they call it happiness while blinking with empty heads (Z "Prologue" §5). Every person that Cook talks to in Vermont, rather than being honest salt of the earth, extorts money from him. Cook says that he could do better, communicate better, "in darkest Africa." Hecht's disgust with the common man, with all his prejudices masquerading as truths, is at work in this scathing look at small-town America.

    Yet in this wilderness, he finds the *Überfrau*, who is the biggest liar of all, Hazel Flagg. Ultimately, she will take her place beside the greatest *Überfrauen* who have ever lived as part of a ludicrous stage show, one that is truth risen and phony as a glass eye.[43] It is important that the only two people that Cook can successfully communicate with in Warsaw are Hazel and Dr. Downer, who are both inveterate liars. The doctor is a drunk and completely delusional. He holds that newspaper men are positively inhuman (which is true but not a criticism in Hecht's universe) and that not even the hand of God could elevate one to the "depths of degradation, not by a million miles." Such hyperbolic nonsense is what allows the doctor to express himself beyond the monosyllabic grunts of the local people. He says that he is "fair minded," but believes that the *Morning Star* owes him $10,000 because twenty-two years ago he entered an essay contest on "the six greatest Americans"—an essay on *Übermenschen*—and did not win. The doctor lies when he says that he saved Hazel "from the jaws of death," but he does save her life by snatching her from the jaws of boredom in Vermont.

We see the reversal of truth again when Hazel worries that if she is marched around New York that people will like her only because she is dying. Cook responds, "That is a cruel way to put it. They will like you because you are a symbol of courage and heroism." Hazel's question is whether people will care about her only out of morbid curiosity, which is technically false because she is not actually dying. But Cook presumably is lying by trying to sugarcoat the situation. Although Cook means to be lying, my suggestion is that he is right. The reason that New York society lays its heart at Hazel's feet is because she *is* a symbol of courage and heroism. Although her courage in the face of death is a lie, there is something brave about her. Her deception is monumental and heedless of its consequences. True, there is something parasitic, superficial, and self-congratulatory in society's reaction to Hazel, but that is just how symbols work. There is no more truthful and less illusory way of hitching oneself to a star. There are only "perspectives and projections—these are neither truth nor appearance," and to attempt to judge them, either within the frame by Cook or through the film's narrative perspective, is a mistake, a sort of revenge against life.[44]

Once we accept Hecht's value-inverted universe, then we see that Hazel has "no relation to any reality whatsoever"—she is her "own pure simulacrum."[45] One feature of the simulation is that it has the power to create "true" or "real" symptoms.[46] A perfect metaphor of this is when Cook and Hazel attend a wrestling match. Cook says that the wrestling match is fake, but of course it seems very real and gives rise to real emotion. Is the match fake, when the men fly out of the ring, land in the crowd, and squash Hazel? Wrestling is framed with fakery, but in fact there really are large men throwing each other around the ring and landing on top of each other. True, they are not trying kill each other. Yet the results of this fakery are "real." The huge arena is filled with people cheering as if it were not fake. Clearly the "truth" that it is "fake" is a complete misunderstanding of the structure of the simulation, which allows the value of the match to emerge for the audience. Cook says that the "wrestlers are a symbol of the whole town, pretending to fight, hate, love and laugh all the time, and they are phonies, all of them." But this enlightened cynicism entirely misunderstands the match and its actual effects. The wrestlers are phony like the glass eye that everyone knows is fake. Ordinary phonies dissimulate or pretend to be something they are not. But the wrestlers blur the line between what is real and what is imaginary. They create a sort of violent art that is still a form of violence. This is the lesson of Nietzsche's early essay "Homer's Contest"—the contest is a simulation and is "necessary to preserve the health of the state" (*HC* p. 36). This is also what Hazel provides. It is not so simple to say that "society is motivated by greed and activated by fraud," for that would keep the idea that lack of fraud is sacred, when the point of the film is that nothing is.[47]

Cook says that he is "head of the list" of phonies by using Hazel to get a bonus and a byline on the front page.[48] Here he is supposedly stating the truth and confessing his guilt, but what he says is in fact false. Firstly, it is not like he has misled Hazel or proclaimed that he had selfless intentions. Hazel does not think that Cook has come to Vermont out of the goodness of his heart. Secondly, he is being suckered by Hazel, so he is not the one taking advantage of anyone, or, at least, she is equally taking advantage of him. He says that she breaks his heart, and when he kisses her hand, we see his tears. That is not phony.[49] But these emotions could happen only *through the phoniness of Hazel*. It was necessary for Hazel to have the health and zest for life that appeared like incredible courage in the face of death to provoke these tears. If she were sickly, sad, and depressed in the face of actual death, it would not have had the emotional effect that it actually has. Cook says that he is tired of the town's "trick tears and phony lamentations." But is there such a thing as fake tears? If one is crying, then is there not sadness or pain? Even if it is simulated, must not it be real enough to cause the tears? This reminds us of Wittgenstein's discussion of pain, fake pain, and pain behavior. Essentially, there is no standard for the truth of an emotional state. The statement that "it is true that I am in pain" is just the assertion that "I am in pain," which is less a claim about what is true and more an expression of pain.[50] What is essential here is the performance. Questioning how it maps onto what is true is a misunderstanding. Truth crushed to earth, mentioned at the start of the film, is a sort of return to the primitive truths, to these feelings, which are real even when they appear as phony. To return to such real and messy truths reminds us of Wittgenstein's remark that we need friction and to return to "the rough ground" rather than to remain attached to the ideal of the True as found in "the crystalline purity of logic."[51]

To say that the feelings at work here are as real (and as phony) as any other expression of them is not to deny that the newspapers are acting like the "ascetic priests" who create an "orgy of feeling" and, in particular, of pity (*GM* III §19). Nietzsche is worried about such phenomena, but not because, as Cook complains, the whole thing is phony. What Nietzsche dislikes is "dishonest mendaciousness," which stems from people who are "all moralized to the very depths," like Alfred Davidson the Christian reformer in *Sadie Thompson* and *Rain* (*GM* III §19). A Dionysian orgy of feeling is a terrible thing when it serves to enervate, exhaust, or turn our feelings against ourselves, when it is an orgy of *ressentiment*. An orgy of pity turns us to hatred, to the "injustice of it all," and does not allow us to forget. Problems occur when the priests are "true believers," who sincerely believe in the nonsense (the gold bricks) that they are peddling and do not see the joke, as Horn puts in in *Rain*. But there presumably can be purgative orgies of emotion that allow us to then see the comedy, to be in on the illusion, and to then forget anything that breeds *ressentiment*. The film's moving images of perspectivism show people genuinely moved to tears by Hazel's heroism in one moment and engaged in laughter and excess the next, proving that illusions can serve a significant function. The spirit of seriousness and "true belief" in morality leads one to be self-flagellating, repetitive, and boring like Cook, although as a journalist he has some skills in deception. The orgy of feeling that Hazel creates is an honest mendaciousness that is an invigorating, even necessary, experience. Cook says that he wants to speak to the readers of the paper to tell them that "we have been their benefactors. We gave them the chance to pretend that their phony hearts were dripping with the milk of human kindness." He fails to understand that phony tears are still real tears. They were not *pretending* to feel. So it is true that Hazel and the newspapers have been their benefactors, but his moral criticism of this process is misguided.

On the ship carrying Cook and Hazel away from New York City, a woman recognizes Hazel and calls her one of "the most gallant girls who ever lived." They convince the woman that Hazel is not *the* Hazel by criticizing the *real* (i.e., the symbolic) Hazel as a fake. In other words, they tell "the truth." The ship passenger then scolds Hazel and Cook and says, "Despite you and your kind the world will never forget Hazel Flagg." It seems that "the truth" is not good enough. Cook assures Hazel that in two months everyone will have forgotten about her: she was a flash in the pan in Manhattan. But most everything Cook says in the film is wrong. The reason Cook is obviously wrong in the final scene is that it will not take two months for the public to forget about her. They have already forgotten about the *actual* Hazel Flagg. After all, the woman is looking directly at Hazel and telling her that she knows nothing about the great Hazel Flagg. The woman is wrong and right. Of course, Hazel knows "the truth" of Hazel, namely, that she is a lie, but she does not know the truthfulness of the lie, namely what the symbol of Hazel means for people. What Cook gets wrong throughout the film is that he does not recognize that what really matters is the illusion. He scolds the public for not being more truthful and sincere, and he tries to reassure Hazel that the illusions will fade so that she can then live a truthful life in peace. But the simulation has been what is real all along. That life of peace is the life of monosyllabism in Vermont. Beneath the simulation, the "real" Hazel has been nothing, even less than nothing. Cook is right that they will forget her but wrong because they have always already forgotten her. It was never about the "real" Hazel. Neither Hazel's fans nor Hazel herself was ever concerned about the difference between reality and appearance, between truth and lies.

Conclusion

Ernst Lubitsch once said of Hecht that if he would "put half as much energy into writing a good script as he does into bamboozling everybody, he would be a really great writer."[52] Lubitsch was right: Hecht was a bamboozler, as were his characters. He used his genius to bamboozle the world. This was because bamboozlement itself was for him the aim of life itself. Hechtian comedies are breakneck affairs and are recreations of the energy of battle that he encountered in the newsrooms in Chicago and that he aimed to recreate in artistic partnerships and deep friendships with men like Charles MacArthur.[53] Hecht's approach to smashing idols is an intriguing mixture of his intellectual idols, the proximate H. L. Mencken and the more distant Nietzsche. Hecht found in Mencken wit, fearlessness, a complete lack of art or contrivance, and the ability to use common language like a cudgel. Hecht found in Nietzsche an invitation to philosophic thinking through wit, poetry, and fiction. Nietzsche showed Hecht how to attack the sacred idols of the world through metaphor, art, and a radical value inversion that turned the world, as Hecht liked to say, all "humpty dumpty." Language and truth are boiled down in Hecht's comedies to a jousting match, a movable host of metaphors, which tests the strength and fearlessness of the other person. But the goal is not simply to conquer or to have power: rather, it is to achieve great things alongside fellow geniuses. It is to bamboozle the world, which is different than simply covering up the truth for some cheap aim. Bamboozlement is to peddle a simulacrum that is better than the truth and, with any luck, will replace and become the so-called truth, at least until the next biggest story in the world comes around.

Hecht himself and the characters that he writes are representative of the life of irony described by Randolph Bourne in 1913. Bourne's Nietzsche-inspired conception of the ironist is the idea of life at its most vivid and intense. The ironist is "always critically awake" and has "an exquisite sense of proportion, a sort of spiritual tact in judging the values and significances of experience."[54] This competing model to the religious life is a life of adventure, lacking any "citadel of truth" to defend, no predestined formulas or "immutable standards."[55] The ironist's courage of critique and self-discipline gives rise to vital human relations and is at the heart of friendship. Bourne offers an intriguing analogy that helps us to see how film can capture the irony of Nietzsche's thought in a way not often found in academic philosophy.

> The ironical method might be compared to the acid that develops a photographic plate. It does not distort the image, but merely brings clearly to the light all that was implicit in the plate before. And if it brings the picture to the light with values reversed, so does irony revel in a paradox, which is simply a photographic negative of the truth, truth with the values reversed. But turn the negative ever so slightly so that the light falls upon it, and the perfect picture appears in all its true values and beauty. Irony, we may say then, is the photography of the soul. The picture goes through certain changes in the hands of the ironist but without these changes the truth would be simply a blank, unmeaning surface. The photograph is a synonym for deadly accuracy.[56]

For an artwork to function according to "ironical method," it must be critically awake and must be actively dissolving the illusions that keep people from truly living through self-creation. The ironist acts like a sort of acid, eating away at the world and leaving a negative image. To simply describe or present the world and its facts as "true" is to present a meaningless surface. The inversions of the ironist may contradict themselves, but they are meaningful as critical activity. Philosophy can hardly revel in paradox without risking incoherence, although Derrida has been willing to take that risk. Irony as photography of the soul may reveal "true values" for Bourne, but for Hecht (and Nietzsche and Derrida) it reveals the untruth of truth, namely, the creativity and deceptiveness required to avoid boredom and be expressive. What I have called the moving image of perspectivism in film is just such a revelry.[57] A remarkable sequence of perspectives shows Hazel's effect on society from a welcome message written in the sky, to the *Morning Star*'s headlines proclaiming her the belle of the city, to her receiving the key to the city and uncouthly shoving it down the front of her dress, to ironworkers reading about her in the paper, to a famous poet writing an ode to her while she looks bored, to that poem in the newspaper being used to wrap fish at a market, and to a deli offering the Hazel Flagg luncheon of cheese and bologna. Hecht presents us with a montage of society through the acidity of his vision and wit, showing the fakery of the common man, the artist, the press, and the politicians, but also showing that life, meaning, art, and the entire city run on and need that fakery to function. Hecht's irony is not in the service, as Bourne suggests, of true values and true beauty. Rather, for Hecht, the only truth is the necessary repetition of untruths in a sequence of self-inventions and bamboozlements.

Film has the traditional verbal ways of maintaining this ironic edge, such as the joke in *The Front Page* in which the wedding certificate and the prostitute both cost two dollars. It has the traditional theatrical ways available to it as well, such as Oscar Jaffe's unnatural hysterics, which are done with a wink to the audience and with the occasional breaking of the fourth wall. But film also offers us the fast-paced montage that can juxtapose values in quick succession and show them in different situations that are neither narratively nor verbally structured.[58] It offers visual gags, like the bag of flour advertising domestic happiness being used to test the gallows. It can show us large crowds and can pick out anonymous members to highlight their responses, like the individuals in the nightclub celebrating Hazel Flagg or the hangmen eating and spitting while testing the gallows for Earl Williams. It shows us the crowd and the individual. It can capture the whole city, whether it is primitive Warsaw, Vermont, fast-paced Chicago, or illusion-hungry New York City. Film, perhaps like no other medium, can take us into multiple worlds and multiple minds with incredible ease and speed. Whether it is the quick juxtaposition of the urban and rural worlds, the world of manners and the ill-mannered, the worlds of the legal and the corrupt—each world is a value system, and film can economically capture and cause a collision between worlds in a way that is supremely ironic. According to Bourne, this sort of contrast in values allows the ironist to deal with "general principles and broad aspects of human nature," which does not simply ridicule but gives people's "souls an airing."[59] The idea of an airing out of our musty souls is surely a Nietzschean one.

6

The Freedom in Fate

The *Übermensch* as Dionysius in the Films of Josef von Sternberg

Introduction

THE FILMS OF JOSEF VON STERNBERG return us to the fated, self-destructive, Dionysian notion of the *Übermensch*, which I began to discuss in the chapter on Stroheim. I should begin by noting that there is no definitive evidence that Sternberg was an admirer of Nietzsche. His own reflections on his art claim that he aimed to place the "full expression of the urgencies" of humanity (and presumably of himself) on film.[1] It is stated in his first film, *The Salvation Hunters* (1925), that he is attempting to photograph "a thought": "There are important fragments of life that have been avoided by the motion picture because Thought is concerned and not the Body. A thought can create and destroy nations—and it is all the more powerful because it is born of suffering, lives in silence, and dies when it has done its work. Our aim has been to photograph a thought—A thought that guides humans who crawl close to the earth—whose lives are simple—who begin nowhere and end nowhere." This poetic introduction tells us that Sternberg wanted, in his first film, to put an existential philosophy onscreen, which is stated as the fact that "it isn't conditions, nor is it environment—our faith controls our lives!" Importantly, there is something like an act of faith in all of Sternberg's films, a faith in what Nietzsche calls "the hidden Yes in you" that is "stronger than all Nos and Maybes that afflict you and your age like a disease" (*GS* §377). Might such a Nietzschean idea be central to Sternberg's thinking? We have already looked at his early film *Underworld*, written by Ben Hecht, which has been referred to as presenting a "quasi-Nietzschean world."[2] Furthermore, source work from Heinrich Mann, who was deeply influenced by Nietzsche in his youth, is used in Sternberg's *The Blue Angel*. Also, his film *An American Tragedy* was based on the novel by Theodore Dreiser, another member, at least for a time, of the American "cult of Nietzsche." Marlene Dietrich is explicit in the inspiration she found in Nietzsche's thought, so it seems likely that his thought was known to Sternberg.[3] After all, his own reflections often have a Nietzschean flavor, as when he rejects the idea that beauty and taste have anything to do with art and, instead, claims that art is a "hygienic search for obscure values, or a cultural memorandum, or an attempt to rival creation, an orderly investigation of chaos, or, at best, a compression of infinite power, spiritual power, into a confined space."[4] It begins to seem almost impossible that he did not have an interest in Nietzsche, having spent much of his spare time as a youth in the New York Public Library reading about philosophy and art.[5]

It is not surprising that the passionate, destructive notion of the *Übermensch* that dominates Stroheim's films finds its way into the films of Sternberg. Not only do the two directors share a certain lyrical style, but we know that Sternberg held Stroheim in high regard and was eventually asked to recut *The Wedding March* and divide it into its, now lost, second half, *The Honeymoon*.[6] Looking at his seven films with Marlene Dietrich, we find the notion of the *Übermensch* as embodying a radical Dionysian form of life. I will focus on *Morocco*, *Blonde Venus*, *The Devil Is a Woman*, *Shanghai Express*, and *The Scarlet Empress*. Entire chapters could and have been written on each of Sternberg's films, so I will have to be selective. My proposal is that Nietzsche's early study in *The Birth of Tragedy* of the contrast between the Apollonian and the Dionysian sheds light on the themes of Sternberg's films, which tend to be overshadowed by concentration on his style.[7] Nevertheless, even his style, his use of light and shadow, can be analyzed in terms of the dichotomy of the Apollonian and Dionysian. But that is a rather nonspecific observation.

More concretely, I would say that his style embodies the Dionysian "lyric genius" who "is conscious of a world of images and symbols—growing out of his state of mystical self-abnegation and oneness" (*BT* §5). There are a multitude of ways that Stroheim accomplishes this, for example through the use of fetishistic objects that symbolize spiritual crises—such as the doll that Amy Jolly carries with her in *Morocco* or the string of pearls she snaps or the music box in *Blonde Venus*—as well as a series of objects that are used to divert attention from such crises such as the constant veils, feathers, and cigarettes or the phonograph in *Shanghai Express*. There is also certainly a connection here to what Schrader has called the transcendental style, a way of attempting to represent "the ineffable, invisible, and unknowable," although the details of the Dionysian transcendent translate into a much more earthy and sensual concept of the transcendent.[8] Moments of crises—animalistic fear, suicidal desperation, flippant nihilism, trembling passion—are given specific behaviors that are spotlighted and tracked by Sternberg's camera but often left unverbalized. The mise-en-scène fluctuates between the cluttered, chaotic public world of crowds and the quiet, private moments of feeling. But this chapter is not a study of Sternberg's notorious style, even if it can be connected to Dionysian lyricism. My concern is the philosophical content of his films, as that is what is often denied to them.

The Dionysian *Übermensch* in Sternberg's films is the person who can overcome the Apollonian world of stabilizing and secure illusions—illusions like marriage, morality, social respectability, and even the self. This means that they must, in a quasi-suicidal moment, come face to face with the suffering of existence. There is a terror that comes from Dionysian ecstatic oneness with life itself and a despair that fills us due to the life-negating, individuating, and, thus, falsifying structures that we impose on ourselves. The result is a rupture that brings to light the *Übermensch*. This figure can say "yes" to the truth of life itself: she submerges herself in the primordial unity of affective life and feeling, in which the self disappears in an ecstatic state that is both terrifying and joyous.[9] This headlong plunge into the metaphysical current of all life is a return to and affirmation of undifferentiated Being. This early part of Nietzsche's philosophy is eventually transformed into the doctrine of *amor fati*, which he describes as a "Dionysian affirmation" of "the same logic and illogic of entanglements" that make up the "world as it is" (*WP* §1041). What we find in Sternberg's work is a meditation on this Nietzschean ideal: "A full and powerful soul not only copes with painful, even terrible losses, deprivations, robberies, insults; it emerges from such hells with a greater fullness and powerfulness; and, most essential of all, with a new increase in the blissfulness of love" (*WP* §1030). It is rare that Nietzsche speaks of love, yet the love of fate and the bliss of absorption into great tasks seem to be an essential feature of the Dionysian ideal.

In contrast to Hecht's use of language to demonstrate the power and genius of his *Übermenschen*, Sternberg's Dionysian films see language as an Apollonian shield rather than the creative tool of genius. Just as Nietzsche saw music as having that more primordial connection to Dionysian states and undifferentiated existence, Sternberg sees his visuals as having such a connection. "Words cannot describe an image in motion, words cannot describe an image."[10] This is an idea that Nietzsche also expresses: "our true experiences . . . could not communicate themselves even if they tried" (*TI* 9 §26). "Whatever we have words for, that we have already got beyond. In all talk there is a grain of contempt. Language, it seems, was invented only for what is average, medium, communicable" (*TI* 9 §26). The Dionysian state of joy and suffering is beyond what is average and communicable. Thus, it takes a unique cinematic style to capture such states, which philosophy cannot do through its powers of reflection and description. While there are many aspects to Sternberg's style that contribute to his transformation of the visible into a record of the incommunicable and invisible, I find his most powerful tool to be his composition of the elements within the frame and, in particular, how he is able to present his characters in a claustrophobic world surrounded by people, things, and animals, but to also and at the same time isolate them from that world—whether it is because they are detached, nauseated, and frozen in time due to the realization that "action could not change anything in the eternal nature of things" or because they alone move with the purpose and passion of the Dionysian *Übermensch* (*BT* §7).

I think it also worth noting how my approach will differ from the influential psychoanalytic analysis offered by Gaylyn Studlar.[11] Studlar's account utilizes the concept of masochistic desire, which concentrates on the pleasure of passivity and the loss of freedom. Although the Dionysian disintegration of subjectivity in these films has the appearance of masochistic desire, I take Sternberg's films to be exploring "metaphysical" (or existential-ontological) themes that can be too easily overlooked if we focus solely on the psychoanalytic interpretation. Rather than being merely the "theatrical play of masochistic desire," I find these works to be largely devoid of the enactment of desire as an *egocentric* activity aimed at some *coherent, pleasurable, erotic* object.[12] Like Greek tragedies, these films show us people who are helpless pawns of fate and not the playful subjects of desire.[13] Studlar does argue that the "masochist longs for and dreads the mystical symbiotic union with the mother in an apotheosis analogous to orgasmic release," which is also linked with death.[14] This sounds close to the Dionysian state that I will be focusing on, but Studlar's reading relies on Freudian concepts, with its concentration on male desire and its union with the Dietrich character, which I take to be rarely the focus of these films. I do not deny that there is the appearance of the masochistic in the Dionysian disintegrations in each film, particularly in *Morocco* and *Blonde Venus*. Yet because of the irrationality of "that place of transcendence where death and desire merge," I find the attempt to model the workings of these characters psychoanalytically as expressing the "masochistic wish for complete symbiosis with the mother" (which works only for male characters) or the noble "sacrifice of the oral mother" (for female characters) to be inadequate.[15] Such an analysis does not do justice to the parity between the sexes as they are inhabited by necessity, fate, and the pre-personal, cosmic forces at work in these films.

When read through the lens of the metaphysics of the Apollonian and Dionysian, we see that what is at stake is not the desire of a subject but the metaphysical collapse of the Apollonian world, including the notion of the subject itself, into the undifferentiated vital being of the Dionysian state. In simpler terms, we can ask, What is the point of Sternberg's films? According to Studlar, "these films do not pay homage to nature or political agendas but to fantasy, to desire, and to the magical thinking of primary [libidinal] process."[16] I would argue that rather than telling us subversive stories about the nature of desire and polymorphous sexuality, they show us that human "desire" and "fantasy"—thought of as governed by the pleasure principle—are just Apollonian illusions. Dionysian oneness is rooted in unjustifiable faith and irrational actions, which are demanded by forces beyond the individual and their desires. Thus, contrary to Studlar, these films do pay homage to "nature," to a terrible fact of nature called fate. This aligns them more with what has been called the transcendental style of filmmaking. This may all seem capturable by the idea of the Freudian death drive, described by Studlar as the "fantasy goal of a return to the beginning, to the womb of rebirth and nothingness."[17] But what is remarkable about Sternberg's films is that they do not present us with the masochistic privileging of inertia and stasis, as Studlar argues.[18] Instead, the characters are extremely active in their own demise through actions that cannot be justified, that they cannot articulate, and that they know go against the instincts of self-preservation and happiness. They embody what Derrida describes as the responsibility "to the one" that is a failure in "responsibility to all the others, to the ethical or political generality," and even to their own self as an ethical or sociopolitical being.¹⁹ Such actions can never be justified and must remain silent. They are indistinguishable from weakness of will and strength of will, because the individual will has been replaced with a cosmic one.

The attempt to understand his films on the model of human psychology, instead of the cosmic, Dionysian indifference to "the human," fails to capture what is so alien about them. Sternberg notes that the motion picture has "not without some justice" presented the human being as the "container of everything that is valuable."²⁰ But it is not entirely justified either, so he adopts the idea that in some sense *everything*, no matter how low or degraded, has dignity, and that the human being in its monstrous enlargement on the screen should be treated as a "landscape."²¹ He entirely rejects a moralistic approach to art and recognizes that it may ignore all "noble and uplifting functions."²² The camera is said to have its own "unlimited and mocking language," as it elevates images and persons to monstrous proportions.²³ If there is one guiding attitude in Sternberg's thoughts, whether it be about actors, the studios, the public, art, critics, or modern life in general, it is a deep cynicism about human beings and a willingness to see their degraded and dehumanized state.²⁴ Rather than making moral proclamations about that degradation or attempting to cover it up with Apollonian illusion or masochistically converting that degradation into pleasure, Sternberg shows us figures willing to literally "let themselves go" and to be swept up in a sacrificial fate "expecting neither response nor recompense, expecting nothing that can be *given back*," or what Derrida calls the gift of death (emphasis in original).²⁵ Contrary to the idea of "the responsibility of a free self" or of one that can be rationally understood as pursuing desire, the Dionysian figure found in these films leads us to the notion of "the sacred as an enthusiasm or fervor for fusion, . . . a form of demonic rapture that has as its effect, and often as its first intention, the removal of responsibility, the loss of the sense or consciousness of responsibility."²⁶ Masochism continues to reek of *ressentiment*, of bad conscience, and of notions of responsibility and punishment that are anathema to Nietzsche's thought and, I believe, to Sternberg's films.

Within Sternberg's universe, the presentation of Apollonian art takes place often in the cabaret.²⁷ This is the space of Apollo as the "ruler over the beautiful illusion of the inner world of fantasy" (*BT* §1). In Apollonian art, the "*principium individuationis*," or "principle of individuation," is central: the individual remains separate, gazing upon the attractive form, delighting in the illusion (*BT* §1). Although such art stimulates, it remains outside the Dionysian state, the state of "wilder emotions" in which individuality breaks down. It is true that Apollonian arts of illusion "make life possible and worth living," in the sense that they distract and enable individuals to feel pleasure and joy (*BT* §1). But they also turn us away from a terrible and crushing truth that is revealed in Dionysian art.

> Dionysian art, too, wishes to convince us of the eternal joy of existence: only we are to seek this joy not in phenomena, but behind them. We are to recognize that all that comes into being must be ready for a sorrowful end; we are forced to look into the terrors of the individual existence—yet we are not to become rigid with fear: a metaphysical comfort tears us momentarily from the bustle of the changing figures. We are really for a brief moment primordial being itself, feeling its raging desire for existence and joy in existence; the struggle, the pain, the destruction of phenomena, now appear necessary to us, in view of the excess of countless forms of existence which force and push one another into life, in view of the exuberant fertility of the universal will. We are pierced by the maddening sting of the pains just when we have become, as it were, one with the infinite primordial joy in existence, and when we anticipate, in Dionysian ecstasy, the indestructability and eternity of this joy. In spite of fear and pity, we are the happy living beings, not as individuals, but as the *one* living being, with whose creative joy we are united. (*BT* §17, emphasis in original)

This passage shows us the confusing state that is revealed and explored in Dionysian art, a state in which joy and fear, pleasure and pain, are mixed as the veil of illusion that keeps us separated from others disappears. It is my claim that Sternberg's difficult and seemingly contradictory films are Dionysian in this sense. They reveal to us this state that is both terrifying and joyful and that leads to the loss of individuality and will. His films also show how the world of Apollonian illusion can eventually come crashing down, and we can be faced with "tremendous *terror* which seizes man [or woman] when he [or she] is suddenly dumbfounded" at a breakdown in the "cognitive form of the phenomena" (*BT* §1, emphasis in original). But that terror is, at the same time, a "blissful ecstasy," in which the principle of individuation is annihilated in a state Dionysian intoxication (*BT* §1).

These films may look like love stories because the union between people is reaffirmed, yet it is more radical than that: "all the rigid, hostile barriers that necessity, caprice, or impudent convention" have fixed between persons are broken (*BT* §1). This is a state of self-abnegation and self-overcoming. Dionysian states provide that "horrible mixture of sensuality and cruelty which has always seemed . . . to be the real 'witches' brew'" (*BT* §2). We find in Sternberg's Dionysian films an inescapable element of sadism, but not as a desire of any person. Rather, sadism appears as a feature of existence and time itself; it is a general feature of the world and manifest within the contradictory relations between love and death, ecstasy and agony.[28] Nietzsche describes this as that state in which "at the very climax of joy there sounds a cry of horror or a yearning lamentation for an irretrievable loss" (*BT* §2). While the Apollonian artist attempts to avoid those extreme, terrifying passions, the Dionysian embraces them, which is ultimately an idea that comes to define the *Übermensch*. In *The Will to Power*, Dionysius is identified with the combination "sensuality and cruelty," and with "an ecstatic affirmation of the total character of life as that which remains the same, just as powerful, just as blissful, through all change; the great pantheistic sharing of joy and sorrow that sanctifies and calls good even the most terrible and questionable qualities of life" (*WP* §1050). That sounds exactly like what Sternberg described as his own cinematic aim.

Morocco (1930) and *Blonde Venus* (1932): Looking into the Abyss

Morocco and *Blonde Venus* are paired together because of numerous structural and thematic parallels between the films. In these two films, Marlene Dietrich's character must overcome the illusory Apollonian world seen in objectifying art, traditional social norms, and luxury. She must ultimately submerge herself in the Dionysian world of intoxication, annihilation of the self, and pure life. The opening scene of *Morocco* is a perfect example of Sternberg's visual language. It begins with a man violently wrestling with a donkey that refuses to move out of a road. The stubborn animal symbolizes nature's resistance to being tamed. These "wild instincts" are called by Nietzsche "wild dogs" in the "cellar" of the soul (Z I "On the Tree on the Mountainside"). The man is wrestling the beast to avoid the soldiers from the Foreign Legion who are marching down the road toward him. Rigid, rule-governed existence, the social straitjacket, and the absurd human attempt to give order to chaos are pressuring him to control the uncontrollable. The man is pulled between the Dionysian instincts of the animal and the Apollonian, civilizing force of the Foreign Legion attempting to cover up that reality and push it to the side. Lining the road are posts with skulls on them, indicating, not so subtly, the presence of death. An audience, almost like a movie audience, stands back in a darkened archway watching. The camera cuts to a woman—perhaps a prostitute—smiling at the soldiers holding on to one of the skull-topped poles. Here the relations between desire and death are made clear, as they will be time and time again in Sternberg's work. He describes the essential formula of film to be that it "always revolves around sex, and its biological associate, violence."[29] In this very simple scene without dialogue, we are presented with the moving image of perspectivism, namely the collision of the Apollonian and Dionysian worlds.

It is really only with the final scene of the film that the opening symbols are revealed as the key to the entire work. In the final scene, Dietrich's Amy Jolly repeats the initial shot of the man's struggle with the uncooperative animal before she marches barefoot into the Sahara Desert while wrangling a goat. Her choice to flee into the Sahara after Gary Cooper's character seems to be both an act of love as well as a sort of suicide, an embrace of suffering, which she neither understands nor explains. She stumbles around, confused, before marching into the abyss, framed again by a doorway. This final scene has puzzled many, thinking it to be ridiculous romanticism or a bizarre reassertion of female subservience to the world of men. While we can easily see how the masochistic reading of the union of pain and pleasure believes such subservience to be the film's fundamental point, I think it insufficient to read it as merely showing us a pleasurable sort of sacrifice, a "fantasy fulfillment" that is noble, "idealized, justified."[30] Instead, the suicidal moment at the end of the film avoids being romantic silliness only if we see that what is happening is that the entire world of illusion is stripped away, leaving the irrational, intoxicated storm of feeling that leads one to rush headlong into death.[31] Studlar wants to deny that this action is "rendered absurd," but surely its absurdity is the very point of it.[32] This idea is found in Nietzsche: "Loving and perishing: that has rhymed for eternities. The will to love, that is to be willing also to die" (Z II "On Immaculate Perception"). Derrida describes the *Übermensch* as one who "awakens and leaves without turning back to what she leaves behind her. She burns her text and erases the traces of her steps. Her laughter then will burst out, directed toward a return which no longer will have the form of the metaphysical repetition of humanism. . . . She will dance, outside the house [of Being], the *active Vergesslichkeit*, the 'active forgetting' and the cruel (*grausam*) feast of which the *Genealogy of Morals* speaks" (emphasis in original).[33] This striking description seems to perfectly describe Amy Jolly, a "suicide passenger" on her one-way trip to Morocco and then into the heart of the Sahara.[34] To read the ending simply as reasserting the traditional female role or providing some sort of libidinal satisfaction fails to see this metaphysical point.

In the first spoken lines of *Morocco*, we overhear the demands of civilization in the voice of the commander of the legionnaires telling them to control their desires and be gentlemen now that they have returned to civilization. Immediately the *adhan* rings out through the town, calling people to prayer. The commands of both military and religious law are trying to control the desires of the village. But the Dionysian undercurrent will not be denied. De Casseres describes this Dionysianism as the fact that "all economical, political and religious programmes fail because of the belief in a rational, ordered future. The future is not like a military road, but is like a pattern in a carpet woven by Puck and Mephistopheles."[35] These commands have little effect on Gary Cooper's character, who seems to both steal from a market vendor and flirt with a woman as the prayer takes place. Cooper's Tom Brown is an egoist, a womanizer, and a loner. He lives a life of isolated hedonism, fixated on women and endless adventure. When he experiences Dionysian intoxication in his initial encounters with Dietrich's Amy Jolly, he responds by throwing himself into the suicidal task of the legionnaire, bringing civilization and violence to the Sahara. This flight may seem simply like "humiliation, suffering, punishment, and denial," but it needs to be seen as a desperate attempt to retain the principle of individuation in the face of the Dionysian abyss, an attempt that Derrida would call autoimmune, which is to say that Tom Brown is essentially killing himself to preserve himself through individuated activity.[36] Thus, these crucial moments of the films are not best thought of as a "game of desire," in which the power of the agent's desire is what transfigures the world "into timeless repetition."[37] Studlar sees appeals to "fate" to be a mere "rationalization" of the "self-humiliating" behavior of the desiring agents: their individual forces are the only forces.[38] My sense is that Sternberg's films capture the metaphysical thought that human beings and their desires are part of a larger, irrational course of events.[39] Brown's flight from her is a manifestation of a traditional sort of love, a sacrifice for her sake. It is a sort of pity because he has nothing to offer her but struggle and perhaps even death. Thus, he is protecting his own ego as well as Amy Jolly's. He refuses to face the terrible Dionysian oneness that she represents.[40] This shows that he is not the Dionysian *Übermensch* of the film, and so I hesitate to say that the film is, in Freudian terms, about his pursuit of unity with a mother figure. After all, that unity never takes place.

Like *Morocco*, *Blonde Venus* opens with a symbol of the Dionysian—an idyllic scene of water nymphs, that is, six naked German actresses swimming in a river, who intoxicate a group of seven men taking a walking tour. Just as *Morocco* shifts from one Dionysian symbol (the man struggling with the wild instincts of the donkey) to another (the smiling woman clinging to the skull-adorned pole), so also does *Blonde Venus*. In particular, a close-up of the nymphs swimming away transitions to the legs of Dietrich's character's child, Johnny, kicking in the bathtub. It is her intoxication with maternal feeling and its closeness to the earth that leads her to abandon herself to a life entirely outside of social morality as she flees her husband, who wants to take Johnny from her.[41] The final scene of *Blonde Venus* repeats the initial scene, albeit in a subtle way. It appears that all six of the Bacchanalian water nymphs from the opening scene are depicted on the top of a porcelain music box that is used to put her son to sleep. It draws Johnny's hand out of the crib; he reaches through the bars of the crib to touch the music box, recalling his father's own intoxicating first meeting with his mother. This circularity suggests the "eternal circulation" that Nietzsche's sees as the nature of time as fate (*WP* §1041).[42]

In *Blonde Venus*, the film shifts from the initial Dionysian scenes of the actresses in the river and Johnny in the tub via an abrupt image of the New York skyline. It then strangely returns to what was cut away from: Johnny Faraday in the bathtub. But now we see Helen Faraday furiously cleaning Johnny and saying that she does not have time for his antics because his father will be home soon. It is her husband, Ned, who, like the skyline of New York or the Foreign Legion, designates the demands of civilization. Ned represents the Apollonian instinct, which Nietzsche tells us eventually withdraws into "the cocoon of logical schematism" out of which science is created (*BT* §14).[43] Given that Ned will die within a year due to radium poisoning, he wants to sell his body to science. Economics, science, the law, misogyny, and Ned's own bad conscience are the forces that ultimately drive Helen into a self-destructive flight into pure instinctual living. This happens when Ned, stung by the debt he owes to Helen and to her lover, played by Cary Grant, must confront the truth of his own weakness and dependency. This confrontation threatens to expose the annihilating truth of the endless circulation of primordial reality. His agency is nonexistent; he is a pawn of fate. Confronted with that terror, Ned, like Gary Cooper's legionnaire, isolates himself from Dietrich's character. He cannot let go of the strictures that maintain his individuality. When Helen gives Ned the gift of life in *Blonde Venus*, she makes him pay a price. The price of the gift of life, for Ned, is the shame of being pitied, which destroys their marriage. Here we see the "logic of the gift" and the idea that gifts contract a debt between the giver and the giftee, leading to an exchange that essentially nullifies the very idea of the gift.[44]

Returning to the Apollonian and Dionysian elements of these films, it is important to note the two different forms of music that can be found in them, because this division between types of music is central to *The Birth of Tragedy*.[45] In *Morocco*, the first music presented is the bugle and drums of the military march. As the opening scene ends and the military marches away, Moroccan folk music is heard, and we see a glimpse of woman playing finger cymbals. The former is clearly representative of Apollonian forms of music that create structure, order, and illusion, whereas the latter is representative of Dionysian forms of music that are communal and that initiate states of pure, undifferentiated feeling. The Dionysian music in *Blonde Venus* can be found in the lullabies that Helen sings to Johnny. In both films, Dietrich's character performs in the cabaret. This is another form of Apollonian music, filled with dreams and illusions. It is staged, fantastical, and controlled. The cabaret is the place where desire and illicitness can be expressed and contained.[46] The individual on the stage must forget about life and enter a dream, a dream that is then shared and projected into the audience. It is a common tendency to fixate on these cabaret scenes in Sternberg's films and regard them as Dionysian scenes, moments of unadulterated desire and the power of female sexuality. I think this is a mistake.[47] The Apollonian arts create palatable symbols of desire that people can sit back and applaud. The cabaret is an extremely staged environment, and in the life of Dietrich's characters it is clearly a sort of degradation or prostitution—a world of dreams and appearances that brings her nausea rather than being expressive of *her* desire. Sternberg's description of the musical theater fits his own visual portraits of them, showing them to represent a sort of nihilistic decadence rather than tapping into the true source of life: "Men assume the garb of women, and women the habits of men, amidst approbation and applause. Every sentiment known to man is served up in song and dance and speech, pantomimed and mimicked by the fit and the unfit, paraded before an assemblage that applauds or hisses, envies or despises the performer."⁴⁸ The cabaret songs, such as "Quand L'amour mourt," "What Am I Bid for My Apple?" and "I Couldn't Be Annoyed" express the Dionysian's nausea and rejection of society. She confesses this to Cary Grant's Nick Townsend in *Blonde Venus*: "I'm not in love with anyone. And I'm completely happy. Nothing means much to me now. It's better this way, no chains at all, no care in the world." It is true that the songs "Hot Voodoo" and "You Little So-and-So" in *Blonde Venus* are expressive of passions, yet we know that in fact these passions are false and that she is devoid of feeling at that moment in the film. They are the mere pantomime of passion for the polite audience.

To the extent that there is any action to speak of in *Morocco*, it concerns Amy Jolly's decision between Gary Cooper's Tom Brown and Adolphe Menjou's La Bessiere. While it may seem like *Blonde Venus* has a similar choice between Herbert Marshall's Ned Faraday and Cary Grant's Nick Townsend, she chooses neither and is instead choosing her son above all else. We might say that in both cases the choice must be made between an easy life of riches without struggle and a life of uncompromising responsibility for and passion toward the One, as Derrida puts it.⁴⁹ I think it is a mistake to think that Dietrich's characters reject La Bassiere and Nick Townsend for being too "feminine," when the feminization of Tom Brown and Ned Faraday is just as evident.⁵⁰ The problem is not their masochism and passivity. It is that they want safety in the preservation of their individual identity rather than the terrifying passion and unity that the Dionysian represents. Sternberg offers his own account of the Dionysian rupture of emotion that disrupts the self.

> The average human being lives behind an impenetrable veil and will disclose his deep emotions only in a crisis which robs him of control. A crisis does not need a great reason. A human being can explode when least expected, as each one has his own way of building a continuity of his admixture of feelings, and his own formula for controlling. . . .
>
> Should a forceful event come along, such as an earthquake, a revolution, an oppressive circumstance, sudden passion or sudden grief, each human being is forced to behave according to a flood of emotions that may have been stored up until then.⁵¹

The irrational forces within us and the whims of fate outside of us conspire to bring the "human being" and their "impenetrable veil" crashing down. In such a crisis one can then look "into the flaws, the faults, and the deficiencies, into the pains and tortures of the human being."[52] It is clear in both films that the earthquake that causes the "veil" to fall is the imminent loss of the Other. In *Morocco*, Amy Jolly has a manic response to the arrival of Tom Brown's company from a grueling march into the desert where it was clear that his commanding officer was going to try to kill him for sleeping with his wife. Amy does not know if Tom has survived and runs out of the home of La Bessiere, snapping the string of pearls that he gave her on the back of a chair. She has the same uncontrollable response to Tom's leaving on another mission, which causes her to run through the Sahara with the Moroccan wives who trail behind the marching legionnaires. These explosions are self-destructive and irrational. They are tragic rather than romantic or sentimental. In *Blonde Venus*, that rupture is caused when her husband threatens to take her son away from her.

Sternberg has been harshly criticized for "directorial incoherence and lack of proportion in dramatic values, due to his ignorance of the relation of man to his environment."[53] It was said that his characters "strut" because of "the falseness of the content in his scenarios" and because of his "amazing ignorance of the moving forces behind human behavior and social reality."[54] But this criticism takes place from the assumption that the moving forces behind human nature are something like practically rational aims. But that is not Sternberg's conception of those moving forces. His characters certainly are contradictory. Take, for example, Gary Cooper's character in *Morocco*: he is the paradox of a noble rogue, a womanizing egoist, who uses women and throws them away, but who immediately forces his fellow legionnaires to show Dietrich's character respect as she performs. He has a lust for life but also seems to throw his life away in a vain attempt to retain his individual self. The same can be seen in many of Dietrich's roles, in which she plays the world-weary jezebel, who has a nobility bordering on saintliness, a strangely nihilistic and self-negating figure, who nevertheless fills the world with coolly apocalyptic love and death. Sternberg suggests that we are only truly ourselves in that moment of extreme crisis where there is little difference between joy and suffering, love and death. As Zarathustra says, "desire—this means to me to have lost myself" (Z 3 "On Involuntary Bliss"). Therefore, Sternberg's films seem false and ignorant of human nature only insofar as we believe that desire retains rather than loses the self. This is the problem with Tom Brown's love. It is an act of cowardice. Rather than embrace her, he carves a heart with the name "Amy Jolly" into a table.

His conception of love is an individuated and distanced one—a love that flees and attempts to retain the self. It is love shielded by morality, which covers up his inability to accept the irrational destruction of the principle of individuation that comes from true intoxication. For Tom, to throw himself into battle and to risk death is not the sort of self-abnegation that results in a Dionysian embrace of naked reality. It is still the Apollonian fiction of the warrior and the isolated individual. It is only with the radical, self-annihilating act that Amy performs in the final scene that we witness the true collapse into Dionysian ecstatic oneness. Both Tom and La Bessiere keep their distance and uphold the Apollonian world. The love of Nick in *Blonde Venus* is no different, keeping its distance and mastery by showering Helen with gifts.

It is clear that the marriage between Helen Faraday and Ned is an Apollonian illusion. Early in the film, they tell the story of their meeting and their romance to their son in terms of a children's bedtime story. This myth-creating activity is an Apollonian act that turns their life together into a bedtime story filled with a dragon and a magic pool filled with princesses. This illusion is literally a sedative for their son but also for themselves. Helen's return to Ned at the end of the film and to that illusion is disappointing, just as Any's flight into the Sahara was in *Morocco*. The return to her family may seem sacrificial, but the Dionysian life that she achieves with her son is both higher and deeper than concerns for her own, personal desires, which will surely not be met by Ned's uninspiring presence.[55] Scholars have puzzled over the mixture of maternal and erotic love in *Blonde Venus*, but we should note, firstly, that from a Nietzschean perspective a person's value is their "pregnancy" (Z 3 "On Involuntary Bliss").[56] Part of being pregnant is being "adventurous, experimental and self-torturing."[57] It is important to notice an essential difference here between two types of sacrifice, which Nietzsche calls the difference between Dionysus and the Crucified (*WP* §1052). The difference is that the Dionysian sacrifice is an affirmation of "life itself, its eternal fruitfulness and recurrence" and "creates torment, destruction, the will to annihilation" (*WP* §1052). It is with this that both films end, which is why many are unsatisfied with them. We misread these films if we see this as a traditional, Christian act of sacrifice that is an "objection to this life" or a "redemption from life" (*WP* §1052). The gifts and sacrifices of the men in these films are attempts to shield themselves and Dietrich from life itself. Their sacrifices are those of the Crucified. It is only Dietrich who is Dionysius.[58]

The Devil Is a Woman (1935): The Abyss Looks Back

I believe that *The Devil Is a Woman* is a profoundly misunderstood film, as the tendency is to read it, much like Sternberg's *The Blue Angel*, as simply the story of a femme fatale, Concha Perez, who destroys a man by the name of Don Pasqual.[59] Contrary to *Morocco* and *Blonde Venus*, where it was Dietrich's character who ran heedlessly into the state of Dionysian oneness, it presumably is now the man's turn to strive for that destructive, metaphysical oneness. But I believe that this is a mistake. This is not the story of Don Pasqual's destructive path toward Dionysian ecstatic oneness. Rather, Don Pasqual has already achieved that before the film has even begun. Instead, Pasqual plays for Concha, as Tom Brown did for Amy Jolly and as Johnny did for Helen Faraday, the genius of the heart, "the tempter god and born pied piper of consciences whose voice knows how to descend into the netherworld of every soul" (*BGE* §295).

> The genius of the heart who silences all that is loud and self-satisfied, teaching it to listen; who smooths rough souls and lets them taste a new desire—to lie still as a mirror, that the deep sky may mirror itself in them—the genius of the heart who teaches the doltish and rash hand to hesitate and reach out more delicately; who guesses the concealed and forgotten treasure, the drop of graciousness and sweet spirituality under dim and thick ice, and is a divining rod for every grain of gold that has long lain buried in the dungeon of much mud and sand; the genius of the heart from whose touch everyone walks away richer, not having received grace and surprised, not as blessed and oppressed by alien goods, but richer in himself, newer to himself than before, broken upon, blown at and sounded out by a thawing wind, perhaps more unsure, tenderer, more fragile, more broken, but full of hopes that as yet have no name, full of new will and currents, full of now dissatisfaction and undertows. (*BGE* §295)

If Pasqual operates in this fashion, then we once more have a story in which Dietrich's character is brought out of a nihilistic state on the edge of the abyss, where she retains a sense of self, and into an ecstatic state that plumets into the abyss. Such a reading requires us to look closely at the final moments, when Pasqual's lack of self finally enacts a fundamental change in Concha's actions and personality. Admittedly, most of the film is about Concha's desperate flight from Pasqual. But the final moments turn the film on its head. The value perspective that has dominated the film, in which Pasqual seems the traditional predatory male and Concha is the prey, is undermined. Pasqual embodies a selfless faith that binds itself to a "singularity," a faith that remains "unjustifiable as the infinite sacrifice" that he makes "at each moment."[60] This sort of responsibility to the One is called demonic and pagan by Derrida (following Patočka) rather than a moral notion of responsibility While the title of the film suggests that Concha is the devil, it is Pasqual's world-destroying passion that is truly demonic.[61]

On the face of it, *The Devil Is a Woman* makes the Dionysian elements of the film rather explicit by placing a large portion of it in a Bacchanalian carnival in Spain that lasts several days. The film was originally entitled *Caprice Espagnol*, and Dietrich's character is certainly absurdly capricious. The mise-en-scène and her behavior are dripping with excess. Concha's cruelty, the amount of money Pasqual spends on Concha, her near instantaneous love of Antonio Galvan, Pasqual's impossible marksmanship, the comedic silliness of the governor, the storm that Pasqual and Galvan fight a duel in, the carnival itself—everything in every scene is hyperbolic and absurd. Dietrich's head tilting and eye fluttering are taken to such an extreme that it could be said that Sternberg creates the first great example of "camp" in cinema, which Susan Sontag describes as converting the "serious into the frivolous" and containing such a level of "artifice" and "exaggeration" as to be unnatural[62]: "The hallmark of Camp is the spirit of extravagance. Camp is a woman walking around in a dress made of three million feathers. . . . Camp is the outrageous aestheticism of Sternberg's six American movies with Dietrich, all six, but especially the last, *The Devil Is a Woman*."[63] This is not to say that films prior to this one, whether by Sternberg or others, are not campy at times, but they are often unintentionally so. True campiness, Sontag argues, "is to understand Being-as-Playing-a-Role."[64] Sternberg clearly constructed *The Devil Is a Woman* to show us Dietrich as inhumanly cruel yet in a strangely stylized and artificial way. While Concha *appears* like a Dionysian genius of the heart, her artificiality and superficiality do not show her to be responding to the terror of Dionysian wisdom. She is actually Apollonian: her capriciousness is a flight away from responsibility to the One. It is Don Pasqual who ultimately has the power to intoxicate Concha and annihilate the Apollonian series of masks that she wears.

This shows an important difference between Sternberg's famous German film *The Blue Angel* and *The Devil Is a Woman*. Lola-Lola's sadism kills Professor Rath, whereas Don Pasqual lives and has Concha return to him. It is clear that Lola-Lola plays the Dionysian genius of the heart. Concha is quite different. She is pure illusion and fantasy, absolute capriciousness and whimsy. All the unsavory, predatory, and cruel aspects of life that Lola-Lola fully accepts are passed off by Concha on to her mother, as she tries to bounce through life like a carefree butterfly. Concha wants everyone to love her because love is how she escapes the world. Ultimately, it is her Apollonian illusionism that must be destroyed by the power of Dionysius. It is tempting to read Concha's capriciousness as representing her embodiment of the Dionysian source of life, of *différance* itself.[65] But that would suggest that Don Pasqual is just another Professor Rath. While Don Pasqual certainly undergoes degradation and almost dies, he not only survives but ends up turning the tables on Concha at the end of the film. He could do this only if, in fact, he is the Dionysian figure, the seducer who has accepted the self-destructive unity at the heart of life itself. Concha appears more like Tom Brown in *Morocco*, continually fleeing the deadly truth that Don Pasqual represents. Some have seen Concha's contradictoriness as reducing her to a "vanishing point, making her impossible to read and this, in turn, sustains an endless proliferation of critical interpretations."[66] Yet Concha actually makes some sense when we see her as the embodiment of the Apollonian image who enacts the continual flight from Dionysian wisdom, namely that love, sex, and life are bound to death, which means that the self crumbles before oneness with the Other.[67]

We gain a clearer sense of Don Pasqual's role in the final scenes of the film. Concha is about to board the train to France with her new lover, Galvan. But rather than flee to France, she decides to return to Don Pasqual, whom she has tortured and fleeced throughout the movie. Concha's final action has puzzled viewers.[68] Scholars are divided between several hypotheses. Perhaps this is a cynical remark about Concha, namely, that she is so inconsistent that she does not even have a mind to change. Perhaps the entire film is an entirely false narration that takes place entirely through the deluded eyes of Pasqual. Perhaps it shows her to be a true devil, preferring to continue to torture Pasqual. Perhaps it is entirely ambiguous and without any clear meaning.[69] No one seems to think that Concha has actually had her illusions shattered. But there is a significant shift in Concha's behavior once she is fleeing Spain. The cool, restrained, and tragic Dietrich from Sternberg's other films emerges. We tend to see Dietrich as the Dionysian goddess and femme fatale, and men, like Don Pasqual, are masochists who are subservient to her power. But that image seems rooted in *The Blue Angel* and does not actually track her transformation in *Morocco, Blonde Venus, The Devil Is a Woman*, or *Dishonored*. While Don Pasqual *is* intoxicated by Concha, the film actually shows how he intoxicates Concha through the infinite nature of his suffering. I do not think that we can attribute Concha's change of heart at the end of the film to mere caprice. Her capriciousness has always been a movement *away from* Don Pasqual and responsibility. By the end of the film, Pasqual's self-abnegation, culminating in a suicidal duel where he allows himself to be shot, shows that he alone has entered into the self-annihilating state of unity with life itself. We can see that it is Concha that is wrapped in Apollonian rationalizations when she misunderstands Don Pasqual and says that he is mistaking his vanity for love. She does not initially see the Dionysian wisdom within Pasqual's complete lack of selfhood and his infinite passion toward her as the singular One. She fully realizes this only when, in the final moments of the film, he sinks into his pillow and believes that his "life is worthless anyway."

My proposal on how to approach *The Devil Is a Woman* is confirmed by the fundamental change that Sternberg made to the story from the source material, Pierre Louÿs's novella *The Woman and the Puppet*. In the novel, Don Mateo (renamed Pasqual in the film) beats Concha until she begs forgiveness. Then he rapes her, and, in spite of all her flirtations, it is revealed that "she was virginal as on the day of her birth."[70] That assault results in her actually fleeing to Paris and leaving him forever. In the film, when Don Pasqual beats her (and presumably also rapes her), she visits him the next day and complains about how rude he was but continues her playful games. In other words, Concha is not a virginal flirt in the film, and Pasqual's violence against her is dismissed as part of the capricious game of illusions. The violence of his suicidal act, which is not even a part of the novella, is the crucial moment for Sternberg. The fact that Concha returns to him in the film is an inversion of the original story and its title *The Woman and the Puppet*, which leads us to recognize that Don Pasqual has become the puppet master.

Like many other scholars, Phillips's recent assessment eschews any attempt to find a substantive, unifying meaning in the film and, instead, claims that it is mere a series of "individual shots and sequences" with "feral independence," in which the "immediacy of the visual attempts to banish all other considerations."[71] Like many who are drawn in by Sternberg's masterful style, Phillips simply denies that the film is attempting to say anything about the world or to "enlist the off-screen in order to press a claim to truth."[72] Sternberg himself says that in his final two films he really pushed the medium to show that "film might well be an art medium" and that he constructed each scene "to form an exact pattern."[73] Yet he rejected the idea that he was all style and no substance or that his film was just an unconnected series of appearances rather than the projection of a thought. He rejected the idea of art for art's sake. Such a notion of art is a superficial escape into Apollonian illusion. The centrality of appearance and illusion, both in terms of the content and the formal aspects of Sternberg's film, does not preclude that he is making a philosophical point about how illusions can be both an escape from and an artistic way of reckoning with the terror of the Dionysian passions. If his films are fragmented and psychologically unrealistic, it seems plausible to think that he is exposing how our lives themselves are a series of fragments, eternally recurring, and that the "normal" and "realistic" are simply a vision of life immured by the individuating forms of escape from Dionysian wisdom.

Shanghai Express (1932): Faithful to the One

In *Shanghai Express*, we find another woman, like Amy Jolly in *Morocco*, who starts the film face to face with the abyss. Her ability to plunge into the abyss of passion and not simply expire shows her to be an *Übermensch*.[74] Unlike the previous films discussed, *Shanghai Express* does show Dietrich to be a genius of the heart, who embodies and can provoke the Dionysian unity that manifests as an infinite responsibility toward the One to the exclusion of the entire world. As Lily states it, the fundamental issue of the film is "a matter of faith"—an idea that we know is central to Sternberg's *The Salvation Hunters*. Rather than faith understood as trust in oneself, *Shanghai Express* concerns faith in the Other. Lily says that she used a "women's trick" to make "Doc" jealous five years ago, and instead of proving his faith in her, he left. Lily then threw her life away, because she did not care "to bargain for love with words."[75] Now she is again attempting to get Dr. Harvey to have faith in her "without proof." She is willing to sacrifice herself to save Harvey from being blinded by the sadistic Chang, but she does not want him to know this. Thus, he believes she is going to run off with the rebel leader for some selfish, perverse reason. The reverend states her point that "love without faith does not amount to very much." To achieve faith is to annihilate the boundaries between herself and Harvey (Doc). Faith in Lily means a loss of faith in the world, in everything the crowd says, and even in one's own individual perceptions. It means a leap into the terrible and an unknown future. We might say that Lily is the demon posing the challenge of the eternal recurrence of the same to Doc, asking him to affirm her, affirm life in all its contradictory forms, in each moment and action. This is the Dionysian test that Lily sets for Harvey and that he finally passes in the final scene. In that scene, they are surrounded by a bustling crowd, but Lily says that there is no one there but the two of them. Effectively, the rest of the world and the crowd have disappeared into nothingness. This is the act of faith and of unity as a responsibility to the "One" that requires a "failing in my responsibility to all the others, to the ethical and political generality."[76] This being bound to "singularities" must take place through an act of faith that is "finally unjustifiable."[77] Lily's actions are here captured in Derrida's account of God's command to Abraham: "Tell me that you love me, tell me that you turn toward me, toward the unique one, toward the other as unique and, above all, over everything else, unconditionally; and in order to do that, make a gift of death."[78] Lily, now thought of as the voice of God to Doc (*qua* Abraham), asks him to "act like a murderer in the eyes of the world and of your loved ones" in order to demonstrate what "absolute duty means, namely how to respond to the absolute other."[79] Doc must die to the world by rejecting the moral code of the crowd and his own emotionally dead but socially "upright" existence, as Dietrich does again and again in Sternberg's films.

Shanghai Express is unique among Sternberg's films because of the number of secondary characters who are living embodiments of the "crowd." Whereas most Sternberg films employ faceless masses, against which the four or five main characters stand out, *Shanghai Express* has several fellow passengers on the train who give voice to what is "human, all too human" within us. These are the gambler Sam Salt (Eugene Pallette), the Reverend Carmichael (Lawrence Grant), the old woman Mrs. Haggerty (Louise Closser Hale), the German trader Eric Baum (Gustav von Seyffertitz), and Major Lenard (Emile Chautard). These characters are full of judgments rooted in traditional morality and concerns about social standing and appearance. The supposedly morally upstanding Mrs. Haggerty is deceitful and has lied about whether she has her dog with her. Reverend Carmichael is a doctor of divinity "in the service of mankind" but loathes the women of low morals on the train. Sam Salt places odds on "everything under the sun going right or wrong." He is completely without principles or faith. Furthermore, his appearance as a high roller is obviously a sham, as all his jewels are fake. Eric Baum proclaims to have a coal mine, but he turns out to be an opium dealer. Major Lenard is dressed as a member of the French military, but in fact he has been forced out and is wearing the uniform to hide his disgrace from his daughter.[80] They all express some form of social superiority relative to Shanghai Lily and Hui Fei, the two prostitutes on board the train. As it turns out, in spite of their low social standing, the two prostitutes are the valuable and honorable members of the party. Sternberg gives a face to the stupidity, passivity, untruthfulness, and immorality of the crowd by showing the secondary characters and their weaknesses. He is then able to show that their social standing is a façade and that they are all wrong in their judgments.

In *Morocco*, *The Devil Is a Woman*, *Dishonored*, and *Blonde Venus*, it is Dietrich's character who must rise above or tunnel under the Apollonian world of appearances. She must come to accept a more radical existence in which the appearance–reality distinction is abandoned. In those films, she must confront the futility of words and their meanings in the face of the irrational pulse of life itself. It is only in *Shanghai Express* (and *The Blue Angel*) that we find that it is the man who must be transformed by the Dionysian genius of the heart, those "pied pipers of consciousness whose voice knows how to descend into the netherworld of every soul" (*BGE* §295). Lily is firmly planted in the Dionysian realm of excess, life, and death throughout *Shanghai Express*. She does not have to move from her starting point. In the other films, it is difficult to say that she acts as the "thawing wind" for the men around (*BGE* §295). Rather, she must move from her starting point and march into the abyss, which appears like the Sahara desert in *Morocco*, the American South in *Blonde Venus*, or the arms of Don Pasqual in *The Devil Is a Woman*. In *Shanghai Express*, Dietrich's "genius of the heart" is more than the simple trope of "the seductress." While this film certainly presents Dietrich in her most seductive light, it is not clear that what she does to awaken faith in Doc is classifiable *as seduction*. In fact, most of Dietrich's moments of beauty and action are revealed to the viewers of the film and not to Doc, who seems to always be gazing off into the distance and from whom her head is often turned and veiled. Can we call what Nietzsche describes as the teaching of silence, hesitation, fragility, and the awakening of both hope and a sense of fate *mere* seduction and the stimulation of sexual desire? But that surely is not what was lost by Doc.

Constable wants to avoid reading Lily either as a seductress or as an empty illusion of a person, "nothing but pure image."[81] I have argued against such a reading even of the even more contradictory figure of Concha in *The Devil Is a Woman*, so I certainly agree with Constable's resistance to the hollowing out of the character of Lily into a pure negation. Constable wants to show that the artificiality and role-playing that Lily does are "linked to the presentation of specific systems of value, allowing her acts of provocation to begin to form a space of critique."[82] She also argues that there is a Nietzschean element in her reading of Lily as "the false raised to a higher power," which is to say her "falseness" becomes a "site of authenticity."[83] Yet I find the idea that Lily undergoes a "reformation" somewhat strange.[84] Unlike the previous Sternberg films discussed, it is not obvious that Dietrich's character undergoes any particular change in this film. Her courage, her strength to endure degradation, her love of Doc, and her rejection of common morality are her consistent and defining features. She tried once before to test Doc's faith, and he failed. She is trying again on the *Shanghai Express*. This time it works. It is not Lily who must reform or find authenticity. Rather, it is Doc who must find his faith in order to no longer care whether it is true or false that she is the notorious man-eater of her reputation. Lily has always had the authenticity and strength to throw her life away rather than "bargain for love with words." Doc must achieve such a state. Lily's willingness to sacrifice, however, should not be seen as a "moral tale."[85] It is not that Doc must see her as *morally* "better than he assumed her to be"; rather, he must abandon these moral notions and unify with her regardless.[86] Doc does not have to come to properly interest Lily as an "ethical subject"; he has to abandon the bargaining about love with words and representations and sink into Dionysian unity with her.[87] It is a mistake to think that the problem here is one to be resolved through some sort of *knowledge*, because Lily is "unknowable" to Doc.[88] These ideas simply do not capture the radical transformation that the genius of the heart demands.

Like most of Sternberg's films, *Shanghai Express* is regularly analyzed only with an eye to its formal features. His films are said to be dominated by "the primacy of style" and "their devotion to surfaces."[89] His stories are supposedly just about Dietrich "manipulating men" and doing unexpected actions for which there is no possible accounting except "the films themselves, and how we experience them."[90] Certainly the angelic lighting, the compositional layering of the fore-, middle-, and background, and abstract shots of shadows, steam, and motion from the train are used to great effect to seemingly transport the film into a spiritual realm, where heaven, love, and faith are struggling against nihilism in a sadistic place where "time and life have no value." But this style is in service to the moving image of perspectivism at work here. Besides the contrasting set of values and symbols already seen in the analysis given so far, Dietrich's character is able to sustain radically distinct selves embodied, on the one hand, in her "devil-may-care" and amoral exterior and, on the other hand, in her capacity for faith and love that manifest as an infinite responsibility to the Other. In other words, her contradictory character, which is regularly dismissed simply as a function of Sternberg's incoherence, is making an important philosophical point and doing so in a way that is unavailable to philosophy itself. Sternberg's tableau is able to capture the self-annihilating mixture of the sacred and profane though his style and through the shifting between Lily's isolation and oneness, which eludes mere description of the Dionysian, even by a philosopher like Nietzsche, who is willing to embrace the poetic and paradoxical as part of his writing style.

The Scarlet Empress (1934): Blood, Lust, and Madness

Although we tend to think of Dietrich as being one of Hollywood's best examples of the *Überfrau* as an enactment of the will to power *qua* seductress, we have seen that in all the Sternberg films discussed so far, her actions do not fit with those relentless women striving for power and success. For such *Überfrauen*, as seen in films like *Red-Headed Woman* and *Female*, human subjectivity and rational agency remain intact. Unclouded by sentiment, they strive for success and greatness. But Dietrich's agency continually seems to be a fleeting shadow as she is drawn to a state of ecstatic oneness in which freedom and enslavement, pleasure and pain, and self and other are combined. More so than any of Sternberg's other movies, *The Scarlet Empress* offers us a tale of the seductress who, like *Übermenschen* from previous chapters, uses her will to achieve power. In spite of this narrative similarity, it is clear that more is going on in this symbolically fraught film than the exercise of the will to power. Although Sternberg never elaborated on what he hoped his films would accomplish, except in the opening frames of *The Salvation Hunters*, one wonders if he would not agree with Antonin Artaud's notion of "pure cinema."[91] This vision of cinema would be an enactment of movement and rhythm that would be aimed at awakening "affective sensation of a nervous order" at an "elementary level."[92] Artaud conceived of film not as an Apollonian "dream" but, in Dionysian terms, as "skin" or flesh. The screen depicts a pure feeling state that defies reason and may even promote a similar, unnerving affective state in the viewer. *The Scarlet Empress*—because of its ambiguity, the repetitiveness of symbols, its campiness, its episodic narrative, and the profound crudeness of the characters in it—perhaps best works as a skin of images that is intended to provoke, I believe, disgust and excitement at the perverse combination of the sacred and the profane. I do not mean to say that the film is empty, incoherent, or mere style, as a philosophic point certainly remains. But the cynicism of that point and the experimentalism of the film suggest an explicit attempt by Sternberg to test the limits of film and its capacity for provocation. I am turning to this film despite the fact that there is no obvious way to see Dietrich's character as having faith in the One or striving for Dionysian oneness as in the other films. In a way, the film's cynicism acts as the acid that presents us with a negative image of the *Übermensch* that we might call the *Untermensch*. It strikes me as very plausible that Sternberg's Russian tale is a variation of Dostoevsky's *Notes from Underground*. She remains a tragically isolated figure throughout the film, and it is perhaps for that reason that her ecstatic passions are converted into murderous insanity. And yet *The Scarlet Empress* is worth discussing alongside Sternberg's other films, because it does have the clearest instance of that "horrible mixture of sensuality and cruelty" that Nietzsche calls "the real 'witches' brew'" (*BT* §2). Furthermore, its disturbing and grotesque visuals are possibly aimed at awakening a Dionysian wisdom in the viewer.

If we construe this as a story about a woman who learns to use her beauty and sexuality to acquire power, like the *Überfrauen* from *Baby Face* and *Red-Headed Woman*, then we have merely a tale of the shift from woman as object to woman as subject.[93] Yet I would argue that it is never clear whether Catherine is a subject at all. She appears in the first half of the film as a doe-eyed imbecile and then in the latter half as a seductive political snake. Is she ever anything but the pawn of destructive forces? The world-historical forces of political survival turn her into Catherine the Great, and the perverse sadism that emerges even when she is a child who asks if she can become the executioner turns her into a lunatic. Her apparent agency is simply a reflection of survival instincts. While Sternberg called the film an exercise in extreme style, it does tell us of the threat that the negation of all agency and selfhood poses. While it may lead to great things, if it takes place in isolation rather than through the love of and faith in the One, then it can lead to madness and murder. The impetus for Dionysian affirmation in Sternberg's films has been through an irrational self-negating love of another person. Lacking any such meaningful connections to others, Catherine slowly devolves into a monster who is no more a "subject" than the vile creatures that surround her. Each is driven by perverse lusts, paranoia, desperation, madness, and history itself. Although she is said to engage in the "ambitious pursuit of power" in the second half of the film, her formation of political alliances is simply the absorption of the cruelty of the Russian court and her attempt to survive. While it is true that the connection between cruelty and the erotic persists in this film, Sternberg's earlier films *show* an important conceptual link between love (desire, sexuality) and cruelty because to truly love requires self-abnegation and degradation. There is no such clear demonstration in *The Scarlet Empress*: in this loveless world, there is nothing but the perverse and cruel.

Although *The Scarlett Empress* is regarded as Sternberg's greatest achievement, there are many ways in which it is an outlier in his oeuvre. One of the features that differentiates it the most is that it is suffused with an atmosphere of paranoia and publicity. There is no private world. From her childhood on, Catherine is publicly paraded, medically examined, and forcefully cajoled. Her every move is scrutinized by others. Eventually, everyone and everything is laid bare in the grotesque gothic pornography of the Russian court. The intimacy, delicacy, and claustrophobia of his other films are replaced with enormity, crudeness, and paranoia. Although Catherine's world is filled with people who are watching her, she is nevertheless entirely alone and isolated for the entire film. Her monadic existence is cold and loveless. The film's sets are grotesque and cluttered. Each room is both cathedral and dungeon chamber. It is as if in every scene, Sternberg aimed to combine the sacred and the profane in order to show how this isolation results in a spiritual void that ends in madness and sadism. If Sternberg's other films are like living flesh, then *The Scarlet Empress* is the flesh of a corpse.[94]

While Dietrich's other characters rush into degradation for the sake of Dionysian ecstatic union, there is never the establishment of any form of agency on her part nor any motivated turn toward an ecstatic, irrational self-abnegation. Instead, the constant echoing of bells and clocks identifies time and history itself with the sadism that dominates the film.[95] She seems little more than a beast driven by instinct and time. The crux of Sternberg's other Dietrich films is that the loss of a practical will and identity can lead to a more fundamental form of life rooted in faith and passion. *The Scarlett Empress* is a cautionary tale that such breaking down of the barriers that constitute a recognizably human social self can also give rise to monsters. It is tempting to read this film on the model of the *Übermensch* as a Machiavellian master of her surroundings. But her wild-eyed grimace at the end of the film suggests that she has become a mirror image of her criminally insane, mentally stunted, and perverse husband, Peter III. Rather than some noble or vital form of *Übermenschlichkeit*, we seem to be entirely in the realm of the *Unmensch*. Sternberg's films have an ironic connection with Nietzsche's philosophy: both were read as being symptomatic expressions of decadence when they were in fact prescribing the path out of modern decadence. Only *The Scarlet Empress* lacks any path out of this decadent world: it reads like the Heideggerian notion of "the They" (*das Man*), which we can understand as the distorting effects of impersonal and, thus, inhuman "publicity" on mood, will, perception, and action.[96]

When asked whether his films were about love as the supreme value of human life—a romantic reading that Marlene Dietrich seems to have accepted—Sternberg rejected the idea. He responded that while "love is a driving element of life," the supreme value is "justice."[97] In effect, *The Scarlet Empress* is a study of a world where any prospect for love or justice is crushed, leaving only survival, revenge, and *ressentiment*. But in what sense is justice at work in his other films? It would appear that Sternbergian justice is to be understood in a very Nietzschean way. Justice is achieved when a person pursues their fate and embraces their most passionate existence even if that goes against reason, society, and morality. This is not a notion of justice in the sense of "calculable right or law" but is instead being bound to "the infinite secret of the other," which points to an unconditional notion of justice that exceeds all performances.[98] Justice in Sternberg's films is found in accepting a Dionysian life of hardship and ecstasy rather than one of comfort and averageness. The idea is not that one gets what one deserves, but that, if one is strong enough and lives life with faith in the infinite value of the Other and in passion, then one will have performed the great task that fate has given. Sternberg's works are tragedies that are critical of injustice that stems from weakness, stupidity, and common morality, but they are not critical of the suffering that stems from strength and will, whether it is self-inflicted or inflicted on others. Such suffering may appear like injustice, but what makes for an *Übermensch* is the capacity to embrace that fate and read it as a sort of justice.

Conclusion

Undoubtedly, Sternberg's films and their unique visual language offer a rich canvas upon which many different interpretative approaches can flourish. Although the standard psychoanalytic approaches can certainly present a plausible narrative of desires and relations at work in these films, I take Sternberg's remark that what is at stake in his films is not love but justice to be informative. Based also on his first film, we know that he was less interested in what film had to say about bodies and desires and was more interested in how film might present to us a philosophical thought, such as the value of transcending the "all, too human" self and the superficial world of Apollonian illusion. That constant theme, the aesthetic vision of the Apollonian world as the world of the ignorant crowd, and the appeal to a deeper, irrational, transpersonal, and vital level of reality are ideas that fit both the films themselves and the suggestions of a governing philosophy found in Sternberg's autobiography. Add to this the prominence of Nietzsche's thought in the culture, and the potential of Nietzsche's influence on Sternberg through the sources of his films, his co-writers, and Dietrich herself, then the case for a Nietzschean reading of these iconic films seems more than justified.

In spite of the richness of these films and their obvious ability to sustain a multitude of different interpretations, my approach stands in contrast to a recent phenomenological study of these films that reads them as a presentation of the human subject, the visualization of "transcendental personhood" and autonomy. There is *something* right about the idea that we find an "ethics of the look" that accepts the materiality of the person and of the image while also gesturing toward "the exceptionalism of the person."[99] The problem is that it is hard to describe what we find here to be an *ethical* presentation of personhood and autonomy. Instead, we see a form of life that embodies the idea of *animae magnae prodigus*, of finding freedom in an enslavement to fate and to the Other.[100] In other words, Sternberg's notion of justice cannot be seen in traditional ethical terms. The conceptual and thematic analysis offered in this chapter could obviously be supported by a more detailed investigation of the formal elements of film that Sternberg uses to capture the mood and look of the distinct worlds and spiritual crises at work in each. That would require a book-length study. What I have attempted to do is to show that, contrary to many leading interpretations that see his films as style and illusionism over substance, there are substantial philosophical concepts at the center of them all, ones that show the influence of Nietzsche, particularly *The Birth of Tragedy*.

7

The Revealing Mask

The *Übermensch* as Free Spirit in the Comedies of Ernst Lubitsch

Introduction

THE FILMS OF ERNST LUBITSCH offer us a sequence of Nietzschean films that I believe shows us a more "humanist" and "free spirited" conception of the *Übermensch*. While it would have made sense to turn to them after the chapter on Hecht, in which *Design for Living* was discussed, there are several reasons not to do so. Firstly, Lubitsch's films end up affirming a more human conception of justice, even while also advocating for an immoral, sometimes even criminal, life of risk, play, and masquerade. Secondly, I turn to Lubitsch in this final chapter because his later films show us the shift of fortunes for Nietzscheanism in films of the late 1930s and early 1940s. While my focus will be on the Nietzschean themes in Lubitsch's films from 1929 to 1937, which were co-written with Samson Raphaelson, Ernest Vajda, and, as already discussed, Ben Hecht, I will conclude with a brief look at his films from 1938 to 1942, where we see a significant shift away from the Nietzschean elements of the earlier works. This shift occurs even in those late Lubitsch films that continue to use Raphaelson as the main screenwriter, such as *The Shop Around the Corner* (1940) and *Heaven Can Wait* (1943), which suggests it was an intentional movement away from the more cynical Nietzschean films of his earlier career.¹ For these reasons, it seems suitable to end our survey of classic Hollywood cinema with Lubitsch.

Lubitsch's silent films were described by Kracauer as farces that emerge from a place of nihilism, offering "a blend of cynicism and melodramatic sentimentality," in which history is "meaningless ... an arena reserved for blind and ferocious instincts, a product of devilish machinations forever frustrating our hopes for freedom and happiness."² This idea helps us to see how Lubitsch's German films align both with the Expressionist tradition and with themes we have seen in the Nietzschean cinematic tradition starting with Stroheim. It seems inevitable that Lubitsch would have some connection to Nietzschean thought, as he was undoubtedly exposed to it via his training in the Reinhardt Theater, that "cathedral of German *Kultur*," which was thoroughly infused with a potent mix of Wagnerian, Schopenhauerian, and Nietzschean philosophy.³ Once he begins to make films with Samson Raphaelson as his lead writer, we see another potential source of Nietzschean ideas. Raphaelson was a student of Stewart Sherman, who championed American Puritanism as an inner restriction of desire and impulse and who was a harsh critic of the Germanic invasion of culture and its free-spiritedness. While Sherman battled against Mencken, Hecht, and Nietzsche, Raphaelson ultimately admits that he felt pulled between these two poles, between the moral and the amoral.⁴

While I do not want to investigate Lubitsch's silent work in detail to determine whether Kracauer's assessment is correct, it is at least superficially accurate. There is surely something inhuman in his early farces, and a detailed exploration of them in relationship to the Nietzschean and Wagnerian ideas of early German cinema would be a valuable study that would further support the thesis of my own work. Yet it is worth having a rough idea of why Kracauer might have seen Lubitsch as creating a nihilistic cinema, as it will help us to see the value perspective of his early sound films. These early films are filled with cartoonish buffoonery and with narcissists who are unable to see past the immediate moment. In *Meyer from Berlin* (1919), *The Oyster Princess* (1919), and *The Wildcat* (1921), it is surely the inhumanity and artificiality of all this comedic stupidity that Kracauer reads as coming from a place of nihilism. These are films of excessive appetites that are at once childlike in their innocence but also animalistic and antisocial. Desire's transformation of the human into a puppet (and vice versa) is seen in *Die Puppe*, or *The Doll* (1919). According to Žižek, the story of *The Doll* tells us the rather Hegelian point that to move from being unfree (a machine or automaton) to being free is like the Fall from the Garden of Eden, both a garnering of knowledge and a fundamental disturbance in desire. That disturbance is a recognition that desire is activated only against the fantasy object or myth; in this case a mechanical, unfree woman is the fantasy backdrop to the real woman.[5] But *The Doll* suggests more cynically that we are all puppets of desires, that the human and the automaton are largely indistinguishable. One of the earliest films that Lubitsch directed, *I Wouldn't Want to Be a Man* (1918), presents us with a gender reversal farce that laughs at rigid class, moral, and gender norms that define the bourgeoisie. His film *Rausch*, or *Intoxication* (1919), based on a Strindberg play performed with the Max Reinhardt company, and his *The Loves of Pharaoh* (1922) show men undone by irrational passions. Madness, hallucination, obsession, hypnotism, suicide, uncontrollable passions, and inescapable fate are found in *The Eyes of the Mummy* (1918). *Carmen* (1918) (also known as *Gypsy Blood*) shows us the Dionysian genius of the heart that bewitches men. The tyrants in *Sumurun* (1920), *Anna Boleyn* (1920) (also known as *Deception*), and *Rosita* (1923), Lubitsch's first American film, are all irrational, criminal, and love-obsessed. While it is difficult to generalize about this collection of fairy-tale-like films with their odd mix of irreverence and exoticism, as well as the many love triangle films of the 1920s that I am not even mentioning, it is not hard to see this work as continuous with left-leaning, depth-psychological, and free-spirited expressions of Nietzschean and Schopenhauerian thought popular in Germany during these years.[6] While it is perhaps easier to see the dark passions of more famous silent German Expressionist film as Nietzschean in nature, I have argued in earlier chapters that cinema that can be childlike, mythical, farcical, fantastical, and joyous may actually better capture Nietzsche's mocking voice.

Lubitsch's early sound films are not as nihilistically farcical as his silents, if only because they are all largely focused one resolving the problem of how freedom and the couple can coexist. For this reason, his works have significant overlap with Cavell's comedies of remarriage. Both are concerned with the epistemic issue of coming to understand the Other, although in Lubitsch's films such understanding takes place only through masks. They are also concerned with overcoming a skeptical relation to the Other, often rooted in a sort of moral harm (disrespect, distrust). The end result is the constitution of the couple. Thus, Lubitsch's films take us toward a more humanistic Nietzscheanism that does not delve into the Dionysian metaphysics of previous chapters, except that they do accept naturalism in contrast to unnatural bourgeois morality.

They also promote an aestheticization of life through the veiling of nature and through the lightness, superficiality, and musicality that we can see as the "Lubitsch touch."[7] Such an underlying philosophy surely draws from sources other than Nietzsche within German Romanticism. But how might such ideas align with the conception of the *Übermensch*? In earlier chapters, I have stressed a conception of the "superhuman" that is related to fate and time as eternal recurrence of the same. I have not been especially concerned with the naturalistic and anthropological themes in Nietzsche's thought that are often found under the idea of "the free spirit." The idea of the free spirit is one that Nietzsche develops in his earlier works, particularly *Human, All Too Human*, which is subtitled *A Book for Free Spirits*, *Daybreak*, and *The Gay Science*. Yet it also the subject of the second chapter of *Beyond Good and Evil*. The idea of the "free spirit," like the idea of the Dionysian, changes across Nietzsche's texts, but also remains present throughout.[8] The free spirit values the changing of opinion and ambitiously strives toward "the forbidden fruits of *spernere se sperni* [to scorn scorning oneself] and *spernere se ipsum* [to scorn oneself]" (*D* §56). What this suggests is that the free spirit is unencumbered by dogma or even their own past. The free spirit is capable of the scorn for oneself that leads to continual advancement beyond the chains of tradition, but they are also capable of scorning self-scorn, in particular, the sort of scorn of self that emerges from guilt, fear, and concern about the opinions of others. There is something innocent in the free spirit's behavior and beliefs because they are beyond repressive notions of sin and guilt. Nothing is sacred for the free spirit except the "will to self-determination, to evaluating on one's own account, this will to *free* will" (*HTH* P §3, emphasis in original).

Of course, Nietzsche does argue that the free spirit is not suited for marriage because such a figure "hates all habituation and rules, everything enduring and definitive" and will continually break "the net" that gives stability to a marriage (*HTH* vol. 1 §427). So it may seem a poor fit for Lubitsch's films. Nietzsche sees love itself to be a rather absolute value judgment "for" the Other and that, while the free spirit may love and take up such a value judgment for a time, they might also shift quite unexpectedly to the opposite position, "against." Nietzsche worries that this instability means that the free spirit will be seen as being poor in love (*HTH* vol. 1 §291). But he does not seem to rule out the possibility of liberated marriages in which "an occasional 'exception'" to its rules is allowed, where "each of the parties seeks to achieve an individual goal through the other," and a "higher conception of marriage" as a sort of "soul-friendship" (*HTH* vol. 1 §399, 402, 424). Thus, we can see why the free spirit is said to "dance right over morality" (*EH* III GS). Changeable and immoral, the free spirit may have started off as scientifically minded debunker, but in *The Gay Science* the will to truth is replaced by a "wish not to see everything naked, or to be present at everything, or to understand and 'know' everything" (*GS* P §4). Such a "good will to appearance" is necessary for life, because it "furnishes us with eyes and hands and above all the good conscience to be *able* to turn ourselves into such a [aesthetic] phenomena" (*GS* §107). Giving such style to one's character is tied to free-spiritedness because we "must discover the *hero* no less than the *fool* in our passion for knowledge" and embrace "all exuberant, floating, dancing, mocking, childish, and blissful art lest we lose the *freedom above things* that our ideal demands of us" (*GS* §107, emphases in original). He calls this figure the free spirit *par excellence*, who can "delight in masks and the good conscience in using any kind of mask" (*GS* §77).[9] How might the ideas translate into Lubitsch's films? As we have already seen from *Design for Living*, at the heart of these comedies is the "dangerous privilege of living *experimentally*" (*HTH* P §4, emphasis in original). Besides the challenge to traditional morality and the aestheticism that informs Lubitsch's presentation of new forms of coupledom, the understanding of and patience before the other person as both hero and fool is of central importance, because it is a way of picturing the complete absence of *ressentiment*. What seems so important to capturing the Lubitsch touch, understood as something substantial rather than merely stylistic, is how it shows us the negative effects of shame and what it is to be without shame. It is in living without shame and *ressentiment* and having an appreciation of appearances rather than trying to tear open all veils and masks that is the common ground between Lubitsch's art and Nietzsche's philosophy of the free spirit.

The first section will discuss *The Love Parade* (1929), *The Smiling Lieutenant* (1931), *One Hour with You* (1932), and *The Merry Widow* (1934), while the next section will discuss *Trouble in Paradise* (1932), which is regarded as the masterwork of middle-period Lubitsch, alongside *Design for Living*. His early musicals do not receive as much attention in the scholarship, and I will not be discussing one of them, *Monte Carlo* (1930), which I take to deviate from his other works insofar as it concludes with tears and the shaming of Jeanette MacDonald's character for her concern for things like money and status. Even if those values are crude and require dissimulation, the moral condemnation she receives from Jack Buchanan's character is not representative of the subtlety of

Lubitsch's filmmaking. I will conclude by contrasting the worlds found in these films to the ones found in Lubitsch's films starting in 1938. By turning to these late works, it will be shown how Nietzschean themes were becoming unpalatable.

Love and Illusion in Lubitsch's Early Musicals

The *Übermensch* as free spirit looks at the supposed seriousness of the human condition and laughs.[10] This is hilariously expressed in the opening scene of *The Love Parade* (1929). Maurice Chevalier's Count Alfred Renard is cheerful while he is seemingly almost killed by the husband of his lover, Paulette. For the audience, it appears that the angry husband has the gun that Paulette has used to kill herself and that the husband has shot Alfred. But for some reason the bullet fails to hurt him. But what we do not know is that this is a regular occurrence for Alfred.[11] He has a desk drawer full of lady's pistols, which means this scene has repeated itself numerous times. We have a simulation of the sort of melodramatic murder-suicide we saw in *Baby Face*, one that Alfred recognizes immediately as a simulation. Although murderous passions are directed against him, Alfred remains helpful, smiling, and joyous. Lubitsch's films are the antithesis to *ressentiment*, which we have already seen in *Design for Living*, and whenever that emotion enters into relationships, tragedy looms. Yet these comedic simulations are not ineffectual in Lubitsch's universe. They have powerful effects on human relations. For example, when Paulette remarkably awakens from her suicide, her husband is so happy that she is not dead that everything seems forgotten. The husband does not come to see the comedic lie at the heart of the situation as Alfred does, which signals Alfred's position as *Übermensch* and the free spirit who can look out across the human condition and see both the heroic and the foolish. The constant repetition of this scene for Alfred means that the idea that events occur "the first time as tragedy, the second time as farce" is expanded to the perspective that Nietzsche calls the eternal recurrence of the same, which makes the farce of each occurrence even that much greater.

Yet the film also shows us how what can appear first as farce can reappear as tragedy. The first scene between Alfred and Queen Louise (Jeanette MacDonald) has her reading a report on his sexual exploits in Paris, for which he has lost his position as military attaché and been sent home to Sylvania. Queen Louise finds his exploits funny and arousing.

They flirt and make jokes while she asks, "Aren't you ashamed of yourself?" But rather than actually shame Alfred, the queen playfully takes on her "queen" role: "I think it's serious. Very serious. And I shall have to punish you. I shall have to punish you very severely. Otherwise, you would start all over again. I shall think of a punishment that will cure you forever. An awful punishment. You shall be ordered to grow a beard. You'll have to be serious in a beard." This playful punishment is to be condemned to seriousness, to which he suggests his own punishment—namely, to continue this playfulness and be by her side at all times. This exchange is repeated in the final scene of the film. But now it is no longer farcical. Queen Louise is penitent and crying. She is asking forgiveness. She has married Alfred and treated him horribly. In effect, she is the one that has grown the beard and become serious. He calls back to that earlier scene by saying, "But how am I going to punish you? You must be punished. And severely. An awful punishment." He does this to show his forgiveness of Louise, who has acted cruelly. He signals that, in spite of the tragic collapse of their love, he is willing to play again, rather than shame her for her seriousness. This repetition is very far away from the fun and gaiety of its first appearance. The difference between the scenes is clear in the punishment that is chosen. In the first scene, she selects the playful punishment of growing a beard and he counters with a proposal that essentially suggests that he be her lover. In the second scene, he offers no playful punishment. She must punish herself. And it is a punishment. She makes him king and releases her power to him. While we saw such a dethroning of an *Überfrau* from her position of power in *Female* and had to resist seeing this as reversion to something traditional, we now see the opposite. The position of power has led the queen to take on traditional roles and turn Alfred into a "husband." Nevertheless, the film also obviously sees such gender role reversal as a sort of anti-naturalism. After all, Alfred's one-sided marriage vow is to "execute his majesty's every wish and every command and to be an obedient and docile husband." The ambassador from Afghanistan is translated as saying, "Man is man. Woman is woman. And that to change that causes trouble. He does not see how any man could stand being a wife. And therefore, he hopes this will be a most unhappy marriage." But most problematic is the fact that she has failed to keep up their games and recognize the heroic and the foolish within these roles.[12] This has caused Alfred to feel both shame and *ressentiment*. The punishment does not come from Alfred; rather, she puts the words in his mouth, telling him that he should say, "From now, *I* shall take command—not only of affairs of the state, not only in the department of the navy but also here at home." By articulating the punishment herself, a sort of minimal mask is retained, allowing her to avoid being shamed and humiliated as Alfred has been.[13] Alfred is clearly playing the role of punisher and king rather than *actually* punishing from a position of power, which might breed *ressentiment*. The free spirit "loves masks," and Alfred can take up this role only insofar as it allows him and Louise to recover their lost playful masquerade (*BGE* §40).

The role of masks and play is essential for the formation of the couple. The free spirit does not want to see nature denuded (*GS* P §4). In this case, that raw nature is the anger, humiliation, and hurt, which is part of their relationship (or any relationship). To attempt to recognize that without a mask would be to come face to face with the unforgivable. Thus, their community and passion can take place only through intentional, playful mask-making and role-construction, for only then can the disruptive passions not be destroyed by the social roles of queen and king, sovereign and subject, husband and wife.[14] To participate in such a game is to share an understanding that remains silent about why the game is necessary (*BGE* §40). If Alfred were to makes these demands and state this punishment himself, he would be removing his mask entirely. All that would be left would be his naked hurt and the revenge that he must take on Louise. For Nietzsche, revenge, an "ill will against time and its 'it was,'" is the opposite of a free and powerful spirit who can allow the past to be nothing (Z II "On Redemption"). To take revenge would be an injury to this marriage from which it may be impossible to recover. The essence of love and marriage is a series of masks. It is through the creation of these shared illusions and roles that "love forgives the lover even his lust" (*GS* §62).

The rawer emotions in the Lubitsch musicals can be given voice only in song. The songs act as masks, moments of unreality, in which one can arrive at more poetic and, thus, more illusory expressions of feeling. Yet these moments are more honest and more revealing than ordinary speech. Nietzsche discusses this theatrical form of the mask when examining the Greeks, who demanded that "passion on the stage" be able to "speak well" in way that is unnatural (*GS* §80). He also looks at the Italians, who had the "unnatural convention" of making "passion that *sings*" (*GS* §80, emphasis in original). "In nature, passion is so poor in words, so embarrassed and all but mute; or when it finds words, so confused and irrational and ashamed of itself" (*GS* §80). Even in this theatrical mask-making, there must be a "residue of *silence*," which is to say that the mask being created and portrayed must give an articulation to passion, but it must also remain silent concerning the crudeness of human passion and the "stammering and screaming" that is the natural expression of passion (*GS* §80, emphasis in original). Ultimately, the marriage problem is resolved by stepping back into a new set of masks, which suggests that romance, love, and married life must be rooted in a playful dance, at once surprising and spontaneous but also choreographed and familiar. Love is made possible through this "imbalance," this call and response, in which one creates a persona that turns desire into a game with unwritten rules that the other must learn in order to offer their own playful persona.[15]

These same ideas are at work in *One Hour with You* (1932), which begins with Dr. Andre Bertier and Colette Bertier acting like young lovers having a secret rendezvous in the park. The problem that emerges in their marriage is then resolved through an elaborate game of illusions in the final scene, which is quite similar to, although more complicated than, the ending of *The Love Parade*. At the end of *One Hour with You*, Andre (Maurice Chevalier, again) must confess to his wife, Colette (Jeanette MacDonald, again), that he has had a sexual rendezvous of an unspecified sort with her best friend, Mitzi (Genevieve Tobin). He must tell her because he is being called to divorce court so that Mitzi's husband (Roland Young) can get out of his marriage. Colette is distraught by this fact. She slaps him, cries, and begins talking about divorce. He asks for forgiveness but is also strangely unrepentant. He claims, "There was nothing wrong with it." Then, changing his tune, he says that he "shouldn't have done it" and, even more strangely, that he did not do it. None of this is helping, and she calls him a liar. They are at an impasse. They need to reconstitute the joy and playful ways that were indicative of their marriage early in the film.

At this point, Andre's friend Adolph shows up. Adolph had thrown himself at Colette repeatedly during a dinner party by confessing his love, suggesting that they run off together, and eventually kissing her. Colette had tried to tell Andre that this had happened earlier in the film, but she said it was all in a dream. Andre did not believe that Adolph could have done this even in a dream. Now she tells Andre that this encounter with Adolph really happened. She too has had a dalliance. Of course, Andre does not believe it. Indeed, it has the appearance of being fake. She feeds Adolph the details of their "twenty-five minutes together," and poor Adolph, who is terribly confused, simply says "yes." Andre gestures laughingly to Adolph to go along with Colette's story. He seems to be saying, "Humor her. Tell her what she wants to hear. I know that this is fake and what she is doing." He is wrong; it is not fake. It did happen. But he is also right. The event was so totally meaningless that her claims that she is "the one that's bad" and that she is a "Cleopatra" to his "Don Juan" are most certainly false. Colette is certainly confessing, but on the other hand she is also lying given that her intent is to say, "See, look. We are even." The fact is that they are not even. "A tooth for a tooth, an eye for an eye, an Adolph for a Mitzi, fifty-fifty." As this charade continues, it is clear that whatever the truth of the situation is, it doesn't matter. What matters is that they are forgiving one another. The use of Adolph is a farcical ploy. They both see that, and it allows them to forgive each other. As they turn to the camera and address the film audience as "ladies and gentlemen," they make it clear, in song, that the truth of the situation is irrelevant. They sing that "he's a Don Juan" and that "she has dreams," but ultimately, they are crazy about each other. So they ask, "What would you do?" and they answer, "That's what I do too" and kiss.[16] A betrayal has taken place. What is important is how they can come together and overcome the spirit of revenge.[17]

Yet having seen how love is provoked, sustained, broken, reconstituted, and deepened through the (mostly) playful use of appearances and self-aware masks, there remains a very puzzling moment in *One Hour with You*. Why does Andre actually have an affair with Mitzi in the first place? It is a moment quite unlike any other in Lubitsch's other musicals. In the film's earlier version, *The Marriage Circle* (1924), we are told that the marriage is ideal and that the encounter with Mitzi remains innocent. In *One Hour with You*, unlike the boring marriage in *The Marriage Circle*, we see a vigorous and inspired romance between husband and wife. He even sings that Collette can do everything that Mitzi can do, and so why should he have this affair? It remains an irrational and inexplainable moment that he is able to express only by saying, "But oh, that Mitzi." *One Hour with You* gives us a stronger picture of the marriage relationship and its romantic playfulness, while forcing it to reckon with an actual infidelity. It has been suggested that the reason for the relationship is that "Andre cannot resist the power of appearance."[18] It is true that the affair in *One Hour with You* seems to happen against Andre's will—a true case of *akrasia*, a sort of zombie love affair. But why this is so is not evident.[19] One significant addition to *One Hour with You* not found in *The Marriage Circle* is an explanation by the professor that helps Andre to feel better about what he did.

Prof. Olivier: My friend, nobody is guilty. I have a theory that nobody is responsible for their actions. Our doings are controlled by circumstances over which we have no control.

Andre: Oh, excellent. Truer words have never been spoken.

Prof. Olivier: Therefore, nobody can be held responsible for his actions.

Andre: Oh, what a beautiful thought, Professor.

On the one hand, we are supposed to find this funny, because Andre seems clearly responsible for his actions. On the other hand, weakness of will can be seen as a compulsion, in which one acts against what one knows to be right and cannot do otherwise. This explanation offered by the professor would be true if it were the case that Andre could not "resist the power of appearance." Yet I do not think that we are supposed to accept that Andre is unfree. The professor's philosophy falls flat. The reason that Andre ultimately cheats on his wife is her suspicious nature. She gives such power to appearances that they are able to transform reality and make an illusory infidelity become a real one. Andre does in fact resist Mitzi and appearances, until he finds himself in a catch-22 situation. Either he goes into the garden with Mitzi and is guilty, or else he goes back to the party with his tie undone and his wife believes him to be guilty. His wife's jealousy is made clear when he switches name cards on the table so that he does not have to sit next to Mitzi, but she takes him to be untrue to her and romantically interested in the person whose name ends up next to his. He is damned if he does and damned if he doesn't. Yet he still has a choice. He can continue to suffer under "the constantly false, namely *shallow*, interpretation of every word, every step, every sign of life he gives," or he can actually be guilty of something (*BGE* §41, emphasis in original). Rather than seeing Andre as predetermined to act and not responsible for his actions, we can conceive of him as freely choosing the dangerous path, as embracing his fate as determined by his wife's suspicions. He takes on real "guilt" or "sin" in order to overcome it, to place his marriage in a position that is beyond such moral notions or at least not subject to the corrosive paranoia that such notions create. There is something both heroic and foolish in his act, and he needs Colette to see that, so that they can return to their shared foolishness that had been interrupted by her bad conscience.

There is an equally puzzling moment in *The Smiling Lieutenant* (1931), in which Chevalier's Niki must marry the rich Princess Anna of Flausenthurm, played by Miriam Hopkins, out of honor and duty. But another love affair exists in the film between Niki and Claudette Colbert's Franzi. It is one of the few Lubitsch romances in which love is not obscured by an ulterior motive (either economic or patriotic) or by a glaring inequality in power. This makes their love rather touching and unusually earnest. Their love is expressed by the song lyrics "Forget everything in the world but me. Forget if it's wrong or it's right. The more that we have to forget, you see, well, the more we'll remember tonight." This depiction of unadulterated love that forgets everything in the world suggests the underlying selfishness of love that Nietzsche describes as intending "nothing less than *excluding* the whole world from a precious good, from happiness and enjoyment" and "the impoverishment and deprivation of all competitors" like a "dragon guarding his golden hoard" (*GS* §14, emphasis in original): "If one considers, finally, that to the lover himself the whole rest of the world appears indifferent, pale, and worthless, and he is prepared to make any sacrifice, to disturb any order, to subordinate all other interests—then one comes to feel genuine amazement that this wild avarice and injustice of sexual love has been glorified and deified so much in all ages—indeed, that this love has furnished the concept of love as the opposite of egoism while it actual may be the most ingenious expression of egoism" (*GS* §14). This is the sort of abandonment of the world that we saw Shanghai Lily demand of Doc, but it seems quite out of place in Lubitsch's world. The pure love of Niki and Franzi in *The Smiling Lieutenant* is of this selfish sort. They sing together a song that is giving voice to a passion that seems to be destroying them: "I love you, I hate you. . . . I'll thrill you, till I kill you. You son of a gun. You devil, say you love me. . . . You brute you, I could shoot you. You son of a gun. You put madness in the moonlight. TNT in each caress. In every sigh you put such high explosive, I send out an SOS. There's dynamite in all your kisses, you and I know this is love." Despite the strength of the attraction, Niki ultimately ends up with Princess Anna (Miriam Hopkins). Why? The answer seems to me to be that the connection between Niki and Franzi is without artifice. Because such unadorned love exposes their finitude and their raw needs, it is too much like a "dragon guarding his golden hoard." Colbert's Franzi expresses why she abandons the love affair with Niki, which allows Niki and Princess Anna to enter into wedded bliss, by stating the fact that "girls who start with breakfast don't usually stay for supper." This is a way of saying that their strong passions, which we are to assume led to her sleeping with him on the first night that they met, will not make for a long-term relationship.[20] They are too honest and unadorned with each other.

But why does the relationship with Princess Anna work? When Niki refuses to make love to Anna on their wedding night, he proclaims that married people do not do that. Anna asks the question that motivates Lubitsch's films of this era, "Then what's the use of getting married?" Niki tells us that "all the philosophers, for three thousand years have tried to find that out and they failed. And I don't think that we'll solve that problem tonight." While many think that Lubitsch's stylistic but superficial films provide no answer to anything of philosophical importance, the obvious answer is that the institution of marriage provides a framework of masks that enables raw nature to be playfully veiled and aesthetically constructed. But there is little evidence that Anna will be able to do this, given how naïve and stupid she is, having gathered all her "knowledge out of the royal encyclopedia, a special edition with all the interesting things left out." Yet this state of innocence allows her to build up her own image of the world, her own fantasies. Niki's relationship with Anna is based on the lie that he was winking, smiling, and laughing at her because she was so beautiful, when in fact she moved in between him and Franzi. This calls to mind the Nietzschean idea that it is only on the "solid, granite foundation of ignorance" that the entire human edifice of knowledge, truth, and morality could be erected—and this includes marriage (*BGE* §24). It is only when Anna is able to meet Niki's level of deceptiveness by creating her own illusions that they are able to love one another. In particular, Anna turns into a sophisticated, cigarette-smoking, jazz-playing woman, aided by a magical and immediate transformation of her entire wardrobe, including her underwear, into something sexy and modern. Although the mythical space of Lubitsch's films has nothing realistic about it, this is a moment of extreme disruption of narrative illusionism, like Chevalier's regular breaking of the fourth wall. Nevertheless, it is difficult to swallow this transformation, which leads us to doubt Anna's capacity to match Niki's ability to keep the playful illusions of marriage active while avoiding shame and revenge.

The Merry Widow (1934) is perhaps Lubitsch's greatest exposition of the need of reciprocity and sensitivity when creating and occupying such romantic illusions. Danilo and Sonia (Chevalier and MacDonald again) continually wear masks. In their first meeting, Sonia is literally wearing a mask (a veil) and Danilo is wearing the mask of a "colossal" and conqueror who wants to sleep with every woman in town. He has, he says, jumped out of every window in town escaping from such trysts. Both are hidden from each other by these masks. Danilo leaves when Sonia sees through this mask and dismisses him, telling him that there is no reason or temptation for her to unveil herself to him. Danilo forgets about her and remarks that he is now "a free man again." But the encounter with Danilo has affected Sonia. The game of this "great lover" mask makes her confront the free spirit and his "delight in masks and the good conscience in using any kind of mask" (*GS* §77). His mask is not so much meant to deceive as it is to express and entertain, and this perhaps leads her to rethink her relationship to her own mask. Thus, Sonia is transformed from literally writing "nothing" in her diary to admitting to herself that her "heart" might learn to dance again. That possibility is what Sonia has seen in Danilo. Quite literally, Danilo belongs among the free-spirited and "noble *traitors* to all things that can in any way be betrayed," insofar as he "advances . . . through one party after another" and feels "no sense of guilt" (*HTH* vol. 1 §637, emphasis in original). The problem is that Sonia takes exception to being just another party who can be betrayed. She deserves more than that.

Sonia wears a mask, but it is neither expressive nor liberating. It is the mask of social rules concerning her mourning and what is respectable for a widow. In their second meeting at the nightclub Maxim's, Sonia is now disguised as Fifi, and Danilo continues with his same charade. He is wearing the mask of Napoleon the conqueror again, and she again calls him out for "attacking too early." Sonia drops her mask and reveals that she is a "society woman" and not a "Maxim's girl" by asking if Danilo loves her. Danilo clearly cannot see past the "Fifi" mask. The mere fact that Sonia is in Maxim's blinds him to what she is trying to express through the mask. Thus, there is no reciprocity in this game of masks. The masks are isolating. Danilo complains about women who "take life too seriously" and "cannot enjoy today without bothering about tomorrow." They ask "silly questions" to which one has "to lie." After seeing that this is just what Sonia has done, he *finally* comes to see that "Fifi" is a mask and that all his preconceptions of what kind of a woman he is dealing with are wrong. Sonia leaves him because of his lack of perception. This leaves Danilo saddened, and he gets drunk and mumbles, "Where are you, Fifi?" Just as their first meeting left an imprint on Sonia, this second meeting leaves its mark on Danilo.

When they meet for the third time, at a party where he is supposed to fulfill his duty to the government and seduce her into marriage so that her money stays in the country, he confesses his love. It seems as if their masks are finally dropping, but their conversation is confrontational. She rejects him. The reasons for this are not immediately clear. I suspect that it is because once both are unveiled, the fire that attracted them to each other in the first place is dampened. They say goodbye to each other. Unexpectedly, they are then swept up by music and begin to dance.[21] Their use of language to negotiate about love is clearly getting in the way of passion. Like Shanghai Lily, bargaining about love with words is an impoverished form of life. Only by shutting up and being carried away by music can their feelings be expressed and reciprocated. Immediately after the dance, however, the government plot that Danilo should marry the widow is revealed. This fact remains a further mask, a set of lies and hidden motives that Danilo was still wearing. Like the social constraint of being a widow in mourning, Danilo has a veil of duty obscuring his expression of passion. Even if his expression of love is true, it is not visible through the mask of his patriotic duty and the fact that he has been *commanded* to love. Perhaps Sonia recognized that Danilo was not yet able to meet her in a way that was reciprocal and sensitive to her vulnerabilities and demands. By remaining true, somewhat, to the government, he is a traitor to her. He is not solely responsible to the One when he remains responsible to the crowd.[22] For Nietzsche, the wearing of masks must be done in good conscience, by which he means without anything shameful.[23] Danilo's love is a mask that hides the shameful fact that he was essentially commanded to be a gigolo and that he has not been able to overcome that shame and tell Sonia this. He could not find the strength to laugh it all off or put a merry face on the situation. It is essential that the free spirit be without shame (*GS* §254, 266). What enthralled Sonia originally was that Danilo was shameless and liberated. But in their second meeting, she essentially says that Danilo was not superficial out of profundity. Instead, he could not see past the masks to find the emotions that were expressed through the masks. He could not see the need for masks, and he took them as truth.[24] But in their third meeting, Danilo attempts to unmask himself and confess his love, but he has a bad conscience. This causes their love to fail.

In their fourth meeting, Sonia appears at his court-martial trial and proceeds to argue for his innocence of the charges of failing to perform his duty. What is interesting about this scene is that she is clearly wearing a mask. She is there to save Danilo's life, which is to say that she still loves him, but her statement to the jury is a criticism of Danilo for lying and deceiving her. He did everything asked of him, which is to say that he did succeed in seducing her. This means he has made her love him. Sonia's character helps us to see what Nietzsche means by saying that the profound free spirit loves masks, but that what is most profound might actually criticize and seem to hate masks (*BGE* §40). Nietzsche sees this as the most sophisticated sort of mask that is trying "to guard something precious and vulnerable" (*BGE* §40). Sonia criticizes all iterations of Danilo and his masks as a way of masking her own fragile, wounded love, having obviously been hurt by the loss of her first husband. It is not that she really hates all masks, for not only is her criticism a mask but she has fallen for Danilo because of his masquerade. So the logic of Sonia's position must be clear to Danilo. If she was really hurt and did not care for him anymore, then she would not show up at the trial at all. If he is not guilty as she argues (he *has* seduced her), then that means she does want to marry him. Since she has shown up at the trial to argue his innocence, then that means her performance, which chastises him for his actions, is a fake. His cross-examination of her exposes this to us, because no one believes that everything about their love was a lie. But this is what she proclaims. The point of this mask is so that Sonia can express her hurt about being lied to, for being treated like something to conquer, and for being treated like just another "Fifi." She expresses, not in words, the vulnerability that her mourning veil was protecting all along. In other words, this mask is there so that Danilo will finally see her. Although Danilo says that he should be "punished without mercy" for falling in love and not simply being a playboy, I think what is actually happening is that he sees that he has hurt her and perhaps lost her. He has not actually paid attention to her or at least not the right type of attention. He has been too superficial and, thus, he should be punished. He has had a moment of self-awareness in which he can no longer simply *be* a playboy: Sonia has shown to him that it is a role that he dons.

In their final meeting, Sonia visits Danilo in his jail cell, which he can seemingly leave at will. They both put on the masks of indifference toward each other, but it is now clear to both that they do so in order to face their love of each other. They are both now finally able to operate with masks that each of them recognizes as a mask. Being able to see what the other is expressing through the mask is the point when they can finally meet in mutual love.[25] Because Lubitsch's films end with the (re)formation of the couple and the establishment of romance, I think it fair to see them as articulating a picture of *Übermenschen*, both men and women, who are superior to the common, "human, all too human" person, who has no self-awareness when it comes to masks. Rather than being pawns of the unnatural and restrictive moralities that promote shame and *ressentiment*, Lubitsch shows us joyful, promiscuous, untrue free spirits who come to understand the alterity of the Other and the need to veil nature with a subtle touch. Such narrative and structural features within the frame are obviously also essential to the framing device of the Lubitsch touch. Ultimately, I see his works as presenting the more humanistic and self-perfectionist conception of the *Übermensch* that I noted in the introduction as being a common view of what this figure is.

Come Lie with Me: *Trouble in Paradise* (1932)

Lubitsch is known to have said that *Trouble in Paradise* was the best of his films "for pure style."[26] What was meant by that? According to Raphaelson, part of the essence of that style is the puzzle of how to do something without doing it or how to show something without showing it.[27] Lubitsch's "touch" is built upon this obliqueness, or his excellence in "*not* showing things, at leaving things unsaid, at absences and ellipses" (emphasis in original).[28] A Nietzschean approach to the question of style—in this case the style of a person—is that all the strengths and weaknesses are fit together according to an "artistic plan" and "even weaknesses delight the eye" (*GS* §290). The clearest example of this in *Trouble in Paradise* is how Gaston Monescu (Herbert Marshall) manages to use his weakness—namely his need of money—to artfully ensnare Madame Mariette Colet (Kay Francis). For the sake of a 20,000-franc reward, he returns a 125,000-franc purse to Colet, which he stole. He could sell the purse, but he wants to return it in order to gain Colet's confidence. Presumably, then, he should just return it and not take the reward to show how upright and noble he is. Instead, Gaston does not refuse the money and is able to play both to Colet's sympathy and her class instincts. This makes Colet feel comfortable, noble, and superior: she says that she is now glad she "lost" the purse, thus revealing her ignorance, which ultimately makes her unsuitable for Gaston. His response appears refreshingly honest, when he confesses to being a member of the recently bankrupted aristocratic class. Of course, this is a lie. He is a long-time criminal and not, as far as we know, a recent victim of the Depression. Yet he makes his weakness and ignobleness appear as strength and courageousness. Unlike the previous Lubitsch films, the male lead is a criminal and master deceiver. We more easily can see this as embodying a Nietzschean notion of the *Übermensch* as genius, which was seen in the chapter on Hecht's comedies.

Giving style means to conceal what is "ugly that could not be removed" and to reinterpret it and make it sublime (*GS* §290). This seems a fair description of the Lubitsch touch. We see this in many ways in the film. The garbage collector in Venice makes the garbage lovely by placing it in a gondola and singing as he works. The world's ugliness—the Great Depression—is turned into something sublime, whether it is through the perfumed and indirect phrase "in times like these" or in how crime itself must be made into a sublime game by Gaston and Lily. The ugliness of their needs as criminals is first covered in the perfume of upper-class manners. When they begin to reveal who they truly are, they do so through a different game, which still works to cover up the ugliness of their situation. Their new game is the demonstration of their skill to one another through impossible feats of thievery. Also, Madame Colet's entire business is the covering and reinterpreting of one's ugliness (one's smell, one's blemishes) with perfume and cosmetics so as to make one appear sublime. But the film itself also must overcome its own ugliness, namely its paper-thin plot, which can be summarized as a thief manipulating his way into being a personal secretary for the rich head of a cosmetics and perfume company. Romance ensues, but he flees with his accomplice and lover when his identity is revealed. But Gaston has his own way of making this plot sublime and describes it as a Casanova suddenly turning out to be Romeo with a Juliet, who might become Cleopatra. The ambiguity of these relations—Casanova and Cleopatra, Romeo and Juliet—and how they are entwined and need to be tested to see which is which—*that* is the stylistic, sublime way of describing the film. Because we know immediately that Gaston and Lily are free spirited *Übermenschen* who can occupy both of these roles, the driving question of the film becomes whether Colet can be a Cleopatra.

I will set aside much of the economic subtext of the film to explore what many have described as the flowering love affair between Colet and Gaston, because this is the root of the "trouble" in the "paradise" of the film. But regarding that economic subtext, Beach argues against reading the film as expressing a "cynical social attitude" because he believes, firstly, that the film continues to enchant with a stylish vision of luxury and, second, that the film ends with a certain "equality" in love between Gaston and Colet.[29] I disagree with that assessment of the Gaston-Colet affair, and this is important for understanding how the film is critical of Colet and, thus, of her class. The so-called "trouble in paradise" is, according to the opening song, "when something is missing." The opening credits suggest that what is missing is something in the bedroom. What is missing in "paradise" in the biblical story is self-knowledge, which is then what allows carnal knowledge.[30] Colet, while not lacking carnal knowledge, shows herself to be strangely narcissistic. The global economy has collapsed, and rather than reckon with this fact she ignores her board of directors and their advice to cut wages, because she is "bored" and has a luncheon. While it seems like she might be showing concern for the workers, that sentiment is shown to be ephemeral if it existed at all in her. She goes out and buys a 125,000-franc handbag (which Gaston appraises to be worth less than half that amount). She is scolded by a Trotskyite for such extravagance as he yells "phooey" at her. But the real problem, at least for Gaston, is that she actually believes in the aristocratic superiority and does not recognize it to be a mask with which one can play. That is why Gaston cannot ultimately choose to be with her. She is simply too naïve and does not share the same free-spirited and changeable nature that would make her a Cleopatra.

As we have seen, one important aspect of love for Lubitsch is that there be "mystery" in the form of the capacity for reinvention, immorality, and the switching of roles. Gaston, masquerading as LaValle, tells Colet that mystery and bouquet are missing from a love letter from the major that he had found in her stolen purse and read. This lack of mystery is why the love affair between Niki and Franzi fails in *The Smiling Lieutenant*. That lack of mystery, or total exposure to the Other, is presumably why Gaston is tempted away from Lily to Madame Colet in *Trouble in Paradise* in the first place. Yet Colet turns out to be more Juliet than Cleopatra. Her excess and capacity for exploitation are results of her class and status rather than her power. She is no "master" or *Überfrau*. Her exploitation is unconscious, and she is easily fleeced by Gaston and the family friend Giron. She lacks the self-awareness that was missing after the Fall from the Garden of Eden and, therefore, is naïvely romantic about carnality. Colet, in the span of two weeks, is ruled by Gaston, who starts by giving her cosmetics tips and ends up running her diet, exercise routine, finances, and entire household. What makes Gaston and Lily (who appears in Colet's household as Mademoiselle Vautier) a more suitable couple is their ability to reciprocally manipulate each other, to enforce their will on each other. Colet appears mysterious because of her social status and her wealth, but these cannot sustain mystery. They soon are shown as hollow. Lily must overcome her exposure to

Gaston and show that her passion, skill, and inventiveness still retain the power of mystery.

It seems like a mistake to say that the "true 'paradisiacal' sexual relationship" would have been the one with Colet.[31] My sense is that the romance, sentimentality, and melancholy surrounding the attraction between Colet and Gaston come from a place of weakness, of a "human, all too human" need to control and be controlled. Marriage in Lubitsch's films must preserve freedom within coupling, but as the Gaston and Colet become more and more entangled, we clearly see their freedom being lost. Gaston would be Colet's Svengali, and, like the marriage in *The Love Parade*, Gaston would lose his life of excitement. Am I saying that the "ultra-romantic sad farewell" between Gaston and Colet is a fake?[32] Yes and no. He does fall for Colet, in large part because the romantic and economic are so intertwined in this film, but he also comes to see "what is missing," which makes a relationship with her impossible. In the Lubitsch universe, more reciprocity *and* more artifice are needed, which is what Lily provides.[33] Lily loves Gaston for his ability to swindle and rob. Colet is attracted to him in part because she believes that she is helping him as part of the nouveau poor and because she seems to like being dominated by him. In other words, her love is mixed with pity and generosity (morality) and the economics of both. Even if love and economics cannot be fully separated in this particular film world, Lily and Gaston are able as free spirits to live joyously immoral lives not constrained by social masks. It may be argued that locating the true possibility for love in the relationship between Lily and Gaston does not do justice to the real attraction between Colet and Gaston or the sadness of their parting.[34] My sense is that the Monsieur LaValle role that he plays with Colet is too ludicrous and too similar to his role as the "baron" earlier in the film to be a life worth living. Colet is exposed as being unable to take that aristocratic role *as a role* when she is willing to immediately call the police if Gaston turns out to be a thief, but she is unwilling to do it to Giron, the chairman of the board of directors at Colet and Company and "distinguished citizen," who has been robbing her blind. Gaston seems to be correct that Colet is classist.

But it is not that simple, because it is not at all clear that Colet's purported difference in how she might handle the two criminals is explainable by class prejudice. Her hesitation to prosecute a friend of the family for forty years versus a man she has known for only two weeks is more than mere class prejudice. Indeed, the real trouble with the relationship is articulated by Colet herself. She could not see that what Gaston wanted was her 100,000 francs; she thought only that he wanted her. She was unable to see how economic and romantic interests are intertwined and how that lack of purity in love requires us to take it, like all things, as a game of illusions.[35] Lily is able to accept the ambiguity of love. She recognizes that it is not clear whether it is serious, comedic, generous, exploitative, good, or evil. It is all of the above. Lubitsch's earlier musical comedies seem to hold that love and desire will be sullied if intermixed with avarice and societal norms. In those works, love has to be beyond the social, the political, and the economic. But the entwinement of these interests and the situatedness of lovers in a social world become more and more a feature of his films.[36] In other words, within Lubitsch's early comedies, lovers cannot come together when there is no mystery, and economic and social interests stand in the way of such mystery. But in *Trouble in Paradise*, we see that the lovers must not simply be able to retain mystery through their clothes, masks, and aristocratic palaces, but they must also maintain it together as they toil and earn their livelihood by their wits. Love and economics must both be subject to the *Bovarysme* of the free spirt.[37]

In the final confrontation between the members of the love triangle, Lily is only partially right to say that the only barrier to the romance between Colet and Gaston is the 100,000 francs that Colet believes that he has stolen from her safe. She is right because Colet's inability to see the interconnectedness of the economic and amorous is the problem.[38] But it is not literally a problem, because if she could forgive Giron a much greater theft, she could do the same for Gaston. After all, her purse cost more than the amount stolen from the safe. She is in fact ready to forgive Gaston even after all the deceptions unravel. So the trouble in paradise is not the money. It is not class. It is Colet's seriousness and her inability to have an ironic, playful distance from life.[39] It is her inability to be both Juliet and Cleopatra simultaneously, to sustain mystery in both private and public. This is what Lily is able to do and to demonstrate in the final scene. She appears like a prideful, moral, and scorned lover (a Juliet) by sacrificing and casting the money aside. She then appears like a vindictive, amoral, and wrathful Cleopatra, by taking the money as the purchase price of Gaston. If Colet could play such roles, she might have immediately seen that he was a crook, just as Lily and Gaston immediately sniffed each other out. This is articulated clearly in his parting remark to Colet. Gaston asks her whether she knows what she is missing, which is the answer to the question of what is the "trouble in paradise." She nods as if she does know. Her seductive nod and refusal to speak impolitely of sex imply that she believes that she is missing the spiritual and sexual pleasure of a life with Gaston as her husband. Again, this shows precisely why she cannot be with Gaston. She does not know what she is missing, and she cannot imagine that the question has any other sort of answer.[40] But of course it does when dealing with a thief. Lily would have known immediately to check for what she was missing. It turns out that Gaston has stolen a necklace to give as a gift to Lily. The necklace is what Colet is missing, and that is the trouble in paradise, in the sense that Colet is unable to think in these terms like a true Cleopatra. That Lily is quite capable of what Colet is not capable of is shown again in the final scene in the taxicab, where we see that Lily has already picked Gaston's pocket, and he has done the same to her. The attempt to argue that the film is socially conservative and merely providing a "utopian form of entertainment" seems to me to fail to understand the basic reasons why Gaston does what he does. The final moments expose that his deeper feelings are for Lily and that Colet remains as witless as she first appears in her company board meeting.[41] The loving theatricality of the one-upmanship of the two crooks is a sharp contrast to the idealized theatricality of the famous "goodbye" scene between Colet and Gaston, which may express true longing on Gaston's part, but it is a longing for ease that stems from weakness to no longer have to perform and invent himself. That the film does not condemn the greed of the criminal and, instead, criticizes the egoism and obliviousness of the wealthy does speak of class critique. In its crudest terms, Gaston shows that the perfume heiress thinks her shit doesn't stink. She believes that love and survival are not ugly and in need of masks. She is wrong about both.

Nietzsche's Cinematic Fate

I want to briefly discuss *Bluebeard's Eighth Wife* (1938), *Ninotchka* (1939), *The Shop Around the Corner* (1940), *That Uncertain Feeling* (1941), *To Be or Not to Be* (1942), and *Heaven Can Wait* (1943). My sense is that these films show us how Lubitsch turns against the anarchical and antisocial elements associated with the free spirit who embraces naturalism against bourgeois morality, illusion against truth, mutability against stability, and the gay couple against society. This shift is a microcosm of how Hollywood in general turned against the sort of ideas that we have seen associated with Nietzsche's thought. Even after hundreds of restrictions on Jews and other minorities in Germany and the controversies around the Munich Olympics, it was really the events of 1938—the *Anschluss* and *Kristallnacht*—that resulted in a cataclysmic shift intellectually, culturally, and cinematically against the radical ideas that I have described as Nietzscheanism in film. Even the cynic Ben Hecht came to embrace religion and his Jewish heritage, although he could not ever escape his low opinion of humanity in general. Hecht's work also shows us this sort of shift. He penned one of the final 1930s screwball comedies, *It's a Wonderful World*, which was released in 1939, and it contains the same themes that we have seen in his other works: two deceptive outcasts, a poet (Claudette Colbert) and a private detective (James Stewart), bamboozle the world and joyously thwart the law. After that, Hecht's work shifts, tackling race in *Lady of the Tropics* (1939), authoritarianism, violence, and the power of press to bring about justice in *Let Freedom Ring* (1939), and race is addressed again when a murderous cult is thwarted in *Gunga Din* (1939). It becomes difficult to find the sort of cynicism of traditional values that characterizes Hecht's early work. In fact, in the 1940s, several of his screenplays become outright patriotic.

None of this should be especially surprising. We see this shift within Jimmy Stewart's films too. After appearing in Hecht's *It's a Wonderful World*, he then fights corruption in *Mr. Smith Goes to Washington* (1939), is a pacifist committed to justice in *Destry Rides Again* (1939), appears in Lubitsch's *The Shop Around the Corner* (1940), which I will discuss below, is persecuted by Nazis in *The Mortal Storm* (1940), and rails against Nietzscheanism in *No Time for Comedy* (1940). In that forgotten film, Stewart plays Gaylord Esterbrook, who becomes a successful playwright through comedies but tries to write a serious "plea for the human race against dictatorship" called *The Way of the World*. He is told it is terrible, and he rages against the "beautiful superiority" and egoistic "self-sufficiency" of elites (namely, his wife), who do not need anybody and who are logical but unfeeling. The critics see his worldview as sentimental, romantic, idealistic, and infantile. Despite the failure of his play, it awakens in his wife a recognition that one must believe in all the humble voices of all those anonymous people in the world who "are kind and only ask to be permitted to live." The decision is made to return to comedy, a satire of all those "smug, contented callous stuffed shirts, the people who think dictators are inevitable, who say that the average man is bloodthirsty and contemptible." That shift in the film represents the film industry's own turn against Nietzscheanism.

Returning to Lubitsch, *Bluebeard's Eighth Wife* alludes to the preludes to war when a department store clerk says that there are enough problems in Europe already without a revolution in selling pajama tops without the bottoms. The film, written by Billy Wilder and Charles Backett, is based on a 1921 play by Alfred Savoir. I am unaware of Savoir's knowledge of Nietzsche, but it should be noted that his play *He* (*Lui*) begins at the International Congress on Free Thought resolving to abolish God. A character named "He" who claims to be God is in attendance. *Bluebeard's Eighth Wife*, like all Lubitsch adaptations, takes little more than the most general scenario from the source material. This film is explicitly a dismemberment of a sort of *Übermensch*. Gary Cooper's Mr. Brandon is the American skyscraper soul personified, a businessman who treats love and marriage like he is merely acquiring oil or tin. Unlike Cooper's crude but still artistic and passionate character in *Design for Living*, Brandon seems to embody H. L. Mencken's conception of the superman as engaged in one thing: exploitation. Colbert's character has to "break him down" and crush his ego, driving him into a nervous breakdown, a divorce, a sanitarium, and a straitjacket. Ironically, Brandon calls his wife an animal and pleads with her to sit down with him and discuss things like a human being. Lubitsch's earlier films typically end with the recognition of *différance*, a recognition of the Other as Other, as continual transcendence. Socially disruptive acts of immorality motivate the formation of a couple committed to play and illusion. This is not true of *Bluebeard's Eighth Wife*, which ends with Colbert saying, "I'm free, independent, rich. We're on equal terms, Michael." This, among many other things, aligns it with the Cavellian remarriage comedy, wherein the main story is the deconstruction of the elite egoist or the inhuman skeptic within us in order to recreate the human capable of standing in relations of equality. For Cavell, the remarriage comedy shows us a response to a "moral cynicism," which Brandon embodies and which tempts us to "give up on a life more coherent and admirable than seems affordable after the compromises of adulthood come to obscure the promise and dreams of youth."[42] Overcoming that threat of moral cynicism and egoism requires that we enter into a sort of self-assessment and conversation with another, in which "I" and "we" engage in "becoming the ones we are."[43] I have already mentioned that the earlier Lubitsch films have affinities with Cavell's analysis of the remarriage genre through their commitment to the formation of the couple. For example, Cavell notes that remarriage is formed by showing the willingness to risk "social station" and employ the "capacity for inventiveness, improvisation," which allows the "marriage partners" to behave "in ways incomprehensible to the rest of society."[44] But *Bluebeard's Eighth Wife* employs this capacity for inventiveness in order to form a couple that will finally, after seven previous marriages, be comprehensible to the rest of society.

While there are Nazis who salute Hitler in *Ninotchka* (1939), the joke is that those Germans appear to the Russians like other Russians. Garbo's Ninotchka has the same problem as Brandon did in *Bluebeard's Eighth Wife*: she is unfeeling and all business. She treats the entire world around her as "an interesting subject of study." She clearly sees herself as a new and superior human. Purges in Russia result in fewer but better Russians, and the capitalists are a type that will soon be extinct. We cannot be sure whether Nietzsche was meant to be associated with the crude materialism that Ninotchka expresses (only Marx is mentioned by name). Both *Ninotchka* and *Bluebeard's Eighth Wife* are written by Billy Wilder and Charles Brackett, and so it is natural to think that the earlier conception of the free spirit, found in the Raphaelson films, is not only absent but is actually exposed as problematic. Something like Mencken's conception of Nietzsche as a naturalist and pragmatic realist can easily support the absurdity of the "barbaric" Ninotchka, who rejects all sentimentality as false and "analyzes everything out of existence." We are certainly no longer dealing with an *Übermensch* in the degenerative, romantic character of Leon, whose free-spiritedness would be valued in the earlier movies. Leon wants Ninotchka to smile and laugh, because, he argues, nothing is worth taking seriously and because of the whole ridiculous spectacle of life. That sort of flippant nihilism is shown to be false. Leon does not even hold such a sentiment and takes his love of Ninotchka very seriously. The point of laughter in the film is that it makes us human—it binds the Russian envoy, French socialite, and the common worker together. It is clear that Swana, the exiled Russian countess, is nearest to the free-spirit figure. She lives by the motto "never complain, never explain" and cynically laughs at the unseriousness of love and at the idea of "regeneration." But unlike the playful, cynical figures of Lubitsch's earlier films, who, from a Nietzschean perspective, *correctly* realize that one should not have to explain nor reveal the hurt behind the mask, Swana is the villain of film.

The Lubitsch-Raphaelson partnership returns in *The Shop Around the Corner* (1940) and *Heaven Can Wait* (1943). *The Shop Around the Corner* is another ode to love and a criticism of both the unfeeling businessman and the immoral cad. James Stewart's Alfred Kralik appears to Margaret Sullavan's Klara Novak as an unsophisticated, low-class clerk. She condemns him as insignificant and forgettable as she fantasizes about the superior, cultured man with whom she has been corresponding, who happens to also be Kralik. Her fantasies of an *Übermensch* and "kulturist" are exposed as petty and snobbish. Rather than praising the playful free spirit who rejects morality, the womanizing clerk Vadas is physically assaulted and publicly humiliated. *Heaven Can Wait* tells us the story of Henry van Cleve, who believes, upon death, that he belongs in hell. His life, he says, was that of a cynic, but the worst that can be said about him is that he appears to have had some minor extramarital affairs of an undisclosed nature. He is called "the great cavalier of the gay '90s," who in his late forties is a "retired Casanova," but the film is not focused on such escapades. Instead, the film presents us the tamest, most boring Casanova ever put to screen. We see nothing but his honest love and mostly traditional marriage, which makes Gene Tierney's character into "the happiest woman in the world." Ultimately, Satan himself decides that this Casanova made everyone around him happy and deserves to be in heaven. So far, each Lubitsch film starting in 1938 makes an explicit turn against the modern Casanovas and Cleopatras of his earlier films. Such free spirits must either disappear or be converted into something traditional.

That Uncertain Feeling (1941) was scripted by Donald Ogden Stewart, whose work on several significant Katharine Hepburn films contributed to Cavell's remarriage comedy sequence. He also wrote the screenplay to the patriotic, anti-fascist film *Keeper of the Flame*. The enemy of *That Uncertain Feeling* first appears as Freud in the guise of Dr. Vengard, the psychologist who introduces a crack in the marriage of the Bakers. The true threat is the entirely neurotic, cowardly pianist and seducer of Mrs. Baker, Alexander Sebastian. This "complete individualist," who is against everything and everybody, is clearly a sort of nihilist whose philosophical equivalent is some amalgamation of Schopenhauer and Nietzsche. He proclaims, "I hate my fellow man and he hates me." According to Sebastian, to be okay with infidelity is to be "modern," and to object to it is to be a "conventional citizen" to whom one needs to lie. But ultimately, the values of the conventional marriage are affirmed via a rejection of all that is "modern"—both modern art, modern psychology, and modern living.

To Be or Not to Be (1942) was scripted by Edwin Justus Mayer, who had earlier screenplays drawn from preexisting work by Ben Hecht and Noël Coward. The need of everyone to be an actor all the time, which was central to both Hecht's comedies and Lubitsch's, is now placed in the serious situation of escaping the Nazis. The acting troupe appears like an earnest group of blue-collar workers, except for the two stars. Rather than living as lithographs, as in Hecht's films, or living in a pure farce in which even an apparent murder-suicide is filled with mirth, as in Lubitsch's earlier films, the actors in this film are brave heroes and resistance fighters. They are committed both to one another and to Poland. As it turns out, the Nazis actually now appear as lithographs, as campy, and as pure farce, which suggests that the sort of nihilism in which the free spirit plays endlessly with masks and overturns all values is now being condemned. That is to say, the weakness of the Nazis' commitments and the superficiality of their concerns show that it is all an act, albeit an especially deadly one. Now we see that free-spiritedness can become rudderless and can act as a collective mask and mass delusion through which horrendous atrocities can be farcically justified.

I certainly do not mean to lessen the importance and richness of these films by briefly showing how they suggest a conscious turn against the radical free-spiritedness of the earlier Lubitsch. But it is rather obvious how they oppose themselves to the sorts of themes we have seen in earlier chapters. This conflict with the Nietzschean cinematic tradition does not lessen the merits of these films. It simply shows them to have reverted to a more traditional moral foundation, as a counterreaction to earlier cinematic excesses. To do so was essential given the cultural and world-historical shifts taking place during these years.

Conclusion

A Nietzschean Film-Philosophy

Nietzschean Films: An Incomplete Historical Picture

In this work, I have offered a reading of early Hollywood film from the late 1910s to the mid-1930s that has shown that Nietzsche's philosophy and his conception of the *Übermensch* were projected with remarkable (and largely unnoticed) frequency. After showing how Nietzsche's philosophy was initially vilified as destructive egoism in socially progressive films and the early horror genre, I gave both historical and interpretive evidence that a Nietzschean series of films emerged. It began with Stroheim's silent films in the late 1910s and early 1920s and then developed in numerous silent films based on literary works, such as those by Jack London, Eugene O'Neill, Hermann Sudermann, Vivente Blasco Ibáñez, Georges Clemenceau, and Somerset Maugham. While I did not engage those 1920s literary adaptations in great depth, it is not hard to see the heroic passions and tragic collapses of these figures as more or less directly inspired by the *Übermenschen* of their source materials. But it was in the development of sound film and with the talent that moved to Hollywood to write for them that the most definitive films of the *Übermensch* emerged. I have shown how this philosophy can be found in the gangster genre, in films depicting liberated women, in the scripts of Ben Hecht, and in the films of Josef von Sternberg and Ernst Lubitsch. I certainly do not mean this to be an exhaustive list of Nietzschean-inspired films even within the pre–World War II films that are my focus. In fact, the writing of Zoe Akins and Anita Loos, the direction of Dorothy Arzner and Howard Hawks, and many of the films of Greta Garbo, Norma Shearer, Barbara Stanwyck, and Katharine

Hepburn could each contribute another chapter to the representation of the *Übermensch* in early 1930s cinema.

It is an undisputed fact that Nietzsche's cultural relevance was profoundly impacted by the Second World War. Even the most radical Nietzscheans, like Ben Hecht, seemed to turn away from his thought, as I have discussed in the concluding chapter. Hitchcock's depiction of the Nietzsche-inspired murder by Leopold and Loeb in *Rope* (1948) is representative of how the culture once again began to portray the *Übermensch*, namely by reverting to misunderstandings of his thought that we saw in 1910s. While I do not think it impossible to find Nietzschean influence and philosophical affinities after the 1930s, it is also the case that psychoanalysis and post-war existentialism would come to become far more culturally influential and cinematically relevant than Nietzsche. The main figures in the Nietzschean "cult" in American culture either moved on to other things or found themselves excluded from Hollywood, as in the cases of Stroheim and Sternberg. The heady mixture of Nietzsche and Mencken, which we know enflamed writers like Hecht, had to adjust to changing realities and maturing visions of the world. One obvious exception to the dilution and eventual disappearance of Nietzsche on film is the work of Orson Welles, which Deleuze has briefly but convincingly argued for as being deeply Nietzschean. I also do not doubt that more general Nietzschean themes than those that I have discussed could be found in many post-war films, especially as a fascist or monstrous threat. Any extended analysis of the continuation of this tradition would have to contend with more traditional moral and humanistic elements that I have said are already present, for example, in Lubitsch's films. My concern is that such analyses would be little more than a series of loose associations that would, at best, allow us to illustrate some philosophical ideas and themes that have affinities with Nietzsche. There would not be the same concerted effort to embody the *Übermensch* idea and its radical inversion of values as found in the films discussed in the previous chapters.

Nietzschean Film-Philosophy

The question of method is an important one in film philosophy. Are we just loosely applying theory to a set of films, or do the films themselves intentionally embody the philosophical themes and offer their own visual method of doing philosophy? I have argued that the latter is case in the sequence of Nietzschean films from the 1930s. But just as there are many ways to do philosophy, so also are there many ways in which films themselves may be said to be philosophical or to do philosophy. I have focused on films for which there is some historical connection to the Nietzsche vogue in the English-speaking world. I have done this because I expect there to be some doubt that films of this era could be engaged in advancing the radical Nietzschean philosophy that I have described. I have wanted to connect these films with Nietzsche's thought in a way that is stronger than the mere fact that Nietzschean theory *can be* imposed on these works. They may also be regarded as embodying a modernist Nietzschean aesthetics. This connection between aesthetic style and philosophical content is obviously strengthened by the historical significance of Nietzsche for the artists involved in these films. But this historical connection also allows us to say that these films are capable of *doing* philosophy in a more significant way than "providing accessible interpretations of key elements" of Nietzsche's theories.[1] While I do not want to say that being illustrative is not a significant way that film can do (contribute to and promulgate) philosophy, Nietzschean philosophy is surely something more than a theoretical activity that stands in need of illustration. It harbors within it challenges to the very values that underlie such theoretical activity. Truth, consciousness, and language are all deconstructed as social and, thus, as *herd* phenomena, which is to say that they carry within them, like an atavism, the history of the will to power. But these notions can be revalued as part of the aesthetic redemption of life from its degraded state. Much like Derrida's concept of the incalculability, heterogeneity, and singularity of the Other, we might say that Nietzschean philosophy aims less for a theory that stands in need of illustrations and more for a series of provocations that stand in need of enactments, of embodiments that both deconstruct attitudes and values and construct the possibilities of alternatives both on film and in the lives of spectators. Illustrations stand as clarifications of theoretical concepts against the standard of some ultimate interpretive truth. But is there one noncontradictory way to understand the *Übermensch*, the eternal recurrence of the same, or the person that loves? Such a form of life might take the form of a world-historical act, as in Sternberg's *Dishonored*, or it might take the form of a journalistic pursuit of the next big story, or it might simply manifest as a new playful formation of the couple. We might say that films that illustrate philosophical theories are attempts to *describe* what there is (reality, the world, Being, etc.). Nietzschean philosophy, at least as it has been presented in this work, is attempting to break down our descriptions of what there is and to challenge the prominence of Being itself, so that Dionysian becoming will manifest both individually, socially, philosophically, and aesthetically. Films that adopt such a philosophy must themselves find ways of disrupting the categories of Being, Truth, and the Good and become provocative, singular performances. While we can always draw generalizations about human life and society from such films, reducing these films to such generalizations will inevitably lose something of the singularity of the voice, performance, and vision within each of them.

I have advanced ideas similar to the ones in the previous sentences in a study of the possibility of a film aesthetics derived from the work of Max Scheler: "We can say that Scheler's aesthetic theory is that art is the construction of an order of love (or of hate) (*ordo amoris, ordo odii*), and aesthetic experience is the intuiting of that order through a conative adoption of it. When we come to inhabit the value universe of an artwork, we grasp the spiritual essence—the order of love and hate—through an 'understanding love' of another being."[2] While Scheler's concepts are not Nietzsche's, the order of love and hate that he takes as the value essence of persons and of their artistic creations marks them as utterly singular in nature, or "personal." Scheler's personalism, his metaphysical account of the reality of value, and his theories of co-feeling that challenge classical conceptions of "the subject" or "the self" result, at least on my account, in a concept of art as the enactment of personal style (or of multiple personal styles if many are involved in the art object's creation) and in an account of the experience of art as the experience of another person or persons in their singularity and alterity. But despite the unique personal order of values that make up the essence of the singular being, Scheler holds that values are themselves objective, universal, and sharable. Nietzsche rejects such a theory of value. While he and Scheler share a commitment to the singular style of the person and to the centrality of value and affect to all expression, Nietzsche sees the singular being as a unique, historical quanta of power whose value orientation is their own nonobjective fate and aesthetic creation. In Deleuze's terms, film is an encounter with the "one" who is "always the index of a multiplicity: an event, a singularity, a life."[3] What this means for the study of film in the previous chapters is that we must try to grasp them in their provocative singularity, as an event and a life, which is manifest both in the content and characters of the film (the singular *Übermensch*) and in the film itself as an expression of the singularity of either the writer, the director, the actors, or all of the above. If film form and film content are enactments of philosophically challenging lives and values, then to think of film as philosophy is to think of how these lives show us the viability of an aesthetic existence that challenges the idols of society, morality, and metaphysics through the singularity of its value creation. Sternberg noted that his films were an attempt to "attract others into my world, but my world is not the form of the crowds."[4] The significance of such enactments is much more than that they illustrate a theory or aid us in understanding reality. While Scheler stresses our conative experience of the Other and their order of love and hate, which is an objective albeit emotionally grasped order of values, Nietzsche's view is a more agonistic approach. Not only must our lives and values confront the unique style and values of the other person, but we must confront the radical, inhuman possibilities that threaten all categories of Being and all our settled values.

This value-focused, radically singular, and agonistic conception of film offers a unique account of "film as philosophy." There are of course many accounts of what film-philosophy is. Wartenberg argues that film as illustration has a "philosophical punch" because of the "immediacy" (compared to other artforms) of its "temporally developing images" that "confront us with a counterfeit of our everyday experience of the world."[5] Mulhall has stressed that films are philosophical when they "engage in systematic and sophisticated thinking about their themes and about themselves" and are subject to "the claims of reason," even if their access to reason is through "imaginative and emotional responses."[6] Pippin has said that he considers "film as a form of moral reflection itself" or, at least, "moral exploration" that operates with "generality" and "illuminating exemplarity . . . but in a way not incorporable in a 'theory.'"[7] Frampton takes a more Deleuzian approach and argues that film offers its own unique form of nonconceptual, poetic, and image-based thinking that can sit alongside philosophy as "a companion in concept-creation."[8] Sinnerbrink has argued that some "cinematic thinking"—in some particularly challenging films—"provokes and defies interpretive coherence" by, at least in some instances, offering a "vertiginous doubling" through "nesting interconnected cinematic worlds, multiple narrative lines, and blurring character identities," while in other cases presenting a traumatic, violent provocation that also creates a "mood of uncanniness, temporal disorientation and visceral dread."[9] There are as many ways of understanding the philosophical significance of film and the philosophical activity of film as there are ways of characterizing what philosophy does and what art does. Moreover, it seems clear that some films can be regarded as "thinking" in several of these ways at once. Because of this, there is no real advantage to trying to sort out which of these different models of film-philosophy is superior. It can simply be said that different broadly philosophical films engage in philosophical activity in different ways.

My primary aim has been to show that a set of early Hollywood films, many of which are not widely recognized as being "philosophical" in any important sense, can be regarded as constituting a sequence of Nietzschean films. I have also suggested that the philosophical work in those films can be regarded as having affinities with Nietzsche's own philosophical activity. I have called this the production of a moving image of perspectivism, which provides a tragicomic and cynical deconstruction of the sacred idols of metaphysics and morality. Sternberg wrote that cinema has placed contrasting values side by side and created social turbulence because "opposites can remain undisturbed only if one doesn't know too much of the other."[10] Broadly speaking, we might call this *moral reflection*, as Pippin does, at least in the sense that Nietzsche's own *On the Genealogy of Morality* is engaged in *moral exploration*. But of course, I have argued that, rather than providing us with generalizable ethical insights, these films offer us images of lives that are immoral, singular, inhuman, and asocial. There is something great, terrifying, and dangerous in the behaviors shown to us. And it is not obvious that we can or should emulate them. Thinking now of the formal features of the films, we also find something disorientating and metaphysically challenging in the dualities and absences of the Lubitsch touch, the claustrophobic visual world of Sternberg, the camp of Marlene Dietrich, the deceptiveness and verbal explosion of Hecht's energetic comedies, the contradictory, self-undermining turns of the gangsters and liberated women, and the jarring repetitive cuts between symbols by Stroheim. So it is not obvious that there is one way that these films make their point. While there are similarities between the different visions of the *Übermensch* that I have explored, there are also significant differences between the degenerative kulturist, the gangster, the liberated woman, the artistic genius, the Dionysian lover of fate, and the free-spirited couple. It is not clear that, combined, they offer anything like a general ethics of how we can be "super" or illustrate a single concept of what a life should be. There simply is no prescriptive ethics of eternal recurrence and the love of fate. The reason for this is that lives are different from each other and contain a heterogeneity of impulses, passions, and possibilities within themselves. Of course, that suggests that we cannot possibly generalize how the spectator might encounter and interpret these provocations. They may use them as invitations for more traditional moral reflection. They may regard them as powerful illustrations of a theory or as engaging in concept creation. Yet a Nietzschean concept of the value of art is that it is intended to work a revolution in the values of a person and to potentially create philosophers (or film directors?) of the future. I have argued that we have good historical reasons to think that the artists and films that I have focused on are part of a broader Nietzschean movement in the arts that thought similarly.

Nietzsche's aesthetics are, like many of his views, hard to pin down. I want to mention several remarks that he makes that support the view I have just articulated. Nietzsche says that art may be monological, which he says "forgets the world" and presents the artist's own life and style in the work rather than being concerned about satisfying the "witness," or audience (*GS* §367). Art of this type emerges from "superabundance" rather than "hunger," and it can take two forms: it can be devoted to "destruction, change, and becoming" and is "pregnant with a future," or it can take up the task of "immortalizing," a spreading of glory and gratitude (*GS* §370). Art is best thought of as "the *good* will to appearance" and the "good conscience to be *able* to turn ourselves" into an "aesthetic phenomenon" while standing "*above* morality" and avoiding "irritable honesty" (*GS* §164, emphasis in original).[11] The task here is not to provide "the sweet sentiments of virtue" (*GS* §381). The artist "transforms things until they mirror" their own power and values, and their art then manifests as a Dionysian excitation and enhancement of the "whole affective system" (*TI* 9 §9–10). Here we see Nietzschean art as an utterly individual expression and as a "great stimulus to life" (*TI* 9 §24). That great stimulation of life can provoke us into our own artistry, awakening within us the power to enter "into any skin, into any affect" and to be capable of "constantly transforming" oneself (*TI* 9 §10). Thus, the task of art is akin to the task of friendship for Nietzsche.

What many accounts of film as philosophy do is figure out how it is that film can occupy the realm of *logos*, how it can stand, as Mulhall puts it, before the claims of reason. It surely can perform such a function. But having argued that Nietzschean philosophy as embodied in these films challenges such logocentrism, we might say that film can be philosophy via its proximity to myth. But myths are not, as Singer puts it, "works of art that purvey a significant level of insight about the world and our concrete involvement in it."[12] According to Nietzsche, Socratism as a manifestation of *logos* was the death of myth, whereas myth represents a Dionysian wisdom, partially shielded in Apollonian imagery. As Blumenberg notes, the roots of myth are poetry and terror.[13] Tragic myth, according to Nietzsche, emerges as a necessary effect of "a glance into the inside and terrors of nature," an effect that uses "the Apollonian aspect of the mask" and is, thus, "appearance through and through" (*BT* §9). Myth is used to capture or symbolize the capacity for terrible anti-natural events by the human. Myth demonstrates heroic destructiveness that brings the "world of phenomena to its limits," such that "every law, every natural order, even the moral world may perish through [the hero's] actions," but the outcome of such destruction is a "higher magical circle of effects which found a new world on the ruins of the old one that has been overthrown" (*BT* §22, 9). Myths live and evolve. They are rooted in feeling, which is lost when they are taken to be about something real, such as a historical fact (*BT* §10). Myth cannot be captured in words by philosophers or poets; rather, the deeper affective core of Dionysian wisdom is found in "the structure of the scenes and the visual images" behind the myth, which is a strikingly cinematic description by Nietzsche (*BT* §17). To reduce them to descriptions of facts robs the myth of its "mythopoeic power" (*BT* §17). Rather than a claim about reality, Nietzsche holds that myth is that through which experiences are seen and interpreted: through myth we press "the stamp of the eternal" on the moments of our lives (*BT* §23).[14] Art that is mythological aims to transfigure the individual in this way, and it works through affective and aesthetic dissonance (*BT* §24).[15]

Rather than dismiss this theory of myth as a piece of Nietzschean juvenilia, I am perhaps in the minority in thinking that it continues to play a significant role in his theory of art.[16] Great art inspires us to "love fate"—it can, like great pain or suffering, lead us to recognize "whatever is necessary" and to "not only bear it" but to "love it" (*NCW* Epilogue §1). Art can be a "teacher of great suspicion," leading us to "put away all trust, all good-naturedness, all that would veil, all mildness, all that is medium" and make us "more profound" (*NCW* Epilogue §1; *GS* P §3). Art should not placate us or confirm who we are; it should drop one into "the abyss of great suspicion" and "self-mastery" whereby "one returns newborn, having shed one's skin, more ticklish and sarcastic, with a more delicate taste for joy, with a more tender tongue for all good things, with gayer senses, with a second dangerous innocence in joy, more childlike and yet a hundred times more subtle than one has ever been before" (*NCW* Epilogue §2; *GS* P §4).[17] This conception of art as a sort of purifying fire is said to be completely opposed to those who dwell on pleasure, particularly "spiritual pleasures" and "passions," which "the educated rabble loves" as it praises what is "elevated" and what is romantically "exaggerated" (*NCW* Epilogue §2; *GS* P §4). One might then assume that Nietzschean art will be ponderous, cold, intellectual, and pedantic, but, in fact, quite the opposite is true. Nietzsche envisions an art that is "a mocking, light, fleeting, divinely untroubled, divinely artificial art, which, like a pure flame, licks into unclouded skies" (*NCW* Epilogue §2; *GS* P §4). All of these ideas can be traced back to the dual impulses of the Apollonian and Dionysian in his early theory of tragic myth and to similar criticisms that he made of the German public.

But how do these claims about art and myth relate to film and to idea that both the content of film and the film itself are encounters with the singularity of another person and their embodiment of their own values and fate? While I do not *simply* want to equate the films that I have discussed with myth, I am suggesting that the way that they can be said to "philosophize" or "think" is through these visions of lives, of bodies in action, that are steeped in affective and mythopoeic power. Each of films that I have discussed offers us images of a life, often both tragic and comedic at the same time. They present us with destructive, heroic figures who press their values into the world, allowing them to forget "what is" in order to pursue a future that may never be. We can see the *Übermensch*'s enactment of value in the world as a constantly creative self-mythologizing, of turning one's acts into a symbolic, eternal struggle. The films themselves are creations of the visionary life of an artist or artists who do the same. But this is not a conception of the individual as a "sovereign individual."[18] That concept, found in Nietzsche's *On the Genealogy of Morality*, does not represent his ideal. Instead, our filmed *Übermenschen* cannot do otherwise; they are fated. How they embrace that fact constitutes their relative freedom compared to those who do not. Film itself mythologizes by trapping time, eternalizing it, allowing it to be replayed again and again. The camera, Sternberg remarks, imprisons the moment: but it does not simply record. The artist's function is to endow the image "with force and power, no matter what the nature of the subject may be."[19] That is, art's function is to mythologize. Ideally, film's imprisonment of the moment embodies the vision and values of its creators. It enlarges and makes monumental moments of a life, turning life into an aesthetic phenomenon, dressed, posed, framed, and laden with significance in the unfolding tragicomedy. The films that I have focused on operate through the dissonance they create via their immoral *Übermenschen* and the rest of the world. These lives move us, enlivening the senses and our affective natures, not because we empathetically and emotionally enter their situation and value orientation, as Scheler would have it. Instead, they present us, through their own dangerous existence, the challenge to eternally justify our existence, as Nietzsche put it in *The Birth of Tragedy*, or to respond to the thought of the eternal recurrence of the same, as he would later put it. We must enact our own genius, press our own values into the world, and, thus, embrace our fate.

The ways of visualizing this imperative are diverse. These films do not offer us a singular way of understanding the world as it appears or as it is. They seem to offer us inhuman and unnatural tales of joyous destruction, imaginings of human possibility beyond its rational limits. We can see this as quite similar to myth, because the purpose of myth is not in the domain of *logos*, or what Nietzsche calls "science" in *The Birth of Tragedy*. Can such imaginative constructions of superhuman possibility be thought of as "thinking" or philosophy? Nietzsche defines philosophy as an art of transfiguration, which takes the individual's states and transposes them into "the most spiritual form and distance" (*GS* P §3). The philosopher for Nietzsche does not have what the "rabble" calls wisdom and, instead, lives "unwisely" and "*imprudently*," living dangerously and playfully, exploring "a hundred attempts and temptations of life" (*BGE* §205, emphasis in original). Philosophers give "an account of themselves" and are committed to "experiment" but are not skeptics: they assert and create their values in the world (*BGE* §210–211). To create art or philosophy in such an experimental, imaginative way is to be an "attempter" (*BGE* §42). Each attempt is also obviously singular, although its presentation as a mythical vision can obviously be theorized about and studied, as I have done. Perhaps this helps to understand Blumenberg's comment that, for Aristotle, *philósophos* and *philómythos* come from the same root, *wonder*.[20] Philosophy, myth, and art are "personal confessions of the authors," a sort of "memoir," a giving of form to a life, and an assertion of value (*BGE* §6). The wonder that underlies philosophy and myth is wonder at the uniqueness of the other person in their singularity.[21]

I recognize that a view such as this does not align with many accounts of philosophy's relation to film. Yet it seems to me to be a straightforward implication of the interpretation of Nietzsche offered by Nehamas, which concentrates on the implications of "perspectivism" and "aestheticism."[22] Perspectivism is the claim that there are only interpretations and are no possible appeals to "the real" or "the world" to settle the interpretive and evaluative activities that different persons pursue. Aestheticism means that one "looks at the world in general as if it were a sort of artwork" and that life is intimately related to artistic creation because it has an output that is "unique."[23] Any particular "interpretation," as an expression of a singular life, "does not provide a model for imitation," as interpretations are dependent on a unique situation, time, inner strength, and values.[24] Nehamas argues that Nietzsche adopts "stylistic pluralism," or the continual "changing of genres and styles in order to make his presence as an author literally unforgettable and in order to prevent his readers from overlooking the fact that his views necessarily originate with him."[25] Nietzsche turns out to be an unreliable narrator, and his work itself is something of a montage. While Nehamas focuses on the agonistic multiplicity of styles and voices or, we might say, Nietzsche's revelation of his perspectivism of form, I would also say that the content of his thought, his attempt to capture the struggle of opposites, leads to a "philosophy of contradictions" and to "insurmountable contradictions in his philosophy."[26] The Apollonian and the Dionysian, the universal and the particular, freedom and fate, strength and weakness, law and disorder, truth and falsity—Nietzsche's philosophy experiments on both sides of the dichotomies, succumbing to the pull of one or the other, in order to reach a position that promotes an "idiosyncratic, recognizable manner" of navigating the field of human possibility, its desires, beliefs, actions, and values.[27] I take all of this to be representative of what myth does for Nietzsche—not myth as a free-floating narrative capturing ideas universal to humanity, but myth as articulated by individual artists who use its symbolic, unnatural, tragic, and divine tales to aestheticize, to interpret their own lives, to embody their own values. Myth allows the individual to reckon with both fate and terror by eternalizing one's experience or, we might say, placing it on a stage of the grandest drama.[28] Like Oscar Jaffe and Lily Garland in *Twentieth Century*, self-mythologization and self-stylization through dramatic, comic, and passionate enactments, inspired by the enactments of others, result in a figure who is, as Hecht calls, a lithograph and even a series of often conflicting lithographs.

Film-Style, Film-Form, and Film-Ontology

Somewhat sporadically throughout these chapters, I have touched on formal aspects of these films and related topics in the ontology of film. Based on what I have just described as Nietzsche's aesthetics and his overall challenge to the traditional philosophical and metaphysical dichotomies that prop up notions of "naturalism" (as opposed to taking the sociality and artificiality of humans as central) and "realism" (as opposed to taking notions like myth, dream, and the future as most "real"), it is not surprising that a fleshed-out Nietzschean film aesthetics would diverge from much traditional film analysis and film ontology.[29] By abolishing the distinction between a "true" world and an "apparent" one, we might say that Nietzsche ends up with a sort of ontological monism in which there is nothing but enactments of will to power. "*This world is the will to power—and nothing besides*" (*WP* §1067, emphasis in original). This would allow us to say, with Cavell, that film consists of "world projections," at least in a very special sense of "world"—namely, projections of an individual's values and personal mythologizing.[30] For Nietzsche, the merely apparent or the false—whether we call this art, subjective experience, consciousness, language, myth, or any other interpretation of the world—are enactments with the same status as their alternatives, called science, objective fact, the world, truth, and so on. This sort of ontological monism can distinguish these enactments according to their value, that is according to how subtly, joyously, skillfully, aesthetically, uniquely, and even deceptively they are performed. That is to say, the issue is not whether something is real or illusion, true or false, but whether it is expressive, revolutionary, and bold in its reckoning with fate and the process of becoming. That means of course that film analysis necessarily will have to deal with the style of such enactments. What is style? We encounter style through our sense of the other as a singular, as a particular piece of fate and value enactment. Style marks the object as the product of the expressive vision of the artist.[31] It can be manifest in both form and content. We should perhaps accept Carroll's point about the heterogeneity of the "film medium," that is, there is no medium-specific way that film must make its point.[32] It could be found in its writing, visual composition, editing, set or sound design, acting performances, and so on, and much of this can be found in other art forms. Furthermore, films are collective works of art, capable of containing the styles of multiple artists—most obviously writer, director, and actor.

My sense is that Nietzsche would agree with Scheler and Merleau-Ponty that the style or singular personality of the human being can be "seen and grasped in one's glance" and the same goes for the artist's personal style in the art object.[33] To grasp the uniqueness of their style is to grasp what separates them from others. This anti-skeptical view is stated by Merleau-Ponty as the fact that we have a gestalt experience of the Other: they are "directly manifest to us as behavior" and in the objects that they fashion.[34] Also, Merleau-Ponty accepts a holism with regards to art; there are no "distinct 'problems'" that can be separated between the form and content: all aspects of an artwork are "branches of Being," and "each entwines the tufts of all the rest."[35] This conception of art is built upon a physiognomic or gestural conception of perception (and, thus, of understanding), which is to say that perception is inseparable from the field of historical and cultural significances that imbue our gestures with meaning and tradition. Each person and art object relates to those significances by a unique series of convergences and divergences expressed in their behavior and body. In this way, the embodied activity of a person is expressive of their individual voice and vision, and this is something that we grasp through our own enculturated life, our affects, and our body. As Merleau-Ponty says, cinema's movement consists not in "the activity of the characters" but in the fact that cinema's moments are "pregnant" with their opposites: the visible and the audible are filled with the invisible and the inaudible. We bring to film our own behavioral, cultural, sensory, and affective fields of significance. The constant interplay between the photographed fragments of a world and the social and behavioral worlds that we inhabit offscreen is what grounds the gestural or expressive movement of film. Whether present in the form or the content of the film, films are an interlaying of behavior, which is expressive of the "questioning" of the singular person "toward the natural and [social] world through divergences."[36] Film itself becomes a "temporal *gestalt*" of expressive human behavior rather than merely a sequence of shots or images.[37] "The meaning of a film is incorporated into its rhythm just as the meaning of a gesture may immediately be read in that gesture."[38] The idea is similarly stated by Agamben that "the element of cinema is gesture and not image," which is to say that "cinema has its center in the gesture and not in the image" and that "it belongs essentially to the realm of ethics and politics (and not simply to that of aesthetics)."[39]

This combination of Nietzsche, Scheler, Merleau-Ponty, and Agamben into a rough outline of a personalist, gestural film aesthetics obviously differs from many other major theories in the field. The one that I want to turn to is Deleuze's, for despite the focus he shares on the singularity of a life and my use of his ideas about Nietzsche, truth and film, I find myself disagreeing with his views on film and its history. I have discussed how I see these Nietzschean films as failing to conform with what he describes as "classic cinema," which is dominated by "movement-images" that are "in accord with our commonsense categories of a uniform temporal succession in a Cartesian, Newtonian space."[40] What is the alternative to this picture? It is a cinema of time-images. One description of that alternative is that it consists of present moments that are doubled, "at once a moment of actual present and virtual past," which I have applied to the films of Stroheim, but which is obviously a feature of all expressive human gestures.[41] Another description is that such cinema offers a "coexistence of compossible and incompossible worlds" that act as "an image of time as a branching labyrinth of possible realities," which is at work in all films that can be called moving images of perspectivism.[42] For even if the individuals of those films are fated, within the conflict of contrasting value systems the labyrinth of possibilities is made visible to the audience. Another description of what films of the time-image do is that they appear as "powers of the false," which means that they express "becoming, dynamic change, metamorphosis, and transformation" and, thus, "undermine fixed identities, thereby falsifying established truths and generating new forms."[43] I have argued that this is present within the histories of degeneration offered by Stroheim, the films of the liberated woman, the tragedies of Sternberg, and the comedies of Ben Hecht and Ernst Lubitsch. Yet another way of describing Deleuze's point is that movement-images try to picture time, whereas a cinema of time-images has "movement subservient to time."[44] I have argued that we see this in how history and degeneration drive the films of Stroheim, how the future drives the gangster, and how the shifting power of masks is the "action" of the superwomen and in Lubitsch's works. With regard to Hecht's comedies, I have said that this priority of time over movement is found in the logorrhea of the characters, offering an unrelenting "sound image," or "sonsign."[45] But we can also find it in the visually striking and often silent images of Sternberg's Dietrich films. These are films in which movement is always secondary to the claustrophobic circle of fated time. A final aspect of the cinema of the time-image is that it has significant "gaps"—the images are "disconnected from their customary sequences," or disconnected from common patterns of "sensory-motor schema."[46] Deleuze describes this as the possibility that characters might find themselves in situations in which their perceptions cannot develop into actions: the situation is "too powerful, or too painful, too beautiful" and "the sensory motor link is broken," resulting in a "purely optical and aural situation."[47] Is this not found in the inaction and breakdowns in *Little Caesar* and *Scarface*, as well as in the moments of crisis in *Baby Face*, and in the Dionysian self-destruction that appears like action but is a force beyond human agency in the films of Stroheim and Sternberg? The fact that these aspects of modern cinema can be found in the Nietzschean films of the classical era is not entirely at odds with Deleuze, who says that "the direct time-image is the phantom which has always haunted the cinema," but he does continue to say that it is given only "a body" in modern cinema.⁴⁸ But from the perspective of the film analyses that I have provided, Deleuze's division seems unsustainable. All human behavior is unnatural, artificial, cultural, filled with the past, a labyrinth of possibilities, and riddled with gaps due to the force of circumstances and the limitations of the human will, our Apollonian consciousness, and our herd language. Could "classical" cinema ever have covered this up?⁴⁹

Another way of moving beyond this distinction of cinema types is to turn to Derrida's remarks on photography. He describes photography as creating an archive, a literal writing with light, that creates a "graphic memory" of something entirely singular, a momentary play of light and darkness that "took place *one time only*, occurred only once," and, thus, shares with the human subject and their gestures the quality of being "unique" (emphasis in original).⁵⁰ He argues that the technology of the photograph "becomes the truth of *physis*" not in the sense that it inscribes reality into a reproducible "archive," but that "in *physis* already, the *interstice* will have been open, like a shutter, so that photography might attest to it" (emphasis in original).⁵¹ I take this to mean that photography is a sort of model of the way in which the physical world is always mediated by human technics—whether that is culture, language, science, or technology. Humans are the sort of being that specializes in the capturing of moments, and what we can capture, for example in art, memory, story, and language, is what comes to define "the Real." This also shows how all revealing, or "archiving," of the moment and of ourselves is marked by *différance*, by the gaps that fragment all identity, because what we are able to "record" or "remember" is always an interpretation. Interpretations are partial because each moment and each thing contain a multitude of possibilities, so the formation of any stable, archived identity is, we might say, a theatrical converting of ourselves into something visible, into an image *for* others.⁵² Photography accentuates this "confusion," in which the real and the artificial cannot be distinguished, both by presenting the event of the singular person and by not presenting it and giving us "the veil, the film, the membrane of the simulacrum."⁵³ This relates photography to desire, to seductiveness, for Derrida, as it is the body and gesture of the Other that are caught on film in a way that is non-reductive or is itself a gesture toward the alterity or transcendence of the Other. This is true even if what is filmed is simply the material world, as the camera itself is a series of gestures.⁵⁴ But photography is also related to death, to a memory of the past, to the "presence of a disappearance."⁵⁵ Photography grasps something "to let it be lost"; it archives what "took place once and is lost," making it "a sort of cenotaph: an empty tomb."⁵⁶

Photography is seen like the act of mourning, "bearing witness" to the surprising "instant of imminence" and making it "an irrecusable past."[57]

Thus, Derrida is less interested in how photography relates to Being, "the world," or to what is real, and is more interested in how it relates to Non-Being, how it is *en abyme*.[58] This leads him to make the linkage between "Dionysianism, philosophy, and photography," but we can also see its Apollonian aspects through its surface of images.[59] Yet to characterize photography flat-footedly as simply archiving, recording, or capturing the moment is not quite accurate. Such a description implies a passive relationship to what is archived or recorded.[60] Derrida argues that photography is ambiguously situated between the idea that it provides a "discovery or a revelation of what is already there" versus an "invention in the sense of production, creation, productive imagination," which "produces the other there where he is not."[61] This suggests that photography is a sort of "performativity" and concerns a "truth to be *made*" that sits alongside and interferes with any attempt to say that photography *simply* reveals, unveils, or exposes the world or others (emphasis in original).[62] Derrida summarizes his view by saying that "the spectral is the essence of photography."[63] At work here is the "right of inspection" to view the Other, to capture "the other in effigy," and to take the "other's piece."[64] While there are many differences between still and moving pictures, I do not see that Derrida's analysis depends on the *stillness* of photography. Thus, I assume that much of his view extends to film.

A Derridian analysis of any cinematic "archive" would be that it exists in a phantasmagoric in-between, neither representing some notion of objective time as quantitative multiplicity (the movement-image) nor the lived-time of duration as qualitative multiplicity (the time-image). The image is not to be modeled on consciousness or intuition, nor on inner or outer experience. Instead, comparing it to a text, a signature, a performance, and an empty tomb, Derrida sees the image as mere fragments of a life, suspended gestures, that retain traces of the style or uniqueness of the Other. A way of summarizing the difference between a Deleuzian analysis of time and the image and a Derridian one (and to do so via a connection to Nietzsche) is to see this as a fundamental difference about the idea of the eternal recurrence of the same and what an art that embodies that actually looks like. My sense is that Deleuze distorts Nietzsche's idea. He describes it as believing in "the being of becoming itself" and as a durational account of time in which the past and future are retained in a present that radiates many possible futures.[65] He denies that the eternal recurrence of the same actually means that "the same" returns, and, instead, converts it merely into the idea of "returning itself," which he describes simply as a "principle which serves as an explanation of diversity."[66] He also translates the resultant value-orientation as an "ethical thought" that the human will is creative, because it is an affirmation of "the existence of becoming-active."[67] Derrida understands Nietzsche's doctrine in more radical terms as a fidelity to "the revolution that bears us along" or *amour fati*, the love of fate.[68] He sees Nietzsche as describing a performance or gesture that relates to the Other and to the abyss, a gesture that promises to "say yes" to whatever emerges but is also capable of willing illusion, deception, and mythologizing whatever emerges. We might call the eternal recurrence of the same the will to mythologize or place every event in the shadow of eternity and fate. This leads Derrida to link "fidelity, parody, forgetting, or recording" as acts of "repetition," in which affirmation can take on different registers or styles.[69] Mythologizing might take the form of melodrama or farce. So the idea of eternal recurrence of the same is, in fact, that the events of our lives and the world itself repeat, as we interpret, reinterpret, photograph, film, and, in general, archive them, and that their affective nature can change with each repetition. Our mythologizing and self-stylization are constructive performances, gestures, in relation to the relentless destruction by which everything passes into its opposite and into the past. I find Agamben more representative of Derrida's approach, when he argues that "the thought of the eternal return, in fact, is intelligible only as a gesture in which power and act, naturalness and manner, contingency and necessity become indiscernible (ultimately, in other words, only as theater)."[70] This is why I have stressed that the *Übermensch* is seen on film through their excessive, inhuman ability to embrace any and every fate or event and to theatricalize it in order to make it both farce and the most important thing in the world at that moment. It is also why we can say that film is doing philosophy because, as theatrical as Nietzsche's writing is, it cannot fully manifest the theatricality of life as eternal return, which is the life of the *Übermensch*.

Admittedly, both Deleuze and Derrida are notoriously obscure and are responding to an obscure concept in Nietzsche. Thus, the power to embody these obscure concepts and gestures on the screen is surely constitutive of a type of philosophy. Nevertheless, a summarization of the past few paragraphs is in order. Deleuze sees classical cinema as merely giving an indirect image of time by constructing an empirical and natural conception of time through spatio-temporal motions, actions, states, and the like. But modern cinema, he contends, presents living time or time as consciousness, thought, or duration, by creating films that abandon the task of resolving their images into a coherent whole. Instead, this type of cinema presents a "sequence of irrational points," in which (a) any sort of outside world is but a trace in the gaps between scenes, (b) narrative and "internal monologue" give ways to free, directionless discourse and vision, and (c) humans and the world are separated.[71] We can call this a cinema that models time as eternal recurrence of the same in terms of the subjective passage of the qualitative activity of thought rather than the quantitative reactive forces of the world. Marking that passage via ruptures is how cinema supposedly results in direct images of time as becoming and repetition. In contrast, Derrida sees within the archiving function of film and photography something like an "*arche-ethical*" gesture of the eternal recurrence of the same or a fidelity and faith, which he describes as "Nietzsche's gesture" toward a "law" that is also a "call [*appel*]" and "reaffirmation" of values (emphasis in original).[72] That notion can be understood as the will to personally affirm some aspect of the text of the world and to maintain fidelity to it by both deconstructing its aspects and preserving it in our creations and gestures.[73] In film, we are faced, regardless of what the content of the image is, with a spectral, moving record of the Other, in their unique singularity. We are given the gesture of their own fidelity and affirmation of this moment. In other words, we are face to face with "a point of singularity that punctures the surface of the reproduction": it addresses us "even though its 'presence' forever escapes" us, yet it also continually returns to us, a "return of the dead," a "spectral arrival in the very space of the photogram."[74] This mythologizing or eternalizing of this loss is at the same time a will to create, even to deceive through the simulacrum. Film and photography are just such performances that challenge us as Nietzsche's demon does to reckon with the possibility of radical affirmation of each moment as fated, as a repeating moment within "tremendous years of recurrence . . . still affirming itself in this uniformity of its courses and years, blessing itself as that which must return eternally, as a becoming that knows no satiety, no disgust, no weariness" (*WP* §1067). Photographic presentations are a "suspending of the Referent" as paradoxically present and absent, and this is pertinent, according to Derrida, "everywhere," not just in these artforms.[75] Faced with presence as absence and absence as presence, the question of the relation of film to "a present or to a real" misses the point: it is a relation "to the other," who is both real and virtual, present and absent, whether on film or not.[76] This is not a conception of time as duration: it is time as "metonymy" as the act of naming, marking, addressing, and substituting. We can look to the films of Sternberg for the clearest expression of this arche-ethical gesture of fidelity, remembrance, desire, forgetting, and death, but it can also easily be seen in the other films that I have discussed as well, albeit in different forms. The faith in the Other seen within those Dionysian films can now be related to the artist's own metonymic archiving or personal way of substituting a curated set of images for the world, as well as the viewer's way of encountering the personal gestures and style of the Other in both film form and film content.

This constructed debate between Deleuze and Derrida regarding cinema and the image has aimed to shed light on a Nietzschean aesthetics. My aim has not been to give a definitive treatment of either Derrida or Deleuze, which, if performed, would surely find deep affinities that may overcome these contrasts. I simply wanted to use this invented debate to aide in illustrating a Dionysian attitude toward film, the rudiments of a gestural, personalist account of film meaning and spectatorship, and to begin to challenge the idea that we can simply partition film history into two different, oppositional regimes of image types. The implication of these contrasting visions for the ontology of film is an emphasis on the singularity and style of artistic creation. We should regard film as an affirmative, constructive valuation for which questions about its truth or relation to "reality" or "the world" seem like the wrong sorts of questions to be asking. Instead, we should be thinking more about our capacities for fidelity to the individuals whose lives and expressions are archived before us. Such an account avoids reducing film into a species of philosophy and illustration, as Mullarkey worries.[77] We have not simply seen one illustration after another of a philosophical idea, which, combined, confirm some truth that Nietzsche also taught us. Rather, we have confronted a number of personal visions and forms of life beyond the "human," which are not entirely compatible with one another. They all present tragic, comic, cynical, and playful expressions of a life outside of traditional morality and committed to the fate of self-invention. They all offer visions critical of the world and capable of challenging us to mythologize or eternalize our own fates through self-overcoming and the enactment of one's own order of value and style. Although I have argued that a specific Nietzschean interpretation of these films is both historically and cinematically justified, I certainly do not mean to have presented anything like an exhaustive treatment of the aesthetic and philosophical values of these films. Many dimensions of the films remain unremarked upon, and the many ways that we may relate to these films and their challenging content remain unexplored.[78] In this sense, the aesthetics outlined above remains "open to the becoming-philosophical of filmic subject matter."[79]

To say much more than this in a conclusion would exceed the function of providing my own gesture at the implications for philosophical film aesthetics of the preceding chapters. This personalist approach to film helps to explain why I have felt the need to focus on talents behind the camera in order to establish a personal vision and connection to Nietzsche that informs the artistic values in the films. But there are other ways that these films could be approached. A more detailed formal approach that also adopts an auteur method to study entire bodies of work would concentrate on the means by which the director addresses us and how we are able to read those directorial gestures situated within our own cultural and embodied existence. Another approach would concentrate on the specific styles and gestures of actors both within individual works and across a body of works. Finally, it is certainly not the case that the film aesthetics that I believe best aligns with Nietzsche's artistic vision must be committed to Nietzsche's specific views about morality. There may well be more objectivity to the values and virtues presentable on screen.

A Final Remark

While this study was inspired by Cavell's *Pursuits of Happiness* and I have borrowed from his claim that film is a "moving image of skepticism" to develop the Nietzschean idea of a "moving image of perspectivism," I have not engaged the substance of Cavell's work as much as I would have liked or as much as I have in earlier drafts.[80] One of the challenges of a sustained, critical encounter with Cavell is that his work on film is explicitly derived from his own singular experience of the films. While his early ontology of film is separable from his later moral perfectionist reading of two film genres, it is not clear that his distinctive style of thinking alongside a set of very specific films can be made to speak to a significantly different set of films. I do think that it is profitable to see the historical sequences of films that he discusses as *responses* to the excesses of this Dionysian tradition, responses that attempt to recover the human and the ordinary. Of course, his readings of some of the films that clearly belong to the remarriage genre can be challenged. My sense is that *His Girl Friday*, the remake of Hecht's *The Front Page*, retains enough of the original to challenge his perfectionist reading of it. Klawans has shown how a film like *The Palm Beach Story* (1942) seems to fit the genre but can actually be read as a "comedy of disillusionment," in which choices do not matter and in which futile and farcical moments create comedy that is more Nietzschean than Emersonian.[81] Might these ideas be extended to unsettle central readings of Cavell's genre analysis, especially *The Lady Eve* (1941)? Might the superhumanity of Hepburn and Grant in *The Philadelphia Story* support a Nietzschean pathos of distance and be more a story about recovering passion than common humanity and ordinary reality? While these are interesting questions, I do not think that we can deny, for the world-historical reasons that I have mentioned, that there is a shift toward (and eventual dominance of) the Capraesque. I think it clear that a Cavellian response to this Nietzschean tradition would see it as still plagued with skepticism, as he often sees Nietzsche—caught within the nihilism that he is attempting to escape. Nevertheless, it would be foolish to deny that Cavell's work has affinities with many aspects of the preceding chapters.

In a way, the difference between a Cavellian viewpoint and the Derridean one that I have leaned on in order to articulate a Nietzschean aesthetics is seen in their distinct employments of Nietzsche when discussing the theory of performatives offered by Cavell's teacher J. L. Austin. Derrida sees the notion of performative speech acts as being free from "the true/false opposition" and, instead, as leading toward an account of "the value of force, of difference of force (*illocutionary* or *perlocutionary force*)," which he says is "nothing less than Nietzschean" (emphasis in original).[82] Cavell says that this is the "reverse" of what he sees in Austin, whose theory of the social context and the felicity of expression and speech behavior can support both the intersubjective aspect of truth as agreement and the idea that, according to the ordinary language account of communication, we are working on a high wire without a net. In other words, we are together, embodied, with no escape from the "unassurance and the opacity" of speech and "the incessant, unending vulnerability of human action."[83] According to Cavell, this is where Austin has a touch of Nietzsche: to abandon the preoccupations of philosophers and metaphysicians, to live out from under the shadow of the death of God, is to return us to the ordinary, sometimes tragic, sometimes felicitous experience of human finitude. But that is not the same as Derrida's (and Nietzsche's) claim that language is innately of the general, a herd phenomenon, and that the address of and force of the Other must be found in the performative, in the agonistic. Another way to state a fundamental contrast here is that for Austin and Cavell, metaphysics is a subset of language invented as a language game by some European philosophers, whereas for Derrida there is no alternative (called "the ordinary") to the metaphysics embedded within language, consciousness, and the oppositional concepts that define all human thought and culture.[84] This difference regarding metaphysics parallels the difference between a philosophical analysis of "the world" in the mode of the "ordinary" and an analysis in the mode of genealogy found in thinkers like Derrida, Nietzsche, and Foucault. This difference of starting points results in a disorienting "turning" of what would appear to be shared concepts, which leads Cavell to say, "I know of no position from which to *settle* this systematic turning" (emphasis in original).[85] As significant as Cavell is to the tradition of film and philosophy within which I am working, I have had to restrain myself from attempting to settle this systematic turning.

Yet we can redescribe this orthogonality. Cavell would likely regard the Nietzschean view adopted for the sake of analyzing this sequence of films as bound to philosophical skepticism, particularly with regard to the Other, because it endorses the flight into something superhuman. Yet it should be clear that these images of the *Übermensch* are not ignoring or expressing horror at our finitude or denying our access to the expressiveness of the Other. I think we can see the contrast between the Nietzschean/Derridean views that I have expressed and Cavell's view by returning to Hecht's cynical world in which expression, affect, and friendship can still flourish. Derrida notes how Austin worries that speech acts are liable to be "infected" by repetitions, deceptions, citations, and other "non-ordinary" and "non-serious" types of speech that are "hollow or void if said by an actor on the stage."[86] Derrida's response, and surely Hecht's too, is that these so-called "parasitic" types of speech are just *what speech is*. Felicity, Austin's stand-in for truth, is possible only through social conformity that shows language, in Nietzsche's terms, to be a herd phenomenon, which is to say, it is an iteration, something *hollow as if said by an actor on a stage*. What Derrida concludes is that every "communication" or "presence" has the "graphematic structure" of *différance*.[87] This means that it is an iteration; each iteration is singular but still an iteration. Does meaning come from these shared iterations, or does it come from the "rupture" or absence that manifests only as the gesture and performance that is marked by the singularity of personal style but also as that which escapes us? Rather than pinning meaning and truth on felicitous expressions and the social, political, and ethical notions of equality that allow us to meet and share the commonplace world, the films and philosophies explored in the previous chapters suggest that it is in the infelicitous, conflictual, and irrational that human and superhuman possibilities lie and enable communication to become multifarious, ambiguous, deceptive, and non-boring.

In spite of Cavell's defense of Austin, Derrida still believes that there is a sort of teleology (and thus metaphysics) at work in the communicative situation that cannot be overcome by a turn to the ordinary. We still "wish to view the world itself," which Derrida sees as the metaphysical, logocentric aspect of the human that cannot be isolated to a subset of language or to a merely modern predicament.[88] Cavell even ascribes this to Nietzsche, calling it "a primordial demand for sense, a demand as original and clear as a baby's cry," which seems to ignore the terrifying, irrational, Dionysianism of that which is "uneducable" and "nonliterate" in us.[89] Again, Cavell would see the denial of this demand for sense as a skepticism that refuses a return to the ordinary, where sense can be found. Derrida would see the hope of escape into the ordinary as retaining the nostalgic, messianic aspects of Heidegger's thought, no matter how phenomenologically rich, partial, tragic, comic, and finite that home in the world is described as being by Cavell. For Derrida, this metaphysical telos can be subverted only by the sort of Nietzschean and deconstructive efforts that are more concerned with being expressions of the value-creative powers of the author than being able to stand up before the claims of reason. But what that also suggests is that the affection of successful communication, especially in art, is not that it is felicitous. It is that is agonistic, challenging, inspiring, rapturous, and, thus, capable of enjoining us to love fate, to be the soul that sacrifices itself to great and terrible things, to be *Übermenschen*.

Notes

Introduction

1. On Nietzsche's early Anglo-American influence, see Patrick Bridgwater, *Nietzsche in Anglosaxony: A Study of Nietzsche's Impact on English and American Literature* (New York: Leicester University Press, 1972); David Thatcher, *Nietzsche in England, 1890–1914* (Toronto: University of Toronto Press, 1970); Manfred Pütz, ed., *Nietzsche in American Literature and Thought* (Columbia, SC: Camden House, 1995); Jennifer Ratner-Rosenhagen, *American Nietzsche: A History of an Icon and His Ideas* (Chicago: University of Chicago Press, 2012); and Hays Alan Steilberg, *Die amerikanische Nietzsche-Rezeption von 1896 bis 1950* (Berlin: de Gruyter, 1996).

2. Gilles Deleuze, *Cinema 2: The Time Image* (Minneapolis: University of Minnesota Press, 1989), 148–49.

3. Stanley Cavell, *Pursuits of Happiness: The Hollywood Comedy of Remarriage* (Cambridge, MA: Harvard University Press, 1981), 262.

4. Mark Steven, "Nietzsche on Film," *Film-Philosophy* 21, no. 1 (2017): 99.

5. Steven, 99.

6. Lea Jacobs, *The Decline of Sentiment: American Film in the 1920s* (Berkeley: University of California Press, 2008), 9.

7. H. L. Mencken, *The Philosophy of Nietzsche*, 3rd ed. (Boston: Luce, 1913), x.

8. Mencken, x. There are different senses of naturalism and animality, and while I tend to avoid these terms, given their opposition to sociality, Lemm interprets them in reference to life as the capacity for deception, forgetting, imagination, and dream. This is more amenable to the views of Nietzsche advanced here rather than many discussions of Nietzsche's naturalism. Vanessa Lemm, *Nietzsche's Animal Philosophy: Culture, Politics, and the Animality of the Human Being* (New York: Fordham University Press, 2009).

9. The idea that film may be "cynical, amoral, nihilistic, politically dubious and antihumanistic" in the sense that it does not present a model of pro-social relations or visions of humanistic freedom is elaborated in Nikolaj Lübecker, *The Feel-Bad Film* (Edinburgh: Edinburgh University Press, 2015), 13. Lübecker points

to how such films have the "capacity to destabilize subjectivities, to overcome distances, to open up bodies" and looks at films that refuse simple emancipatory or redemptive possibilities (Lübecker, 13, 168). In spite of providing an analysis of such antihumanistic films, Lübecker says that we can see them as contributing to "humanism XL," which has a richer, more problematized conception of the human psyche, yet can still contribute to a general human project of *Buildung* (cultural education) (Lübecker, 170). While one can always convert cynical or antihumanist works into lessons on how improve our humanist traditions, it is not clear to me that that is the aim of the Nietzschean project of the *Übermensch*.

10. Stanley Cavell, *Contesting Tears: The Hollywood Melodrama of the Unknown Woman* (Chicago: University of Chicago, 1996), 9.

11. Stanley Cavell, *Cavell on Film* (Albany: SUNY Press, 2005), 89, 55.

12. Cavell, *Contesting Tears*, 11.

13. Gilles Deleuze, *Pure Immanence: Essays on A Life* (New York: Zone Books, 2001), 30.

14. Jacques Rancière, *The Intervals of Cinema* (London and New York: Verso, 2014), 25.

15. Jules de Gaultier, *Bovarysm* (New York: Philosophical Library, 1970), 173.

16. Rancière, *Intervals*, 35.

17. Mary Devereaux, "Oppressive Texts, Resisting Readers and the Gendered Spectator: The New Aesthetics," *Journal of Aesthetics and Art Criticism* 48, no. 4 (1990): 342. While I will not engage the theory of spectatorship in detail, it does not seem difficult to imagine that Nietzsche's unique, often personal, direct, and autobiographical way of addressing his audience translates into a theory of film spectatorship that is individualized and, therefore, heterogenous and historical. On such an approach, see Judith Mayne, *Cinema and Spectatorship* (London and New York: Routledge, 1993).

18. Devereaux, "Oppressive Texts," 342.

19. Devereaux, 343.

20. That model is said to be reliant on "notions of decorum, proportion, formal harmony, respect for tradition, mimesis, self-effacing craftsmanship, and cool control of the perceiver's response." David Bordwell, Janet Staiger, and Kristin Thompson, *The Classical Hollywood Cinema: Film Style and Mode of Production to 1960* (New York: Columbia University Press, 1985), 3–4.

21. Cavell, *Cavell on Film*, 91.

22. Lotte Eisner, *The Haunted Screen: Expressionism in the German Cinema and the Influence of Max Reinhardt* (Berkeley: University of California Press, 1969), 11.

23. Important English works on the early cultural influence of Nietzsche in Germany are Steven Aschheim, *The Nietzsche Legacy in Germany* (Berkeley and Los Angeles: University of California Press, 1992); Seth Taylor, *Left-Wing Nietzscheans: The Politics of German-Expressionism 1910–1920* (Berlin: De Gruyter, 1990); and Carol Diethe, *Nietzsche's Women: Beyond the Whip* (Berlin: De Gruyter, 1996).

24. The details of Nietzsche's influence in France, which flourished prior to the First World War, are given in Christopher Forth, *Zarathustra in Paris: The Nietzsche Vogue in France 1891–1918* (Dekalb, IL: Northern Illinois University Press, 2001).

25. Oscar Levy, "The Nietzsche Movement in England," in *The Complete Works of Friedrich Nietzsche*, vol. 18, *Index to Nietzsche*, ed. Oscar Levy (London: T. H. Foulis, 1913), x. For an overview of Levy's Nietzscheanism, see Dan Stone, "An 'Entirely Tactless Nietzschean Jew': Oscar Levy's Critique of Western Civilization," *Journal of Contemporary History* 36, no. 2 (2001): 271–92.

26. Grace Neal Dolson, *The Philosophy of Friedrich Nietzsche* (New York: MacMillan, 1901), iii.

27. Julius Goldstein, "The Keynote to the Work of Nietzsche," *Mind*, 11, no. 42 (1902): 216.

28. Charles Bakewell, "The Teaching of Nietzsche," *International Journal of Ethics* 9, no. 3 (1899), 314; Herbert Stewart, "Some Criticisms on the Nietzsche Revival," *International Journal of Ethics* 19, no. 4 (1909): 427–43.

29. Paul Elmer More, *The Drift of Romanticism: Shelburne Essays, Eighth Series* (Boston and New York: Houghton Mifflin, 1913), 147.

30. Grace Neal Dolson, "Review: *Nietzsche the Thinker*—A Study by William Mackintire," *International Journal of Ethics* 28, no. 4 (1918): 554.

31. Dickie Loeb was obsessed with Ben Hecht and invited him to hold a literary debate at the Loeb family mansion in 1919. Rather than Nietzsche, Stuart Sherman (screenwriter Samuel Raphaelson's literature professor at the University of Illinois) argued that these "two young supermen" were ripped from the pages of Ben Hecht's novels, *Erik Dorn* and *Humpty Dumpty*. William MacAdams, *Ben Hecht: A Biography* (New York: Barricade Books, 1990), 54.

32. On Nietzsche's relation to the theater and the Nietzscheanism of Strindberg, Shaw, and O'Neill, see David Kornhaber, *The Birth of the Theater from the Spirit of Philosophy: Nietzsche and the Modern Theater* (Evanston, IL: Northwestern University Press, 2016).

33. Thomas Stockham Baker, "Contemporary Criticism of Friedrich Nietzsche," *Journal of Philosophy, Psychology and Scientific Methods* 4, no. 15 (1907): 409, 414.

34. Walter Kaufmann, *Nietzsche: Philosopher, Psychologist, Antichrist*, 4th ed. (Princeton: Princeton University Press, 1974), 308.

35. Bernd Magnus, "Perfectability and Attitude in Nietzsche's 'Übermensch,'" *Review of Metaphysics* 36, no. 3 (1983): 633.

36. Leo Berg, *The Superman in Modern Literature* (London: Jarrold and Sons, 1915).

37. Jacques Derrida, *The Beast and the Sovereign*, vol. 1 (Chicago: University of Chicago Press, 2009), 260.

38. Kaufmann, *Nietzsche*, 309–310.

39. Kaufmann, 316. This superman strives to achieve an integration of their desires and actions, which amounts to a sort of freedom and, with that, an acceptance of responsibility; see Alexander Nehamas, "How One Becomes What One Is," *Philosophical Review* 92, no. 3 (1983): 407.

40. Arthur Danto, *Nietzsche as Philosopher* (New York: Columbia University, 1965), 199.

41. Richard Schacht, *Nietzsche* (London and New York: Routledge, 1983), 340.

42. Schacht says in 1983 that the "metaphor" of the *Übermensch* is made meaningful insofar it designates "the essence of his notion of such higher humanity" (Schacht, 340). The idea that it is a metaphor or an educational image, akin to myth, which is part of a ladder that we climb up and dispense within order to achieve higher humanity ourselves, is stated in his most recent work. See Richard Schacht, *Nietzsche's Kind of Philosophy: What It Is—and Isn't* (University of Chicago Press, forthcoming), chapter 3.

43. A. R. Orage, *Friedrich Nietzsche: The Dionysian Spirit of the Age* (Chicago: A. C. McClurg, 1911), 67, 72.

44. Orage, 75. See also the idea that animal, human, and superhuman constitute fundamentally different types of species in A. R. Orage, *Consciousness: Animal, Human and Superman* (London and Benares: Theosophical Publishing Society, 1907).

45. Orage, *Friedrich Nietzsche*, 81.

46. This view is found in Bertram's influential 1918 interpretation, with which I agree. "Nietzsche's great men . . . are prismatic refractions of the Platonic primal light called 'overman': even their sum total would not yield the original image. . . . The overman is an entirely future reality, never an actually existent one." Ernst Bertram, *Nietzsche: Attempt at a Mythology* (Urbana, IL: University of Illinois Press, 2009), 174. I find this reading to align with the postmodern Nietzsche, where the *Übermensch* is thought of as an unimaginable "break with humanity," a being that is "radically different from any *human* type we might be able to describe." See Michel Haar, "Nietzsche and Metaphysical Language," in *The New Nietzsche*, ed. David Allison (Cambridge: MIT Press, 1977), 24. Also Michel Haar, *Nietzsche and Metaphysics* (Albany: SUNY Press, 1996), 22–27.

47. An excellent account of the rhetorical nature of the idea and of its "danger and horror," albeit one that fails to emphasize the alternatives to a cruel and tyrannical reading, is found in Michael Allen Gillespie, *Nietzsche's Final Teaching* (Chicago: University of Chicago Press, 2017), 59.

48. Stambaugh's work remains an invaluable study of the relations of the superhuman to art, the will to power, and the idea of the eternal recurrence of the same. Joan Stambaugh, *Nietzsche's Thought of Eternal Return* (Baltimore and London: Johns Hopkins University Press, 1972). The "will to power" idea is a far more general one that applies to all life and not simply to the *Übermensch*.

49. Bordwell, Staiger, and Thompson, *Classical Hollywood Cinema*, 231.

50. Such an idea of subordination to impersonal forces was found in radical thinkers such as Sorel and Hulme. See Henry Mead, *T. E. Hulme and the Ideological Politics of Early Modernism* (London: Bloomsbury, 2015), 190. While this idea can easily lead to fascistic subordination of the individual will to the people, nation, or history, this is not necessarily the implication of Nietzsche's view because our fate is always singular or personal.

51. Devereaux, "Oppressive texts," 345. Thus, I will be challenging the idea that the spectators of these films were "supposed, in one way or another, to *believe in it*, to not be placed above the fable, above the lure" (emphasis in

original). Jean-Louis Comolli, *Cinema against Spectacle: Technique and Ideology Revisited* (Amsterdam: Amsterdam University Press, 2015), 107.

52. Comolli, 100.

53. Janko Lavrin, *Nietzsche and Modern Consciousness: A Psycho-critical Study* (London: W. Collins and Sons, 1922), 8, 61.

54. Comolli, *Cinema against Spectacle*, 72.

55. Comolli, 61.

56. Cavell, *Cavell on Film*, 118.

57. Cavell, 117–18.

58. Cavell, 116.

59. Stanley Cavell, *The World Viewed*, rev. ed. (Cambridge, MA: Harvard University Press, 1979), 22.

60. Cavell, 22.

61. Cavell, *Cavell on Film*, 116.

62. For a view of Nietzsche's perspectivism that emphasizes its pluralism rather than its nihilism, see Debra Bergoffen, "Nietzsche's Madman: Perspectivism without Nihilism," in *Nietzsche as Postmodernist: Essays Pro and Con*, ed. Clayton Koelb (Albany: SUNY Press, 1990), 57–71.

63. Maurice Merleau-Ponty, *Phenomenology of Perception* (London and New York: Routledge, 1962), 169.

64. Stanley Cavell, *In Quest of the Ordinary: Lines of Skepticism and Romanticism* (Chicago and London: University of Chicago Press, 1988), 57.

65. Cavell, *Cavell on Film*, 117.

66. Robert Solomon, "Nietzsche *Ad Hominem*: Perspectivism, Personality, and *Ressentiment*," in *The Cambridge Companion to Nietzsche*, eds. Bernd Magnus and Kathleen Higgins (Cambridge: Cambridge University Press, 1996), 183.

67. Maurice Merleau-Ponty, "The Film and the New Psychology," in *Sense and Non-Sense* (Evanston, IL: Northwestern University Press, 1964), 58.

Chapter 1

1. The depiction of Wolf Larsen in the 1941 film of London's *The Sea Wolf* anachronistically makes the *Übermensch* figure into a stand-in for Nazism. Saverio Giovacchini, *Hollywood Modernism: Film and Politics in the Age of the New Deal* (Philadelphia: Temple University Press, 2001), 127.

2. For an excellent overview of interpretations of Nietzsche in relation to evolution and several of the biological theories of his day, see Robert Holub, *Nietzsche in the Nineteenth Century: Social Questions and Philosophical Interventions* (Philadelphia: University of Pennsylvania Press, 2018), chapter 7.

3. On the fact that Nietzsche would oppose eugenics, see Donovan Miyasaki, "Nietzsche's Naturalist Morality of Breeding: A Critique of Eugenics as Taming," in *Nietzsche and the Becoming of Life*, ed. Vanessa Lemm (New York: Fordham University Press, 2015), 194–213.

4. Martin Heidegger, *Nietzsche*, vol. 3 (New York: Harper & Row, 1991), 41, 45.

5. Eugene Fink, *Nietzsche's Philosophy* (London: Continuum, 2003), 12. Such a Schopenhauerian picture is rejected by scholars who see Nietzsche as the enemy of all metaphysical systems, but my sense is that those interpretations needlessly abandon any sort of philosophical ontology because of Nietzsche's condemnation of *transcendent* metaphysics. Two recent works developing Nietzsche's ontology are Paul Loeb, *The Death of Nietzsche's Zarathustra* (Cambridge: Cambridge University Press, 2010) and Bevis McNeil, *Nietzsche and Eternal Recurrence* (Cham, CH: Palgrave Macmillan, 2021). On a more "unitarian" reading of Nietzsche connecting his early and late works, see Tracy Strong, "The Optics of Science, Art, and Life: How Tragedy Begins," in *Nietzsche and the Becoming of Life*, ed. Vanessa Lemm (New York: Fordham University Press, 2015), 19–31.

6. Gianni Vattimo, *Beyond the Subject: Nietzsche, Heidegger, and Hermeneutics* (Albany: SUNY Press, 2019), 4.

7. Jacques Derrida, *Negotiations: Interventions and Interviews, 1971–2001* (Stanford: Stanford University Press, 2002), 221.

8. Nietzsche appropriates this phrase from Horace's *Odes* (1: xii).

9. H. G. Wells, "Human Evolution," *Natural Science* (April 1897): 244.

10. H. G. Wells, *Anticipations of the Reaction of Mechanical and Scientific Progress upon Human Life and Thought* (London: Chapman & Hall, 1902), 318.

11. Heinrich Goebel and Ernest Antrim, "Friedrich Nietzsche's Uebermensch," *Monist* 9, no. 4 (1899): 566–67.

12. Goebel and Antrim, 568.

13. Goebel and Antrim, 570.

14. Sinclair was a reader of Nietzsche who confesses in his autobiography to infusing Nietzsche into his 1903 work *The Journal of Arthur Stirling* and credits himself with launching "the Nietzsche cult in America." Upton Sinclair, *The Autobiography of Upton Sinclair* (New York: Harcourt, Brace, & World. 1962), 86–87.

15. Mencken, *Nietzsche*, 102.

16. Mencken, 138.

17. Mencken, 137.

18. George Santayana, *Winds of Doctrine: Studies in Contemporary Opinion* (New York: Charles Scribner's, 1913), 188.

19. Bruce Barton, *The Man Nobody Knows: A Discovery of the Real Jesus* (Bobbs-Merrill, 1925), 179.

20. George Santayana, *Egotism in German Philosophy* (New York: Charles Scribner's, 1916), 134.

21. Colin Schindler, *Hollywood in Crisis Cinema and American Society, 1929–1939* (London and New York: Routledge, 1996), 9. For an excellent overview of how 1930s cinema combined opposites and exploded cultural divisions in the wake of the economic meltdown, see Lary May, *The Big Tomorrow: Hollywood and the Politics of the American Way* (Chicago and London: University of Chicago Press, 2000), chapter 2.

22. John Warbeke, "Friedrich Nietzsche, Antichrist, Superman, and Pragmatist," *Harvard Theological Review* 2, no. 3 (1909): 371.

23. Scott Nearing, *The Super Race: An American Problem* (New York: Huebsch, 1912), 20–23.

24. Albert Edward Wiggam, *The Next Age of Man* (New York: Blue Ribbon Books, 1927), 121–22.

25. Phil Lonergan, "A Disciple of Nietzsche," *Reel Life* (September 18, 1915): 16.

26. Mencken, *Nietzsche*, 107–108.

27. Mencken, 103.

28. David Ritchie, *Darwinism and Politics* (London: Swan and Sonnenschein, 1891).

29. Bertram Laing, "The Origin of Nietzsche's Problem and Its Solution," *International Journal of Ethics* 26, no. 4 (1916): 520. For a current reading of Nietzsche's criticism of Darwin, see Virginia Cano, "Is Evolution Blind? On Nietzsche's Reception of Darwin," in *Nietzsche and the Becoming of Life*, ed. Vanessa Lemm (New York: Fordham University Press, 2015), 51–66.

30. Laing, "The Origin of Nietzsche's Problem," 521.

31. Laing, 526.

32. Shelley Stamp, *Lois Weber in Early Hollywood* (Berkeley: University of California Press, 2015), 118–20. Other early films that explore eugenics are detailed in Angela Smith, *Hideous Progeny: Disability, Eugenics, and Classic Horror Cinema* (New York: Columbia University Press, 2011), 17.

33. Margaret Sanger, "Family Limitation," 6th ed. (1917), 3.

34. See Melissa Ooten and Sarah Trembanis, "Filming Eugenics: Teaching the History of Eugenics through Film," *Public Historian* 29, no. 3 (2007): 145–55.

35. A dismissal of attempts to de-biologize Nietzsche and to continue to read him as a Darwinian of sorts is found in Peter J. Woodford, *The Moral Meaning of Nature: Nietzsche's Darwinian Religion and Its Critics* (Chicago: University of Chicago Press, 2018), 29.

36. David Strauss, *The Old Faith and the New: A Confession* (London: Asher, 1873), 274–75.

37. David Starr Jordan, *The Heredity of Richard Roe: A Discussion of the Principles of Eugenics* (Boston: American Unitarian Association, 1911), 15.

38. Eugene Talbot, *Degeneracy: Its Signs, Causes and Results* (London: Walter Scott, 1898), 63.

39. Dana Seitler, *Atavistic Tendencies: The Culture of Science in American Modernity* (Minneapolis: University of Minnesota Press, 2008), 130–31. See also Thomas Doherty, *Pre-Code Hollywood: Sex, Immorality, and Insurrection in American Cinema 1930–1934* (New York: Columbia University Press 1999), 256–74.

40. Edgar Rice Burroughs, *Tarzan of the Apes* (New York: A. L. Burt, 1914), 325. On the positive form of atavistic return to our "animal heritage," see David Gerstner, *Manly Arts: Masculinity and Nation in Early American Cinema* (Durham, KY: Duke University Press, 2006), 133–37.

41. See Gerstner, chapter 2.
42. Hudson Maxim, *Defenseless America* (New York: Hearst's International Library, 1915), v, vii, xvi.
43. Maxim, 29, 41.
44. Maxim, 139.
45. Maxim, 42.
46. Maxim, 237.
47. Ralph Waldo Emerson, *The Works of Ralph Waldo Emerson: Miscellanies* (Boston and New York: Fireside Edition: 1878), 180.
48. Maxim, *Defenseless*, 274.
49. J. Stuart Blackton, *The Battle Cry for Peace* (Brooklyn: M. P. Publishing, 1915), 27.
50. Blackton, 56.
51. James Giles Beneficial, "Atavism in Frank Norris and Jack London," *Western American Literature* 4, no. 1 (1969): 15–27.
52. On London's Nietzscheanism, see Ishay Landa, *The Overman in the Marketplace: Nietzschean Heroism in Popular Culture* (Lanham: Rowan and Littlefield, 2007), 118–19. Also Geoffrey Harpham, "Jack London and the Tradition of Superman Socialism," *American Studies* 16, no. 1 (1975): 23–33.
53. Paul Zweig, *The Adventurer* (New York: Basic Books, 1974), 207, 219.
54. Jack London, *Before Adam* (New York: Macmillan, 1915), 179.
55. London, 94–95.
56. Sue Matheson, "The 'True Spirit' of Eating Raw Meat: London, Nietzsche, and Rousseau in Robert Flaherty's *Nanook of the North* (1922)," *Journal of Popular Film and Television* 39, no. 1 (2011): 12–19.
57. Racist depictions of primitivism in the Pacific and Africa can be found in *Lost and Found on a South Sea Island* (1923), *Moana* (1926), *White Shadows in the South Seas* (1928), *The Pagan* (1929), *Tabu* (1931), and *Kongo* (1932, a remake of Tod Browning's *West of Zanzibar*). See Doherty, *Pre-Code Hollywood*, chapter 9.
58. James Chandler, *An Archaeology of Sympathy: The Sentimental Mode in Literature and Cinema* (Chicago: University of Chicago Press, 2013), 250–51.
59. Mary Shelley, *Frankenstein; or, The Modern Prometheus* (London: Puffin Books, 1989), 65, 111.
60. Obviously, the Nietzschean themes continue in 1930s Frankenstein films. This is noted in Michael Sevastakis, *Songs of Love and Death: The Classical American Horror Film of the 1930s* (Westport, CT: Greenwood Press, 1993), 59–74.
61. Edward Said, "Conrad and Nietzsche," in *Joseph Conrad: A Commemoration*, ed. N. Sherry (London: Palgrave, 1976), 65–76. On Conard's engagement with the theme of degeneration, see Daniel Pick, *Faces of Degeneration: A European Disorder, c. 1848–c. 1918* (Cambridge: Cambridge University Press, 1989), 160–62.
62. Joseph Conrad, *Victory* (New York: The Modern Library, 1915), viii.

63. Eisner links the 1916 German Film *Homunculus*, the 1914 and 1920 versions of *The Golem*, and the creation of artificial life in Fritz Lang's *Metropolis* (1926) to the notion of the superman. See Eisner, *Haunted Screen*, 50.

64. John T. Soister and Henry Nicolella, with Steve Joyce and Harry Long, *American Silent Horror, Science Fiction and Fantasy Feature Films, 1913–1929*, vol. 1 (Jefferson, NC: McFarland, 2012), 322.

65. W. Somerset Maugham, *The Magician* (New York: George H. Doran, 1908), 147.

66. Maugham, 179–80.

67. Pick, *Faces of Degeneration*, 165–67.

68. Max Nordau, *Degeneration* (New York: D. Appleton, 1895), 18.

69. Daniel Pick, *Svengali's Web: The Alien Enchanter in Modern Culture* (New Haven, CT: Yale University Press, 2000).

70. Frank Norris, "Lauth," *Overland Monthly* 21, no. 123 (March 1893): 244.

71. Norris, 260.

72. This obviously calls to mind werewolf films, the first of which is *Wolf Blood* (1925), in which a blood transfusion also brings about an atavistic return. An obvious influence on this discourse of human-animal intermixing is Serge Voronoff, who attempted regeneration of humans by grafting animal glands (thin slices of monkey testicles) into the scrotum of men, to improve their sex drive, memory, and eyesight and to reverse a variety of ailments. It was all obviously a fraud, but it was turned into two films, *Black Oxen* (1923) and *Vanity's Price* (1924), featuring women who were revitalized by such human-animal experiments. America had its own version of this, the so-called "goat gland doctor" John Brinkley, who was exposed as a fraud by Dr. Morris Fishbein, an acquaintance of Ben Hecht. The most explicit of these animal-mixing horror films is the odd Bela Lugosi film *Murders in the Rue Morgue* (1932).

73. H. G. Wells, *The Invisible Man: A Grotesque Romance* (New York and London: Harper & Brothers, 1897), 230.

74. Wells, 234.

75. The screenplay of this film was written by Philip Wylie, who wrote the novel *The Gladiator*, in which a doctor creates a superhuman baby through a serum that genetically modifies the fetus that his wife is carrying. This work is credited for inspiring the DC Comics character of Superman. He also wrote works of social criticism (*Generation of Vipers*) and ethics (*An Essay on Morals*), which can easily be seen as Nietzschean in spirit but which have no mention of Nietzsche, given that they were written after all things German had fallen out of favor. Philip Wylie, *Gladiator* (Lincoln, NE: University of Nebraska Press, 2004).

76. H. G. Wells, *The Island of Dr. Moreau: A Possibility* (New York: Stone & Kimball, 1896), 144.

77. As Nietzsche argues, morality is a sort of "official lie" that turns the human against the animal and leads humans to have "contempt" for "the slave as a non-man, as a thing" (*HTH* vol. 1, §40).

Chapter 2

1. Lea Jacobs, *The Decline of Sentiment: American Film in the 1920s* (Berkeley: University of California Press, 2008), 28.

2. "*Différance* points to a *relationship* . . . —a relation to what is other, to what differs in the sense of alterity, to the singularity of the other—but 'at the same time' it also relates to what is to come, to that which will occur in ways which are inappropriable, unforeseen, and therefore urgent, beyond anticipation." Jacques Derrida, "The Deconstruction of Actuality: An Interview with Jacques Derrida," *Radical Philosophy* 68 (Autumn 1994): 31.

3. As Bazin remarked, Stroheim's work is "dominated by sexual obsession and sadism, and that it develops under the aegis of violence and cruelty." See André Bazin, *The Cinema of Cruelty* (New York: Seaver Books, 1982), 6.

4. Drucilla Cornell, *The Philosophy of the Limit* (New York and London: Routledge, 1992), 80.

5. "In his films reality lays itself bare like a suspect confessing under the relentless examination of the commissioner of police. He has one simple rule for direction. Take a close look at the world, keep on doing so, and in the end it will lay bare for you all its cruelty and ugliness." André Bazin, *What Is Cinema?*, vol. 1 (Berkeley: University of California Press, 1967), 27. See also Arthur Lennig, *Stroheim* (Lexington, KY: University of Kentucky Press, 2000), 131.

6. Gilles Deleuze, *Cinema 2: The Time Image* (Minneapolis: University of Minnesota Press, 1989), 141.

7. There are many instances in the following chapters in which connections can be made between the Nietzschean ideas regarding fate, agency, time, and the individual with similar ideas explored by Pippin in the film noir genre, ideas that he summarizes as "the weakness and even futility of our attempts to direct the future rationally (in the face of the conventions of classic realist film and American optimism in general)." Robert Pippin, *Fatalism in American Film Noir: Some Cinematic Philosophy* (Charlottesville and London: University of Chicago Press, 2012), 8. While Pippin traces many different historical reasons for why agents in film noir "look so different," I wonder whether they are so different from the agents in the films that I will discuss. Many of the historical reasons behind film noir apply equally to the historical situation after the first World War and after the Great Crash of 1929.

8. Erich von Stroheim, "In the Morning," *Film History* 2 (1988): 295. Max Nordau, *Paradoxes* (Chicago: L. Schick, 1886).

9. Stroheim, "In the Morning," 293.

10. Frank Norris, *Novels and Essays* (New York: The Library of America, 1986), 241–42.

11. Norris, 241–42.

12. E. Ray Lankester, *Degeneration: A Chapter in Darwinism* (London: Macmillan, 1880), 29. The same ideas of loss of complexity, structure, and function,

as well as the example of parasitism, are found in Eugene Talbot, *Degeneracy: Its Signs, Causes and Results* (London: Walter Scott, 1898), 12–14.

13. As Nietzsche makes clear, there is no single notion of "corruption" or degeneration and it is "something totally different depending on the organism in which it appears" (*BGE* §258). For one organism it may, out of "extravagance of its own moral feelings" fail to pursue a "higher state of *being*" (*BGE* §258, emphasis in original). To abandon such striving is a corruption of "the foundation of the affects, which is called 'life'" (*BGE* §258). For Nietzsche, parasitism is a sort of invalidism or vegetative state, in which society exists for its own sake and we all just merely survive (*TI* "Skirmishes" §36). Ironically, corrupted life continues to live, while uncorrupted life rushes into death.

14. Nordau, *Degeneration*, 261–262, 16.

15. Nordau, 18.

16. Nordau, 18–19.

17. Nordau, 243.

18. Nordau, 260.

19. One source of influence that I will not discuss relates to Stroheim's second film, *The Devil's Pass Key* (1920). It may have received an infusion of Nietzschean ideas from the Baroness Mahrah (Olga) de Meyer, whose short story "Clothes and Treachery" was its foundation. There is the possibility that Stroheim knew Mahrah de Meyer personally. Richard Koszarski, *Von: The Life and Films of Erich Von Stroheim* (New York: Limelight Editions, 2001), 58. We have neither the original story nor the film to determine whether Meyer's work contains the same explicit praise of Nietzschean ideas that are found in her semi-autobiographical novel *Nadine Narska* (New York: Wilmarth Publishing Co., 1916).

20. John Orr, *Cinema and Modernity* (Cambridge: Polity Press, 1993), 16.

21. Orr, 16–17.

22. It has been suggested that *Blind Husbands* essentially creates the *Bergfilme* genre, although the credit cannot be given all to Erich von Stroheim. The story of *Blind Husbands* in fact owes much to his brother, who had published a collection of romantic and religiously symbolic stories about life in the woods and mountains, in which guilty and predatory persons find their doom while the innocent, just, and repentant characters find redemption and peace. Lennig, *Stroheim*, 18–19.

23. Lennig, 114.

24. On the notion of the Dionysian man as actor who stands between the satyr's "all-too-natural" connection to the horror of the abyss and the Apollonian man of reason and culture, see Michel Haar, *Nietzsche and Metaphysics* (Albany: SUNY Press, 1996), 170.

25. Deleuze, *Cinema 2*, 133.

26. Gilles Deleuze, *Cinema 1: The Movement-Image* (Minneapolis: University of Minnesota Press, 1986), 134.

27. Deleuze, 137.

28. Lennig, *Stroheim*, 107.

29. Deleuze, *Cinema 2*, 131.

30. Deleuze, 126–27, 132.//
31. Deleuze, 132.//
32. A broad notion of the uncanny, its literary roots, and its application to film is found in Siegbert Salomon Prawer, *Caligari's Children: The Film as Tale of Terror* (Oxford and New York: Oxford University Press, 1980), 108–137.//
33. Lennig, *Stroheim*, 131.//
34. Lennig, 147, 149.//
35. Lennig, 148.//
36. Lennig, 6.//
37. On this metaphor for degeneration, see Modris Eksteins, "History and Degeneration: Of Birds and Cages," in *Degeneration: The Dark Side of Progress*, ed. J. Edward Chamberlin and Sander Gilman (New York: Columbia University Press, 1985), 1–23.//
38. Frank Norris, *The Octopus* (New York: Doubleday, Page, 1903), 634.//
39. "The dominant hereditary or 'external' forces which often control the lives of his characters shows Stroheim retaining the determinist philosophy of the Naturalist." Joel Finler, *Stroheim* (Berkeley: University of California Press, 1968), 132. On the continued pessimism of Nietzsche and the idea that life is a useless squandering, see Scott Jenkins, "Life, Injustice, and Recurrence," in *Nietzsche and the Becoming of Life*, ed. Vanessa Lemm (New York: Fordham University Press, 2015), 121–36.//
40. Deleuze, *Cinema 1*, 125–27.//
41. Deleuze, 130.//
42. Deleuze, *Cinema 2*, 81–82.//
43. Deleuze, *Cinema 1*, 130, 133.//
44. Thus, I agree with Coates that Stroheim's films must be seen as "mythical, allegorical and naturalistic simultaneously" and even approaching "surrealism" at times. Paul Coates, *Screening the Face* (Basingstoke and New York: Palgrave MacMillan, 2012), 116. However, it seems misleading to identify Mac simply with the emotion of greed, as Coates does. The world external to Mac is far more dominated by this emotion, and he succumbs to it only after a great struggle to live more freely.//
45. In Stroheim's original scenario, when the First World War breaks out, the merry-go-round is controlled by the God of War, Mars. Eventually, he planned for a "personification" of death via a monstrous "crawling animal" representing disease, which would march toward the camera in another moment of dark symbolism. Lennig, *Stroheim*, 177.//
46. See Jacqueline Vansant, *Austria: Made in Hollywood* (Rochester, NY: Camden House, 2019), 23–38.//
47. Georges Lewys, *Merry-Go-Round* (Privately Printed, 1923), prefatory note.//
48. Nordau develops a (rather Schopenhauerian) theory of love in which the lover, stirred by the "sex-centre" of the brain, searches for the embodiment of the "inward ideal" of traits in another individual that would best fit with oneself, and, when found, results in "love on the spot, in an instant" or the snap of a

violin string. Nordau, *Degeneration*, 251. Similarly, love appears in "the matter of an instant" and is "blind" and "unreasoning" in Frank Norris, *McTeague* (New York: Norton, 1997), 104–106.

49. "The Dionysian world . . . is a chaotic world that resembles a sea, agitated by eternally changing yet always self-identical forces." Paul Valadier, "Dionysius versus the Crucified," in *The New Nietzsche*, ed. David Allison (Cambridge, MA: MIT Press, 1985), 248.

50. Ben Hecht, *The Ben Hecht Show: Impolitic Observations from the Freest Thinker of 1950s Television* (Jefferson, NC: McFarland, 1993), 50–51.

51. Ben Hecht, "The Rival Dummy," in *The Collected Stories of Ben Hecht* (New York: Crown, 1945), 458.

52. This idea of non-self-identity is discussed by Mulhall, drawing upon Sartre, but also recognizing in Nietzsche the "dynamics of self-identity as a process of endless self-overcoming." Stephen Mulhall, *The Self and Its Shadows: A Book of Essays on Individuality as Negation in Philosophy and the Arts* (Oxford: Oxford University Press, 2013), 73.

53. "But the double is precisely not a prosthesis: it is an imaginary figure, which, just like the soul, the shadow, the mirror image, haunts the subject like his other, which makes it so that the subject is simultaneously itself and never resembles itself again, which haunts the subject like a subtle and always averted death. This is not always the case, however: when the double materializes, when it becomes visible, it signifies imminent death." Jean Baudrillard, *Simulacra and Simulation* (Ann Arbor, MI: University of Michigan Press, 1994), 95.

54. Jacques Derrida, *Negotiations: Interventions and Interviews, 1971–2001* (Stanford: Stanford University Press, 2002), 226. Because of this, Nietzsche's notion of strength has been called incoherent, but that charge assumes it was his intention that it be a stable category in the first place. See Frederick Olafson, "Nietzsche's Philosophy of Strength: A Paradox in *The Will to Power*," *Philosophy and Phenomenological Research* 51, no. 3 (1991): 557–72.

Chapter 3

1. Jacques Derrida, *Acts of Religion* (New York and London: Routledge, 2002), 236.

2. Derrida, 241.

3. Eugene Fink, *Nietzsche's Philosophy* (London: Continuum, 2003), 70. Fink's view of the will to power as constitutive of all finite things and as the dynamic of opposition and strife in general is opposed, for example, to the neo-Kantian view of some scholars, such as Kain, who argue that the "will to power is a theory of how we construct structures that hide chaos and the horror of existence." Philip Kain, *Nietzsche and the Horror of Existence* (Lanham, MD: Lexington Books, 2009), 39, 31–34. This would seem to identify the will to power with the Apollonian power to bring order and beautiful illusion to existence.

4. Henry Mead, *T. E. Hulme and the Ideological Politics of Early Modernism* (London: Bloomsbury, 2015), 84.

5. The identification of the will to power with a simple doctrine of "force" and a "moral poison" led it to be identified with German militarism and "the justification of every brutality war carries with it." James DeNormandie, "Nietzsche and the Doctrine of Force," *Proceedings of the Massachusetts Historical Society* 3, no. 48 (1915): 171–72.

6. Referring to "The Three Evils" section of *Zarathustra*, Fink points out how power and dominance are revalued as "the principle of restlessness that stirs up individuals and people and pushes them on to the path of history" and as "the openness . . . towards the unpredictable" that manifests as "a generous virtue of an overflowing soul." Fink, *Nietzsche's Philosophy*, 84.

7. Benjamin de Casseres, *The Superman in America* (Seattle: University of Washington Bookstore, 1929), 7.

8. John D. Rockefeller, *Random Reminiscences of Men and Events* (New York: Doubleday, Page, 1909), 71.

9. De Casseres, *Superman in America*, 30.

10. Ralph Waldo Emerson, *Essays: First and Second Series* (New York: Vintage Books/The Library of America, 1990), 176.

11. Emerson, 181–82.

12. Gilles Deleuze, *Cinema 2: The Time Image* (Minneapolis: University of Minnesota Press, 1989), 90–91.

13. Deleuze, 94.

14. Deleuze, 142.

15. An extremely detailed analysis of crime movies and the cultural politics surrounding the film industry from 1906 until 1914 is found in Lee Grieveson, *Policing Cinema: Movies and Censorship in Early-Twentieth-Century America* (Berkeley: University of California Press, 2004). On the development of the genre: William Everson, *American Silent Film* (New York: Oxford University Press, 1978), 227–34.

16. Grieveson notes that the earliest cycle of crime film was focused on "surveillance and policing," which then turned into films focused on "the reformation of gangsters in connection with psychological, sociological, and environmental discourse about crime and city space." Lee Grieveson, "Gangsters and Governance in the Silent Era," in *Mob Culture: Hidden Histories of the American Gangster Film*, ed. Lee Grieveson, Esther Sonnet, and Peter Stanfield (New Brunswick, NJ: Rutgers University Press, 2005), 15.

17. Havelock Ellis, *The Criminal* (New York: Scribner & Welford, 1890), 2. The possibility that there are some Nietzschean influences on Walsh's work is not outlandish. One possible connection will be shown in the next chapter.

18. Raoul Walsh, *Each Man in His Time: The Life Story of a Director* (New York: Farrar, Straus and Giroux, 1974), 115.

19. Owen Kildare, *My Mamie Rose: The Story of My Regeneration: An Autobiography* (New York: Baker and Taylor, 1903).

20. For more details on the crime films of the 1920s, see Kevin Brownlow, *Behind the Mask of Innocence: Sex, Violence, Prejudice, Crime: Films of Social Conscience in the Silent Era* (Berkeley: University of California Press, 1990), 142–211.

21. Gouverneur Morris IV, *The Penalty* (New York: Charles Scribner's and Sons, 1919).

22. Gregory Moore, *Nietzsche, Biology and Metaphor* (Cambridge: Cambridge University Press, 2002), 188.

23. "Those claiming the life of philosophical genius or inspiration can be said to be bad citizens . . . not because they are necessarily lawbreakers or violators of the principles of justice, but because they necessarily criticize the life of these laws, and so seem malcontent . . . they seem to live *against* the spirit, or rather against the actual life, of the laws" (emphasis in original). Stanley Cavell, *Cities of Words: Pedagogical Letters on a Register of the Moral Life* (Cambridge, MA: Harvard University Press, 2004), 225.

24. On the ateleological nature of the will to power, see Christopher Cox, *Nietzsche and Naturalism: Naturalism and Interpretation* (Berkeley: University of California Press, 1999), 229–35.

25. Obviously, that is a controversial claim. Some attribute it to the lost film *The City Gone Wild* (1927). See Julien Gorbach, *The Notorious Ben Hecht: Iconoclastic Writer and Zionist Militant* (West Lafayette: Purdue University Press, 2019), 52. That film was directed by James Cruze (director of *The Great Gabbo*) and written by Charles and Jules Furthman. Of these two Chicago brothers, Jules would go on to be an important screenwriter for both Joseph von Sternberg and for Howard Hawks. But based on the descriptions of its plot, it appears to be a tale of a lawyer (admittedly a crooked one) out for justice and revenge in a world surrounded by gangsters.

26. Ben Hecht, *A Child of the Century* (New York: Simon & Schuster, 1954), 479–80. Gorbach, *Notorious Ben Hecht*, 53. Bull Weed's name is presumably derived from the criminal "Blackie Weed," whom Hecht knew. See Ben Hecht, *Gaily, Gaily* (New York: Doubleday, 1963), 87.

27. Hecht, *A Child of the Century*, 167.

28. Hecht, 167–68.

29. Ben Hecht, *Humpty Dumpty* (New York: Boni and Liveright, 1924), 222.

30. Hecht, *The Ben Hecht Show*, 155.

31. Hecht, 21.

32. For an insightful reading of this notion, see Robert Gooding-Williams, *Zarathustra's Dionysian Modernism* (Stanford: Stanford University Press, 2001), 124–28. Also, Vanessa Lemm, *Nietzsche's Animal Philosophy: Culture, Politics, and the Animality of the Human Being* (New York: Fordham University Press, 2009), 80–85.

33. Deleuze recognizes the cinematic possibility of the transformation of an action, such as a crime, into a series of time-images when it is an "action in a whole network of relations," a transferring or passing of this act "to someone else," which makes these into "symbolic acts that have a purely mental existence

(gift, exchange, and so on)." Gilles Deleuze, *Negotiations* (New York: Columbia University Press, 1995), 54. This strikes me as clearly at stake in the films that are my focus.

34. Everson, *American Silent Film*, 230.

35. The concept of justice will emerge when talking about the films of Sternberg also. On a Nietzschean conception of justice that is not a "passive instrument of measuring or evaluating in the service of science" but is, instead, "an active force of life invested in the becoming of future life," see Vanessa Lemm, "Life and Justice in Nietzsche's Conception of History," in *Nietzsche and the Becoming of Life*, ed. Vanessa Lemm (New York: Fordham University Press, 2015), 105–20. See also Lemm, *Nietzsche's Animal Philosophy*, 75.

36. W. R. Burnett, *Little Caesar* (New York: The Dial Press Burnett, 1958), 18.

37. Burnett, 18.

38. Burnett, 19–20.

39. Burnett, 20.

40. Burnett, 13.

41. It is worth noting that the novel presumably means for the gangster to appear as the embodiment of modern vanity and as the ignoble worship of nobility, whereas the film seems much closer to seeing the gangster as noble and as possessing the "vanity of the *ancient régime*," which is "gay, unconcerned, and frivolous." See René Girard, *Deceit, Desire, and the Novel: Self and Other in Literary Structure* (Baltimore: Johns Hopkins Press, 1965), 120.

42. Jack Shadoian, *Dreams and Dead Ends: The American Gangster Film*, 2nd ed. (Oxford: Oxford University Press, 2003), 43.

43. Shadoian, 40.

44. On the idea of self-overcoming as change and development rather than asceticism and self-denial, see Fink, *Nietzsche's Philosophy*, 70.

45. Burnett, *Little Caesar*, 124.

46. Burnett, 26.

47. Jacques Derrida, *Margins of Philosophy* (Chicago: University of Chicago Press, 1982), 17.

48. Fran Mason, *American Gangster Cinema: From Little Caesar to Pulp Fiction* (Houndsmills and New York: Palgrave Macmillan, 2002), 11.

49. Ben Hecht, "The Sermon in the Depths," *Little Review* 2, no. 3 (1915): 40.

50. Hecht, 40.

51. Hecht, 41.

52. Hecht, 41.

53. It strikes me as rather moralistic to think that Tony is simply a "primordial savage, a Frankenstein's monster bourne of the modern era" and "suggestive of Hitler." Gorbach, *Notorious Ben Hecht*, 59.

54. Mason, *American Gangster Cinema*, 27.

55. James Huneker and Vance Thompson, *M'lle New York* 1, no. 1 (1895): 7.

56. Hecht, *Child of the Century*, 147. Also, Gorbach, *Notorious Ben Hecht*, chapter 2.

Chapter 4

1. Thomas Wartenberg, *Thinking on Screen: Film as Philosophy* (London and New York: Routledge, 2007), chapter 3. I will have more to say about Wartenberg's notion of illustration in the conclusion.

2. Wolfgang Müller-Lauter, *Nietzsche: His Philosophy of Contradictions and the Contradictions of His Philosophy* (Urbana, IL: University of Illinois Press, 1999), 5.

3. Stephen Mulhall, *On Film*, 3rd ed. (London and New York: Routledge, 2016), 89.

4. Mulhall, 87.

5. Gilles Deleuze, *Cinema 2: The Time Image* (Minneapolis: University of Minnesota Press, 1989), 131.

6. Deleuze, 132.

7. Deleuze, 133–34.

8. Jacques Derrida, *Spurs: Nietzsche's Styles* (Chicago: University of Chicago Press, 1979), 97, 101.

9. Derrida, 97, 101.

10. Derrida, 97.

11. It seems to me false that this figure is simply reconstituting the notion of the woman as vamp or *femme fatale* or showing that "any woman who has rational power will invariably use it to destroy man." Catherine Constable, *Thinking in Images: Film Theory, Feminist Philosophy and Marlene Dietrich* (London: BFI, 2005), 117. This figure is not necessarily as manipulative as Constable suggests. That is but one way in which she might appear.

12. On the connection between women and the superhuman, see Debra Bergoffen, "Toward the Body of the Overman," in *Nietzsche and the Becoming of Life*, ed. Vanessa Lemm (New York: Fordham University Press, 2015), 161–76.

13. Derrida, *Spurs*, 97.

14. It is possible to raise a criticism here of Cavell's stress on the "unknown" nature of certain women on film within the genre that he calls the melodrama of the unknown woman. For Cavell, these women want "to be known, or to know that her separateness is acknowledged," but they come to judge that "the world" is "unfit" for such love. Stanley Cavell, *Contesting Tears: The Hollywood Melodrama of the Unknown Woman* (Chicago: University of Chicago, 1996), 17–19. Certainly, he recognizes that this ideal of recognition amounts to the openness to be allowed "to tell and not to tell what she knows," but the limits of this epistemic reading and its connection to a notion of truth, albeit an interpersonal and constructive one, would still be considered as operating within the realm of the phallogocentric philosophy of presence. I take this to be a problem also with Doane's interpretation, when she says that "for Derrida, woman incarnates the *mise-en-abyme* structure of truth." Mary Anne Doane, *Femmes Fatales: Feminism, Film Theory, Psychoanalysis* (New York and London: Routledge, 1991), 59. This formulation still operates under the shadow of the "real world" or of "truth" as a

lost, unattainable mystery. Derrida's terminology of "depthless depth" or "abysmal divergence" points to the fact that only from the *metaphysical* perspective does woman appear as depth and abyss. Derrida, *Spurs*, 51. From the perspective of the text of the Other, women (and men) appear both depth*less* and deep, which is to say that we are confronted with the ambiguous divergence of masks. From the perspective of the logocentric tradition, this ambiguity is an abyss, but from the Dionysian perspective these masks are just affirmative actions and do not "deprive the woman of subjectivity," although the notion of subjectivity undergoes critique and revaluation. Doane, *Femmes Fatales*, 59, 68. Thus, the criticism of both Derrida's and Nietzsche's discussion of the woman and truth as still having "metaphysical baggage" strikes me as a mistaken interpretation that does not follow the tale of how the "real world became myth" to its end. Doane, 60.

15. Derrida, *Spurs*, 101, 97.

16. Derrida, 99.

17. Haskell describes the liberated women of this era, from flappers in the 1920s to the fast-talking dames and gold-diggers of the 1930s, as "Dionysian" in their approach to life. Molly Haskell, *From Reverence to Rape: The Treatment of Women in the Movies*, 2nd ed. (Chicago and London: University of Chicago Press, 1987), 44.

18. Constable is one of the few film scholars who takes up this Derridean and Nietzschean idea of "the radical potential of woman's presentation as the icon of illusion, fiction and fakeness." She also draws upon Derrida's "analysis of the configurations of woman and truth." Constable, *Thinking in Images*, 4, 99–103.

19. "One could indeed characterize Nietzsche's 'ontology' as feminine, or even as gynecological, for this ontology speaks of being as a woman who has no being, as appearance and disguise, as the illusion and mystery of a woman who has no nature, who is pure spectacle." Eric Blondel, "Nietzsche: Life as Metaphor," in *The New Nietzsche*, ed. David Allison (Cambridge, MA: MIT Press, 1985), 156.

20. We might regard these moments as "gaps of a text" and "not only, as signs of elision but as aporias representing important points of articulation between its inside and outside." Peter Brunette and David Wills, *Screen/Play: Derrida and Film Theory* (Princeton: Princeton University Press, 1989), 59. Thus, they stand as counterexamples to Deleuze's claim that such gaps appear only after the classical period.

21. Derrida, *Spurs*, 51–53.

22. Derrida, 57.

23. Jacques Derrida, *Margins of Philosophy* (Chicago: University of Chicago Press, 1982), 10–11.

24. See Hecht's mention of him in his autobiography. Ben Hecht, *A Child of the Century* (New York: Simon & Schuster, 1954), 339, 373. Scola and Markey collaborated on eight films: *Luxury Liner* (1933), *Midnight Mary* (1933), *Lilly Turner* (1933), *Baby Face* (1933), *Female* (1933), *A Modern Hero* (1934), *The Merry Frinks* (1934), and *A Lost Lady* (1934). Nietzschean themes can be found in all

of them. For example. *Lilly Turner* is a strange Depression-era story of survival, scam artists, love, and self-sacrifice, in which the *Überfrau* and *Übermensch* are paraded out as models of health for a con man's traveling "clean living" and self-help scam. My focus is on the more clearly amoral tales rather the moral ones, such as *Midnight Mary*, where Loretta Young gets involved with gangsters but is really quite honest and innocent.

25. She says that she "drifted into a set of intellectuals," including H. L. Mencken, and members of his circle, including Ernest Augustus Boyd, whose books *H. L. Mencken* (New York: Robert M. McBride, 1925) and *The Sacred Egoism of Sinn Fein* (Dublin and London: Maunsel, 1918) show knowledge of and influence by Nietzsche), the novelist Joseph Hergesheimer, and the critic George Jean Nathan. Anita Loos, *Kiss Hollywood Good-By* (New York: Viking Press, 1974), 12. Indeed, Loos's most famous work, *Gentlemen Prefer Blondes*, was inspired by her friendship with Mencken and his falling for a blonde. See Anita Loos, *Anita Loos Rediscovered: Film Treatments and Fiction* (Berkeley: University of California Press, 2003), 45.

26. Loos, *Anita Loos Rediscovered*, 83–86.

27. I do not have any evidence that the author of the source material, Katharine Brush, intended to write on Nietzschean themes, but her forgotten work is an intriguing cynical sort of feminism. It would be used in the early Claudette Colbert and Ginger Rogers film *Young Man of Manhattan* (1930), in which the former is a journalist and the latter a flapper. Her work was also used in the convoluted *Lady of Secrets* (1936), scripted by Zoë Akins. It would be quite easy to regard the hardworking, independent women in the other two films based on Brush's work to be *Überfrauen*, Joan Crawford in *Mannequin* (1937) and Madeleine Carroll in *Honeymoon in Bali* (1939).

28. Loos, *Kiss Hollywood Good-By*, 39.

29. On the vamp as "the enemy" created by a "puritanical impulse," see Haskell, *From Reverence to Rape*, 102.

30. Mary MacLane, *I, Mary MacLane: A Diary of Human Days* (New York: Frederick A. Stokes, 1917), 1–4, 90–91.

31. Mary MacLane, *Human Days: A Mary MacLane Reader* (Austin, TX: Petrarca Press, 2014), 305.

32. Mary MacLane "The Movies—and Me," *Photoplay* (January 1918): 25.

33. MacLane, 25.

34. For his influence on feminism and anarchism in Germany, see R. Hinton Thomas, *Nietzsche in German Politics and Society 1890–1918* (Manchester: Manchester University Press, 1983), chapters 5 and 7. His influence on feminism is also discussed in Steven Ascheim, *The Nietzsche Legacy in Germany: 1800–1900* (Berkeley: University of California Press, 1992), 85–93.

35. "Did Nietzsche predict the Superwoman as well as the Superman?," *Current Literature* 43 (1907): 643–44. For the superwoman notion in British feminism, see Lucy Delap, "The Superwoman: Theories of Gender and Genius in Edwardian Britain," *Historical Journal* 47, no. 1 (2004): 101–26.

36. Jennifer Ratner-Rosenhagen, *American Nietzsche: A History of an Icon and His Ideas* (Chicago: University of Chicago Press, 2012), 83.

37. Maude Petre, "Studies on Friedrich Nietzsche: Nietzsche the Anti-Feminist," *Catholic World* 83 (1906): 162.

38. On the political uses of Nietzsche during this time, see Tracy Strong, "Nietzsche's Political Misappropriation," in *The Cambridge Companion to Nietzsche*, eds. Bernd Magnus and Kathleen Higgins (Cambridge: Cambridge University Press, 2006), 119–47.

39. Ratner-Rosenhagen, *American Nietzsche*, 115–16. Katharine Hepburn's *A Woman Rebels* (1936) is perhaps referencing Margaret Sanger's "A Woman Rebel" in its title.

40. Dora Marsden, "Bondwomen," *Freewoman* 1, no. 1 (November 23, 1911): 1.

41. Marsden, 2.

42. Dora Marsden, "Commentary on Bondwomen," *Freewoman* 1, no. 2 (November 30, 1911): 21.

43. Marsden, 22.

44. Georges Clemenceau, *The Strongest* (Garden City and New York: Doubleday, Page, 1919), 235–36.

45. Clemenceau, 240.

46. Clemenceau, 241.

47. Clemenceau, 176–77, 292.

48. On the tragic nature of "irrevocable" choices and the nearly pagan glorification of love as an impersonal force in these films from the 1920s, see Haskell, *From Reverence to Rape*, 89.

49. W. Somerset Maugham, *A Writer's Notebook* (Garden City, NY: Doubleday, 1949), 24–34.

50. While an enormous amount of literature on the "New Woman" concept exists, an excellent treatment of its importance to this particular time in American history is found in Lynn Dumenil, *The Modern Temper: American Culture and Society in the 1920s* (New York: Hill and Wang, 1995), chapter 3.

51. Some connections between the Sinclair Lewis and Nietzsche are made in Steven Michels, *Sinclair Lewis and America Democracy* (Lanham, MD: Lexington Books, 2017), 57–58, 64, 92. Two other films based on Lewis's work, which take a more liberal-progressive approach than a Nietzschean one, are *Main Street* (1923), criticizing America's genteel values, and *Babbitt* (1924), criticizing its "skyscraper" or capitalist values.

52. Harold Stearns, ed., *Civilization in the United States: An Inquiry by Thirty Americans* (New York: Harcourt, Brace, 1922), vii.

53. Mark Steven, "Nietzsche on Film," *Film-Philosophy* 21, no. 1 (2017): 98.

54. Deleuze, *Cinema 2*, 133–34.

55. As Jacobs notes, one of the main things that the censors wanted to remove from the film was talk of Nietzsche's philosophy. It seems like mere mention of Nietzsche was more dangerous to depict than a jealous ex-lover killing Lily's current

lover and then himself. See Lea Jacobs, *The Wages of Sin: Censorship and the Fallen Woman Film, 1928–1942* (Berkeley: University of California Press, 1995), 74–75. And yet to censor explicit references to Nietzsche did little to excise the philosophy from the film; essentially all that it did was turn Cragg into a contradictory voice.

56. The following passage seems to capture Lily's mindset. "The great liberation comes for those who are thus fettered suddenly, like the shock of an earthquake: the youthful soul is all at once convulsed, torn loose, torn away—it itself does not know what is happening. A drive and impulse rules and masters it like a command; a will and a desire to go off, anywhere, at any cost; a vehement dangerous curiosity for an undiscovered world flames and flickers in all its senses. 'Better to die than to go on living *here*'—thus responds the imperious voice and temptation: and this 'here,' this 'at home' is everything it had hitherto loved!" (*HTH* P §3, emphasis in original).

57. The advice given to her by Mr. Cragg in the edited version qualifies her power and says, "But there is a right and a wrong way. Remember the price of the wrong way is too great." The edited version does not say to use men; rather it says, "Don't let people mislead you. You must be a master, not a slave. Be clean, be strong, be defiant and you will be a success."

58. H. L. Mencken, *The Philosophy of Nietzsche*, 3rd ed. (Boston: Luce, 1913), 93.

59. Mencken, 115. In any case, the censors cut all of this out and replaced it with a letter: "Dear Lily, I can see from your letters that my advice was for nothing. You have chosen the wrong way. You are still a coward. Life will defeat you unless you fight back and regain your self-respect. I send this book hoping that you will allow it to guide you right. Merry Christmas—Adolf Cragg."

60. For an excellent account of the mask relative to the expressivity and elusiveness of the face, see Paul Coates, *Screening the Face* (Basingstoke and New York: Palgrave MacMillan, 2012), 6–12.

61. Steven, "Nietzsche on Film," 99.

62. Derrida, *Spurs*, 97.

63. Thus, I do not think that Lily is being "situated as evil" and "punished" as a "symptom of male fears about feminism." Doane, *Femmes Fatales*, 2–3. This would make *Baby Face* into little more than reboot of the older vamp films.

64. Jacobs, *Wages of Sin*, 71.

65. Jacobs, 79.

66. Jacobs, 18.

67. John Orr, *Cinema and Modernity* (Cambridge: Polity Press, 1993), 24–25.

68. This perhaps challenges Derrida's idea that the counterfeit can work only if it is not shown to be certainly counterfeit, for only then does it retain the "perhaps" and "faith" that generates the institution of money. See Jacques Derrida, *Given Time: I. Counterfeit Money* (Chicago: University of Chicago Press, 1992), 94.

69. Loos describes this as an atavistic hunger for mistreatment, captured in the idea that a kiss on the hand makes a girl feel respected, while a slap to the face expresses ardor. See Loos, *Kiss Hollywood Good-By*, 19.

70. See William Everson, *American Silent Film* (New York: Oxford University Press, 1978), 199.

71. Cavell argues that when "the terms of one's intelligibility are not welcome to others," then the alternative is "a certain choice of solitude." Cavell, *Contesting Tears*, 11–12. But doesn't *Female* show a third alternative—namely, to remain unintelligible to the Other but to have the power to present an intelligible mask? While *Female* strikes me as one-sided, in that the man cannot see the mask or come to terms with the unintelligibility of the Other, the comedies of Hecht and Lubitsch suggest a sort of friendship of mutual unintelligibility that comes from unrelenting deceptiveness and play.

72. Deleuze, *Cinema 2*, 137.

Chapter 5

1. Several lesser Hecht comedies could be used to support the reading in this chapter, such as *Hallelujah I'm a Bum!* (1933), *Turn Back the Clock* (1933), *Soak the Rich* (1936), *The Scoundrel* (1935), and *It's a Wonderful World* (1939).

2. Ben Hecht, *Fantazius Mallare: A Mysterious Oath* (Chicago: Covici-McGee, 1922), 41. See a similar idea in "Cinders" by Hulme in T. E. Hulme, *The Collected Writings of T. E. Hulme* (Oxford: Clarendon Press, 1994). See also Henry Mead, *T. E. Hulme and the Ideological Politics of Early Modernism* (London: Bloomsbury, 2015), 26.

3. Benjamin de Casseres, "The Philosophy of Hypocrisy," *International* 9, no. 7 (July 1915): 222.

4. H. L. Mencken, *The Impossible H. L. Mencken* (New York: Anchor/Doubleday, 1991), 618.

5. Mencken, 619.

6. See also *TI* 9 §31.

7. Gilles Deleuze, *Cinema 2: The Time Image* (Minneapolis: University of Minnesota Press, 1989), 128.

8. Ben Hecht, *A Child of the Century* (New York: Simon & Schuster, 1954), 49.

9. Hecht, 49.

10. Hecht, 53.

11. Hecht, 141–42.

12. Stanley Cavell, *Cavell on Film* (Albany: SUNY Press, 2005), 337.

13. Cavell, 340.

14. Cavell, 340.

15. Stanley Cavell, *Pursuits of Happiness: The Hollywood Comedy of Remarriage* (Cambridge, MA: Harvard University Press, 1981), 172.

16. Although such ideas might strike us as particularly postmodern, they were part of modernist culture in America that was inspired by Nietzsche. For example, Bourne, who was a student of Dewey, argues that "concepts are indis-

pensable—and yet each concept falsifies." In fact, the idea of contagion is found in Bourne as well when he states that "our minds are so unfortunately arranged that all sorts of belief can be accepted and propagated quite independently of any rational or even experiential basis at all." Randolph Bourne, "The Life of Irony," *Atlantic Monthly* (March 1913): 360–61.

17. Cavell, *Pursuits of Happiness*, 164.

18. Cavell, 165. Similarly, there is no real evidence to say that these characters are "cynical but noble newshounds." Thomas Doherty, *Pre-Code Hollywood: Sex, Immorality, and Insurrection in American Cinema 1930–1934* (New York: Columbia University Press 1999), 188.

19. Stephen Mulhall, *On Film*, 3rd ed. (London and New York: Routledge, 2016), 6.

20. On the need for society to mirror the cruelty of nature to create genius, see Paul Franco, *Nietzsche's Enlightenment: The Free-Spirit Trilogy of the Middle Period* (Chicago: University of Chicago Press, 2011), 49.

21. "Genius is said to be morbidly egotistic. It assumes, in fact, a still higher form of psychological development than egotism. It is impersonal. It not only believes in itself utterly, but it subdivides itself ad infinitum that it may worship itself under a myriad forms and revel in its own luminous magnificences. It worships itself in the third person plural." Benjamin de Casseres, "The Divinity of Genius," *Sun* (August 14, 1911): 4.

22. Jules de Gaultier, *Bovarysme* (New York: Philosophical Library, 1970); Benjamin de Casseres, "Jules de Gaultier: Super-Nietzschean," *Forum* (January 1913): 86.

23. When engaged in high deception, Colbert kisses Stewart in *It's a Wonderful World*, and says, "from one wizard to another."

24. Hawks's films have a fixation on this part of the human body, which Cavell points out on occasion. Cavell, *Pursuits of Happiness*, 117. In fact, Oscar's first scene shows him gazing at his secretary's behind when she bends over.

25. Jacques Derrida, *Geneses, Genealogies, Genres, and Genius: The Secrets of the Archive* (New York: Columbia University Press, 2006), 1–2.

26. Derrida, 1–2.

27. Derrida, 1–2.

28. Derrida, 79.

29. "The individual is not a substance, but exists and constitutes itself by entering various roles. . . . Hence the idea that the human being is an actor, and that every actor has *several roles*." See Michel Haar, *Nietzsche and Metaphysics* (Albany: SUNY Press, 1996), 95.

30. "To live is to lie. To act is to pose. Sincerity, strictly speaking, cannot exist. . . . It is the pose, Gullibus, that makes our lives romantic and supportable. On arising each morning, we, all of us, prepare our pose for the day. In the freshness of the morning each being conceives an artificial and impossible vision of himself or herself—no different from the egocentric visions induced in the brain by opium or alcohol. The day dies and the dream—the pose—dies with it. It is

like the "morning after" of a debauch. This is the eternal comedy of the daily tragedy—trying to make ourselves and others believe that we are other than we are. Hypocrisy generates the beautiful in character. The pose is the Lie Beautiful and gives reality to our ideals and ennobles our weaknesses and imperfections by straining them to the breaking point. Bottoms all, we conceive ourselves to be Prosperos and Don Juans. Tartuffes, we pose as Jobs and supermen of varying degrees. If you have not your pose you are as uninteresting as a cow. It is your artificial self that I fall in love with." Benjamin de Casseres, "Insincerity: A New Vice," *Camera Work* no. 42–43 (April–July 1913): 16.

31. "All human beings, in all cultures, preserve a division between their self-identities and the 'performances' they put on in specific social contexts. But in some circumstances the individual might come to feel that the whole flow of his activities is put on or false." Anthony Giddens, *Modernity and Self-Identity: Self and Society in the Late Modern Age* (Stanford: Stanford University Press, 1991), 58.

32. De Casseres, "Divinity of Genius," 4.

33. Benjamin de Casseres, "The Stage-Instinct," *Theater* 7, no. 79 (September 1907): 234.

34. Eyman is no fan of Hecht and refers to "Hecht's touch" as being "crinkly cellophane aphorisms that make every character sound like a literate but childish narcissist fending off self-awareness." Scott Eyman, *Ernst Lubitsch: Laughter in Paradise* (New York: Simon and Schuster, 1993), 210–11.

35. In Hecht's original screenplay it read, "This is New York, Skyscraper Champion of the World . . . With a Silk Hat for a Soul and a Mammy Song for a Heart . . . This is Bagdad, Babylon, and Podunk in a Cake-Walk between Two River Banks. This is Where the Slickers and the Smart Alecks hang their Gold Hats. This is Where the Sky is a Forgotten Sign left in the Wind by a Defunct Firm . . . where the Handwriting on the Wall is just Part of the Daily Menu . . . This is New York . . . Where Goliath Got the Decision . . . New York . . . the Fortress of Sophistication with a Price-Tag for a Flag . . . where nothing is too Strange, too Macabre, too Humpty Dumpty or too Ooh-La-La if it happened in New York." Obviously this is not suitable for an opening title due to its length, and we do not know who was responsible for the succinct statement actually found at the start of the film. See Katharine Best, "Horseplay into Photoplay," *Stage* (November 1937): 63. These original lines from Hecht seem to me to be more focused on the contradictions and superficiality of New York than the actual lines from the film, which are about the nature of truth.

36. Deleuze, *Cinema 2*, 146.

37. We can call it a "naked pretence" in which "no one is fooled." Russell Grigg, "The Joyful Art of Ernst Lubitsch: *Trouble in Paradise*," in *Lubitsch Can't Wait*, ed. Ivana Novak, Jela Krečič, and Mladen Dolar (Ljubljana: Slovenian Cinematheque, 2014), 40.

38. The phrase *morning star* has several significant meanings. Besides signaling the coming of dawn, it is also one of the names by which Lucifer is identified (Isaiah 14:12). Also, Jesus refers to himself in this way (Revelation 22:16). Thus,

it is a name that holds profound ambiguity, not only because it (mis)identifies Venus as a star and does so in a way that falsely differentiates it from itself as the evening star. Yet it also calls to mind one of Cavell's favorite quotes from Thoreau, the final lines of *Walden*, "The light which puts out our eyes is darkness to us. Only that day dawns to which we are awake. There is more day to dawn. The sun is but a morning star." See Henry David Thoreau, *Walden; or, Life in the Woods* (Boston and New York: Houghton, Mifflin, 1919), 367.

39. It is very likely that Ernest Walker is a gesture toward a real character that Hecht regularly fictionalized. Grover Cleveland Redding was part of a "Back to Africa" movement and called himself "the Grand Exalted Mysterious Ruler of the Star Order of Ethiopia and the Princes of Abyssinia." He was hanged for murdering someone when his parade exploded into the "Abyssinia riot" in Chicago in 1920. When Hecht retold this story in various works, he made this character into a split-personality schizophrenic who was parading around as "Prince Mulbo of Abyssinia." In Hecht's original script, it is said that he has an uncontrollable Sultan complex. For the backstory and Hecht's versions of it, see Robert Schmuhl, "History, Fantasy, Memory: Ben Hecht and a Chicago Hanging," *Illinois Historical Journal* 83, no. 3 (1990): 146–58. Hecht sometimes changed the name of Redding to Samuel Williams or Howard Givin, and sometimes made him a physician or a dentist. See Ben Hecht, *Gaily, Gaily* (New York: Doubleday, 1963), 17–33.

40. In Hecht's retelling of this episode, the "Negro Knights of Africa" movement, of which Dido de Long and Redding/Williams/Givin were a part, was going to set up a kingdom in Liberia, where they could be "human beings" and rulers. So, what appears as lies is perhaps truer than what is "real." See Hecht, *Gaily, Gaily*, 21–23.

41. Jacques Derrida, *Writing and Difference* (Chicago: University of Chicago Press, 1978), 129–30.

42. Derrida, 130.

43. On the notorious Frank Fay, who is the master of ceremonies of the tribute to Hazel Flagg, see Gerald Weales, *Canned Goods as Caviar: American Film Comedy of the 1930s* (Chicago: University of Chicago Press, 1985), 249–50.

44. Deleuze, *Cinema 2*, 144, 133, 139.

45. Deleuze, *Cinema 2*, 144, 133, 139.

46. Deleuze, *Cinema 2*, 3.

47. Weales, *Canned Goods*, 265.

48. I think it is a rather serious mistake to think that this film offers "moral scorn" for "the newspaper industry" because it is "exploitative, heartless, and fundamentally dishonest." Allen Larson, "1937: Movies and New Constructions of the American Star," in *American Cinema of the 1930s: Themes and Variations*, ed. Ina Rae Hark (New Brunswick, NJ: Rutgers University Press, 2007), 203. On such mistaken views, see Weales, *Canned Goods*, 248–49.

49. Weales points out that the wise city slicker is, contrary to stereotype, made into the sentimental sap before the country bumpkin. Weales, *Canned Goods*, 256. He sees Cook's character as something like the mirror opposite of

the characters from *The Front Page*. But it is not that Cook is simply naïve and honest. Instead, he is operating within the dichotomy of truth and lies and has yet to graduate to the more cynical perspective in which there is nothing but simulations.

50. Ludwig Wittgenstein, *Philosophical Investigations*, 2nd ed (Oxford: Blackwell, 1958), §246.

51. Wittgenstein, §107.

52. Scott Eyman, *Ernst Lubitsch: Laughter in Paradise* (New York: Simon & Schuster, 1993), 208.

53. For his touching and funny memoir about MacArthur, see Ben Hecht, *Charlie: The Improbable Life and Times of Charles MacArthur* (New York: Harper & Brothers, 1957).

54. Bourne, "Life of Irony," 358.

55. Bourne, 359.

56. Bourne, 360. On Bourne's theory of irony, this metaphor of photography, and a connection to the "Nietzschean 'transvaluation of values,'" see Matthew Stratton, *The Politics of Irony in American Modernism* (New York: Fordham University Press, 2014), 28. Admittedly both Hecht and Nietzsche are less likely to see the ironist as democratic, as Bourne does.

57. A supporting analysis of ironic method in cinema is found in James MacDowell, "Interpretation, Irony and 'Surface Meanings' in Film," *Film-Philosophy* 22, no. 2 (2018): 261–80.

58. There are of course many different types of montage, and the sort that I am focusing on in these films is both what is sometimes called "intellectual" montage as well as "tonal" montage, which gives rise to a critical or cynical attitude toward conflicting value sets. On the ability of montage to do this, see Sergei Eisenstein, *The Film Sense* (New York: Meridian Books, 1957), 4.

59. Bourne, "Life of Irony," 362.

Chapter 6

1. Josef von Sternberg, *Fun in a Chinese Laundry* (New York: MacMillan, 1965), 3.

2. Herman Weinberg, *Josef von Sternberg: A Critical Study of the Great Film Director* (New York: E. P. Dutton & Company, 1967), 31.

3. Noël Coward, *The Letters of Noël Coward* (New York: Vintage Books, 2007), 324. See also her mentions of Nietzsche in Marlene Dietrich, *Marlene Dietrich's ABC* (New York: Ungar Publishing, 1984).

4. Sternberg, *Chinese Laundry*, 2. See also his claim that he tried to show that "film might well be an art medium," particularly regarding his final two Dietrich films. Sternberg, 264.

5. John Baxter, *Von Sternberg* (Lexington, KY: University Press of Kentucky, 2010), 16.

6. See Richard Koszarski, *Von: The Life and Films of Erich Von Stroheim* (New York: Limelight Editions, 2001), 222; Sternberg, *Chinese Laundry*, 34–35.

7. This division between the Apollonian and Dionysian is one major way that Nietzsche's thought was appropriated by the films of the Nazi era. See Laura Heins, *Nazi Film Melodrama* (Urbana, IL: University of Illinois Press, 2013), 84–87.

8. Paul Schrader, *Transcendental Style in Film: Ozu, Bresson, Dreyer* (New York: De Capo Press, 1972), 8.

9. These Dionysian notions are often not seen as central to the superhuman, but there are readings that emphasize it, such as Jill Marsden, "Sensing the Overhuman," *Journal of Nietzsche Studies* 30 (2005): 102–14.

10. Josef von Sternberg, *The Blue Angel: Authorized Translation of the German Continuity* (New York: Simon & Schuster, 1968), 9.

11. Gaylyn Studlar, *In the Realm of Pleasure: Von Sternberg, Dietrich, and the Masochistic Aesthetic* (New York: Columbia University Press, 1988).

12. For a criticism of Studlar's view, see Catherine Constable, *Thinking in Images: Film Theory, Feminist Philosophy and Marlene Dietrich* (London: British Film Institute, 2005), 59–63.

13. Studlar recognizes that the masochist appeals to fate but denies that this is at work here. Instead of fate, it is all "self-willed misery" caused by "the subterranean network of masochism's demands." Studlar, *In the Realm of Pleasure*, 117.

14. Studlar, 61. It is this (rather male/Oedipal) notion of union with the mother that Constable thinks undermines Studlar's feminist approach by not really accounting for desire in a way that includes women.

15. Studlar, 123.

16. Studlar, 91.

17. Studlar, 124.

18. Studlar, 124.

19. Jacques Derrida, *The Gift of Death and Literature in Secret* (Chicago: University of Chicago Press, 2008), 71. On a Nietzschean conception of such "responsibility to the other," see Vanessa Lemm, *Nietzsche's Animal Philosophy: Culture, Politics, and the Animality of the Human Being* (New York: Fordham University Press, 2009), 149.

20. Sternberg, *Chinese Laundry*, 323.

21. Sternberg, 323.

22. Sternberg, 329.

23. Sternberg, 337.

24. It seems misguided to say that Sternberg was "no cynic." James Phillips, *Sternberg and Dietrich: The Phenomenology of Spectacle* (Oxford and New York: Oxford University Press, 2019), 49. Only *The Salvation Hunters* is non-cynical. Every other major film he made is deeply cynical, and his autobiography is an exercise in cynicism. Phillips thinks that *Underworld* is not cynical because Bull Weed's jealousy is not justified, but the fact that the *Übermensch* is subject to such "all too human" concerns is a cynical moment. And *Underworld* is not the film upon which to judge whether Sternberg was cynical or not.

25. Derrida, *Gift of Death*, 96.

26. Derrida, 3–4.

27. Support of the idea that the cabaret is more Apollonian than Dionysian is found in the idea that it represents "mass culture" and even film itself. See Barbara Kosta, *Willing Seduction: The Blue Angel, Marlene Dietrich, and Mass Culture* (New York: Beghahn Books, 2009), chapter 1.

28. "The seed of decline is already implanted in all becoming. The pleasure of death and decay resonates in the pleasure of generation and love." Eugene Fink, *Nietzsche's Philosophy* (London: Continuum, 2003), 23.

29. Sternberg, *Chinese Laundry*, 67.

30. Studlar, *In the Realm of Pleasure*, 122.

31. The irrational is a theme that could be brought up in many contexts in previous chapters, but it is most evident in Sternberg's films. One Nietzschean theorist of the irrational was De Casseres. "The Intellect is bankrupt. It is only a park pond. The Mississippi and the Amazon flow through the heart. All ends are myths. Life itself explains life. Chance, danger and the irrational constitute the new Trinity. Dionysus dances in menadic frenzy on the skulls of Darwin, Spencer, Taine, Buckle and Haeckel. . . . The irrational is the groundwork of all existence. Life is itself an error." Benjamin de Casseres, "The Renaissance of the Irrational," *Camera Work* (June 1913): 23.

32. Studlar, *In the Realm of Pleasure*, 122.

33. Jacques Derrida, *Margins of Philosophy* (Chicago: University of Chicago Press, 1982), 136.

34. This is a point where the intersection with Pippin's analysis of "passive agency" in film noirs is especially relevant. I maintain that at its extremes, some figures in the Nietzschean film tradition, especially in Stroheim and Sternberg, begin to lose all agency, but Pippin is right to stress that there are degrees of agency and that these compromised figures expose the complexities of both the psychological and social preconditions of agency. See Robert Pippin, *Fatalism in American Film Noir: Some Cinematic Philosophy* (Charlottesville and London: University of Chicago Press, 2012), 17–22.

35. De Casseres, "Renaissance of the Irrational," 23.

36. Carole Zucker, *The Idea of the Image: Josef von Sternberg's Dietrich Films* (Rutherford, NJ: Fairleigh Dickinson University Press 1988), 53.

37. Studlar, *In the Realm of Pleasure*, 126–27. For example, Studlar talks of a "masochistic urge towards death" and the idea of "a return to the beginning, to the womb of rebirth and nothingness," which would seem to align very well with my reading. Studlar, 123–24. This idea is also endorsed by Kosta, *Willing Seduction*, 64. My disagreement is with the characterization of this as an act of the agent, part of a "self willed liberation" to both achieve pleasure and also "control desire and contain pleasure." Studlar, *In the Realm of Pleasure*, 123–24, 159. From a Dionysian perspective, this is not a choice or an act of desire or self-determination dominated by the pleasure principle.

38. Studlar, *In the Realm of Pleasure*, 118.

39. I think that part of the reason that masochism is taken as the key to Sternberg's film is partially a result of the fact that his films seem to be read through *The Blue Angel*, which is much easier to be read through that psychoanalytic lens because it focuses on male humiliation. See Paul Coates, *The Gorgon's Gaze: German Cinema, Expressionism, and the Image of Horror* (Cambridge: Cambridge University Press, 1991), 62–72.

40. The radical, destructive force of the Dionysian supports the idea of films as "progressive texts," and *Morocco* was an early example of such a text. The "progressive text" shows discontinuity and fissures in experience generally and in the film experience particularly. See Veronica Pravadelli, *Classic Hollywood: Lifestyles and Film Styles of American Cinema, 1930–1960* (Urbana, IL: University of Illinois Press, 2014), 10.

41. On the Oedipal reading of the mother-child relationship in *Blonde Venus*, see Studlar, *In the Realm of Pleasure*, 76.

42. The opening scene of *Blonde Venus* is commented upon by Studlar. She argues that there is an erotic unification between Dietrich's character and her son, as well as an association of both of them with the goddess Venus and with fish as some sort of phallic symbol. Studlar, *In the Realm of Pleasure*, 146–147. I do not find this terribly plausible as a reading. Instead, the unification of the two scenes comes from the notion of Dionysian intoxication and the loss of the self (including the loss of desire as an egological act). As for the Nietzschean use of the symbol of the fish, it appears in *Zarathustra* to symbolize the man speaking to the "unfathomable woman," who laughs at his stupidity and "virtue" (Z II "The Dancing Song").

43. Kain argues that the problem with the Dionysian is the "pure raging torrent of life which includes death for the individual," which (Apollonian) art allows us to avoid. Philip Kain, *Nietzsche and the Horror of Existence* (Lanham, MD: Lexington Books, 2009), 9. But the life of the *Übermensch* is not a passive one, where one contemplates the flux of existence: it is to actually enter into and embrace that flux as a part of fate. The role of art is to provoke action and the acceptance of the eternal return, which means to accept and embrace death rather than to flee it.

44. Jacques Derrida, *Given Time: I. Counterfeit Money* (Chicago: University of Chicago Press, 1992), 13.

45. See Michel Haar, *Nietzsche and Metaphysics* (Albany: SUNY Press, 1996), 178.

46. Thus, I hold the completely opposite position from Phillips, who claims that the "stage throws open the doors to unearthly powers and to revolutionary futures." James Phillips, *Sternberg and Dietrich: The Phenomenology of Spectacle* (Oxford and New York: Oxford University Press, 2019), 47. In Sternberg's films, true revolutionary futures are inseparable from a form of death and happen outside the sphere of the theater.

47. Studlar sees the cabaret scenes as taking up the viewpoint of female desire and as simply reversing gender divisions. Studlar, *In the Realm of Pleasure*,

64. I think that this misunderstands the scenes significantly. We should consider the harsh words that Sternberg had for such low, merely sensual entertainment of the crowd.

48. Sternberg, *Chinese Laundry*, 60.

49. Derrida, *Gift of Death*, 80, 71.

50. Studlar, *In the Realm of Pleasure*, 59.

51. Sternberg, *Chinese Laundry*, 56. This passage is discussed by Wilson, who finds its notion of a deep unconscious essence to be in conflict with Sternberg's own aesthetic fixation on "opaque, superficial, and distorting exteriors of the human specimens he directs." But he then recognizes that those images are meant to provide insight into the "basic strata of the hidden self" through a symbolist aesthetics from "the traditions of expressionism and surrealism." George Wilson, *Narration in Light: Studies in Cinematic Point of View* (Baltimore and London: Johns Hopkins University Press, 1986), 146–47.

52. Sternberg, *Chinese Laundry*, 56–57.

53. Peter Baxter, ed., *Sternberg* (London: British Film Institute, 1980), 31.

54. Baxter, 33.

55. Cavell sees this return as a "negation of the unknown woman genre" and a sort of "remarriage," but, as he himself mentions, this return is not for the husband but for the sake of her child. Stanley Cavell, *Contesting Tears: The Hollywood Melodrama of the Unknown Woman* (Chicago: University of Chicago, 1996), 14–15.

56. "For from the depths one loves only one's child and work: and where there is great love of oneself it is a sign of pregnancy" (Z 3 "On Involuntary Bliss").

57. A. R. Orage, *Nietzsche in Outline and Aphorism* (Edinburgh: T. N. Foulis, 1911), 43.

58. Since the masochistic fantasy is not available to women, to read the film through this renders Dietrich's character into the nurturing, oral mother. Studlar, *In the Realm of Pleasure*, 15. Although she nurtures in *Blonde Venus* and, in a deceptive sense, in *Shanghai Express*, she certainly does not in any of the other films. Nor can we say that those two films reduce her to such a nurturing figure.

59. On this standard connection between these films, see Studlar, *In the Realm of Pleasure*, 61.

60. Derrida, *Gift of Death*, 71.

61. Derrida, 4–5.

62. Susan Sontag, "Notes on Camp," in *Against Interpretation and Other Essays* (London: Penguin, 2009), 275. Of course, the acting (perhaps it is closer to puppetry given Sternberg's control) is always artificial in these films. See Zucker, *Idea of the Image*, 94.

63. Sontag, "Notes on Camp," 283. I consider camp more along the lines of what Sontag describes as "deliberate Camp."

64. Sontag, 280.

65. Constable, *Thinking in Images*, 134. She is said to be "the prototype of the *femme fatale*" in George Wilson, *Narration in Light: Studies in Cinematic Point of View* (Baltimore and London: Johns Hopkins University Press, 1986), 147. She is also called a *femme fatale* in Erica Carter, *Dietrich's Ghosts: The Sublime and the Beautiful in Third Reich Film* (London: BFI Publishing, 2004), 151.

66. Constable, *Thinking in Images*, 134.

67. I disagree with Wilson, who says that it is "nearly impossible to say anything enlightening about the general *conception* that informs" the film's "elliptical and apparently illogical plot" (emphasis in original). Wilson, *Narration in Light*, 164.

68. Andrew Sarris, *The Films of Josef von Sternberg* (Garden City: Doubleday, 1966), 42.

69. Constable, *Thinking in Images*, 133; Studlar, *In the Realm of Pleasure*, 163.

70. Pierre Louÿs, *Woman and Puppet* (London: Greening, 1908), 48.

71. Phillips, *Sternberg and Dietrich*, 74. This is a common approach to Concha's character. Unable to see an underlying rationale (responsibility to the One, with its terrifying Dionysian consequences, and the flight from this), Doane says that there is no "motivation beyond that of pure exhibitionism, pure show" in this character. Mary Anne Doane, *Femmes Fatales: Feminism, Film Theory, Psychoanalysis* (New York and London: Routledge, 1991), 49.

72. Phillips, *Sternberg and Dietrich*, 76.

73. Sternberg, *Chinese Laundry*, 267.

74. Much of what I will say also applies to *Dishonored*, in which Dietrich's character is nihilistically alienated from life because her husband has died. She is then bound in faith to his memory as she becomes a spy before shifting her passions to his replacement in Colonel Kranau. But that film is the only Dietrich-Sternberg film in which she dies because of her Dionysian embrace of passion. And while that is not reason alone to set the film aside, I do think it is the least effective of this film sequence for a variety of reasons that I will not discuss.

75. Such a remark is a clue perhaps to Sternberg's approach in the film. He too does not want to bargain with some simple form of love that can be put into words and wants instead to visualize the paradoxical nature of a love that can be both holy and profane, selfish and selfless.

76. Derrida, *Gift of Death*, 71.

77. Derrida, 71.

78. Derrida, 72.

79. Derrida, 73.

80. These figures are mentioned as fakes in Phillips, *Sternberg and Dietrich*, 30.

81. Constable, *Thinking in Images*, 152. I should point out that I believe that Constable does not fully appreciate Derrida's view. She continually attributes to him the idea that the "ideal woman" is "the untruth of truth, who is also defined in terms of absence." Constable, 142. But this seems to me to not recognize that

Derrida moves past the logic of "presence" and its negative, to the more radical idea of woman as "an affirmative power, a dissimulatress, an artist, a dionysiac." Jacques Derrida, *Spurs: Spurs: Nietzsche's Styles* (Chicago: University of Chicago Press, 1979), 97.

82. Constable, *Thinking in Images*, 147.
83. Constable, 160.
84. Constable, 155.
85. Phillips, *Sternberg and Dietrich*, 25.
86. Phillips, 25.
87. Phillips, 26. Phillips then does go on to talk about this as a leap of faith, but that is simply not the same thing as recognizing her as an "ethical subject."
88. Phillips, 40.
89. Imogen Sara Smith, "Mistress of Confessions," in *Dietrich and Von Sternberg in Hollywood* (Criterion Collection, 2018), 27.
90. Gary Giddins, "The Devil is in the Details," In *Dietrich and Von Sternberg in Hollywood* (Criterion Collection, 2018), 47.
91. Antonin Artaud, "Cinema and Reality," in *French Film Theory and Criticism: A History/Anthology: 1907–1939*, vol. 1, ed. Richard Abel (Princeton: Princeton University Press, 1988), 411.
92. Artaud, 411.
93. This seems to be Constable's approach in *Thinking in Images*, 63–80. In spite of their disagreements, this emphasis on her agency is shared with Studlar, *In the Realm of Pleasure*, 152.
94. It is for this reason that I cannot agree with the veiling of Dietrich, particularly in her bed after giving birth, in this film as being a component in Sternberg's (male) gaze to make her more erotic, more desirable, and more envious. Doane, *Femmes Fatales*, 74. Instead, it seems to me that the connection between veils and death is here more important than their eroticizing function.
95. Studlar, *In the Realm of Pleasure*, 143–44; Constable, *Thinking in Images*, 65.
96. Martin Heidegger, *Being and Time* (New York: Harper & Row, 1962), H169–170/E213–214.
97. Herman Weinberg, *Josef von Sternberg: A Critical Study of the Great Film Director* (New York: E. P. Dutton), 130. It has been said that a central Sternbergian theme is "love . . . as degradation, as a 'deal,' as physical and emotional suffering, as betrayal and faithlessness." See Zucker, *Idea of the Image*, 14.
98. Jacques Derrida, *Rogues: Two Essays on Reason* (Stanford: Stanford University Press, 2005), 52, 88, 151.
99. Phillips, *Sternberg and Dietrich*, 4, 100.
100. It seems like a mistake to describe Dietrich's characters as hedonists and "unshackled sensualists." Molly Haskell, *From Reverence to Rape: The Treatment of Women in the Movies*, 2nd ed. (Chicago and London: University of Chicago Press, 1987), 109. They may be unshackled from traditional morality, but they are shackled to forces outside their control, forces that cannot be simply thought of as a drive for sensual pleasure.

Chapter 7

1. It has also been claimed that Hecht did an anonymous rewrite of *The Shop Around the Corner*. Doug Fetherling, *The Five Lives of Ben Hecht* (Toronto: Lester & Orphen, 1977), 113.

2. Siegfried Kracauer, *From Caligari to Hitler: A Psychological History of the German Film* (Princeton: Princeton University Press, 1947), 52–53.

3. Scott Eyman, *Ernst Lubitsch: Laughter in Paradise* (New York: Simon & Schuster, 1993), 36. On these themes and, in particular, the influence of Wagner, see J. L. Styan, *Max Reinhardt* (Cambridge: Cambridge University Press, 1982), 11–12.

4. Samson Raphaelson, *The Human Nature of Playwriting* (New York: Macmillan, 1949), 192–93.

5. Slavoj Žižek, *Absolute Recoil: Towards a New Foundation of Dialectical Materialism* (London and New York: Verso, 2014), 301–4. Slavoj Žižek, "Lubitsch, the Poet of Cynical Wisdom?" in *Lubitsch Can't Wait*, ed. Ivana Novak, Jela Krečič, and Mladen Dolar (Ljubljana: Slovenian Cinematheque, 2014), 187–91.

6. See Seth Taylor, *Left-Wing Nietzscheans: The Politics of German-Expressionism 1910–1920* (Berlin: De Gruyter), 1990.

7. There is a tension between Nietzschean aestheticism and naturalism, where the latter is taken in a scientific or explanatory sense that then wants to bind Nietzsche's normative project to some nearly "natural law" conception of what is valuable and what the virtues are. See Tracy Strong, "Optics of Science, Art, and Life,: How Tragedy Begins," in *Nietzsche and the Becoming of Life*, ed. Vanessa Lemm (New York: Fordham University Press, 2015), 19–31. See also Lawrence Hatab, "Nietzsche, Nature, and the Affirmation of Life," in *Nietzsche and the Becoming of Life*, ed. Vanessa Lemm (New York: Fordham University Press, 2015), 32–33.

8. So while I agree that some uses of the notion of the free spirit cannot be related to the notion of the *Übermensch*, there certainly is some overlap. Nevertheless, I am not defending the idea that free-spiritedness is a good way to read the concept of the *Übermensch*. But it is a plausible way that the idea was understood and taken up in the culture and by writers and directors. See Michael Allen Gillespie, *Nietzsche's Final Teaching* (Chicago: University of Chicago Press, 2017), 44–45.

9. "We can say that one of Nietzsche's projects is to let the mask show itself as mask. Before this can happen, his interpretations must do more than call attention to themselves as interpretations. They need to move in such a way that their force is not one of systematic self-maintenance or instance upon their own truth. Their force is rather one that withdraws their truth and meaning by the power that establishes their claim to truth and meaning. It must be a force of self-overcoming that makes evident the masking process in the manner in which that process goes on." Charles Scott, "The Mask of Nietzsche's Self-Overcoming," in *Nietzsche as Postmodernist: Essays Pro and Contra*, ed. Clayton Koelb (Albany: SUNY Press, 1990), 217–18.

10. "Nietzsche sees the essential connection between lightness, creative excess, self-realization and the cosmos. The spirit of heaviness contrasts with all of these. It condemns man to self-alienation, burdens him with the weight of a transcendental God and morality and chains him to the ontic world. Gravity becomes the symbol of an oppressed life for which everything is heavy." Eugene Fink, *Nietzsche's Philosophy* (London: Continuum, 2003), 85.

11. The "bottom line of comedy" is that "repetition comes first. Double comes first. It foreshadows the original." Mladon Dolar, "To Be or Not to Be? No, Thank You," in *Lubitsch Can't Wait*, ed. Ivana Novak, Jela Krečič, and Mladen Dolar (Ljubljana: Slovenian Cinematheque, 2014), 127.

12. "Authority is always staged and performed." Gregor Moder, "The Beard, the Bust, and the Plumed Helmet," in *Lubitsch Can't Wait*, ed. Ivana Novak, Jela Krečič, and Mladen Dolar (Ljubljana: Slovenian Cinematheque, 2014), 155.

13. This demonstrates the idea that there is no "pure immediacy" in the Lubitsch universe, although I would say that there can be such immediacy but that it is best to avoid it because it has catastrophic results. Ivana Novak and Jela Krečič, "Introduction: The Importance of Being Ernst," in *Lubitsch Can't Wait*, ed. Ivana Novak, Jela Krečič, and Mladen Dolar (Ljubljana: Slovenian Cinematheque, 2014), 1.

14. As Haskell says of Lubitsch's films, they show "the multiplicity of women's roles as a primary condition of her being." She also points out how the shifting roles and masks of Lubitsch's films point out that part of what it is to be an "active role-player" who is "perpetrating an illusion" is also to be "a passive receptacle" who is subject to the Other's selective appreciation and interpretation. Molly Haskell, *From Reverence to Rape: The Treatment of Women in the Movies*, 2nd ed. (Chicago and London: University of Chicago Press, 1987), 97–98.

15. Novak and Krečič, "Importance of Being Ernst," 7.

16. While one might read this as a sexist moment in which the "naïve" and innocent wife must suffer and forgive her husband, I would argue that this overlooks the catch-22 that leads to the infidelity in the first place and that a similar outcome happens in *Angel*, with the gender roles reversed, which suggests that Lubitsch's point cannot be so easily dismissed. Sabine Hake, *Passions and Deceptions: The Early Films of Ernst Lubitsch* (Princeton: Princeton University Press, 1992), 75.

17. Haskell points out that the function of the love triangle in these films is to expose multiple sides of the person and that "no one person is the complete complement to any other." Haskell, *From Reverence to Rape*, 99. Thus, the dalliances and affairs are essential for recovering a sense of the Other as Other, as transcendence, which is what makes them attractive in the first place.

18. Novak and Krečič, "Importance of Being Ernst," 4.

19. Novak and Krečič argue that language and appearances have a certain autonomy for Lubitsch, but this implies a sense of antihumanist fatalism that, while obvious in Sternberg's films, does not sit well with Lubitsch. Therefore,

I think it important to seek what actually motivates Andre's affair. Novak and Krečič, "Importance of Being Ernst," 4.

20. Again, one could read this as a very misogynistic moment in which "loose women" simply do not make for good wives. Sabine Hake, *Passions and Deceptions: The Early Films of Ernst Lubitsch* (Princeton: Princeton University Press, 1992), 75. But that would significantly cheapen their true affection for one another and the fact that it is Franzi that states this. I propose instead that it is more accurately seen as a comment on the brutal, unadorned honesty of their relationship and a recognition that life needs its masks.

21. "The Dionysian ideal, however, is to strive for the mastery of the accomplished dancer who can forget his own body—not out of lack or insufficiency, but by supreme mastery." Paul Valadier, "Dionysius versus the Crucified," in *The New Nietzsche*, ed. David Allison (Cambridge, MA: MIT Press, 1985), 249. On the fact that song and dance are synonymous with "the expression of sexual desire and love" in his musicals, see Hake, *Passions and Deceptions*, 164.

22. It seems to be false that Lubitsch's films (with the exception of the Hechtian *Design for Living*) are "revolutionary" in their denial of the ability for love to be contained in the institution of marriage, given that nearly all his films end with either a marriage or a remarriage. Novak and Krečič, "Importance of Being Ernst," 7.

23. "For Nietzsche, these phenomena are not masks attached to a thing in itself, some lesser beings, or nothingness, or facts; their being belongs to an interpretive process, which consists only in the difference between an interpreting activity and a text. Being *is* a text. It appears and makes sense; and the sense is multiple" (emphasis in original). Jean Granier, "Nietzsche's Conception of Chaos," in *The New Nietzsche*, ed. David Allison (Cambridge: MIT Press, 1985), 135.

24. "The phenomenon masks what it manifests, *without enabling us to dissociate dissimulation from manifestation*. The phenomenon *is* a mask; it turns its own appearing into an appearance—i.e., it appears as pretense. Beyond it, one would find *nothing*." Granier, "Nietzsche's Conception of Chaos," 136, emphasis original.

25. Thus, I find it an exaggeration to say that the field of love in Lubitsch's universe is "the field of an impossible encounter" that acts as a "riddle which never finds its 'correct' answer." Novak and Krečič, "Importance of Being Ernst," 8. That more postmodern response is more in line with Hecht's comedies rather than the more humanist conclusions of Lubitsch's films, even as they conclude with a sense of the repetition of this task of meeting the Other continually anew and through masks.

26. Eyman, *Ernst Lubitsch*, 200.

27. Samson Raphaelson, *The Human Nature of Playwriting* (New York: Macmillan, 1949), 190.

28. Aaron Schuster, "Comedy in Times of Austerity," in *Lubitsch Can't Wait*, ed. Ivana Novak, Jela Krečič, and Mladen Dolar (Ljubljana: Slovenian Cinematheque, 2014), 20.

29. Christopher Beach, *Class, Language, and American Film Comedy* (Cambridge: Cambridge University Press, 2002), 20–23.

30. Žižek argues that the "paradise" of the title is a "full sexual relationship" and that what is missing is sexual rapport. Žižek, *Absolute Recoil*, 306; Žižek, "Lubitsch, the Poet of Cynical Wisdom?," 192. This seems to be a mistake to me. What is missing is what hinders the formation of such a relationship between Gaston and Colet, namely sufficient duplicity on the part of Colet.

31. Žižek suggests that this is a valid reading of the irreducible ambiguity of the film. Žižek, *Absolute Recoil*, 306; Žižek, "Lubitsch, the Poet of Cynical Wisdom?," 192. Paul argues that both relations are "equally valid notions of love," in part because Colet's passivity acts as a temptation for Gaston, but as Paul notes that is "a kind of oblivion, a removal, a dissipation." William Paul, *Ernst Lubitsch's American Comedy* (New York: Columbia University Press, 1983), 65, 67. I do not see the relationship with Colet as viable at all. Haskell agrees that the more traditional and less sexually liberated relationship would be to Kay Francis rather than Miriam Hopkins. Haskell, *From Reverence to Rape*, 93. The same point is made in James Harvey, *Romantic Comedy in Hollywood from Lubitsch to Sturges* (New York: Kopf, 1987), 56.

32. Žižek, *Absolute Recoil*, 310; Žižek, "Lubitsch, the Poet of Cynical Wisdom?," 195.

33. Again we see the idea that artificiality has priority. This idea is discussed (in Lacanian terms) and linked with Derrida's reflections on language, presence, speech and writing in Moder, "The Beard, the Bust, and the Plumed Helmet," 155–56.

34. I do not see that one needs to attribute deep sincerity to the goodbye with Colet in order that it match Lily's "cynical despair" or "Gaston's outburst about the hypocrisy of the rich." Remember that Gaston is robbing her of a necklace during this scene. Žižek, *Absolute Recoil*, 310; Žižek, "Lubitsch, the Poet of Cynical Wisdom?," 192.

35. This weakness in Colet, her inability to see the value of things and the economic relations between people, has been noted. Russell Grigg, "The Joyful Art of Ernst Lubitsch: *Trouble in Paradise*," in *Lubitsch Can't Wait*, ed. Ivana Novak, Jela Krečič, and Mladen Dolar, 39–64 (Ljubljana: Slovenian Cinematheque, 2014), 60–61.

36. Paul, *Ernst Lubitsch's American Comedy*, 12–14.

37. Hake recounts how interpretations of the film have seen it as criticizing the wealth and the elite but also have argued that Lubitsch's superficial style has obscured any real social commentary. Hake herself seems to endorse the idea that the film has an "inherent ambivalence," and that theft, economics, and filmmaking are interwoven. Hake, *Passions and Deceptions*, 183–85. My sense is that Lubitsch never simply condemns institutions, whether they be matrimonial, economic, or political, but holds that any mask can hinder life and love if it is not recognized for what it is and treated sensitively. This changes in his films that are made in the shadow of the Second World War.

38. Zupančič's analysis of the two love interests in Lubitsch's final film, *Cluny Brown*, "one that excludes the impossible object, and one that includes it; one in which love follows a fantasy scenario, and one that involves a different king of love (a genuine 'comic love')," can easily be applied to *Trouble in Paradise*. Alenka Zupančič, "Squirrels to the Nuts, or, How Many Does It Take to Not Give up on Your Desire?" in *Lubitsch Can't Wait*, ed. Ivana Novak, Jela Krečič, and Mladen Dolar (Ljubljana: Slovenian Cinematheque, 2014), 171. Obviously, if I took up a more Lacanian analysis, I would have to give significantly more weight to how (phallic) objects prop up desire and so in this case would have to focus more on the exchanges of money here.

39. Another way of putting it is that the trouble is that "imbalance and disharmony are the very soul of desire." Schuster, "Comedy in Times of Austerity," 28. Colet does not recognize that. Gaston recognizes it: he is drawn to Colet because of the imbalance she causes—or, equally, that her world results in a balanced world that unbalances his ordinarily imbalanced life. So I disagree with those who attempt to validate the Colet-Gaston relationship because opposites attract or because Lily is too similar and too much a friend. Grigg, "The Joyful Art of Ernst Lubitsch," 54. As Pfaller states, "the new, modern twist here is that love now happens between 'parallel' partners who are in the same business . . . not between opposed partners who complement each other." Robert Pfaller, "What Is So Funny about Multiple Love? The Polygamous Lubitsch Touch," in *Lubitsch Can't Wait*, ed. Ivana Novak, Jela Krečič, and Mladen Dolar (Ljubljana: Slovenian Cinematheque, 2014), 76.

40. As Grigg points out, the trite dialogue here suggests that there is a distance from "any authentic emotional involvement," but I would say that applies to Gaston but not to Colet, who clearly shows through her ignorance that she has no ironic distance from these romantic notions. Grigg, "The Joyful Art of Ernst Lubitsch," 65.

41. Beach, *Class, Language, and American Film Comedy*, 22.

42. Stanley Cavell, *Cities of Words: Pedagogical Letters on a Register of the Moral Life* (Cambridge, MA: Harvard University Press, 2004), 23–24.

43. Cavell, 49.

44. Cavell, 154.

Conclusion

1. Thomas Wartenberg, *Thinking on Screen: Film as Philosophy* (London and New York: Routledge, 2007), 53.

2. Matthew Rukgaber, "Phenomenological Film Theory and Max Scheler's Personalist Aesthetics," *Studia Phaenomenologica* 16 (2016): 218.

3. Gilles Deleuze, *Pure Immanence: Essays on A Life* (New York: Zone Books, 2001), 30–31.

4. Josef von Sternberg, *Fun in a Chinese Laundry* (New York: MacMillan), 85.

5. Wartenberg, *Thinking on Screen*, 137.

6. Stephen Mulhall, *On Film*, 3rd ed. (London and New York: Routledge, 2016), 6, 93.

7. Robert Pippin, *Filmed Thought: Cinema as Reflective Form* (Chicago and London: University of Chicago Press, 2020), 68, 7.

8. Daniel Frampton, *Filmosophy* (London and New York: Wallflower Press, 2006), 10–11.

9. Robert Sinnerbrink, *New Philosophies of Film: Thinking Images* (London and New York: Bloomsbury, 2011), 148, 151, 163, 147.

10. Sternberg, *Chinese Laundry*, 53.

11. I should mention that this conception of Nietzschean aesthetics is somewhat at odds with the interpretation that it is part of a tradition that aims at "'disclosure' of the real, of being as such, not empirical or social reality." See Robert Pippin, *Philosophy by Other Means: The Arts in Philosophy and Philosophy in the Arts* (Chicago and London: University of Chicago Press, 2021), 12.

12. Irving Singer, *Cinematic Mythmaking: Philosophy in Film* (Cambridge, MA: MIT Press, 2008), 2.

13. Hans Blumenberg, *Work on Myth* (Cambridge, MA: MIT Press, 1985), 59.

14. For a sophisticated treatment of the different notions of myth and how they can be used in the analysis of film, as well as their translation into the practical via ritual, see John Lyden, *Film as Religion: Myths, Morals, and Rituals* (New York and London: New York University Press, 2003).

15. While this is not the place to discuss it at length, I think it worth contrasting Nietzsche's view here to Blumenberg, who argues that myth is "the earliest way of processing the terrors of the unknown and of overwhelming power" and thus "contributes to the humanization of the world." Blumenberg, *Work on Myth*, 388. While this shows the Apollonian aspect of myth, that is not the whole of myth for Nietzsche. When he says that it is through art and myth that "existence and the world are eternally *justified*," I take this to mean that what myth and art do is not "humanize"—they "eternalize" and place us in the shadow of a cosmic, dialectical struggle that he will rename the eternal recurrence of the same (*BT* §5, emphasis in original).

16. Young argues that Nietzsche returns (perhaps he never left it) to the "illusionism" of *The Birth of Tragedy* in his final works and again favors the Dionysian. Julian Young, *Nietzsche's Philosophy of Art* (Cambridge: Cambridge University Press, 1992), 148.

17. Obviously, this is connected to the idea of the *Übermensch* as child in *Zarathustra*.

18. Matthew Rukgaber, "The 'Sovereign Individual' and the 'Ascetic Ideal': On a Perennial Misreading of the Second Essay of Nietzsche's *On the Genealogy of Morality*," *Journal of Nietzsche Studies* 43, no. 2 (2012): 213–39.

19. Sternberg, *Chinese Laundry*, 26, 310.

20. Blumenberg, *Work on Myth*, 26.

21. The notion of singularity appears in Nietzschean form in Lemm, *Nietzsche's Animal Philosophy: Culture, Politics, and the Animality of the Human Being* (New York: Fordham University Press, 2009), 40, 57, 73–80.

22. Alexander Nehamas, *Nietzsche: Life as Literature* (Cambridge, MA: Harvard University Press, 1985), 3.

23. Nehamas, 3–4.

24. Nehamas, 8.

25. Nehamas, 37.

26. Wolfgang Müller-Lauter, *Nietzsche: His Philosophy of Contradictions and the Contradictions of his Philosophy* (Urbana, IL: University of Illinois Press, 1999), 5.

27. Nehamas, *Life as Literature*, 38.

28. If this work were more focused on the development of an aesthetic theory, then I would appeal significantly to Hatab's Nietzsche-inspired work on myth and its connection to reason, truth, and art. Lawrence Hatab, *Myth and Philosophy: A Contest of Truths* (La Salle, IL: Open Court, 1990). The remarks that I make here are intended to be compatible with Hatab's insights.

29. There are many different types of film realism. Kania describes three: film creates an illusion of reality; we are literally seeing real objects; and our perception of films is "like our experience of the world." Andrew Kania, "Realism," in *The Routledge Companion to Philosophy and Film*, ed. Paisley Livingston and Carl Plantinga (London and New York: Routledge, 2009), 237. Although the last one seems phenomenologically false, there surely are films that are realistic in the first two senses. I just do not think that the Nietzschean films that are my focus are. Certainly, other people and their expressive styles do actually exist, are real, or are in the world, so I would prefer Cavell's articulation that "reality" is "photographed, projected, screened, exhibited, and viewed," where "reality" is taken in a bland sense of "the visible" or "the presence of things," although I would also say that the invisible or the absence of things is also photographed, projected, and so on. Cavell, *The World Viewed: Reflections on the Ontology of Film*, enlarged edition (Cambridge, MA: Harvard University Press, 1979), 192.

30. Cavell, *World Viewed*, 105.

31. Bordwell describes style "in the narrowest sense" as "a film's systematic and significant use of techniques of the medium" or the "texture of the film's images and sounds," but that is surely also linked to what he calls "individual style," which seems to be the style of directors across their works and which goes on to include things like "narrative strategies and favored subjects or themes." David Bordwell, *On the History of Film Style* (Cambridge, MA and London: Harvard University Press, 1997), 4.

32. Noël Carroll, *Engaging the Moving Image* (New Haven and London: Yale University Press, 2003), 7.

33. Maurice Merleau-Ponty, "Cezanne's Doubt," in *Sense and Non-Sense* (Evanston, IL: Northwestern University Press, 1964), 16.

34. Maurice Merleau-Ponty, "Film and the New Psychology," in *Sense and Non-Sense* (Evanston, IL: Northwestern University Press, 1964), 53.

35. Maurice Merleau-Ponty, "Eye and Mind," in *The Primacy of Perception* (Evanston, IL: Northwestern University Press, 1964), 188.

36. Maurice Merleau-Ponty, *The Sensible World and the World of Expression* (Evanston, IL: Northwestern University Press, 2020), 126–27.

37. Maurice Merleau-Ponty, "Film and the New Psychology," 54.
38. Merleau-Ponty, 57.
39. Giorgio Agamben, *Means without End: Notes on Politics* (Minneapolis: University of Minnesota Press, 2000), 55–56. This concept is elaborated in Janet Harbord, *Ex-centric Cinema: Giorgio Agamben and Film Archeology* (New York and London: Bloomsbury, 2016), 57–99. The centrality of gesture is also elaborated by Rancière in his analysis of how Chaplin's performance achieves a unique immediacy and mode of expression by transforming expectations and engaging in what I would call the moving image of perspectivism. Jacques Rancière, *Aisthesis: Scenes from the Aesthetic Regime of Art* (London and New York: Version: 2013), 191–206.
40. Ronald Bogue, "Deleuze," in *The Routledge Companion to Philosophy and Film*, ed. Paisley Livingston and Carl Plantinga (London and New York: Routledge, 2009), 371.
41. Bogue, 372.
42. Bogue, 373.
43. Bogue, 374.
44. Bogue, 372; Gilles Deleuze, *Cinema 2: The Time-Image* (Minneapolis: University of Minnesota Press, 1989),41.
45. Deleuze, *Cinema 2*, 22.
46. Bogue, "Deleuze," 734.
47. Gilles Deleuze, *Negotiations* (New York: Columbia University Press, 1995), 51. Deleuze remarks that "there's still movement, of course" in that there are people in space doing things, but it is a kind of "wandering" that he sees linked specifically to the aftermath of the Second World War (Deleuze, 51).
48. Deleuze, *Cinema 2*, 41.
49. A valuable critique of this division and the fact that the two types of images inseparably bleed into one another is found in Jacques Rancière, *Film Fables* (Oxford and New York: Berg, 2006), 107–23.
50. Jacques Derrida, "Aletheia," *Oxford Literary Review* 32, no. 2 (2010): 171.
51. Derrida, 172.
52. Derrida, 173.
53. Derrida, 175.
54. It is not possible to work through all the connections that Derrida makes here, but an account of cinema's relation to touch and gesture, as well as the way in which the body is shot through by "technicity," is elaborated through the work of Nancy and Derrida in Laura McMahon, *Cinema and Contact: The Withdrawal of Touch in Nancy, Cresson, Duras and Denis* (Abingdon and New York: Routledge, 2012). These specific connections between "tactile visuality," the erotic, and mourning are found also in Laura Marks, *The Skin of the Film: Intercultural Cinema, Embodiment, and the Senses* (Durham, KY: Duke University Press, 2000), 192–93.

55. Jacques Derrida, *Athens, Still Remains: The Photographs of Jean-François Bonhomme* (New York: Fordham University Press, 2010), 27.
56. Jacques Derrida, *Copy, Archive, Signature: A Conversation on Photography* (Stanford: Stanford University Press, 2000), 19.
57. Derrida, "Aletheia," 176.
58. Derrida, *Athens, Still Remains*, 19.
59. Derrida, 67.
60. Cavell too rejects the idea that film "records" reality and says that "reality" is not really "a candidate" for being recorded, as what is recorded is in principle "indistinguishable" from the recording, as in the example of a musical performance. But reality and what is "projected" in film are distinguishable. Cavell, *World Viewed*, 183. If I had to interpret this, I would say that Cavell means that the frame of the film and other formal and technical features of it do something quite different than "record" or faithfully reproduce "the world" that they photograph and project.
61. Derrida, *Copy, Archive, Signature*, 43.
62. Derrida, 5.
63. "C'est l'essence de la photographie, le spectral." Jacques Derrida and Marie-Francoise Plissart, *Droit de Regards* (Paris: Editions de Minuit, 1985), 6.
64. Derrida and Plissart, 13.
65. Gilles Deleuze, *Nietzsche and Philosophy* (New York: Columbia University Press, 1983), 48.
66. Deleuze, 48–49.
67. Deleuze, 72. This reading is supported in Dorthea Olkowski, *Gilles Deleuze and the Ruin of Representation* (Berkeley: University of California Press, 1999), 185.
68. Derrida, *Negotiations*, 219.
69. Derrida, 247.
70. Agamben, *Means without End*, 53.
71. Deleuze, *Cinema 2*, 187–88.
72. Derrida, *Negotiations* 222.
73. Derrida, 222–23.
74. Jacques Derrida, *The Work of Mourning* (Chicago and London: University of Chicago Press, 2001), 39, 54. On these connections, see Peter Brunette and David Wills, *Screen/Play: Derrida and Film Theory* (Princeton: Princeton University Press, 1989), 114–15.
75. Derrida, *Work of Mourning*, 49.
76. Derrida, 48.
77. John Mullarkey, *Refractions of Reality: Philosophy and the Moving Image* (Houndmills and New York: Palgrave Macmillan, 2009), 6.
78. We might adopt Babich's conception of Nietzsche's style to describe this approach to film—as being "concinnous"—meaning a style that enacts a "harmony of disparate or dissonant themes" while initiating a play between different texts

and being also "reader-specific" or hyper-aware of the relation to the historical situation of the reader. Babette Babich, "Nietzsche and the Condition of Postmodern Thought: Post-Nietzschean Postmodernism," in *Nietzsche as Postmodernist: Essays Pro and Con*, ed. Clayton Koelb (Albany: SUNY, 1990), 252.

79. Babich, 13.

80. An excellent statement of Cavell's notion of film as reproducing a sort of skepticism that can be called the "theatricalization of our own reality" and, thus, as a "distance from the everyday world" is given by Bronfen. Elizabeth Bronfen, "Hurray for Hollywood: Philosophy and Cinema according to Stanley Cavell," in *Film as Philosophy*, ed. Bernd Herzogenrath (Minneapolis: University of Minneapolis Press, 2017), 181.

81. Stuart Klawans, "Habitual Remarriage: The Ends of Happiness in *The Palm Beach Story*," in *Film as Philosophy: Essays in Cinema After Wittgenstein and Cavell*, ed. Rupert Read and Jerry Goodenough (Houndmills and New York: Palgrave Macmillan, 2005), 162.

82. Jacques Derrida, *Limited Inc.* (Evanston: Northwestern University Press, 1988), 13.

83. Stanley Cavell, *Philosophical Passages: Wittgenstein, Emerson, Austin, Derrida* (Oxford and Cambridge: Blackwell, 1995), 61, 53, 50.

84. Cavell, 77.

85. Cavell, 47.

86. Derrida, *Limited Inc.*, 16–17.

87. Derrida, 16–18.

88. Cavell, *World Viewed*, 102.

89. Stanley Cavell, *Cities of Words: Pedagogical Letters on a Register of the Moral Life* (Cambridge, MA: Harvard University Press, 2004), 218.

Bibliography

Agamben, Giorgio. *Means without End: Notes on Politics*. Minneapolis: University of Minnesota Press, 2000.
Artaud, Antonin. "Cinema and Reality." In *French Film Theory and Criticism: A History/Anthology: 1907–1939*. Vol. 1, edited by Richard Abel, 410–12. Princeton: Princeton University Press, 1988.
Ascheim, Steven. *The Nietzsche Legacy in Germany: 1890–1990*. Berkeley: University of California Press, 1992.
Babich, Babette. "Nietzsche and the Condition of Postmodern Thought: Post-Nietzschean Postmodernism." In *Nietzsche as Postmodernist: Essays Pro and Con*, edited by Clayton Koelb, 249–66. Albany: SUNY, 1990.
Baker, Thomas Stockham. "Contemporary Criticism of Friedrich Nietzsche." *Journal of Philosophy, Psychology and Scientific Methods* 4, no. 15 (1907): 406–19.
Bakewell, Charles. "The Teaching of Nietzsche." *International Journal of Ethics* 9, no. 3 (1899): 314–31.
Barton, Bruce. *The Man Nobody Knows: A Discovery of the Real Jesus*. Indianapolis: Bobbs-Merrill, 1925.
Baudrillard, Jean. *Simulacra and Simulation*. Ann Arbor, MI: University of Michigan Press, 1994.
Baxter, John. *Von Sternberg*. Lexington, KY: University Press of Kentucky, 2010.
Baxter, Peter, ed. *Sternberg*. London: British Film Institute, 1980.
Bazin, André. *What Is Cinema?* Vol. 1. Berkeley: University of California Press, 1967.
———. *The Cinema of Cruelty*. New York: Seaver Books, 1982.
Beach, Christopher. *Class, Language, and American Film Comedy*. Cambridge: Cambridge University Press, 2002.
Beneficial, James Giles. "Atavism in Frank Norris and Jack London." *Western American Literature* 4, no. 1 (1969): 15–27.
Berg, Leo. *The Superman in Modern Literature*. London: Jarrold and Sons, 1915.
Bergoffen, Debra. "Nietzsche's Madman: Perspectivism without Nihilism." In *Nietzsche as Postmodernist: Essays Pro and Con*, edited by Clayton Koelb, 57–71. Albany: SUNY Press 1990.

———. "Toward the Body of the Overman." In *Nietzsche and the Becoming of Life*, edited by Vanessa Lemm, 161–76. New York: Fordham University Press, 2015.

Bertram, Ernst. *Nietzsche: Attempt at a Mythology*. Urbana, IL: University of Illinois Press, 2009.

Best, Katharine. "Horseplay into Photoplay." *Stage* (November 1937): 63–65.

Blackton, J. Stuart. *The Battle Cry for Peace*. Brooklyn: M. P. Publishing, 1915.

Blondel, Eric. "Nietzsche: Life as Metaphor." In *The New Nietzsche*, edited by David Allison, 150–75. Cambridge, MA: MIT Press, 1985.

Blumenberg, Hans. *Work on Myth*. Cambridge, MA: MIT Press, 1985.

Bogue, Ronald. "Deleuze." In *The Routledge Companion to Philosophy and Film*, ed. Paisley Livingston and Carl Plantinga, 368–77. London and New York: Routledge, 2009.

Bordwell, David. *On the History of Film Style*. Cambridge, MA and London: Harvard University Press, 1997.

Bordwell, David, Janet Staiger, and Kristin Thompson. *The Classical Hollywood Cinema: Film Style and Mode of Production to 1960*. London: Routledge and Kegan Paul, 1985.

Boyd, Ernest Augustus. *H. L. Mencken*. New York: Robert M. McBride, 1925.

———. *The Sacred Egoism of Sinn Fein*. Dublin and London: Maunsel, 1918.

Bourne, Randolph. "The Life of Irony." *Atlantic Monthly* (March 1913): 357–65.

Bridgwater, Patrick. *Nietzsche in Anglosaxony: A Study of Nietzsche's Impact on English and American Literature*. New York: Leicester University Press, 1972.

Bronfen, Elizabeth. "Hurray for Hollywood: Philosophy and Cinema according to Stanley Cavell." In *Film as Philosophy*, edited by Bernd Herzogenrath, 180–99. Minneapolis: University of Minneapolis Press, 2017.

Brownlow, Kevin. *Behind the Mask of Innocence: Sex, Violence, Prejudice, Crime: Films of Social Conscience in the Silent Era*. Berkeley: University of California Press, 1990.

Brunette, Peter, and David Wills. *Screen/Play: Derrida and Film Theory*. Princeton: Princeton University Press, 1989.

Burnett, W. R. *Little Caesar*. New York: The Dial Press, 1958.

Burroughs, Edgar Rice. *Tarzan of the Apes*. New York: A. L. Burt, 1914.

Cano, Virginia. "Is Evolution Blind? On Nietzsche's Reception of Darwin." In *Nietzsche and the Becoming of Life*, edited by Vanessa Lemm, 51–66. New York: Fordham University Press, 2015.

Carter, Erica. *Dietrich's Ghosts: The Sublime and the Beautiful in Third Reich Film*. London: BFI Publishing, 2004.

Carroll, Noël. *Engaging the Moving Image*. New Haven and London: Yale University Press, 2003.

Cavell, Stanley. *The World Viewed: Reflections on the Ontology of Film*. Enlarged edition. Cambridge, MA: Harvard University Press, 1979.

———. *Pursuits of Happiness: The Hollywood Comedy of Remarriage*. Cambridge, MA: Harvard University Press, 1981.

———. *In Quest of the Ordinary: Lines of Skepticism and Romanticism*. Chicago and London: University of Chicago Press, 1988.
———. *Philosophical Passages: Wittgenstein, Emerson, Austin, Derrida*. Oxford and Cambridge: Blackwell, 1995.
———. *Contesting Tears: The Hollywood Melodrama of the Unknown Woman*. Chicago: University of Chicago, 1996.
———. *Cities of Words: Pedagogical Letters on a Register of the Moral Life*. Cambridge, MA: Harvard University Press, 2004.
———. *Cavell on Film*. Albany: SUNY Press, 2005.
Chandler, James. *An Archaeology of Sympathy: The Sentimental Mode in Literature and Cinema*. Chicago: University of Chicago Press, 2013.
Clemenceau, Georges. *The Strongest*. Garden City and New York: Doubleday, Page, 1919.
Coates, Paul. *The Gorgon's Gaze: German Cinema, Expressionism, and the Image of Horror*. Cambridge: Cambridge University Press, 1991.
———. *Screening the Face*. Basingstoke and New York: Palgrave MacMillan, 2012.
Comolli, Jean-Louis. *Cinema against Spectacle: Technique and Ideology Revisited*. Amsterdam: Amsterdam University Press, 2015.
Conrad, Joseph. *Victory*. New York: The Modern Library, 1915.
Constable, Catherine. *Thinking in Images: Film Theory, Feminist Philosophy and Marlene Dietrich*. London: British Film Institute, 2005.
Cornell, Drucilla. *The Philosophy of the Limit*. New York and London: Routledge, 1992.
Coward, Noël. *The Letters of Noël Coward*. New York: Vintage Books, 2007.
Cox, Christopher. *Nietzsche and Naturalism: Naturalism and Interpretation*. Berkeley: University of California Press, 1999.
Danto, Arthur. *Nietzsche as Philosopher*. New York: Columbia University, 1965.
De Casseres, Benjamin. "The Stage-Instinct." *Theater* 7, no. 79 (Sept. 1907): 234–35.
———. "The Divinity of Genius." *Sun* (August 14, 1911): 4.
———. "Jules de Gaultier: Super-Nietzschean." *Forum* (January 1913): 86–90.
———. "Insincerity: A New Vice." *Camera Work* no. 42–43 (April–July 1913): 15–17.
———. "The Renaissance of the Irrational." *Camera Work* (June 1913): 22–24.
———. "The Philosophy of Hypocrisy." *International* 9, no. 7 (July 1915): 222–23.
———. *The Superman in America*. Seattle: University of Washington Bookstore, 1929.
De Gaultier, Jules. *Bovarysm*. New York: Philosophical Library, 1970.
De Meyer, Mahrah. *Nadine Narska*. New York: Wilmarth Publishing, 1916.
Delap, Lucy. "The Superwoman: Theories of Gender and Genius in Edwardian Britain." *Historical Journal* 47, no. 1 (2004): 101–26.
Deleuze, Gilles. *Nietzsche and Philosophy*. New York: Columbia University Press, 1983.
———. *Cinema 1: The Movement-Image*. Minneapolis: University of Minnesota Press, 1986.
———. *Cinema 2: The Time-Image*. Minneapolis: University of Minnesota Press, 1989.

———. *Negotiations*. New York: Columbia University Press, 1995.
———. *Pure Immanence: Essays on A Life*. New York: Zone Books, 2001.
DeNormandie, James. "Nietzsche and the Doctrine of Force." *Proceedings of the Massachusetts Historical Society* 3, no. 48 (1915): 170–76.
Derrida, Jacques. *Writing and Difference*. Chicago: University of Chicago Press, 1978.
———. *Spurs: Nietzsche's Styles*. Chicago: University of Chicago Press, 1979.
———. *Margins of Philosophy*. Chicago: University of Chicago Press, 1982.
———. *Limited Inc*. Evanston: Northwestern University Press, 1988.
———. *Given Time: I. Counterfeit Money*. Chicago: University of Chicago Press, 1992.
———. "The Deconstruction of Actuality: An Interview with Jacques Derrida." *Radical Philosophy* 68 (Autumn 1994): 27–41.
———. *Copy, Archive, Signature: A Conversation on Photography*. Stanford: Stanford University Press, 2000.
———. *The Work of Mourning*. Chicago and London: University of Chicago Press, 2001.
———. *Negotiations: Interventions and Interviews, 1971–2001*. Stanford: Stanford University Press, 2002.
———. *Acts of Religion*. New York and London: Routledge, 2002.
———. *Rogues: Two Essays on Reason*. Stanford: Stanford University Press, 2005.
———. *Geneses, Genealogies, Genres, and Genius: The Secrets of the Archive*. New York: Columbia University Press, 2006.
———. *The Gift of Death and Literature in Secret*. Chicago: University of Chicago Press, 2008.
———. *The Beast and the Sovereign*. Vol. 1. Chicago: University of Chicago Press, 2009.
———. "Aletheia." *Oxford Literary Review* 32, no. 2 (2010): 168–88.
———. *Athens, Still Remains: The Photographs of Jean-François Bonhomme*. New York: Fordham University Press, 2010.
Derrida, Jacques, and Marie-Francoise Plissart. *Droit de Regards*. Paris: Editions de Minuit, 1985.
Devereaux, Mary. "Oppressive Texts, Resisting Readers and the Gendered Spectator: The New Aesthetics." *Journal of Aesthetics and Art Criticism* 48, no. 4 (1990): 337–47.
"Did Nietzsche Predict the Superwoman as Well as the Superman?" *Current Literature* 43 (1907): 643–44.
Diethe, Carol. *Nietzsche's Women: Beyond the Whip*. Berlin: Walter de Gruyter, 1996.
Dietrich, Marlene. *Marlene Dietrich's ABC*. New York: Ungar Publishing, 1984.
Doane, Mary Anne. *Femmes Fatales: Feminism, Film Theory, Psychoanalysis*. New York and London: Routledge, 1991.
Doherty, Thomas. *Pre-Code Hollywood: Sex, Immorality, and Insurrection in American Cinema 1930–1934*. New York: Columbia University Press, 1999.

Dolar, Mladon. "To Be or Not to Be? No, Thank You." In *Lubitsch Can't Wait*, edited by Ivana Novak, Jela Krečič, and Mladen Dolar, 111–129 (Ljubljana: Slovenian Cinematheque, 2014).
Dolson, Grace Neal. *The Philosophy of Friedrich Nietzsche*. New York: MacMillan, 1901.
———. "Review: *Nietzsche the Thinker*—A Study by William Mackintire." *International Journal of Ethics* 28, no. 4 (1918): 554–58.
Dumenil, Lynn. *The Modern Temper: American Culture and Society in the 1920s*. New York: Hill and Wang, 1995.
Eisenstein, Sergei. *The Film Sense*. New York: Meridian Books, 1957.
Eisner, Lotte. *The Haunted Screen: Expressionism in the German Cinema and the Influence of Max Reinhardt*. Berkeley: University of California Press, 1969.
Eksteins, Modris. "History and Degeneration: Of Birds and Cages." In *Degeneration: The Dark Side of Progress*, edited by J. Edward Chamberlin and Sander Gilman, 1–23. New York: Columbia University Press, 1985.
Ellis, Havelock. *The Criminal*. New York: Scribner & Welford, 1890.
Emerson, Ralph Waldo. *The Works of Ralph Waldo Emerson: Miscellanies*. Boston and New York: Fireside Edition, 1878.
———. *Essays: First and Second Series*. New York: Vintage Books/The Library of America, 1990.
Everson, William. *American Silent Film*. New York: Oxford University Press, 1978.
Eyman, Scott. *Ernst Lubitsch: Laughter in Paradise*. New York: Simon & Schuster, 1993.
Fetherling, Doug. *The Five Lives of Ben Hecht*. Toronto: Lester & Orphen, 1977.
Fink, Eugene. *Nietzsche's Philosophy*. London: Continuum, 2003.
Finler, Joel. *Stroheim*. Berkley: University of California Press, 1968.
Forth, Christopher. *Zarathustra in Paris: The Nietzsche Vogue in France 1891–1918*. Dekalb, IL: Northern Illinois University Press, 2001.
Frampton, Daniel. *Filmosophy*. London and New York: Wallflower Press, 2006.
Franco, Paul. *Nietzsche's Enlightenment: The Free-Spirit Trilogy of the Middle Period*. Chicago: University of Chicago Press, 2011.
Gerstner, David. *Manly Arts: Masculinity and Nation in Early American Cinema*. Durham, KY: Duke University Press, 2006.
Giddens, Anthony. *Modernity and Self-Identity: Self and Society in the Late Modern Age*. Stanford: Stanford University Press, 1991.
Giddins, Gary. "The Devil Is in the Details." In *Dietrich and Von Sternberg in Hollywood*. The Criterion Collection, 2018.
Gillespie, Michael Allen. *Nietzsche's Final Teaching*. Chicago: University of Chicago Press, 2017.
Giovacchini, Saverio. *Hollywood Modernism: Film and Politics in the Age of the New Deal*. Philadelphia: Temple University Press, 2001.
Girard, René. *Deceit, Desire, and the Novel: Self and Other in Literary Structure*. Baltimore: Johns Hopkins Press, 1965.
Goebel, Heinrich, and Ernest Antrim. "Friedrich Nietzsche's Uebermensch." *Monist* 9, no. 4 (1899): 563–71.

Goldstein, Julius. "The Keynote to the Work of Nietzsche" *Mind* 11, no. 42 (1902): 216–26.
Gooding-Williams, Robert. *Zarathustra's Dionysian Modernism*. Stanford: Stanford University Press, 2001.
Gorbach, Julien. *The Notorious Ben Hecht: Iconoclastic Writer and Zionist Militant*. West Lafayette, IN: Purdue University Press, 2019.
Granier, Jean. "Nietzsche's Conception of Chaos." In *The New Nietzsche*, edited by David Allison, 135–141. Cambridge: MIT Press, 1985.
Grieveson, Lee. *Policing Cinema: Movies and Censorship in Early-Twentieth-Century America*. Berkeley: University of California Press, 2004.
———. "Gangsters and Governance in the Silent Era." In *Mob Culture: Hidden Histories of the American Gangster Film*, edited by Lee Grieveson, Esther Sonnet, and Peter Stanfield, 13–40. New Brunswick, NJ: Rutgers University Press, 2005.
Grigg, Russell. "The Joyful Art of Ernst Lubitsch: *Trouble in Paradise*." In *Lubitsch Can't Wait*, edited by Ivana Novak, Jela Krečič, and Mladen Dolar, 39–64. Ljubljana: Slovenian Cinematheque, 2014.
Haar, Michel. "Nietzsche and Metaphysical Language." In *The New Nietzsche*, edited by David Allison, 5–36. Cambridge, MA: MIT Press, 1977.
———. *Nietzsche and Metaphysics*. Albany: SUNY Press, 1996.
Hake, Sabine. *Passions and Deceptions: The Early Films of Ernst Lubitsch*. Princeton: Princeton University Press, 1992.
Harbord, Janet. *Ex-centric Cinema: Giorgio Agamben and Film Archeology*. New York and London: Bloomsbury, 2016.
Harpham, Geoffrey. "Jack London and the Tradition of Superman Socialism." *American Studies* 16, no. 1 (1975): 23–33.
Harvey, James. *Romantic Comedy in Hollywood from Lubitsch to Sturges*. New York: Knopf, 1987.
Haskell, Molly. *From Reverence to Rape: The Treatment of Women in the Movies*. 2nd ed. Chicago and London: University of Chicago Press, 1987.
Hatab, Lawrence. *Myth and Philosophy: A Contest of Truths*. La Salle, IL: Open Court, 1990.
———. "Nietzsche, Nature, and the Affirmation of Life." In *Nietzsche and the Becoming of Life*, edited by Vanessa Lemm, 32–48. New York: Fordham University Press, 2015.
Hecht, Ben. "The Sermon in the Depths." *Little Review* 2, no. 3 (1915), 40–42.
———. *Fantazius Mallare: A Mysterious Oath*. Chicago: Covici-McGee, 1922.
———. *Humpty Dumpty*. New York: Boni and Liveright, 1924.
———. "The Rival Dummy." In *The Collected Stories of Ben Hecht*, 454–62. New York: Crown Publishers, 1945.
———. *A Child of the Century*. New York: Simon & Schuster, 1954.
———. *Charlie: The Improbable Life and Times of Charles MacArthur*. New York: Harper & Brothers, 1957.
———. *Gaily, Gaily*. New York: Doubleday, 1963.

———. *The Ben Hecht Show: Impolitic Observations from the Freest Thinker of 1950s Television*. Jefferson, NC: McFarland, 1993.
Heidegger, Martin. *Being and Time*. New York: Harper & Row, 1962.
———. *Nietzsche*. Vols. 1–4. New York: Harper & Row, 1991.
Heins, Laura. *Nazi Film Melodrama*. Urbana, IL: University of Illinois Press, 2013.
Holub, Robert. *Nietzsche in the Nineteenth Century: Social Questions and Philosophical Interventions*. Philadelphia: University of Pennsylvania Press, 2018.
Hulme, T. E. *The Collected Writings of T. E. Hulme*. Oxford: Clarendon Press, 1994.
Huneker, James, and Vance Thompson. *M'lle New York*. No. 1, vol. I, 1895.
Jacobs, Lea. *The Decline of Sentiment: American Film in the 1920s*. Berkeley: University of California Press, 2008.
———. *The Wages of Sin: Censorship and the Fallen Woman Film, 1928–1942*. Berkeley: University of California Press, 1995.
Jenkins, Scott. "Life, Injustice, and Recurrence." In *Nietzsche and the Becoming of Life*, edited by Vanessa Lemm, 121–36. New York: Fordham University Press, 2015.
Jordan, David Starr. *The Human Harvest: A Study of the Decay of Races through the Survival of the Unfit*. Boston: Beacon Press, 1907.
Kain, Philip. *Nietzsche and the Horror of Existence*. Lanham, MD: Lexington Books, 2009.
Kania, Andrew. "Realism." In *The Routledge Companion to Philosophy and Film*, edited by Paisley Livingston and Carl Plantinga, 237–48. London and New York: Routledge, 2009.
Kaufmann, Walter. *Nietzsche: Philosopher, Psychologist, Antichrist*. 4th ed. Princeton: Princeton University Press, 1974.
Kildare, Owen. *My Mamie Rose: The Story of My Regeneration: An Autobiography*. New York: Baker and Taylor, 1903.
Klawans, Stuart. "Habitual Remarriage: The Ends of Happiness in *The Palm Beach Story*." In *Film as Philosophy: Essays in Cinema After Wittgenstein and Cavell*, edited by Rupert Read and Jerry Goodenough,149–63. Houndmills and New York: Palgrave Macmillan, 2005.
Kornhaber, David. *The Birth of the Theater from the Spirit of Philosophy: Nietzsche and the Modern Theater*. Evanston, IL: Northwestern University Press, 2016.
Kosta, Barbara. *Willing Seduction: The Blue Angel, Marlene Dietrich, and Mass Culture*. New York: Berghahn Books, 2009.
Koszarski, Richard. *Von: The Life and Films of Erich Von Stroheim*. New York: Limelight Editions, 2001.
Kracauer, Siegfried. *From Caligari to Hitler: A Psychological History of the German Film*. Princeton: Princeton University Press, 1947.
Laing, Bertram. "The Origin of Nietzsche's Problem and Its Solution." *International Journal of Ethics* 26, no. 4 (1916): 510–27.
Landa, Ishay. *The Overman in the Marketplace: Nietzschean Heroism in Popular Culture*. Lanham, MD: Rowan and Littlefield, 2007.
Lankester, E. Ray. *Degeneration: A Chapter in Darwinism*. London: Macmillan, 1880.

Larson, Allen. "1937: Movies and New Constructions of the American Star." In *American Cinema of the 1930s: Themes and Variations*, edited by Ina Rae Hark, 182–205. New Brunswick: Rutgers University Press, 2007.

Lavrin, Janko. *Nietzsche and Modern Consciousness: A Psycho-Critical Study*. London: W. Collins and Sons, 1922.

Lemm, Vanessa. *Nietzsche's Animal Philosophy: Culture, Politics, and the Animality of the Human Being*. New York: Fordham University Press, 2009.

———. "Life and Justice in Nietzsche's Conception of History." In *Nietzsche and the Becoming of Life*, edited by Vanessa Lemm, 105–20. New York: Fordham University Press, 2015.

Lennig, Arthur. *Stroheim*. Lexington: University of Kentucky Press, 2000.

Levy, Oscar. "The Nietzsche Movement in England." In *The Complete Works of Friedrich Nietzsche*. Vol. 18, *Index to Nietzsche*, ix–xxxvi. London: T. H. Foulis, 1913.

Lewys, Georges. *Merry-Go-Round*. Privately Printed, 1923.

Loeb, Paul. *The Death of Nietzsche's Zarathustra*. Cambridge: Cambridge University Press, 2010.

Loos, Anita. *Kiss Hollywood Good-By*. New York: The Viking Press, 1974.

———. *Anita Loos Rediscovered: Film Treatments and Fiction*. Berkeley: University of California Press, 2003.

London, Jack. *Before Adam*. New York: Macmillan, 1915.

Lonergan, Phil. "A Disciple of Nietzsche." *Reel Life*. September 18, 1915: 16.

Louÿs, Pierre. *Woman and Puppet*, London: Greening, 1908.

Lübecker, Nikolaj. *The Feel-Bad Film*. Edinburgh: Edinburgh University Press, 2015.

Lyden, John. *Film as Religion: Myths, Morals, and Rituals*. New York and London: New York University Press, 2003.

MacAdams, William. *Ben Hecht: A Biography*. New York: Barricade Books, 1990.

MacDowell, James. "Interpretation, Irony and 'Surface Meanings' in Film." *Film-Philosophy* 22, no. 2 (2018): 261–80.

MacLane, Mary. *I, Mary MacLane: A Diary of Human Days*. New York: Frederick A. Stokes, 1917.

———. "The Movies—and Me." *Photoplay* (January 1918): 24–25.

———. *Human Days: A Mary MacLane Reader*. Austin, TX: Petrarca Press, 2014.

Magnus, Bernd. "Perfectability and Attitude in Nietzsche's 'Übermensch.'" *Review of Metaphysics* 36, no. 3 (1983): 633–59.

Marks, Laura. *The Skin of the Film: Intercultural Cinema, Embodiment, and the Senses*. Durham, KY: Duke University Press, 2000.

Marsden, Dora. "Bondwomen." *Freewoman* 1, no. 1 (Nov. 23, 1911): 1–2.

———. "Commentary on Bondwomen." *Freewoman* 1, no. 2 (Nov. 30, 1911): 21–22.

Marsden, Jill. "Sensing the Overhuman." *Journal of Nietzsche Studies* 30 (2005): 102–14.

Mason, Fran. *American Gangster Cinema: From Little Caesar to Pulp Fiction*. Houndsmills and New York: Palgrave Macmillan, 2002.

Matheson, Sue. "The 'True Spirit' of Eating Raw Meat: London, Nietzsche, and Rousseau in Robert Flaherty's *Nanook of the North* (1922)." *Journal of Popular Film and Television* 39, no. 1 (2011): 12–19.

Maugham, W. Somerset. *The Magician*. New York: George H. Doran, 1908.

———. *A Writer's Notebook*. Garden City, NY: Doubleday, 1949.

Maxim, Hudson. *Defenseless America*. New York: Hearst's International Library, 1915.

May, Lary. *The Big Tomorrow: Hollywood and the Politics of the American Way*. Chicago and London: University of Chicago Press, 2000.

Mayne, Judith. *Cinema and Spectatorship*. London and New York: Routledge, 1993.

McMahon, Laura. *Cinema and Contact: The Withdrawal of Touch in Nancy, Cresson, Duras and Denis*. Abingdon and New York: Routledge, 2012.

McNeil, Bevis. *Nietzsche and* Eternal. Cham, CH: Palgrave Macmillan 2021.

Mead, Henry. *T. E. Hulme and the Ideological Politics of Early Modernism*. London: Bloomsbury, 2015.

Mencken, H. L. *The Philosophy of Nietzsche*. 3rd ed. Boston: Luce, 1913.

———. *The Impossible H. L. Mencken*. New York: Anchor/Doubleday, 1991.

Merleau-Ponty, Maurice. *Phenomenology of Perception*. London and New York: Routledge, 1962.

———. "The Film and the New Psychology." In *Sense and Non-Sense*, 48–59. Evanston, IL: Northwestern University Press, 1964.

———. "Cezanne's Doubt." In *Sense and Non-Sense*, 9–25. Evanston, IL: Northwestern University Press, 1964.

———. "Eye and Mind." In *The Primacy of Perception*, 159–90. Evanston, IL: Northwestern University Press, 1964.

———. *The Sensible World and the World of Expression*. Evanston, IL: Northwestern University Press, 2020.

Michels, Steven. *Sinclair Lewis and America Democracy*. Lanham, MD: Lexington Books, 2017.

Miyasaki, Donovan. "Nietzsche's Naturalist Morality of Breeding: A Critique of Eugenics as Taming." In *Nietzsche and the Becoming of Life*, edited by Vanessa Lemm, 194–213. New York: Fordham University Press, 2015.

Moder, Gregor. "The Beard, the Bust, and the Plumed Helmet." In *Lubitsch Can't Wait*, edited by Ivana Novak, Jela Krečič, and Mladen Dolar, 151–64. Ljubljana: Slovenian Cinematheque, 2014.

Moore, Gregory. *Nietzsche, Biology and Metaphor*. Cambridge: Cambridge University Press, 2002.

More, Paul Elmer. *The Drift of Romanticism: Shelburne Essays*. 8th series. Boston and New York: Houghton Mifflin, 1913.

Morris IV, Gouverneur. *The Penalty*. New York: Charles Scribner's and Sons, 1919.

Mulhall, Stephen. *The Self and Its Shadows: A Book of Essays on Individuality as Negation in Philosophy and the Arts*. Oxford: Oxford University Press, 2013.

———. *On Film*. 3rd ed. London and New York: Routledge, 2016.

Mullarkey, John. *Refractions of Reality: Philosophy and the Moving Image.* Houndmills and New York: Palgrave Macmillan, 2009.
Müller-Lauter, Wolfgang. *Nietzsche: His Philosophy of Contradictions and the Contradictions of His Philosophy.* Urbana, IL: University of Illinois Press, 1999.
Nehamas, Alexander. "How One Becomes What One Is." *Philosophical Review* 92, no. 3: (1983): 385–417.
———. *Nietzsche: Life as Literature.* Cambridge, MA: Harvard University Press, 1985.
Nearing, Scott. *The Super Race: An American Problem.* New York: Huebsch, 1912.
Nietzsche, Friedrich, *The Collected Works of Friedrich Nietzsche*, edited by Oscar Levy. Edinburgh and London: T.N. Foulis, 1909–1913.
———. *Basic Writings of Nietzsche*, translated by Walter Kaufmann. New York: Modern Library, 2000.
———. *The Portable Nietzsche*, translated by Walter Kaufmann. New York: Penguin Books, 1982.
———. *Daybreak*, translated by R. J. Hollingdale. Cambridge: Cambridge University Press, 1982.
———. *Philosophy and Truth*, translated by Daniel Breazeale. Amherst, MA: Humanity Books, 1999.
———. *On the Genealogy of Morals and Ecce Homo*, translated by Walter Kaufmann. New York: Vintage Books, 1967.
———. *The Gay Science*, translated by Walter Kaufmann. New York: Vintage Books, 1974.
———. *The Will to Power*, translated by Walter Kaufmann. New York: Vintage Books, 1968.
———. *Human, All Too Human*, translated by R. J. Hollingdale. Cambridge: Cambridge University Press, 1996.
Nordau, Max. *Paradoxes.* Chicago: L. Schick, 1886.
———. *Degeneration.* New York: D. Appleton, 1895.
Norris, Frank. "Lauth." *Overland Monthly* 21, no. 123 (Mar. 1893): 241–60.
———. *The Octopus.* New York: Doubleday, Page, 1903.
———. *Novels and Essays.* New York: The Library of America, 1986.
———. *McTeague.* New York: Norton, 1997.
Novak, Ivana, and Krečič, Jela. "Introduction: The Importance of Being Ernst." In *Lubitsch Can't Wait*, edited by Ivana Novak, Jela Krečič, and Mladen Dolar, 1–17. Ljubljana: Slovenian Cinematheque, 2014.
Olafson, Frederick. "Nietzsche's Philosophy of Strength: A Paradox in *The Will to Power*." *Philosophy and Phenomenological Research* 51 no. 3 (1991): 557–72.
Olkowski, Dorthea. *Gilles Deleuze and the Ruin of Representation.* Berkeley: University of California Press, 1999.
Ooten, Melissa and Trembanis, Sarah. "Filming Eugenics: Teaching the History of Eugenics through Film." *Public Historian* 29, no. 3 (2007): 145–55.
Orage, A. R. *Consciousness: Animal, Human and Superman.* London and Benares: Theosophical Publishing Society, 1907.

———. *Friedrich Nietzsche: The Dionysian Spirit of the Age*. Chicago: A. C. McClurg, 1911.
———. *Nietzsche in Outline and Aphorism*. Edinburgh: T. N. Foulis, 1911.
Orr, John. *Cinema and Modernity*. Cambridge: Polity Press, 1993.
Paul, William. *Ernst Lubitsch's American Comedy*. New York: Columbia University Press, 1983.
Petre, Maude. "Studies on Friedrich Nietzsche: Nietzsche the Anti-Feminist." *Catholic World* 83 (1906): 159–70.
Pfaller, Robert. "What Is So Funny about Multiple Love? The Polygamous Lubitsch Touch." In *Lubitsch Can't Wait*, edited by Ivana Novak, Jela Krečič, and Mladen Dolar, 65–82. Ljubljana: Slovenian Cinematheque, 2014.
Phillips, James. *Sternberg and Dietrich: The Phenomenology of Spectacle*. Oxford and New York: Oxford University Press, 2019.
Pick, Daniel. *Faces of Degeneration: A European Disorder, c. 1848–c. 1918*. Cambridge: Cambridge University Press, 1989.
———. *Svengali's Web: The Alien Enchanter in Modern Culture*. New Haven, CT: Yale University Press, 2000.
Pippin, Robert. *Fatalism in American Film Noir: Some Cinematic Philosophy*. Charlottesville and London: University of Chicago Press, 2012.
———. *Filmed Thought: Cinema as Reflective Form*. Chicago and London: University of Chicago Press, 2020.
———. *Philosophy by Other Means: The Arts in Philosophy and Philosophy in the Arts*. Chicago and London: University of Chicago Press, 2021.
Pravadelli, Veronica. *Classic Hollywood: Lifestyles and Film Styles of American Cinema, 1930–1960*. Urbana, IL: University of Illinois Press, 2014.
Prawer, Siegbert Salomon. *Caligari's Children: The Film as Tale of Terror*. Oxford and New York: Oxford University Press, 1980.
Pütz, Manfred, ed. *Nietzsche in American Literature and Thought*. Columbia, SC: Camden House, 1995.
Rancière, Jacques. *Film Fables*. Oxford and New York: Berg, 2006.
———. *Aisthesis: Scenes from the Aesthetic Regime of Art*. London and New York: Version: 2013.
———. *The Intervals of Cinema*. London and New York: Verso, 2014.
Raphaelson, Samson. *The Human Nature of Playwriting*. New York: Macmillan, 1949.
Ratner-Rosenhagen, Jennifer. *American Nietzsche: A History of an Icon and His Ideas*. Chicago: University of Chicago Press, 2012.
Ritchie, David. *Darwinism and Politics*. London: Swan and Sonnenschein, 1891.
Rockefeller, John D. *Random Reminiscences of Men and Events*. New York: Doubleday, Page, 1909.
Rukgaber, Matthew. "The 'Sovereign Individual' and the 'Ascetic Ideal': On a Perennial Misreading of the Second Essay of Nietzsche's *On the Genealogy of Morality*." *Journal of Nietzsche Studies* 43, no. 2 (2012): 213–39.
———. "Phenomenological Film Theory and Max Scheler's Personalist Aesthetics." *Studia Phaenomenologica* 16 (2016): 215–31.

Said, Edward. "Conrad and Nietzsche." In *Joseph Conrad: A Commemoration*, edited by N. Sherry, 65–76. London: Palgrave, 1976.
Sanger, Margaret. *The Woman Rebel*. Vol. 1, no. 1 (March 1914).
———. "Family Limitation." 6th ed. (1917).
Santayana, George. *Winds of Doctrine: Studies in Contemporary Opinion*. New York: Charles Scribner's, 1913.
———. *Egotism in German Philosophy*. New York: Charles Scribner's, 1916.
Sarris, Andrew. *The Films of Josef von Sternberg*. Garden City, NY: Doubleday, 1966.
Schacht, Richard. *Nietzsche*. London and New York: Routledge, 1983.
———. *Nietzsche's Kind of Philosophy: What It Is—and Isn't*. Forthcoming.
Schindler, Colin. *Hollywood in Crisis Cinema and American Society, 1929–1939*. London and New York: Routledge, 1996.
Schmuhl, Robert. "History, Fantasy, Memory: Ben Hecht and a Chicago Hanging." *Illinois Historical Journal* 83, no. 3 (1990): 146–58.
Schrader, Paul. *Transcendental Style in Film: Ozu, Bresson, Dreyer*. New York: De Capo Press, 1972.
Schuster, Aaron. "Comedy in Times of Austerity." In *Lubitsch Can't Wait*, edited by Ivana Novak, Jela Krečič, and Mladen Dolar, 19–38. Ljubljana: Slovenian Cinematheque, 2014.
Scott, Charles. "The Mask of Nietzsche's Self-Overcoming." In *Nietzsche as Postmodernist: Essays Pro and Contra*, edited by Clayton Koelb, 217–229. Albany: SUNY Press, 1990.
Seitler, Dana. *Atavistic Tendencies: The Culture of Science in American Modernity*. Minneapolis: University of Minnesota Press, 2008.
Sevastakis, Michael. *Songs of Love and Death: The Classical American Horror Film of the 1930s*. Westport, CT: Greenwood Press, 1993.
Shadoian, Jack. *Dreams and Dead Ends: The American Gangster Film*. 2nd ed. Oxford: Oxford University Press, 2003.
Shelley, Mary. *Frankenstein; or, The Modern Prometheus*. London: Puffin Books, 1989.
Sinclair, Upton. *The Autobiography of Upton Sinclair*. New York: Harcourt, Brace, & World, 1962.
Singer, Irving. *Cinematic Mythmaking: Philosophy in Film*. Cambridge, MA: MIT Press, 2008.
Sinnerbrink, Robert. *New Philosophies of Film: Thinking Images*. London and New York: Bloomsbury, 2011.
Smith, Angela. *Hideous Progeny: Disability, Eugenics, and Classic Horror Cinema*. New York: Columbia University Press, 2011.
Smith, Imogen Sara. "Mistress of Confessions." In *Dietrich and Von Sternberg in Hollywood*. The Criterion Collection, 2018.
Soister, John T., and Henry Nicolella, with Steve Joyce and Harry Long. *American Silent Horror, Science Fiction and Fantasy Feature Films, 1913–1929*. Vol. 1. Jefferson, NC: McFarland, 2012.
Solomon, Robert. "Nietzsche *ad hominem*: Perspectivism, Personality, and *Ressentiment*." In *The Cambridge Companion to Nietzsche*, edited by Bernd Magnus and Kathleen Higgins, 180–222. Cambridge: Cambridge University Press, 1996.

Sontag, Susan. "Notes on Camp." In *Against Interpretation and Other Essays*, 275–92. London: Penguin, 2009.
Stambaugh, Joan. *Nietzsche's Thought of Eternal Return*. Baltimore and London: Johns Hopkins University Press, 1972.
Stamp, Shelley. *Lois Weber in Early Hollywood*. Berkeley: University of California Press, 2015.
Steven, Mark. "Nietzsche on Film." *Film-Philosophy* 21, no. 1 (2017): 95–113.
Steilberg, Hays Alan. *Die amerikanische Nietzsche-Rezeption von 1896 bis 1950*. Berlin: de Gruyter, 1996.
Stearns, Harold, ed. *Civilization in the United States: An Inquiry by Thirty Americans*. New York: Harcourt, Brace, 1922.
Sternberg, Josef von. *Fun in a Chinese Laundry*. New York: MacMillan, 1965.
———. *The Blue Angel: Authorized Translation of the German Continuity*. New York: Simon & Schuster, 1968.
Stewart, Herbert. "Some Criticisms on the Nietzsche Revival." *International Journal of Ethics* 19, no. 4 (1909): 427–43.
Stone, Dan. "An 'Entirely Tactless Nietzschean Jew': Oscar Levy's Critique of Western Civilization." *Journal of Contemporary History* 36, no. 2 (2001): 271–92.
Stratton, Matthew. *The Politics of Irony in American Modernism*. New York: Fordham University Press, 2014.
Strauss, David. *The Old Faith and the New: A Confession*. London: Asher, 1873.
Stroheim, Erich von. "In the Morning." *Film History* 2 (1988): 283–95.
Strong, Tracy. "Nietzsche's Political Misappropriation." In *The Cambridge Companion to Nietzsche*, edited by Bernd Magnus and Kathleen Higgins, 119–147. Cambridge: Cambridge University Press, 1996.
———. "The Optics of Science, Art, and Life: How Tragedy Begins." In *Nietzsche and the Becoming of Life*, edited by Vanessa Lemm, 19–31. New York: Fordham University Press, 2015.
Studlar, Gaylyn. *In the Realm of Pleasure: Von Sternberg, Dietrich, and the Masochistic Aesthetic*. New York: Columbia University Press, 1988.
Styan, J. L. *Max Reinhardt*. Cambridge: Cambridge University Press, 1982.
Talbot, Eugene. *Degeneracy: Its Signs, Causes and Results*. London: Walter Scott, 1898.
Taylor, Seth. *Left-Wing Nietzscheans: The Politics of German-Expressionism 1910–1920*. Berlin: De Gruyter, 1990.
Thatcher, David. *Nietzsche in England, 1890–1914*. Toronto: University of Toronto Press, 1970.
Thomas, R. Hinton. *Nietzsche in German Politics and Society 1890–1918*. Manchester: Manchester University Press, 1983.
Thoreau, Henry David. *Walden; or, Life in the Woods*. Boston and New York: Houghton, Mifflin, 1919.
Valadier, Paul. "Dionysius versus the Crucified." In *The New Nietzsche*, edited by David Allison, 247–261. Cambridge, MA: MIT Press, 1985.
Vansant, Jacqueline. *Austria: Made in Hollywood*. Rochester, NY: Camden House, 2019.

Vattimo, Gianni. *Beyond the Subject: Nietzsche, Heidegger, and Hermeneutics.* Albany: SUNY Press, 2019.
Walsh, Raoul. *Each Man in His Time: The Life Story of a Director.* New York: Farrar, Straus and Giroux, 1974.
Warbeke, John. "Friedrich Nietzsche, Antichrist, Superman, and Pragmatist." *Harvard Theological Review* 2, no. 3 (1909): 366–85.
Wartenberg, Thomas. *Thinking on Screen: Film as Philosophy.* London and New York: Routledge, 2007.
Weales, Gerald. *Canned Goods as Caviar: American Film Comedy of the 1930s.* Chicago: University of Chicago Press, 1985.
Weinberg, Herman. *Josef von Sternberg: A Critical Study of the Great Film Director.* New York: E. P. Dutton, 1967.
Wells, H. G. *The Island of Dr. Moreau: A Possibility.* New York: Stone & Kimball, 1896.
———. *The Invisible Man: A Grotesque Romance.* New York and London: Harper & Brothers, 1897.
———. "Human Evolution." *Natural Science* (April 1897).
———. *Anticipations of the Reaction of Mechanical and Scientific Progress upon Human Life and Thought.* London: Chapman & Hall, 1902.
Wiggam, Albert Edward. *The Next Age of Man.* New York: Blue Ribbon Books, 1927.
Wilson, George. *Narration in Light: Studies in Cinematic Point of View.* Baltimore and London: Johns Hopkins University Press, 1986.
Wittgenstein, Ludwig. *Philosophical Investigations.* 2nd ed. Oxford: Blackwell, 1958.
Woodford, Peter. *The Moral Meaning of Nature: Nietzsche's Darwinian Religion and Its Critics.* Chicago: University of Chicago Press, 2018.
Wylie, Philip. *Gladiator.* Lincoln, NE: University of Nebraska Press, 2004.
Young, Julian. *Nietzsche's Philosophy of Art.* Cambridge: Cambridge University Press, 1992.
Žižek, Slavoj. *Absolute Recoil: Towards a New Foundation of Dialectical Materialism.* London and New York: Verso, 2014.
———. "Lubitsch, the Poet of Cynical Wisdom?" In *Lubitsch Can't Wait*, edited by Ivana Novak, Jela Krečič, and Mladen Dolar. Ljubljana: Slovenian Cinematheque, 2014, 181–205.
Zucker, Carole. *The Idea of the Image: Josef von Sternberg's Dietrich Films.* Rutherford, NJ: Fairleigh Dickinson University Press, 1988.
Zupančič, Alenka. "Squirrels to the Nuts, or, How Many Does It Take to Not Give Up on Your Desire?" In *Lubitsch Can't Wait*, edited by Ivana Novak, Jela Krečič, and Mladen Dolar, 165–179. Ljubljana: Slovenian Cinematheque, 2014.
Zweig, Paul. *The Adventurer.* New York: Basic Books, 1974.

Index

abyss, 7, 44, 46, 49, 89, 106, 149–150, 156, 160, 162, 204, 212–213, 231n24, 237–238n14
aesthetics: expressionism, 5, 11, 56, 65, 170–171, 250n51; Nietzschean, 4, 10, 13, 37, 64, 199, 203–207, 215–219; sentimentalism, 1–2, 18–19, 43–44, 48, 56, 86, 170. *See also* art
aestheticism, 4, 10, 172, 173, 199, 203, 206
affect, 7, 44, 62, 143, 164–165, 200–201, 203–205, 209, 218–219, 231n13, 252n93; and crisis, 153–155; expressions of, 135–136. *See also* shame; uncanny
Agamben, Giorgio, 209, 213
agency, 68, 79, 230n7, 248n34, 248n37, 252n93; lack of, 51, 152, 164–166, 210. *See also* fate
agonism, 38, 65, 119, 201, 207, 217, 219
akrasia, 178–179
amor fati. *See under* fate: love of
animae magnae prodigus, 16–17, 25, 39, 64, 86, 89, 168, 219
aristocracy, 17, 21, 27–29, 50, 54, 80, 99, 187–188. *See also* pathos of distance
art, 7, 11–13, 141–142, 173, 200–209; for art's sake, 160; and existence, 125, 258n15; and gesture, 209, 211–214; for the masses, 9–10; and morality, 146; and self-alienation, 57–58; and sublimation of passion, 124, 135; will to, 116. *See also* aesthetics; Dionysian and Apollonian
atavism, 16, 29, 32–34, 42, 52, 54, 199, 229n72; Jack London on, 25–26; positive and negative forms of, 23–27, 59, 227n40
autonomy, 168; of appearances, 254n19; as sovereignty, 205; and women, 87, 92, 110

Baby Face, 1, 73, 96–103, 105, 106, 165, 174, 210, 238n24, 241n63
Battle Cry for Peace, The, 23–25
Bazin, André, 230n3, 230n5
becoming, 8–9, 16, 37, 38, 44, 71, 111–112, 116, 203, 208, 210, 248n28; versus being, 11, 67, 75, 90, 199–200, 212–214
Blind Husbands, 41–46
Blonde Venus, 151–155, 159, 162 249n41–42, 250n58
Bourne, Randolph, 138–140, 242–243n16, 246n56
Bovarysm, 3, 114, 125, 189, *See also* aestheticism

camp, 157 165 195 202, 250n62–63

277

capitalism, 18–19, 48, 186–187, 192–193, 240n51; and the *Übermensch*, 63
Catherine the Great, 108, 111, 165
Cavell, Stanley, 1, 5, 12–13, 119–120, 122, 208, 217–219, 235n23, 243n24, 259n29, 261n60, 262n80; on art and selfhood, 11–12; and remarriage comedies, 2–3, 105, 123, 171, 192, 194, 216; and melodrama of the unknown woman, 237n14, 242n71, 250n55. *See also* skepticism
Clemenceau, Georges, 92–93
Comolli, Jean-Louis, 11, 224–225n51
Conrad, Joseph, 30–31, 228n61
Constable, Catherine, 162–163, 237n11, 238n18, 247n12, 247n14, 251n65, 251–252n81, 252n93
counterfeit, 46–47, 49–50, 52, 87, 102–103, 129, 201, 241n68
crime, 19, 69, 78–79, 116, 120, 122, 169, 186; in film history, 65–66, 234n15, 234n16, 235n20; revolutionary action as, 63–64; two types of, 67, 70–71
crowd, the, 57, 73, 93, 97, 139, 160–162, 167, 168, 183, 201, 204, 206, 250n47; and the herd, 7, 9, 31, 39, 55, 67 80, 88, 90, 101, 128, 199, 211, 217–218

Darwin, Charles, 16, 34, 227n29, 227n35; and evolutionary theory, 26, 31, 115, 225n2; and social Darwinism, 16–17, 19, 21–24, 28, 32
De Casseres, Benjamin, 63, 114, 129, 130, 150, 243n21, 243–244n30, 248n31
death, 16, 31, 56–57, 122, 134, 155, 252n94; and boredom, 114; courage in the face of, 78, 134–135; created by fiction, 121; and degeneration, 32, 33, 45–47, 49, 50–53, 231n13; 232n45; gift of, 146, 161, 215; of God, 217; and love, 154, 158; and pleasure, 144–145, 148–149, 248n28, 248n37; and photography, 211; and self-overcoming, 73–75, 94, 149, 233n53, 249n43, 249n46
deception, 103–6, 111, 114–119, 122, 126, 130–131, 134, 136, 181, 186, 213, 218, 221n8; and women, 88–90, 97, 103; and self-deception, 109, 123
degeneration, 33–34, 38, 44–46, 50–51, 59, 61, 210, 228n61, 230–231n12, 231n13; and criminality, 61, 66–67; of Europe, 47–48; interpretations of, 40–42; symbols of, 37–38, 52, 232n37; versus regeneration, 46, 52–54
Deleuze, Gilles, 1, 64–65, 198, 200, 215; on action-images and time-images, 51, 75, 117, 209–210, 213–214, 235–236n33, 238n20, 260n47; and the autoimmune, 150; on eternal recurrence, 212–214; on power of the false, 38, 44, 47, 65, 87, 131, 209; on Stroheim, 44, 51
DeMille, Cecile B., 23, 27–29
Derrida, Jacques, 16, 58, 131, 133, 138–139, 199, 215, 217–219, 238n20, 241n68, 260n54; and autoimmunity, 150; on death, 146, 161; on eternal recurrence, 212–214; on genius, 127; on justice, 61–62; on photography, 211–214; on responsibility, 145–146, 153, 157, 161; on the *Übermensch*, 7, 149–150; on women, 87–90, 97–98, 107, 109, 237–238n14, 238n18, 251–252n81; see also *différance*
Design for Living, 115, 123–125, 169, 173, 174, 192, 255n22

Devereaux, Mary, 4, 10, 222n17
Devil is a Woman, The, 156–160, 162
différance, 37–38, 75, 90, 122, 127, 158, 192, 211, 218, 230n2
Dionysian, 10, 68, 79, 101, 105–106, 146, 150, 171, 172, 200, 203, 215, 219, 233n49, 238n17, 249n40, 255n21; and Apollonian, 59, 142–145, 149, 162, 164, 203–205, 207, 212, 231n24, 247n7, 248n27, 249n43; art, 4, 147; and ecstasy, 59, 94, 107, 136, 251n74; as loss of individuality, 46, 148, 151, 153, 155–156, 160–166, 248n37, 249n42; and symbols of, 43, 44, 148–152; *Übermensch* as, 8, 16, 53, 96, 141–142, 247n9; wisdom, 43, 49, 143, 157–160, 165, 203–204; woman as, 88–89, 100, 106–107, 111
Disciple of Nietzsche, A, 20–21
Dr. Jekyll and Mr. Hyde, 32–33, 57, 81 91

egoism, 16, 18–19, 25, 28, 30–32, 34, 37, 40, 45, 55, 57–58, 62, 90–92, 97, 115, 125, 129–130, 150, 154, 180, 190–192
Eisner, Lotte, 5, 229n63
Emerson, Ralph Waldo, 2, 6–7, 24, 64, 217
eternal recurrence of the same, 9, 13, 16, 62–63, 64, 86, 121, 127, 155, 161, 199, 202, 206, 212–214, 224n48, 258n15; life as 10; as repetition, 51–53, 75, 80, 87, 95, 103, 106, 123, 130, 150–151, 174–175, 213, 218, 254n11, 255n25. *See also* fate, time
eugenics, 3, 16–17, 19–22, 225n3, 227n32

faith, 122, 141–142, 145, 157, 160–167, 214–215, 241n68, 251n74, 252n87; cinematic, 3; traditional forms of, 17, 22, 41, 49
farce, 4, 27, 41, 87, 103, 105–106, 127, 170–171, 174, 195, 213, 217
fate, 2–4, 9–10, 12, 16, 18, 19, 37–38, 46, 51–54, 58–59, 63, 74, 85–87, 90, 121–122, 144–146, 150–153, 167–168, 172, 200, 205–208, 224n50, 247n13, 249n43; love of, 9, 13, 64, 68, 93, 143, 202, 213, 219
Female, 90, 107–111, 124, 164, 175, 238n24, 242n71
femme fatale, 156, 158, 237n11, 251n65. *See also* vamp
film: Artaud on, 164–165; classical Hollywood model of, 5, 9, 65, 85, 209–210, 213, 222n20; as moving image of perspectivism, 12–13, 38–39, 43–44, 52, 59, 64, 71, 83, 107, 117, 121–122, 123, 124, 136, 139–140, 163–164, 202, 216; as moving image of skepticism, 11–13, 216–217, 262n80; and myth 203–205; as philosophy, 2, 86, 198–201, 213, 215–216; and transcendental style, 143, 163. *See also under* Deleuze, Gilles: on action-images and time-images
Fink, Eugene, 16, 233n3, 234n6, 248n28, 254n10
Foolish Wives, 46–50, 52
forgetfulness, 4, 26, 27, 70, 77, 83, 85, 104, 136–137, 150, 180, 203, 205, 213, 215, 221n8
Frankenstein, 30, 34, 44, 66, 228n60, 236n53
free spirit, 96, 172–174, 176, 182–188, 190, 193–195, 253n8; and isolation, 30–31
friendship, 8, 69, 99, 117, 138, 173, 203, 218, 242n71
Front Page, The, 115–123, 125, 139, 216, 245–246n49

gender: and equality, 87, 92, 96, 107, 111; reversal, 107, 109, 171, 175–176, 249–250n47, 254n16; as role, 107–112, 150, 254n14. *See also under* truth: women as symbols of
genius, 6–7, 21, 40, 50, 53, 55–57, 92, 113–116, 118–119, 123, 125–128, 130, 144, 186, 206, 235n23, 243n20–21; of the heart, 156–158, 160, 162, 163, 171; lyric, 142
gesture, 13, 209–216, 218, 260n39
Great Gabbo, The, 55–58, 64, 71, 81
Greed, 50–54, 232n44
Griffith, D. W., 21, 23, 26, 43, 65

Hawks, Howard, 78, 125, 197, 235n25
Hecht, Ben, 55, 68–69, 71, 78–82, 90, 125, 137–139, 144, 169, 191, 194, 198, 207, 210, 223n31, 229n72, 244n34–35, 245n39–40, 253n1, 255n25; and cynicism, 119, 122, 133, 218; on eternal recurrence of the same, 121; on marriage, 117; on morality, 123; on truth and deception, 118, 126–128, 131–132, 139; on the *Übermensch*, 113–116, 186
Heidegger, Martin, 16, 167, 219
history, 40–41, 54, 62, 71, 94, 166, 170, 224n50, 234n6; and fate, 10, 37–38, 59

illusion, 87, 107, 111, 118, 136–137, 162, 176–177, 181, 189, 192, 208, 213, 238n18–19, 254n14; Apollonian, 143, 145–147, 149, 152, 155, 158–160, 168, 233n3; and film, 4, 81, 106, 259n29; life as, 114, 125–129; and presence, 90; time as, 47; and truth, 3, 12, 131–132. *See also* counterfeit, deception, reality, simulacrum, truth

irony, 138–140, 246n56

Jacobs, Lea, 1–2, 103, 240n55
justice, 45, 62, 67, 72, 80, 82, 87, 96, 122, 167–168, 169, 191, 235n23, 236n35

knowledge, 30–31, 33–34, 163, 171, 173, 181, 185, 187

language, 86–98, 90, 113–114, 123, 127, 137, 144, 183, 199, 208, 211, 217–219, 254n19; and speech 133, 218, 256n33; and writing, 117, 119, 121–122
laughter, 27, 41, 53, 57, 69, 71–72, 79, 82, 107, 109, 115, 134, 136, 149, 174, 183, 193, 249n42
Lebensphilosophie, 5, 39–40
Lemm, Vanessa, 221n8, 236n35, 247n19, 258n21
life, 2, 4, 5, 8–13, 16–17, 22, 23, 31, 35, 41, 46, 50, 55, 62–63, 67–68, 71, 74, 80, 90–91, 96, 98–99, 103, 105, 108, 111–112, 113–114, 116, 121–122, 124–125, 130, 134, 137, 138, 143, 147–148, 152–155, 158–159, 162, 166, 167, 172–173, 200, 203, 205–206, 213, 221n8, 224n48, 231n13, 232n39, 236n35, 248n31, 249n43, 255n20, 256n37; as degeneration and regeneration, 37–38, 39, 44, 48–49, 52
Little Caesar, 62–64, 68, 72–79, 83, 124, 210
London, Jack, 25–26, 225n1
Loos, Anita, 90, 105, 106, 197, 239n25, 241n69
love, 8, 16, 28, 42, 44, 46, 54, 66, 69–70, 72, 79, 80, 91, 93–94, 102, 105, 108, 115, 117, 124, 129, 143, 149–150, 154–5, 158, 160–165, 172, 176–178, 180–181, 183–184,

187–190, 200–201, 232–233n48, 237n14, 240n48, 250n56, 251n75, 255n21–22, 255n25, 256n31, 257n38–39; as destructive, 55–58, 248n28; lack of, 30–31, 166–167; perverse, 79, 166, 252n97
Love Parade, The, 174–177, 188

Male and Female, 27–29, 109
marriage, 2, 105–106, 109–110, 117–119, 122, 143, 152, 171–172, 175–179, 181, 188, 191–194, 255n22
Marsden, Dora, 92–93, 98, 107
masks, 10, 101–102, 125, 127, 132, 157, 171, 173, 176–178, 181–190, 195, 204, 210, 237–238n14, 241n60, 242n71, 253n9, 254n14, 255n20, 255n23–25, 256n37; and masquerade, 41, 89, 169, 176, 184
Maugham. W. Somerset, 31–32, 79, 91, 95
Mencken, H. L., 2, 17, 20–21, 80, 92, 96, 98–100, 114, 137, 192–193, 239n25
Merleau-Ponty, Maurice, 12–13, 208–209
Merry Widow, The, 53, 173, 181–185
modernity: 194; as cool apocalypse, 104–105, 154; and decadence, 23, 42, 56, 67, 81, 94, 152, 167; as tragicomedy, 41, 46, 59, 86, 202
morality, 32, 45, 55–56, 95, 107, 126, 129, 132, 155, 171, 188, 190, 201–202, 216, 229n77, 236n53, 238–239n24; Christian, 17, 27–29, 95–96, 105, 136, 161–162, 254n10; and criticism of the gangster, 66–67, 73; and criticism of the liberated woman, 91, 93, 103–105, 151; and immorality, 40, 49 123, 187, 192, 203; Strauss's naturalistic, 22; Nietzsche's non-prescriptive, 8, 22, 58–59, 86, 202; and *Übermensch*, 3–4, 7, 96, 114, 143, 163, 167–168, 173, 215
Morocco, 143, 145, 148–155, 158, 159, 160, 162, 249n40
music, 144, 152–153, 261n60; and musicals, 56, 176, 183, 255n21
myth, 38, 44–45, 59–60, 75, 85, 90, 124, 155, 171, 203–208, 213–215, 232n44, 248n31, 258n14–15, 259n28

narrative, 4, 37, 65, 85, 139, 181, 201, 214, 259n31; false, 89, 101
naturalism, 1–2, 15, 21, 22, 27, 64, 86, 171–172, 190, 193, 207, 221n8, 253n7; in Stroheim, 37–38, 44, 51–52, 59, 232n39, 232n44
Nazism, 6, 15, 190–191, 193–195, 225n1, 247n7
nihilism, 3, 22, 143, 163, 170–171, 193–195, 217, 221n9, 225n62
Nordau, Max, 33, 39–40, 50, 232–233n48
Norris, Frank, 33–34, 39–40, 50–51, 233n48
Nothing Sacred, 115, 130–137, 139

One Hour with You, 177–179
O'Neill, Eugene, 2, 22, 93, 223n32
ordinary, the, 4, 176, 216–219
Other, the, 12, 13, 63–64, 115, 154, 158, 164–165, 167–168, 171–172, 184–185, 187, 192, 217–218, 237–238n14, 242n71, 254n17, 255n25; as singular, 145, 157, 159, 160–161, 199–201, 206, 208, 211–215, 230n2, 247n19

pathos of distance, 29, 57, 128, 217; as effect of philosophy, 206
perfectionism, 2, 20, 68, 119, 185, 216; in horror films, 30–31, 34

perspectivism, 12–13, 59, 206, 211, 225n62
pity, 17, 20, 24, 31, 96–98, 101, 136, 147, 150, 152, 188
philosophy, 2, 11–12, 86–87, 112, 121, 138, 144, 164, 201, 203, 206–207, 213; conservative, 39; elitist, 90, 93; progressive humanist, 19; Nietzschean, 3–5, 16–17, 20–21, 30, 40, 59, 67, 68, 75, 90, 97–98, 170, 172, 197–199. *See also under* film: as philosophy
photography, 11, 138–139, 141, 211–214, 259n29, 261n60, 261n63
Pippen, Robert, 201–202, 230n7, 248n34, 258n11
play, 2, 10, 26, 41, 88–90, 110–111, 113, 127, 129, 144, 169, 175–178, 181, 189, 192–193, 199, 206, 215, 242n71, 261–262n78
power, 10, 19, 21, 31, 34, 38, 41, 47, 50, 59, 92–3, 95, 100–101, 104, 108–112, 117, 124, 175–176, 187–188, 200, 203, 213, 258n15; will to, 43–44, 62–65, 66–77, 79, 82–83, 86–89, 97–98, 116, 122, 125–126, 133, 164–166, 199, 208, 224n48, 233n3, 234n5–6, 235n24, 236n44

Rancière, Jacques, 3, 260n39, 260n49
Raphaelson, Samson, 169–170, 185, 193, 223n31
reality versus appearance, 3–4, 10–12, 38, 47, 87, 101, 116, 118, 122–127, 132, 134–137, 160, 162, 173, 178–179, 199, 204, 207–208, 215, 259n29, 261n60
realism, 3, 9–10, 13, 41, 51, 64, 75, 85, 106–107, 207, 211, 215; versus symbolism, 38, 52, 59–60
Red-Headed Woman, 90, 103–107, 164, 165

repetition. *See under* eternal recurrence of the same
ressentiment, 65, 70, 73, 76–77, 82–83, 94, 136, 146, 167, 173–176, 185

Sanger, Margaret, 21, 92, 240n39
Santayana, George, 18–19, 48
Scarlet Empress, The 164–167
Scheler, Max, 200–201, 205, 208, 209
self, the, 2–3, 7–8, 10–12, 22, 130, 168, 200, 250n51, 254n10; destruction of, 25, 46, 59 73, 81, 141–145, 148, 150–151, 153–155, 158–159; as divided, 32–33, 56–58, 81–82, 112, 192; highest form of, 115, 118–119, lack of, 111, 156–157, 165–166, 233n52, 243–244n30–31; and *principium individuationis*, 58, 146, 150; self-invention, 38–40, 52, 60, 74, 76, 88–89, 97, 105, 111, 138–139, 203, 207, 215; and self-scorn, 172
sentiment, 19, 72, 78, 99–102, 104; lack of, 57, 64, 106, 108, 164; as weakness, 55–56, 64, 69, 74, 77, 188, 193. *See also* affect, love
seriousness, 26, 115, 119, 136, 157, 174–175, 182, 189, 193, 218
sexuality, 43, 45–46, 89, 95–96, 101, 104–105, 124, 145, 152, 180–181, 188, 190, 230n3, 255n21, 256n30–31; and death, 148–149, 158, 165–166
shame, 152, 173, 175–176, 181, 183, 185
Shanghai Express, 143, 160–164, 180, 183, 250n58
silence, 70, 133, 141, 156, 162, 176–177
simulacrum, 88, 100, 134–135, 138, 211, 214, 233n53
skepticism, 11–13, 89, 119, 171, 206, 216–219, 262n80; moral, 33, 40

Smiling Lieutenant, The, 180–181, 187
spectatorship, 4, 9–10, 65, 199, 202–203, 215, 222n17, 224n51
Studlar, Gaylyn, 144–145, 149, 150, 247n12–14, 248n37, 249n42, 249–250n47
style, 186, 199–201, 203, 207–208, 212–213, 215–216, 218, 259n31, 261–262n78; in character, 7, 173, 185; Lubitsch's, 185–186, 256n37; Sternberg's, 142–144, 159–160, 163–165

theater, 9–10, 170, 213, 223n32, 249n46
time, 2, 9, 38, 41–42, 46–47, 51–53, 64–65, 69, 71, 74–76, 80, 85, 93, 104, 106, 117, 148, 150–151, 166, 172, 176, 205, 209–214. *See also* fate, eternal recurrence of the same
Trouble in Paradise, 185–190, 257n38
truth, 11–12, 40, 65, 104, 116, 120–121, 178, 181, 183, 199, 208, 212, 217–218, 253n9, 259n28; and boredom, 113; of bourgeois existence, 105; and cinema, 4, 11, 200, 209–210, 215; inversion of, 118–119, 123–124, 127–139; and language, 114, 120, 137; of Nietzsche, 4; revaluing, 67; as terrible, 143, 147, 151–152, 158; will to, 173; women as symbols of, 87–90, 96, 100, 237–238n14, 238n18, 251–252n81. *See also* deception, Deleuze: on power of the false, Dionysian: wisdom, illusion, perspectivism
Twentieth Century, 115, 125–130, 207

Übermensch: as beast, 15, 17, 19–20, 27, 32, 59, 198; as childlike, 27, 70, 80, 170–171, 173, 204, 258n17; criticisms of, 13, 79, 192; Danto on, 7; as Dionysian, 16, 53, 59, 141–144, 148, 160; as degenerate, 38–39, 45, 50, 53, 59, 85; and eternal recurrence, 53, 224n42; and fate, 9, 18–19, 38, 74–75, 167, 205, 249n43; as free spirit, 96, 169, 174, 186, 253n8; and gift-giving, 69–70, 72, 114–115, 234n6; humanistic interpretation of, 21, 185, 223n39; history of interpretation, 3, 5; as indeterminate, 2, 8, 64, 199, 202, 224n46; as inhuman, 7, 15, 23, 80, 85–86; and Jesus, 18, 155; Kaufmann on, 7; Schacht on, 7–8, 224n42; as spur, 44, 59; and theatricality, 213; as tragic, 38–39, 49–50, 80; *Untermensch* and *Unmensch*, 41, 165, 167; and value creation, 63, 77, 82–83, 205. *See also under* fate: love of, genius, power: will to
uncanny, 7, 47, 65, 201, 232n32
Underworld, 68–72, 75, 82–83, 94, 115, 124, 142, 247n24

vamp, 34, 42, 89, 91–92, 94, 237n11, 239n29, 241n63. *See also* femme fatale

war, 22–24, 31, 47, 54, 67, 80, 94, 115, 120, 198, 232n45, 234n5
Wells, H. G., 16–17, 21, 29, 32, 34

Žižek, Slavoj, 170–171, 256n30–31

www.ingramcontent.com/pod-product-compliance
Lightning Source LLC
Chambersburg PA
CBHW030527230426
43665CB00010B/797